GLOBAL
HEALTH

GLOBAL HEALTH

Why Cultural Perceptions, Social Representations, and Biopolitics Matter

MARK NICHTER

THE UNIVERSITY OF ARIZONA PRESS

TUCSON

The University of Arizona Press
© 2008 The Arizona Board of Regents

Library of Congress Cataloging-in-Publication Data

Nichter, Mark.
  Global health : why cultural perceptions, social
representations, and biopolitics matter / Mark Nichter.
    p. ; cm.
  Includes bibliographical references and index.
  ISBN 978-0-8165-2573-7 (hardcover : alk. paper) —
ISBN 978-0-8165-2574-4 (pbk. : alk. paper)
  1. World health. 2. World health—Social aspects.
3. Biopolitics. I. Title.
  [DNLM: 1. World Health. 2. Cross-Cultural
Comparison. 3. Health Policy. 4. Social Medicine.
5. Social Sciences. WA 530.1 N629g 2008]
RA441.N53 2008
362.1—dc22   2007045614

Manufactured in the United States of America on acid-free,
archival-quality paper.

Publication of this book is made possible in part by a grant from
the Provost's Author Support Fund of the University of Arizona.

13 12 11 10 09 08   6 5 4 3 2 1

Book and jacket design: David Alcorn, Alcorn Publication Design

To Mimi Nichter for her support,
patience, love, and inspiration

CONTENTS

PREFACE

In 2001 I was commissioned to write a short report on social science contributions to international health for the Social, Economic, and Behavioural Research (SEB) committee of the UNICEF–UNDP–World Bank–World Health Organization Special Programme for Research and Training in Tropical Diseases (TDR). In the report, I was asked to briefly review what the past twenty-five years of health social science research had contributed to a cultural understanding of the ten "tropical" diseases encompassed by the TDR program and allied programs related to child survival and women's health. I was directed to focus my attention on health-related perceptions and representations, originally presented to me as "health beliefs" and "explanatory models" of illness, leaving the issues of health care seeking and social stigma to other reviews. In addition, I was asked to critically examine common theoretical approaches that drive the practice of health social science research in international health and provide direction for a next generation of research.[1]

I initially declined the request because I saw the task as enormous and my time limited, given heavy teaching and research commitments. Johannes Sommerfeld from TDR proved to be very persuasive. And so, to make a long story short, I agreed to take up the challenge, and the report provided the impetus for this book. Here I explore health- and health care–related perceptions and representations maintained by three groups: local populations living in developing countries, public health practitioners working in the field of international health, and health planners and policy makers. I reflect on the course of qualitative research in international health and identify important lessons learned from the study of both local cultures and the cultures of those in the fields of medicine, public health, and development. The "social life" of representations maintained by the latter groups is as important for social scientists to study as local perceptions that guide thinking about health and illness. Finally, I chart what I see to be a next generation of health social science research contributing to global health—a representation in its own right that can reframe the way we think about linkages, the politics of responsibility, and foreseeable futures.[2]

This book addresses two audiences: those interested in the application of social science in global health, and those interested in studying the social science of global health (Parker and Harper 2005).[3] The first audience is composed of practitioners hailing from the social and behavioral sciences, public health, and medicine who are interested in learning practical lessons from qualitative research that may assist them in community-based problem solving. The second audience is a growing group of scholar-activists from these same disciplines who are interested in what social science theory contributes to the critical assessment of public health practice and health and development policy. Discussions with members of both groups of colleagues have contributed to my growth as a scholar-activist and engaged anthropologist (Nichter 2006a).

The book is designed to have two layers. For those interested in practical lessons, the text should suffice. I have tried not to encumber the text with too many details or too much jargon. For those wishing to follow up on issues presented and theoretical positions drawn upon or critiqued, and for instructors searching for case studies to illustrate points raised, extensive endnotes and bibliography provide a second layer of useful resources.[4] In the book, I draw upon my experience as a medical anthropologist and a trainer of health social science researchers and graduate students in India, Indonesia, the Philippines, Sri Lanka, and Thailand and as a consultant to projects in Africa and Latin America. As a rhetorical strategy, a number of questions demanding future research are posed throughout the book. It is my hope that these questions and the lessons highlighted will contribute to the emerging field of global health.

NOTES

1. I use the phrase "health social science" throughout this book to refer to social science research broadly applied to health- and health care–related topics. This encompasses studies that focus on *social science in health* and on *social science of health* alike. My review of the literature covers research conducted by social scientists hailing from many different fields and is filtered through my experience as a medical anthropologist trained and working in international health for more than twenty-five years. I have attempted to respect what Porter (2005) has referred to as the "dignity of difference" that is required for multi- and transdisciplinary problem solving.

2. In the first chapters of this book, I describe health social science contributions to international health, broadly conceived. In the last section of the book, I draw an important

distinction between international and global health and argue that we engage a global health agenda that is biopolitical.

3. Parker and Harper (2005) have recently applied a distinction long made between "social science in and of medicine" to social science in and of public health. I employ this distinction in this book as a heuristic, but I would argue that a hallmark of engaged anthropology is the reflexive application of both (Nichter 2006a). There is a tendency in anthropology to broadly classify anthropologists in two groups. For example, Cooper and Packard (1997) and Ferguson (1990) have noted that anthropologists studying development fall into two broad camps: applied anthropologists who do development work and whose work is focused on the exigencies of fulfilling contractual obligations, and anthropologists who critically examine and critique development work and call attention to inequality but end up doing little about it. Many anthropologists engage in real-world problem solving and maintain a critical perspective.

4. Janes (2003) has recently argued for the importance of introducing theory into the practice of global health and encouraged anthropologists to play a translation role. Although I think of my role as being a facilitator, more than a consultant (his term), I wholeheartedly agree with him. To some extent, this book, with its extensive endnotes for those who want to follow up on theoretical issues, is an experiment in line with this agenda.

ACKNOWLEDGMENTS

This monograph distills many of the themes I present in a year-long graduate seminar on anthropology and global health at the University of Arizona. I would like to thank current and former graduate students who commented on a working draft of the original report (Heide Castañeda, Karin Friederic, Namino Glantz, Vinay Kamat, Jen Pylypa, Laura Tesler, and David Van Sickle) and an early draft of this book (Lauren Carruth, Ben McMahan, Sara Raskin, and Alyson Young). Arachu Castro and Peter Winch provided constructive comments on the original report, leading me to rethink the scope of the current project. Mimi Nichter and Lenore Manderson provided me with a careful reading and much-needed reality check in the final stages of writing. My sincere thanks also go to Charla Dain and Carol Gifford for editorial assistance along the way. Charla, thanks for helping me stay the course. I, of course, take full responsibility for all positions advanced in the book, any errors made, and the footnotes within the footnotes. Finally, let me thank the many people I have worked with, learned from, and been inspired by in the fields of medical anthropology and international health and development. There are too many to name here, but you know who you are.

GLOBAL HEALTH

INTRODUCTION

COMMUNITY MEMBER: Mark, can you please explain to this sir what it is that you do? We have told him you are an anthropologist and not a doctor. What kind of *shastra* [discipline] is this anthropology, he wants to know? What benefit is it to the Indian people, or is this just research for writing books?

MARK: *Anubhava shastra.* I study the *anubhava* [experiences] of others. I study how people think about and try to solve problems. I learn from their experiences and share these lessons with people in other places trying to solve similar problems. I study what people say they do, what they actually do, and why there is a difference between the two. What benefit is anthropology? Mutual understanding, respect, and new ways of thinking about problems.

LOCAL POLITICIAN: Your government gives money for such research? Why then does it understand so little outside its own gates?

MARK: We are trying to learn, sir.

This vignette is drawn from my field notes in 1980 and was written following an encounter I had with a local South Indian politician who had come to visit one of the villages in which I was conducting research.[1]

What contributions have social science *in* international health and the social science *of* international health made to our local understanding of health problems in developing countries, public health initiatives, and local response to both? In this three-part book, I identify lessons that matter, learned from qualitative and more in-depth ethnographic studies of health-related perceptions and social representations commonly found in health and development discourse.[2] Part I (chapters 1–4) is devoted to research on health-related perceptions maintained by local community members.[3] Part II (chapters 5–7) examines representations of health and social formations maintained by members of an international health and development "community of practice."[4] Each set of perceptions and representations frames thinking about health-related problems and guides the way in which people develop and assess health interventions, allocate resources, and evaluate outcomes. After taking stock of lessons learned and demonstrating why perceptions and representations that frame health problem solving matter, I consider future directions for health social science. Part III (chapter 8) identifies important areas of research in the emerging field of global health, a field that I argue is fundamentally biopolitical.

In Part I, I review *social science in health* investigations of popular health culture. Popular health culture (Chrisman and Kleinman 1983; Kleinman 1980) encompasses local perceptions of bodily processes (ethnophysiology); factors thought to cause or render one vulnerable to illness; the local classification and language of illness; perceptions of pluralistic healing modalities, modes of divination, and diagnosis; pharmaceutical practice; and local responses to public health efforts to prevent and manage disease.[5] Investigations of popular health culture entail both the study of contemporary folk health concerns and practices and local interpretations of biomedical terms, concepts, resources, and practices.[6] My review of major contributions from social science research is largely drawn from ethnographic studies of child survival (primarily acute respiratory infections [ARI], diarrheal disease, and vaccinations) and the ten diseases covered by the World Health Organization's Tropical Disease Research program: African trypanosomiasis, dengue fever, Chagas disease, leishmaniasis, leprosy, lymphatic filariasis, malaria, onchocerciasis, schistosomiasis, and tuberculosis. I also draw on research on women's health, contraception, and HIV/AIDS to make a few important points about perceptions of risk,[7] harm reduction practices, and the need for a more culturally aware approach to evidence-based public health.[8]

In Part II of the book, I engage *social science of health* research to critically assess six of the key social representations that circulate in international health and development discourse ("development speak"). As part of master narratives (Roe 1991), these representations frame and justify national and international health initiatives. I draw attention to (1) representations of the health status and disease burdens of populations, (2) representations of health priorities and groups at risk produced by epidemiology and evidence-based medicine (a representation of "best practice"), (3) representations of the household and community that underlie public health rhetoric on community participation, (4) representations of social capital currently gaining prominence in neoliberal discourse on development, (5) representations of nongovernmental organizations (NGOs) as providing a new foundation for the emergence of civil society, and (6) representations of social justice that call attention to health as a human right and the politics of responsibility for the control of diseases that threaten global health.

In Part III, I look to the future of health social science in—and of— global health, a field of engagement demanding a biopolitical perspective. Continuing research is clearly needed on communicable and vector-borne diseases, and new research needs to be mounted to investigate behavioral dimensions of noncommunicable diseases and chronic illness. These research agendas must also take into account the important linkages between communicable and noncommunicable diseases, defective modernization (e.g., uncontrolled antibiotic use), unhealthy lifestyles (e.g., rising tobacco use, obesity, etc.), community responses to clinical trials, new forms of public health interventions, and emerging threats of pandemic disease (such as new avian flu strains). Reflecting on studies noted in Part I, I draw attention to the limitations of social science research that is disease-specific. I argue that such a focus misses important lessons that may be learned from a critical assessment of risk factors that are perceived or demonstrated to link several illnesses together, as well as from an examination of structural and ecosocial factors that contribute to the distribution of health problems and health care resources.

I identify and introduce the reader to several key concepts that will prove useful in the next generation of health social science research, including global health; syndemics and ecosocial epidemiology; popular epidemiology and participatory global information systems; local biology, life span biology, and life-course epidemiology; technologies of governance and audit; medical citizenship; and biosocial value. I suggest how these concepts can serve as useful lenses through which to study emerging and synergistic health problems; new assemblages of people, social movements, and stakeholders influencing the course of global health; and health care transitions that are affecting us all.

The research issues highlighted in this book are complex. I hope to provide the reader with an understanding of the role each plays in framing health problems and guiding the actions of the afflicted and their families, health care providers, and policy makers. An appreciation of how problems are conceptualized by multiple stakeholders is necessary if we are to develop culturally sensitive and socially responsible health programs and policies. As noted in the vignette that opens this introduction, I see my role as a medical anthropologist as rendering the perceptions and representations, experiences and agendas of different stakeholders visible, thereby facilitating critical thinking, meaningful dialogue, and more fully informed problem solving.

Theories of Representations

Let me begin by clarifying how I am using the terms *representation* and *perception*. My use of the term *representations* is informed by two distinct but complementary theoretical perspectives. On the one hand, the term refers to collective representations in Emile Durkheim's sense of meanings (intellectual and emotional) that are commonly shared by members of a social group as social facts (Durkheim 1974 [1896]).[9] This usage of representation draws attention to a group's distinctive history and collective experiences. Collective representations are collective ideas and sentiments that give a group its uniqueness and sense of social cohesion. Intragroup variation occurs as individuals construct personal meanings from collective representations during their life and in accord with their experiences. People who share a common culture learn similar ways of talking and thinking about or representing things, but their knowledge "of, about, and how" varies. Here the work of social theorists such as Moscovici (1984, 2000) is useful in pointing out the practical value of studying the ways in which social representations enable individuals and groups to construct a coherent vision of reality that facilitates action by constituting commonsense knowledge. Moscovici modernized Durkheim's notion of collective representations in recognizing how complex societies and global flows result in a multiplicity of social groups. As societies become more diverse and fragmented, their representations become less stable and uniform.[10] His research, along with that of others, draws our attention to how social representations are created in the course of communication and how, once established, representations lead a life of their own.[11]

A second theoretical perspective reminds us that representations also need to be thought about in terms of knowledge production and the work of advancing and solidifying ideological positions as well as the "politics of othering," which often entails one group using negative representations to devalue another group.[12] This theoretical perspective calls for a critical assessment of the power of representations and the motivation behind the framing of people, events, problems, and solutions in particular ways using particular images. Representations may be used to justify as well as reinforce relations of power, inequality, and subordination. Representations enable governmentality (defined as the exercise of power through information and regulation) by justifying certain institutions, procedures, analyses, calculations, and programs.[13] Science is replete with representations that take on truth value when presented as facts that go unquestioned and appear compelling as conventional wisdom (Latour 1987).[14]

Representations may also be used strategically, managed, or resisted by those who bear them.[15] This point is well illustrated by a recent study of a community of lepers in South India (Staples 2004). People with leprosy formed a union to protect the way they were represented to the public by the media and NGOs.[16] They joined together through a shared sense of biosociality,[17] a common identity afforded by their disease and its complications. At the same time, they recognized that representations of their illness had exchange value in the market.[18]

I have long been interested in the social life of health-related representations as social facts employed strategically in cultural projects, be they the interpretation of ill health or the justification of health interventions or policies. Thinking about representations in this way leads me to ask questions that most public health researchers would not ordinarily think to ask about health beliefs, cultural models, or statements populating health discourse and taken for granted as true. It is important to recognize that representations are employed in discourse not just to communicate ideas but also to reproduce and strengthen interpretative frameworks and social positions.[19] The popularity of representations and the rationalities they propagate beg examination given cultural heterogeneity, unequal distribution of knowledge and power within societies, contests of meaning, and the subtle and not-so-subtle agendas of stakeholders. Ecological and epidemiological studies of why some health-related ideas and representations are more contagious or virulent than others in particular contexts are needed, as are studies of why some representations are more or less resistant to change and reinterpretation.[20]

PERCEPTIONS

My use of the term *perception* also demands some explanation. Perception is the process of gathering information through any or all of our senses, followed by the acts of organizing this information and making sense of it. Health and illness are perceived in both cognitive and visceral ways, and the two are often co-extensive or perceived by a "mindful-body" (Lock and Scheper-Hughes 1987).

But what predisposes people to perceive an experience in particular ways? An obvious answer would be past experience, which has a "family resemblance" to what one is currently in the process of experiencing; but then what about that previous experience? I have found the social theorist Pierre Bourdieu (1990) helpful here. Bourdieu suggests that people draw upon an accumulated stock of durable, largely unconscious, dispositions, termed *habitus*. Habitus is embodied during the course of everyday life. Within social fields (networks of social positions), perceptions are structured by repeated and reinforcing practices and sanctions that lead one to acquire predisposed ways of thinking, classifying, acting, and feeling, from one's position within local worlds. One gains a feel for the "game of life," having embodied practical knowledge as a form of common sense; one then learns to improvise in novel circumstances. Acquired practical logics, dispositions, and skills in improvising influence the way people relate to their world.[21]

One's perceptions of and interactions with the physical and social environment are closely tied to habitus as well as structured by polythesis. *Polythesis* is a term used by Bourdieu to describe the organizational power of generative schemes (core concepts, such as ways of orienting one's body) applied to multiple domains in life, such that life has a sense of continuity. A good example might be the broad application of the "hot" and "cold" conceptual framework within many popular health cultures in Asia and Latin America. For many, domains of experience are thought about and viscerally experienced in terms of perceptions of hot and cold.[22]

Bourdieu's writings also draw attention to the fact that the perceptions of different groups of people within society (composed of networks of "social fields") may well differ in relation to their social position. Perceptions of diet, health, and illness or preferences for particular healing modalities, medications, and so on may not be generalizable within whole societies but may instead reflect class or caste or other aspects of habitus. Bourdieu reminds us that we need to be attentive to the study of both habitus, which lends order to customary life within societies, and differences of perception and preference that reflect cultivated predispositions and social positionality.[23]

SOCIAL SCIENCE RESEARCH IN INTERNATIONAL HEALTH: FROM BLUNT INSTRUMENTS TO MORE-REFINED STUDIES

Before identifying major lessons learned from qualitative studies conducted on issues of relevance to international health, I shall briefly discuss the range of studies that one encounters in the literature and provide a short critical assessment of research motivated by public health agendas and driven by practical concerns but limited by a rather narrow agenda. During the period 1975–2000, most social science research in international health relied upon "knowledge, attitude, behavior, and practice" (KABP) surveys, rapid assessment procedures (RAP), and brief focused ethnographic studies (FES) of diseases.[24] Typically, these studies were carried out in the service of public health programs having distinct needs and agendas and limited resources. As blunt instruments, they informed policy by drawing attention to particular dimensions of culture that influenced health behavior and identified gaps in health knowledge. These studies do, however, have inherent problems and limitations.

In general, public health interest in collecting data on health beliefs has been motivated toward two ends. First, baseline data are collected on what a population does not know, enabling the measurement of knowledge and practice change following an intervention. Second, data are collected to identify cultural barriers to health programs associated with noncompliance. There are inherent limitations in the collection of data narrowly focused on identifying ignorance or misconception on the part of a population. Although collecting information on behaviors and perceptions that place a population at risk for particular health problems is important, employing a single biomedical lens to view what people say and do leads to a skewed perception of local worlds: it filters out context, pays too little attention to the reasons for actions taken and not taken, and ignores life contingencies. Moreover, placing emphasis on what a population does not know deflects attention away from the important issues of what people do know and how they learn. This information is important to consider when engaging a population in problem solving and promoting trust in new ideas and practices.[25] It is a practice that privileges biomedical knowledge and pays little attention to local practical knowledge and the role this knowledge might play in health promotion as well as disease prevention and management.

We must also be wary of the simplistic and misleading use of health representations in "cultural barrier"–type explanations for why public health projects have failed or should not be initiated.[26] Such explanations often blame the victim and use culture as a scapegoat for other, more compelling reasons for failure, including poor program planning and implementation, cultural insensitivity on the part of practitioners, an inconsistent supply of resources, poor access to information, and forms of structural (institutional, systemic) violence (Farmer 1999, 2003; Ogden et al. 1999).[27] Cultural-barrier explanations are commonly based on (mis-)representations of culture as monolithic and the "local" as both stagnant and somehow juxtaposed to the modern.[28] Although cultural reasoning and practical logic certainly influence the local reception of public health programs, it is wrong to assume that cultural reasoning is generally conservative, static, and unaffected by local politics and the global flow of products, ideas, desires, and possibilities.[29] Experience teaches us that this is generally not the case. People tend to be pragmatic; they appropriate, reinterpret, and make use of new resources following a process of cultural assessment. This process has as much to do with the way in which information and resources are introduced and who introduces them as with the extension of existing conceptual frameworks. Moreover, local response to the entry of public health programs and health resources introduced in the private sector has as much to do with microeconomics, the social relations of health care provision, and the practicalities of everyday living as with cultural perceptions of illness causality and the like.

I emphasize this point at the beginning of the book to make a case for evaluating the importance of cultural perceptions and representations of health in relation to local contingencies, economics, and the politics of responsibility, not as isolated or independent variables. Failing to view perceptions and representations in this way is to adopt a reified perception of culture that is static and ahistorical instead of dynamic, processual, lived, and contested.[30] Much public health research exemplifies this failure, treating culture as if it has an independent etiological role in the epidemiology of disease.[31] This use of culture is misleading and counterproductive and has been amply critiqued by anthropologists and other social scientists. Appreciating that health ideas and behaviors are interlinked with other aspects of culture (norms, values, institutions, roles, identity) is important, but of equal importance is the recognition that particular stakeholders have vested interests in maintaining some cultural practices more than others.[32] As such, an assessment of culture (and popular health culture) must address social, economic, and power relations and not just beliefs.[33] When investigating what appear to be prototypical cultural models of illness and how life should be lived, researchers must consider factors that limit or facilitate an individual's ability to actually act on those models (Dressler and Bindon 2000).[34]

Rapid assessments and focused ethnographies of illness typically identify explanatory models (cognitive schema) for illnesses and vary widely in sophistication from those that survey health beliefs to studies that have used more-rigorous modes of investigation involving multiple methods and data triangulation.[35] Some researchers have attempted to correlate core cultural components of explanatory models (such as perceptions of illness etiology) with outcomes (such as severity of disease, stigma, and compliance).[36] Relatively little research has investigated differences in the way illness is thought about and responded to in the same society by different age groups, genders, social classes, castes, ethnic groups, people living in rural or urban areas, and so on.[37] Those studies that have attended to difference typically rely on surveys that sample groups for comparison based on assumptions about which subjects to investigate, as distinct from ethnographic research that looks into how groups should be selected and what variables might matter the most in sample selection.

It is not good enough to simply sample different social groups and conduct surveys of explanatory models for hypothetical illnesses. Such studies do reveal patterns in how representative illnesses are thought about, but the studies are severely limited.[38] They produce mental maps and stereotypes, but they do not describe how individuals understand and respond to illness in context. More-processual approaches to the study of illness representations are required (Farmer 1990), as are circumstantial ethnographies (Lock and Nichter 2002) that explore contingencies, hard choices, and, in situations in which little choice exists, the coping strategies that favor illness being interpreted in particular ways.[39]

What do surveys and rapid assessment procedures focusing on "explanatory models of illness" not tell us? And what do the more in-depth ethnographies contribute?[40] To answer, let us return to the original intent of explanatory-model research. Explanatory models of illness, as originally conceptualized by medical anthropologists such as Arthur Kleinman (1983, 1986), are not fixed. They emerge out of rich, multidimensional semantic illness networks. Semantic illness networks (Good 1977) are ensembles comprised of ideas about what symptoms characterize an illness, the causes of different types of illness, memories of past illness experiences, emotional and social responses to these illnesses, and associations with moral identity, treatment expectations, and perceptions of prognosis. Explanatory models emerge out of semantic illness networks and are dynamic and subject to change.

One of the shortfalls of rapid assessment studies that draw on explanatory models of ideal-type illness categories is that they often gloss over the fact that peoples' ideas about illness are not monolithic. Indeed, people's ideas about health and illness are emergent, ad hoc, and subject to change through time in accordance with the processual nature of illness and the response of illness to different therapeutic modalities both used and imagined. Longitudinal studies of illness and illness narratives (stories people tell about illness) have suggested that interpretations of illness often shift through time (Hunt et al. 1989).[41] Illness stories end up being much like revisionist histories, which take on meaning in context (Kleinman 1988; Kleinman and Kleinman 1991). They differ from telling to retelling depending on the audience and agenda for representing an illness in a particular manner. As such, the more in-depth approaches to understanding illness experiences and illness representations have centered on how the diagnosis and classification of illness are negotiated within therapy management groups (action sets mobilized to respond to illness), in accord with the shifting priorities and agendas of members (Janzen 1978, 1987; Nichter 2002a),[42] and how different types of illness are responded to by others in one's community.[43]

People's illness experiences are too complex and dynamic to be captured through questionnaires or short one-time interviews. Anthropologists who have carried out longitudinal case studies of sickness have noted that illness taskonomy (illness classification based on tasks the afflicted seeks to accomplish) is as important to consider as illness taxonomy (classification by inclusion and exclusion criteria). Taskonomic studies of illness (Bhattacharyya 1997; Chand and Bhattacharyya 1994; Nichter 1991a; Whittaker 2002) attend to the provisional ways in which illness is classified and the tentative way illness is treated with the resources at hand and constraints on time (enabling factors);[44] the ways in which illness is presented to others to get valued resources (strategic factors); and issues of entitlement, moral identity, and stigma.[45] Ethnographies of illness also remind us how often indeterminacy is a part of the illness experience and how often "diagnosis by treatment" or diagnosis based on the positive or negative outcome of treatment, and not just illness characteristics, occurs.[46] Ambiguity in illness labeling is important to acknowledge, not only as a lack of specificity but also as a state of indeterminacy sensitive to the politics of illness labeling, especially when a stigmatized condition is involved (Nichter 1989b).

Uses and Abuses of Social Science in International Health Research

Health social science has made several contributions to international health. Before I list reasons for carrying out social science in international health research, let me voice four notes of caution to those eager to conduct research in developing countries as a contribution to public health practice. First, beware of unrealistic expectations related to how your research may be used, and do not misconstrue the significance of research on one group at one point in time for a population at large over time. Second, bear in mind that it may be simplistic to think that your research on health-related perceptions and illness representations will enable public health practitioners to predict the health care–seeking behavior of particular individuals at any given time. Qualitative data can be suggestive or explanatory of larger patterns, yet there is often *not* a close fit between how people understand an illness and the treatment they seek for an illness at any one moment in time, owing to other life considerations.

Third, do not entertain false hopes that somehow identifying "cultural misconceptions" about health or illness will lead to health education that can quickly foster behavior change. Local ideas are embedded in larger systems of knowledge and practice, and they have social valence. What may appear to be a misconception to you may be a cornerstone of an important social construction. For example, belief in spirits or evil eye might bear an important moral message about social obligations, constitute an idiom of distress, deflect responsibility for a child's ill health from a young mother, or communicate collective anxiety about social change. Remember, perceptions of etiology are often an expression of ideology. Fourth, bear in mind that behavior change may be less related to changes in knowledge than economics or social relational factors that index such issues as masculinity, moral identity, responsibility, being seen as modern, and so on—all issues that demand social science investigation beyond the purview of most rapid assessment studies.

What do studies of health-related perceptions and representations bring to the international health table that is of practical use and social value? The following are seven reasons for carrying out "qualitative" research.[47]

Risk Perception Affects Illness Prevention

Qualitative research sheds light on local perceptions of vulnerability that entail various aspects of material, social, emotional, and spiritual life. Research on risk perception helps us better understand cultural ways of viewing developmental stages and reproductive cycles; climatic conditions and environmental changes; poverty and food availability; the toll of different types of work on the body; positive and negative aspects of different lifestyles and consumption patterns; popular understanding of worms, germs, and disease vectors; concepts of illness resistance and hereditary disease; and so on. Risk perception affects primary, secondary, and tertiary prevention in that it may be engaged in prior to, during, and after illness.

Illness Perceptions Influence Health Care Seeking

Long-standing, emergent, and hybrid ideas about illness etiology influence but do not determine health care seeking. They constitute predisposing factors that may influence perceptions of illness course and severity.

Predisposing factors figure into health care seeking along with enabling factors (time, access, economics), service-related factors (how service is rendered), past illness treatment experiences, and the social status of the afflicted and caretakers. Just as it is necessary to account for the relationships between host, environment, and agent when conducting an epidemiological study, accounting for the interaction between predisposing, enabling, and service variables is essential to studies of health care seeking.

Local Impressions of Public Health Interventions Affect Community Participation

Local perceptions of public health interventions influence whether interventions are embraced as effective or deemed ineffective, dangerous, or useful for some people but not others. Representations of interventions that involve technical fixes (such as vaccinations) may reflect perceptions of what interventions do and how they do it or may be associated with the reputation of those promoting interventions, or trust in the government. Local participation in family-planning programs may be influenced by a weighing of perceived benefits against risks as well as trust and power relations. Participation in vector control programs may be influenced by perceptions of responsibility for different spaces.

Expectations and Fears of Medication Affect Pharmaceutical Behavior

Local perceptions of pharmaceutical compatibility, effectiveness, side effects, and safety (in the short and long run) influence acceptance and adherence to medical recommendations. Expectations influence adherence, and unmet expectations may foster practitioner shopping.

Illness Identity Affects the Illness Experience of the Afflicted and Their Caretakers

How an illness is viewed by society at large—and how it is viewed by one's immediate family—affects the biosocial experience of illness. The ill are doubly afflicted with disease and cultural representations of their illness, and the two are mutually constitutive. Family members and caretakers are also affected by illness representations, although much less is known about them.

Illness Representations Are Employed in the "Politics of Othering" and Complicate Public Health Practice

Association between particular groups and negatively valued illnesses has long been used in the "politics of othering" (Said 1978). Likewise, those in public health who seek to diagnose, investigate, and educate the public about certain diseases can easily become complicit in "othering projects" if they do not remain vigilant, pay attention to intergroup tensions, and take rumor seriously.

Illness Representations Affect Community Response to Epidemics

Public reactions to previous epidemic disease, warnings about impending disease with which a population is or is not familiar, and threats of pandemic disease provide valuable insights into community preparedness. There are important lessons to be learned from past history related to how the public and medical practitioners are likely to respond to epidemics, what sources of information are trusted, what the public expects from the government, and so on.

NOTES

1. This confrontation occurred while I was a scholar funded by the Indo-U.S. subcommission on Education and Culture and piloting "Project Community Diagnosis," described in Nichter 2006a. In 1980, the Indian government began expelling many U.S. diplomats and researchers from the country for political reasons. Despite being confronted about the nature of our research, Mimi Nichter and I were graciously allowed to stay and continue this participatory research project. We are grateful for the support of J. P. Naik, former director of the Indian Council of Social Science Research.

2. Although the terms *qualitative research* and *ethnography* are often used interchangeably, there are important differences. Qualitative research can be thought of as an overarching methodological framework, with ethnography defined as one approach/methodology within the larger framework of qualitative research. Some of the key defining characteristics of ethnography, such as participant observation, holism, attention to social context (space and place, time, social interaction, etc.), and sociocultural description, are typically not included in a study defined as utilizing qualitative methods. In ethnography, the production of knowledge and shifts in behavior in different contexts is a key concern, as is the study of contingency and circumstance. During the past decade, the use of qualitative research as part of larger quantitative studies in the health field has become commonplace. Often, the qualitative methods employed in such studies are semistructured focus groups or semistructured interviews conducted at one point in time. The hallmark of good qualitative research is aptly summarized by Agar:

> In traditional research, one observes a situation, notices a variable of interest, and sets out to design a measure for it, where "measure" means a procedure to assign a number to the phenomenon. The procedure should allow for the isolation and measurement of that same variable in other situations where it occurs so that the values can be compared. In qualitative research, one notices something of interest, but then takes a different approach. Instead of isolating it, one first wonders what other aspects of the situation it might be connected to. This linking of an observation with other features of the situation distinguishes a concern with context.

Let me put that more strongly. When an observation is linked to other features of context, and that linkage holds up across additional cases, we are on the way to a qualitative explanation of that observation. (Agar 2003:979)

3. It is not my intent to present an illness-by-illness account of health social science contributions to international health; instead, I focus on broad lessons learned across studies. Illness-specific reviews already exist: see disease/condition-specific reviews in Ember and Ember 2004; reviews of HIV/AIDS-related behavior in Parker 2001; reviews of acute respiratory illness (ARI) in Nichter et al. 1994; reviews of malaria in McCombie 1996 and 2002, in Mwenesi 2005, and in Williams and Jones 2004; and reviews of women's health in Inhorn 2006. I also do not present contributions to the field in terms of the theoretical orientation of authors: that is, as being cultural constructivist, biocultural, or critical medical anthropology. Up until the mid-1990s, there was a general imbalance in studies that favored cultural analysis of illness over political economic analysis of factors contributing to health inequality. Straw-man debates pitted one type of study against the other (see, for example, Farmer 1997, 1999; and a response by Barnhoorn and Van der Geest [1997]). I support a more biosocial synthesis that sees all three approaches as valuable and mutually informative. See other attempts to move in this direction in the edited volume by Goodman and Leatherman (1998).

4. Members of "communities of practice" are individuals bound together by informal relationships. They typically share common goals, a sense of identity gained through participatory learning, and the adoption of common language and core practices (Wenger 1996, 1998; Wenger et al. 2002). Those participating in public health and clinical epidemiology in developing countries form a loose community of practice. My separation of the "local community" and the "community of practitioners and policy makers" is a heuristic device. Clearly, individuals participate in and are members of both groups.

5. The terms *disease*, *illness*, *illness experience*, *sickness*, and *suffering* have distinct meanings that have now become conventional in medical anthropology (Hahn 1983; Young 1982). The term *disease* refers to a pathology or disorder as defined by a medical system (e.g., biomedicine, Ayurvedic medicine) on the basis of inclusion and exclusion criteria. The term *illness* denotes the subjective experience of being unwell—a personal, phenomenological experience that may or may not correspond to a clinically identifiable disorder and that can be experienced in a multitude of ways within one's personal, social, and cultural context. The term *illness experience* refers to how the afflicted and members of their household (and significant others) perceive, live with, and respond to symptoms, pain, diagnoses, and treatment. *Sickness* is used to refer to the social-relational and performative dimension of the disease and illness experience. The study of sickness includes a consideration of how the act of diagnosing and constructing diagnostic categories is motivated and influenced by social processes and power relations. It also examines how illness is experienced in relation to the disruption of social roles that define one's position in society. Suffering is not reducible to the experience of immediate pain. It entails a loss of coherence that accompanies a challenge to one's identity and valued social relationships. The suffering that an individual experiences is related not only to a loss of immediate capacities, roles, and so forth, but also to the loss of an anticipated future and hopes for a better life.

6. In this book I acknowledge but avoid using the term *health beliefs*, for epistemological reasons well articulated by Good (1994). The term *health beliefs* conveys a static and limited sense of culture that overlooks history. It also leads to three common misconceptions found in the international health literature: (1) a tendency to oversystematize local

knowledge, which is often applied in an ad hoc manner; (2) an assumption that there is far more consensus in conscious thought than is often the case; and (3) an underestimating of the presence and importance of ambiguity.

7. I do not attempt to review the vast literature on HIV/AIDS but draw upon this literature to highlight a few important issues of broad relevance to health social science.

8. Evidence-based public health differs from evidence-based medicine as the latter is commonly understood. Evidence-based medicine is based on statistical abstractions in which "average" people suffering from "average" diseases are indistinguishable. It assumes that all illness is largely biological—separate from social context and manageable by a common set of treatment guidelines, making audit possible.

   This model of disease investigation reinforces the reductionistic tendency of modern medicine and works best for discrete, biological diseases (e.g., bacteriological disease) treatable by specific, usually biological interventions (e.g., antibiotics). Clinical epidemiology is often associated with evidence-based medicine, clinical trials (the gold standard of double-blind randomized controlled trials within evidence-based medicine), and meta analysis. The International Clinical Epidemiology Network (INCLEN), which I have participated in for more than twenty years, took a much broader vision of evidence-based medicine, recognizing the importance of other types of evidence for research and examining the effectiveness (as well as efficacy) of possible treatment options for different populations (and patients), in keeping with the original and evolving mandate of evidence-based medicine (Guyatt et al. 2004; Sackett et al. 1996, 2000). Evidence-based public health adopts a broad-based approach to evidence-based problem solving. It calls for an informed, explicit, and judicious use of evidence derived from the biosciences, the social sciences, and evaluation research (Rychetnik et al. 2004). I would add that evidence-based public health also acknowledges that illness is not randomly distributed or experienced and that health is biocultural, not just biological.

9. Durkheim was interested in the study of collective life. He described social facts as having an existence in and of themselves and not bound to the actions of individuals; social facts have a life of their own, much like rumors. Once social facts come into existence, they circulate and influence the way members of groups think and act. Social facts influence social relations.

10. See Howarth et al. 2004 for a discussion of the relevance of Moscovici's theories of social representation for health social science.

11. Other theoretical frameworks also provide insights into how we use representations. Let me mention two. Sewell (1992, 2005) describes social life as an interplay between overlapping and interlocking structures (habitus, recurrent social patterning, expectations, etc.) and contingency. Within structures, people creatively employ schemas (habits of thought, representation) to orient action and interpretation. Tannen and Wallat's (1993) discussion of frames is also instructive. They note that frames are "structures of expectation" that include both knowledge schema and interactive frames of interpretation subject to negotiation and revision. Interactive frames interface with familiar schema and give birth to new representations through such modalities as stories.

12. Othering often involves stigmatization (Goffman 1963) and a politics of social distinction and distancing. Perceived difference from a societal norm or ideal is the grounds for social distance. Othering can also foster coalition building by bringing together those distanced by a dominant group. See Canales 2000 for an accessible discussion of exclusionary and inclusionary aspects of othering.

13. Foucault's writing has been instrumental to thinking about how governmentality is established (see, for example, Foucault 1979, 1991). Foucault invites us to consider the

interconnection between knowledge and power and emphasizes the importance of expert knowledge as a form of productive power (biopower) distinct from restrictive power. Expert knowledge creates the conditions for measurement, surveillance, and calculation as a means of managing and regulating populations as forms of governance. Through the exercise of biopower, representations of population norms as well as deviance have emerged. Many social theorists have extended the work of Foucault, as in presenting analyses of risk as a means of regulating and thereby governing human life (see Rose and Miller 1992). For a detailed discussion of biopower that addresses its centrality to Foucault's thinking about governmentality, and how the concept has been used by other contemporary social theorists, see Rabinow and Rose 2006.

14. Representations may come to solidify an ideological position in subtle ways, such as through the use of metaphor in science (Stepan 1993). Emily Martin's (1990, 1992, 1994) research on medicine in the United States is instructive. It suggests that scientific explanations of bodily processes are often framed in salient cultural terms, for example as metaphors that mirror dominant economic models. Martin does not suggest that scientists intentionally choose economic models as the basis for their thinking about the body, but certain models seem compelling because they permeate society at a given juncture of time. As these models are applied to body processes in books, schools, clinics, the media, and advertising, they become internalized and, over time, naturalized. They are no longer perceived as metaphor but are taken as objective scientific fact available in an easy-to-understand form. Notably, Martin recognizes that individuals engage with but do not blindly accept scientific metaphors made popular by the media and other sources of information. People actively employ scientific images according to their individual needs, concerns, and social contexts. In this sense, science acts as a cultural resource for mediating a complex world. Martin points out that individuals personalize metaphors of health and the body to cope with and create meanings of illness that make sense for their lives. Her work holds valuable lessons for social scientists working in global health.

15. For a powerful example of how visual representations of the body may be used for political purposes, see Petchesky's (1997) analysis of the film *The Silent Scream*. She describes the manipulation of visual imagery of the fetus by antiabortion activists in which unborn fetuses are represented as self-sufficient entities that are robbed of their life by abortion. Antiabortionists in the United States used this strategy to make the fetus a public presence in a visually oriented culture.

16. This case speaks to the conflicting needs of different stakeholders in what clearly emerges as a politics of disease representation. The conflict is between lepers who rely on a stigmatized representation of leprosy for their livelihood and "beneficent others" who are rewarded in their own social sphere for destigmatizing leprosy and integrating lepers into the broader community. The case leads us to think about how stigma may be appropriated as a resource and used positively by the afflicted for their own benefit. This is the reverse of the politics of othering, in which one group uses negative representations to devalue another.

17. Rabinow (1996) introduced the concept of biosociality to suggest the emergence of associational communities around particular biological conditions.

18. The commodification of a good, service, sign (representation), or idea involves the worth of the aforementioned in a trade or exchange. The trade may be influenced by social, economic, political, or cultural factors and involve property rights. The exchange value of *X* represents what quantity of other commodities (or money) it may be exchanged for, if traded.

19. Discursive analysis considers not only how discourse is used to construct representations of what is true, valued, and normative but also who gets to say what about whom, and

with what consequences. Attention is drawn to discursive fields in which a number of competing discourses coexist, each having varying degrees of power to give meaning to events and organize social processes and institutions. Which "voices" (positions, rationalities) get privileged and which get silenced is explored, along with who benefits from prevailing representations and in what ways. These questions address relations of power, hierarchy, and domination.

20. Sperber (1985, 1990, 1996) introduced the possibility of an epidemiology of cultural representations. Indeed, he posits that ideas that persist and become widely shared are what anthropologists call culture. Although I think this is a somewhat simplistic vision of culture, I do find his idea of an epidemiology of representations productive and worth pursuing. Along these lines, I suggest later in this book that spatial representations of risk perception might be possible to map and compare to gradients of epidemiological risk. Doing so might better enable us to study the impact of public health interventions.

21. Local knowledge entails what Bourdieu (1990) has termed the "logic of practice." Practical logic is commonsense reasoning about one's world engaged in by agents who share a common embodied history (habitus) and set of transposable dispositions. These dispositions act as guiding principles and are adapted as well as adopted by actors in ways that are polythetic, especially when populations are presented with novel situations and new products. See Craig 2000 and Williams 1995 for accessible overviews of Bourdieu's relevance for health-related research. Craig provides a useful discussion of how different multiple practical logics may coexist. On this point, also see Hausmann and Ribera's (2003) discussion of "recipe-knowledge" and malaria treatment and of why people continue to engage in indigenous treatment even when they accept new ideas from health educators. Recipe-knowledge draws upon the work of the social theorist Alfred Schutz.

22. For example, see Nichter 1986 on how hot and cold conceptualization as well as several other health concerns highlighted in this book influence South Indian notions of health, diet, illness, and health care.

23. This is a very simplistic overview of Bourdieu's ideas about how one gets a "feel for the game" in social fields in which different forms of capital (economic, cultural, social, symbolic, physical) are at stake (Bourdieu 1986). According to Bourdieu, a person's position within social fields is heavily influenced by social class, which in turn predisposes that person to preferences, tastes, and other cultivated dispositions. As such, bodies and desires reflect class position, and hierarchies of control and privilege become naturalized at the level of perception.

24. Focused illness ethnographies often make use of rapid assessment procedures popularized in the 1980s–1990s. For a description and critical assessment of rapid assessment procedures, see Herman and Bentley 1992; Lambert 1998; Manderson and Aaby 1992a, 1992b; Scrimshaw and Gleason 1992; Utarini et al. 2001. I cite specific disease ethnographies throughout this book and point out the limitations of focused illness ethnographies. Others have commented on why such studies are a good beginning point but hardly sufficient to yield in-depth knowledge about health care behavior; see, for example, Williams et al. 2002.

25. Research that focuses attention on what people do not know also sets us up to underestimate what people do know. An emphasis on health beliefs as barriers to change leads us to underappreciate the propensity for local populations to be practical when faced with new information and resources. Lack of use of resources is as often attributable to reasons related to trust, economics, and power relations as to traditional beliefs. Placing an emphasis on what people do not know also portrays culture (cultural institutions, norms) in a negative light as a source of risk. In the international health literature, it is far more

common to find culture spoken about in relation to risk factors for disease transmission than to find cultural institutions or knowledge spoken about as protective factors. When presented with data on disease prevalence associated with culture or ethnicity, we must remember to ask two questions. First, what social, economic, and cultural factors increase the likelihood of members of this population becoming ill? Second, what cultural factors have prevented this public health problem from being far more common or serious? Also missing from studies and surveys that ask participants to identify health beliefs is an appreciation for tacit knowledge (Polanyi 1967), that which is known but not readily articulated out of context.

26. Studies of cultural barriers, like studies of compliance, tend to presume that intervention/treatment failures are community/patient failures. Social scientists must resist simplistic analyses that blame the victim and should broadly consider reasons for why interventions are not responded to in the way imagined by planners.

27. As noted by Farmer (1999), one way in which attention is diverted away from forms of structural violence is by ascribing more personal agency to the afflicted than they actually have while living under conditions of dire poverty. This may take the form of health education efforts that target risky behavior or lifestyle and underplay the structural conditions that place people in environments of risk. Another way of diverting attention is to use culture as an alibi and conflate cultural difference with structural violence.

28. Anthropologists have gone to great lengths to demonstrate that the "local" is dynamic, not static; porous, not bounded; and the product of both a unique history and global flows of people, resources, and ideas. Pigg and Adams (2005:18) note that "global processes undo and remake the very particularism of the local as it stands in contrast to the seeming transcendence of the global." They go on to observe that "older models of pre-existing 'cultures,' arrayed in well-defined territories and eventually penetrated by 'outside forces' lead inevitably to an attempt to winnow an artificially reified authentic tradition from inauthentic borrowings." Beck (2002:17), in an essay on cosmopolitanism (internal globalization), emphasizes that "globalization is a non-linear, dialectic process in which the global and the local do not exist as cultural polarities, but as combined and mutually implicating principles."

29. As Janes (2006) has argued, we must avoid looking at culture as being independently causal or deterministic; instead, we should examine cultural systems as part of changing social and political processes.

30. Writing against a reductionist notion of culture, Kleinman (1995:56) encourages those in medicine and medical ethics to view culture "not as shared canonical meanings that are distributed equally throughout a community, but rather as lived meanings that are contested because of gender, age cohort, and political difference."

31. See Wardlow 2002 for a good critique of the "etiologizing" of culture in HIV research. Wardlow aptly calls attention to the essentializing of culture while at the same time calling for us not to abandon the culture concept in its entirety.

32. In addition to looking at cultural institutions through the optic of power relations, health social scientists must balance an interest in cultural relativity with a consideration of universal human rights. Marchione (2007) notes that a position of vulgar cultural relativism that overlooks power relations within cultures has given dictatorial regimes and elites cover to abuse their own people. As a case in point, Marchione cites the case of Malawi under the regime of Banda. Cultural relativism was used by the Banda government to deny ratification of the International Covenant on Economic, Social, and Cultural Rights. Marchione suggests that the same tactic is being used today by politicians in Malawi and other countries as a shield against demands to comply with global programs that secure universal human rights.

33. Many medical anthropologists have critiqued the tendency in public health circles to treat culture as if it were in people's heads as a template for behavior; see, for example, Pigg 1995.

34. Dressler and Bindon (2000) use the term *cultural consonance* to describe the degree to which individuals are able, in their daily lives, to approximate in their own behaviors widely shared and prototypical cultural models of how life is to be lived. Working from a cognitive theory of culture, Dressler and Bindon argue that there are a number of cultural models (e.g., of material lifestyles, social support, family life, diet, illness management, and others) that are widely shared and define how life is to be lived. These shared cognitive representations guide behavior and enable others' behaviors to be interpreted. Of equal importance is Dressler and Binden's observation that economic factors can simultaneously intervene to limit an individual's ability to act on those models. Cultural consonance in a given domain may be widely distributed because of wide individual differences in the way in which people enact those behaviors. Dressler argues that low cultural consonance, or the inability to act on a cultural ideal, is a profoundly and chronically stressful experience and can lead to deleterious health outcomes (Dressler 1995, 1999, 2004). The study of cultural consonance complements as well as deepens social epidemiological studies such as those conducted by Wilkinson (1996) that examine population health and well-being in developed societies in relation to social cohesion, egalitarian values, and income distribution as much as economic well-being. Where these studies fall short is in closely examining social relational dimensions of life that influence one's capacity to act in consonance with particular cultural aspirations inclusive of social support networks. Social support networks can buffer the impact of poor consonance, enabling those with social resources to cope better and in some cases construct new social fields and forms of counterculture.

35. Many of those in public health exposed to health social science in the 1980s–1990s began substituting the term *explanatory model of illness* for the term *health beliefs*. In some cases, this signaled a change of research methodology and thinking about local illness perceptions, but in other cases, a change in terminology was merely cosmetic and deemed politically correct.

36. For example, see studies by Weiss (1985, 1988, 1997, 2001) that employ an EMIC (Explanatory Model Interview Catalog) approach to cultural epidemiology, drawing heavily on interviews and attempting to identify representations of illness that influence illness experience. Weiss has become well known for his studies of stigmatized illness. Exemplary of his approach is a study that found that perceived causes of leprosy emphasizing fate and karma were associated with high rates of clinical depression (Weiss et al. 1992). For critiques of the approach adopted by Weiss that call attention to limitations in the way culture is operationalized (largely as homogeneous), undertheorized, and not problematized (in terms of class, caste, gender, generation, and so on), see Dressler 2006; Janes 2006; Waldram 2006. Biocultural anthropologists such as Dressler have called for studies that investigate the distribution of particular illnesses (especially chronic diseases associated with stress) among different segments of society through methods that are attentive to measures of cultural consensus and cultural consonance ("local" shared models of what is culturally important) and "lifestyle incongruity." See Dressler 1995, 1999, 2004, and 2005. See also note 34.

37. Some anthropologists have attempted to use cultural consensus analysis to study the extent to which "cultural beliefs" are shared (Romney 1999). This cognitive approach to studying the distribution of knowledge within a culture has been applied to both local conceptions of disease of biomedical significance and folk illnesses (Ruebush et al. 1992; Weller 1983, 1984a, 1984b; Weller et al. 1993). Such studies are insightful; however, they

are insufficient because they do not get at how knowledge is actually produced, applied, and evaluated in contexts.

38. These types of ethnographic studies take time; in the world of international health, what is valued are rapid studies that are good enough for the task at hand. This is fair enough. My point is that rapid studies that get at perceptions of illnesses need to be complemented by in-depth ethnographic studies that provide insights into social relational factors significantly influencing health-related behavior.

39. Circumstantial ethnographies also attend to the way current events influence interpretations and representations of illness. Consider, for example, a context of heightened concern about chemical and biological weapons and how this might influence public response to sudden illness. A few years ago in Manila, a thousand students in several schools deluged local clinics with mundane flu-like symptoms as a result of rumors about bioterrorism spread by students text messaging each other on cell phones (Wessely et al. 2001).

40. Focused illness ethnographies and rapid assessments identify core cultural concepts and broad behavior patterns, but they are not designed to study the processual nature of illness experiences and responses to illness. Coupled with short training courses (Vlassoff and Manderson 1994), they do expose medical and public health colleagues to qualitative research, fostering productive partnerships with social scientists.

41. Many health social scientists tend to use the term *narrative* very loosely, often as a synonym for *story*. Problems occur when narratives are presented as coherent stories (Bruner 1991; Garro and Mattingly 2000). Illness narratives collected by medical anthropologists are generally not monologues told at one point in time in a linear progression to a passive audience. They are often a collaborative event that involves more than one teller. They are also multivoiced (Bakhtin 1981 [1935]) in the sense that a narrator often adopts a variety of subject positions in the service of identity management (see also Goffman 1959).

42. Although a meaning-centered approach can inform us how an illness event is symbolically constituted, it cannot tell us why particular associations are selected from among a repertoire of meanings. A performative approach to language use (Bauman and Briggs 1990; Jacoby and Ochs 1995) can be used to further examine the co-construction of identity through language. One afflicted with an illness and his or her significant others actively use symbols to fashion an identity appropriate for that moment. For examples, see Price 1987 and Garro 2000.

43. Important to study is both what people say about those afflicted, especially those afflicted by stigmatized illness, and what behavior people exhibit toward the afflicted and family members. How does behavior vary by social relationship to the afflicted? See Weiss and Ramakrishna 2006 and Weiss et al. 2006 for an introduction to the study of stigmatized diseases. See Macq et al. 2006 for a critical assessment of methods used to study stigma related to TB that identifies major dimensions of stigma in need of assessment.

44. See, for example, Sauerborn et al. 1996b for an observation on significant seasonal differences in health care seeking in Burkina Faso. In the rainy season, when resources are scarce, illnesses are less likely to be interpreted as severe, fewer sick people are taken to practitioners, and people are more likely to frequent less-expensive types of practitioners or engage in home care.

45. A taskonomic approach to understanding illness behavior takes account of divergent rationalities that may be used to explain an illness and guide action as well as nonmedical factors that may influence decision making (Hunt and Mattingly 1998; Nichter 1991b). It also pays attention to the way in which mothers present sick children to health care practitioners so as to receive valued medical resources. Vinay Kamat (2004, 2006) pro-

vides a powerful example that illustrates this point. He notes that women in Tanzania will not give babies tepid water baths to reduce fever before taking a child to a health post, for fear that the child's fever will not be high enough to warrant the best medicine available.

46. McCombie (2002) reminds us that not only are illness episodes defined in terms of successful forms of treatment, but also, illness classifications are revised when medicines fail. She cites an unpublished study by Kachur on malaria in Malawi wherein a local illness category that overlaps with the signs of malaria is rejected in favor of another local illness category when common medicines for malaria do not work.

47. In this book, I focus on social science research conducted in developing countries. Many of the issues covered are just as relevant in developed countries. A burgeoning literature exists on popular health culture, lay epidemiology, and ethnomedicine in the West. Lessons learned in developing countries have relevance to lessons learned in the West and vice versa. Public health researchers have long recognized the importance of studying "lay epidemiology" (the study of cultural perceptions of disease etiology and risk perception) and have articulated concerns that popular health culture may conflict with public health interventions (e.g., Allmark and Tod 2006; Davison et al. 1992; Hunt and Emslie 2001; Rose 1985; Weed 1995). The field of medical anthropology also has a long history of investigating popular health culture (e.g., Martin 1994), perceived risk and harm reduction (e.g., Nichter 2003a), and pharmaceutical practice (e.g., Nichter and Thompson 2006; Vuckovic and Nichter 1997). For an expanded list of interest areas within the field of medical anthopology, see the Web site of the Society for Medical Anthropology: www.medanthro.net. In this book, I selectively cite research conducted in the West, when useful, to introduce concepts not widely applied by social scientists working in developing countries.

PART I
POPULAR HEALTH CULTURE

Owing to his lack of knowledge, the ordinary man cannot attempt to resolve conflicting theories or conflicting advice into a single organized structure. He is likely to assume that the information available to him is on the order of what we might think of as a few pieces of an enormous jigsaw puzzle. If a given piece fails to fit, it is not because it belongs to a different puzzle or because it is fraudulent; more likely the contradictions and inconsistencies within his information are due to his lack of understanding and to the fact that the [*sic*] possesses only a few pieces of the puzzle. Differing statements about the nature of things, differing medical philosophies, differing diagnoses and treatments—all of these are to be collected eagerly and to be made a part of the individual's collection on puzzle pieces.

—ALAN R. BEALS

What aspects of popular health culture have health social scientists drawn attention to in the past three decades? In the four chapters that follow, I highlight a set of themes that emerge from both a close reading of the international health and medical anthropology literature and my own field experience in South and Southeast Asia. I profile a few key points related to each theme as a means of giving a sense of why the theme matters, and I cite references guiding the reader to exemplary studies that unpack or illustrate points made. The themes selected draw attention to local understandings of the body, health, diet, risk, illness, and pharmaceuticals as well as the emergence of hybrid health ideas associated with local interpretations of public health messages. I also briefly consider representations of the quality of care in private and public health sectors.

1

Perceptions of Ethnophysiology Matter

You cannot just treat diseases, you have to treat bodies, and you cannot just treat bodies unless you understand the lives bodies have become accustomed to living. What is healthy for one man may not be healthy for another. One man may be accustomed to taking a *peg* [a drink] every day and it is good for his health, but it would not be good for my health. The diet of my caste and the castes of fisherfolk is different, we require different things to remain healthy besides the basics of clean water, clean air, and sanitation. Ayurvedic medicine recognizes the importance of diagnosing people, their needs, hungers, and excesses, not just diseases. This is why you cannot just export Ayurvedic medicine to the United States without adjusting to place and population. . . . (sighs) Treating people today is more difficult than before. The climate has changed, the food has become adulterated with chemicals, and people are becoming hybrid. Even people living in rural areas want to live like those living in Bombay or even America. People are adjusting to a life of growing desires and adulteration. They look for medicine to reduce the *dosa* [trouble] of the world they live in. See, we are becoming like you Americans.

—65-year-old practitioner of Ayurveda,
rural South India, 2000

Before one can begin to understand how health and illness are comprehended in different cultures, one must appreciate how the body is thought about and "sensed" (Nichter 2008). Ethnophysiology is the study of how bodily processes are understood in different cultures and how such understanding influences perceptions of health, physical development, illness, medicines, and diet.[1] Perceptions of bodily process influence what physical symptoms are deemed normal and abnormal at particular times and which ones are deemed serious enough to warrant treatment beyond simple palliative care. Ethnophysiology contributes to the meaning accorded to particular symptoms and plays an important role in determining thresholds of symptom tolerance.

An appreciation of ethnophysiology requires a consideration of bodily states associated with the rhythm of everyday life and notions of illness causality. Within popular health cultures, there are coexisting ideas about internalizing and externalizing factors that cause or are an outcome of illness (Young 1976). Internalizing factors involve ethnophysiological processes that are often explained through analogical reasoning. For example, digestion may be described as an internal cooking process, a process of churning, or a hydraulic process that may become blocked.[2] Externalizing factors (discussed shortly) involve agents of illness that may or may not act with intention and tend to be explained through narratives. Let me briefly illustrate how ideas about ethnophysiology are associated with perceptions of illness during child development, the seasons, synergistic relationships with worms, reproductive health, illness presentation and progression, pharmaceutical practice, and folk dietetics.

EXAMPLES OF ETHNOPHYSIOLOGY

Afflictions Tied to Child Development

In many cultures, certain afflictions are expected and viewed as milestone illnesses that occur during the course of child development (Nichter 1996a). Diarrhea has been linked to transitional periods such as teething and weaning, and acute respiratory infections (ARIs) have been linked to child development, as well as other factors such as changes in diet and the effects of climate. Because such illnesses are expected and related to developmental processes, caretakers may delay seeking medical attention for them. This is especially the case if the caretaker considers a trip to a health provider something that might further exacerbate a condition by exposing a sick child to heat, cold, or the wind—one reason sick children are often bundled up even in tropical countries.

Other developmental changes are associated with signs of illness. For example, in Cameroon, Ghana, and Nigeria, the presence of blood in the urine (hematuria) is associated with puberty and normal development among both adolescent boys and girls. A perception of "male menstruation" coexists with female menstruation. This has been reported to lead to delays in seeking treatment for schistosomiasis and other diseases that manifest with blood in the urine (Amazigo et al. 1997; Bello and Idiong 1982; Huang and Manderson 1992; Hunter 2003; Kloos 1995; Nash et al. 1982).

Seasons

Perceptions of ethnophysiology are sometimes modeled after local ecology. For example, in South India, humoral ideas about the body are modeled on observations of the seasons, the movement of winds, and the behavior of plants and animals. In these contexts, people anticipate bodily changes and illnesses that are commonly associated with seasonal changes in heat and cold, rainfall and dryness. As is noted in some detail shortly, fevers in different cultures may be expected at different times of the year; such expectations may influence diagnosis and patterns of treatment. Fevers may be expected in the hot season or when fruit is ripening, and respiratory symptoms may be expected during the rainy season or times of relative coolness. In some cases, such expectations are based on observation of illness prevalence, whereas in other cases, explanatory models are understood in humoral terms.

Times of seasonal change or changes in wind direction are often tied to general ill health as well as increased incidence of particular illnesses.[3] In locations where malaria and dengue fever are endemic and seasonal, fevers may be associated with spirits and winds that are prevalent at times of the year when illness is common. For example, among the Shipibo in Peru, it is thought that malaria and dengue spirits travel with the rain all over the world and that these diseases appear in their locality only during the rainy season (Doreen Montag, unpublished data).

Synergistic Relationships with Worms

Understanding ethnophysiology requires thinking ecologically. The cultural perceptions of worms present a case in point. In many parts of the world, including parts of the Caribbean, Ethiopia, India, Indonesia, and Latin America, a limited number of worms are thought to exist in the body from birth and to play a necessary role in digestion.[4] In cultural contexts where roundworms are ascribed a physiological function, people attempt to control the number of worms they have in their gut as well as the migration of worms within the body. However, despite this desire to control worms, they may not be keen to rid the body of all worms, because worms are perceived to serve a bodily function. It is widely recognized that children are especially prone to worm problems, and local explanations for this may focus on notions of ethnophysiology that differentiate child and adult bodies and draw more attention to children's diet than to hygiene, especially children's propensity to eat more sweet foods than adults do.[5]

Notions of ethnophysiology affect perceptions of other types of worms as well. In regions of both Nigeria and Ghana, the guinea worm is viewed as present in all human bodies, and thus unpreventable (Bierlich 1995; Brieger and Kendall 1992; Brieger et al. 1991). Children and elders in Ghana are thought to be less resistant to illness from the guinea worm than adults are because children have not yet developed sufficiently "strong blood" and the blood of elders has lost strength (Bierlich 1995). Ideas that symptoms such as swelling are signs of worm activity affect the diagnosis of diseases having overlapping characteristics. In Nigeria, Brieger and colleagues (1986) found that onchocerciasis was commonly mistaken for guinea worm, owing to the belief that all swelling was caused by guinea worm, even if a worm was never expelled from the skin.

Reproductive Health

Ethnogynecology, the study of local perceptions of woman's bodily processes, further illustrates the far-reaching importance of investigating local representations of physiology and pathology.[6] Ethnogynecology influences perceptions of menstruation, fertility, pregnancy, the postpartum period, contraception decisions, and the impact of reproductive health and women's health over the life course.[7] Much has already been written about cultural interpretations of menstruation as it relates to fertility, as a barometer for health, and as a means of bodily purification (e.g., Buckley and Gottlieb 1988; Castaneda et al. 1996; de Bessa 2006; Shail and Howie 2005; Sobo 1993a, 1993b). Let me cite a few other examples that illustrate how important ideas about ethnogynecology are and how they influence women's health care practices and decisions.

In the Gambia, fertility is thought about by women in biosocial terms that take into account both ethnophysiology and life contingencies (Bledsoe 2002; Bledsoe et al. 1994, 1998). Bledsoe and her colleagues found that women's decisions about when to have children and when to "space" child-bearing were based on their understanding of ethnogynecology, reproductive capacity throughout the life course, and their self-evaluation of health given the harshness of their lives.[8] Reproductive capacity and physical aging are not seen as strictly linear but are considered to be contingent on a woman's reproductive and health histories. Reproductive mishaps are viewed as more taxing to the body than normal pregnancies and birthing experiences. Bledsoe found that women use contraceptives to prevent this wearing down of the body and to conserve their strength, muscle, and blood for desired pregnancies in the future with their current or future partner.

Other studies have drawn attention to perceptions of ethnogynecology that influence when in the month women think they are most and least likely to become pregnant. In several cultures, perceptions of fertility are associated with time periods prior to or following menstruation, with the best times to avoid pregnancy being the middle of the month (de Bessa 2006; Maynard-Tucker 1989; Nichter and Nichter 1987, 1996a; Victora and Knauth 2001). In some cultures, procreation is thought to involve an ethno-physiological process that requires more than just one act of insemination. Males and females grow a baby through multiple acts of sexual exchange thought to nourish a fetus (Meigs 1986; Taylor 1988).[9]

Several studies have documented how perceptions of ethnogynecology influence the use of hormonal contraceptives and other family-planning modalities (Hardon 1997).[10] In a study of family planning in Sri Lanka, we (Nichter and Nichter 1996a) determined that many women who wanted to space their children were reluctant to use temporary methods of birth control. They feared that such methods would result in permanent infertility.[11] Their reasoning involved analogical thinking about agricultural seeds needing moist, fecund soil to sprout. The pill was thought to work by drying out the womb so that "seeds" could not take root. Women feared that drying of the womb might result in "dry rot" and render a woman unable to become moist again, thus preventing seeds from "sprouting" in the future. Similar analogical reasoning has been reported in the Middle East (Good 1980) and Cambodia (Sadana and Snow 1999). Further, Johnson-Hanks (2002) in Cameroon and de Bessa in Brazil (2006) document how fear of contraceptives is related to contraceptives' perceived effect on sexual desire, as this would affect both physical and social well-being.

Perceptions of how medicines affect bodily processes also affect the willingness of pregnant and lactating women to consume preventive medicine. In some areas of Nepal, night blindness (nyctalopia) is thought to be part of the pregnancy experience, much like morning sickness. Since night blindness is culturally associated with a "hot" body state, women are afraid to treat it with Western medicines, which are also generally thought to be heating (Christian et al. 1998).

Such ideas influence women's responses to "tropical diseases" as well.[12] Although malaria is particularly dangerous for pregnant women, pregnant women are often the least willing to take prophylactic medications. Helitzer-Allen and colleagues (1993) found that many Malawian women consider malaria-like symptoms to be normal during pregnancy, thus requiring no treatment. Although taking chloroquine in small doses to relieve symptoms is considered safe, its use for prevention during pregnancy is thought to be too risky (Helitzer-Allen and Kendall 1992). So-called bitter medicines such as chloroquine are often thought to cause abortions and miscarriages (e.g., Glik et al. 1987; Ndyomugyenyi et al. 1998; Reuben 1993; Ruebush et al. 1992; Spencer et al. 1987). Fear of taking medicines during pregnancy extends to iron supplementation programs. In several countries (Bahrain, Bolivia, Burkina Faso, East Africa, Honduras, India, and Indonesia), women have expressed concern about taking iron tablets during pregnancy, out of fear that doing so will cause increased birth weight and a difficult delivery (Aldarazi 1987; Bexell 1990; Galloway et al. 2002; Nichter and Nichter 1996b; Tripp et al. 2001). Similarly, fears of the potentially abortive effects of tuberculosis (TB) medicines have also been documented (Conanan and Valeza 1988; Liefooghe et al. 1995; Nichter 1997).

Women also fear that malaria and TB medicines may dry up breast milk or harm breast-fed children (Nichter 1997; Ruebush et al. 1992). For impoverished women who lack viable alternatives to breast-feeding, this concern about reduced lactation is especially high. The perception that TB medicines reduce lactation has been well documented as a contributor to nonadherence, although there is no evidence to suggest that TB medicine negatively affects breast-feeding or the quality of breast milk (American Academy of Pediatrics 2001; Lawrence and Lawrence 2004; Mathew 2004).[13] TB programs have yet to address this concern in educational materials (Nichter 2002b).

Given that women may be pregnant or lactating for a significant portion of their lives, ideas that medications are risky during these times can significantly affect disease control programs. For example, clinical guidelines exclude pregnant women, as well as breast-feeding women for the first one to nine weeks postpartum, from being treated with ivermectin for onchocerciasis. Some women and even some primary health care workers perceive ivermectin to be dangerous well beyond these nine weeks. Left untreated, infected women who breast-feed for one to two years between intermittent pregnancies become an important reservoir for the disease in Sierra Leone (Yumkella 1996).

When pregnant or breast-feeding women are reluctant to take medications or when women should be cautioned, research might explore whether special culturally sensitive messages are needed to assure them that the medicines being provided are safe for them in terms of their preexisting concerns, or whether new medicines (in appearance or in strength) need to be provided that are safe for pregnant and lactating women. This would make it easier for health staff to follow treatment guidelines as well.[14]

Health concerns related to ethnogynecology are not limited to fertility, pregnancy, and lactation. In many Latin American and Asian cultures, a woman's postpartum experience is linked to her future health. In northeastern Thailand, Whittaker (1996) and Boonmongkon and colleagues (2001) discuss the practice of lying on a bed suspended over hot coals (*yu fai*) for a number of days following delivery as a health promotion and harm reduction practice. "Staying by the fire" cleanses the womb of spoiled blood and waste fluids that have accumulated in the body during pregnancy and "dries out" the womb. If these fluids are not expelled, they are thought to remain within the body and cause weakness, chills, and infertility. It is thought that if the uterus is not dried out, women's risk of reproductive tract infections increases. Notably, women associate gynecological and health complaints ranging from weakness and body pain to prolapsed uterus with not staying by the fire at all or staying by the fire for an inadequate period of time. In many cultures, health complaints experienced later in life are associated with not having followed postpartum care practices.

Postpartum health concerns highlight an important lesson. Illness is not thought about only in relation to recent events and immediate causal factors; women recognize that inattention to health during a time of vulnerability may result in lifelong problems. Postpartum care is an example of preventive health care thinking and incorporates harm reduction practices that are oriented toward the future, not simply the present. As discussed, local practices are related to perceptions of ethnogynecology that take account of a woman's body over the life course.

Illness Presentation and Progression

Ideas about how an illness manifests itself are often related to perceptions of pathophysiology. For example, in many cultures there exists a concept of "inside fever," which is an internal fever undetectable by touching the outside of the body or measurement with a thermometer. Inside fever has been associated with rashes and diarrhea in India as well as dry cough in the Philippines (Nichter and Nichter 1996c) and hydrocele in Ghana (Gyapong et al. 1996). In Ghana, cumulative experiences with inside fever among men are believed to cause it to settle in the scrotum and cause swelling (hydrocele) when not treated effectively. Similarly, among women, inside fever is believed to settle in the breasts.

For impoverished people in developing countries, health is relative and prevention may largely be conceived in terms of preventing minor illnesses from becoming more serious ones (Nichter 2003a). Three notable examples involve reproductive health, TB, and dengue fever. The reproductive health example is particularly poignant and illustrates how iatrogenic notions of pathophysiology related to illness progression may emerge when public health programs are introduced without appropriate attention to popular health culture. In northeastern Thailand, women's concerns about reproductive health problems (including reproductive tract infections and abdominal pains of various etiologies that are culturally associated with the uterus) grew steadily during the 1990s (Boonmongkon et al. 1999). Concern escalated following a government-sponsored screening program for cervical cancer that drew local attention to this disease. Medical anthropological research showed that the perceived prevalence of cervical cancer grew to be several orders of magnitude higher than the prevalence rate estimated by epidemiologists. Women came to imagine that both vaginal discharge and pain associated with the uterus were evidence of wounds or ulcers forming within the body that might eventually progress to cancer.[15] As a result, many women suffering from easily treatable problems, such as recurrent fungal infections, experienced psychological distress that disrupted their lives and sexual relationships with husbands. They also engaged in inappropriate self-medication with antibiotics for a wide range of symptoms in an attempt to reduce their risk of cancer. This example dramatically illustrates that ethnographic data on local health concerns are as important to address in evidence-based public health programs as epidemiological data when considering what constitutes serious threats to well-being.[16]

A second instance of an illness representation involving the progression of one illness to another is the category of "weak lungs" in the Philippines. In Mindoro and southern Luzon, minor respiratory conditions are widely imagined to be capable of developing into more-serious illnesses, including "pulmonia" and bronchitis (illnesses that often, but not always, overlap with pneumonia), whooping cough, weak lungs and TB, and eventually lung cancer (Alonzo et al. 1991; Nichter and Nichter 1996c).[17] In the case of weak lungs, mucus is thought to coat and dry on the lungs like coats of paint until the afflicted has difficulty breathing (Nichter 1997). Yet weak lungs are held to be fairly common and are considered a precursor to TB if not treated. For this reason, a diagnosis of weak lungs is not stigmatized like a diagnosis of TB, and members of the community as well as some practitioners tend to label TB that is not advanced as weak lungs. The ramifications of this conception of weak lungs as a TB precursor require further study. One observation made in the early 1990s was that it leads some people who were prescribed TB medication (mostly isoniazid, or INH) to share it with other family members who had respiratory infections, or for people to buy INH over the counter as a form of harm reduction (Nichter 1997). If people take INH to prevent persistent respiratory illnesses from progressing, resistance to INH may follow, limiting the effectiveness of an essential drug in the treatment of TB. I observed similar behavior in Tamil Nadu, India, in the 1980s (Nichter, unpublished data), but additional research is needed on the extent to which other curative drugs are used to prevent minor illness from progressing to more serious illnesses.

A third example involves progressions of fevers. In several different parts of the world, there is a belief that minor fevers may transform into major febrile illnesses such as pneumonia, typhoid, malaria, and dengue. For example, in the Yucatán region of Mexico, it is commonly believed that a minor fever can progress to become dengue if left untreated (Winch et al. 1991). I discuss fever and fears of its progression in greater depth shortly.

Pharmaceutical Practice

As already noted, ethnophysiology can significantly influence medication usage. Let me cite a few other examples, this time related to children. Mothers in several Asian countries (e.g., Indonesia, India, Philippines, Thailand) are reluctant to give Western medications, especially injections, to children with measles (Serquina-Ramiro et al. 2001). For measles to be cured, it is thought that heat and toxins need to be expelled from the body. Taking medicine that might impede this process is considered dangerous. In the Philippines, we (Nichter and Nichter 1996c) documented cases of children dying from pneumonia while suffering from measles because of a delay in seeking health care. Mothers postponed taking children to clinics that they would have normally visited more rapidly had their child not had measles.

Measles is not the only illness that mothers are afraid to treat with biomedicine because of a fear that such medicine might obstruct or delay the process of healing. In her ethnography of "fruit fever" (*khai makmai*) in northeastern Thailand, a region with one of the highest prevalence rates for both malaria and dengue fever in Thailand, Pylypa (2004, 2007) identified a folk illness that complicates the diagnosis and treatment of malaria and dengue among ethnic Lao. In the season when fruits are ripening, people treat all fevers with caution. When fever is experienced during this time, people may wait a few days to see whether a rash emerges before consulting a health care provider. If such a rash appears, fruit fever may be suspected and herbal medicine taken, while Western oral medications may be avoided. Western medications are believed to trap the symptomatic bumps within the body, placing the person in greater danger. Furthermore, intravenous fluid and intramuscular injections are especially feared in cases thought to be fruit fever; these are thought to lead to death by interfering with the natural progression of the disease.

In northern Ghana, some medicinal injections are at once valued and feared among the Dagomba. For the rather ambiguous illness category *jogu*, which is associated with boils (especially those black in color) and excess body heat, injections are considered deadly because they are seen to exacerbate already-dangerous body heat. As a result, injections are thought to cause the blood within the body to clot (Bierlich 2000).

Despite such instances, injections remain popular in developing countries but not for everyone equally. In many contexts, injections are preferred for school-age children and adults but not for younger children, because their bodies are not thought able to withstand strong medicines. Concern that young children will be given injections when ill has led to reluctance on the part of parents to take their children to health clinics or hospitals. For example, in Zambia and Tanzania, injections are generally believed to be more efficacious than oral medications for severe malaria. However, when a young child is seriously ill, injections are avoided. Anticipating that clinic staff will attempt to administer an injection has led families to avoid seeking care at government health facilities (Baume et al. 2000; Oberlander and Elverdan 2000; Williams et al. 1999). What underlies fear of injections for malaria when young children are already exposed to vaccination programs? Is it primarily a perception of the strength of injections at a time when the child is weak that has led to concern? Or are other ideas about how injections work in the body or perceptions of the course of illness involved?

Folk Dietetics

Representations of health are often framed in terms of a population's perceptions of appropriate diet. In most parts of the world, people depend on one staple, such as rice, that provides an embodied sense of well-being based on predictable food transit time, routine digestive cycles, and associated bodily signs, such as urine color and the consistency of feces. Perceptions of a basic minimal diet (how much of a staple food household members require; see Nichter and Nichter 1981) underlie household production of health strategies and local evaluations of food security (Messer 1997).

The importance of staple foods and representations of a healthy diet are aptly illustrated by the experience of refugee programs. During a crisis in Rwanda in the 1990s, many refugees fled to Tanzania, where camps were supplied with maize, even though most rural Rwandans previously relied on root crops and cassava flour. In the Ngara camp, Pottier (1996) reported that most of the maize distributed was an unprocessed whole grain. Rwandans do not traditionally eat loose grain; even when it is boiled and turned into porridge, it is not deemed a healthy food source. Rwandan refugees complained that they were being forced by aid agencies to eat food that would make them sick. The incidence of diarrhea in the camps was blamed directly on maize by the refugees. This is not an isolated incident. Reed and Habicht (1998) studied use of food aid by refugees in Zaire and found the same cultural aversion to maize. Refugees there complained that many children died due to diarrhea and vomiting because they were forced to eat maize and lentils, both unfamiliar and undesirable foods. While refugees welcomed any help they could get in the early days of the camps, their sense of well-being over time was tied to their staple diet.

Cultural representations of the properties of specific foods and when foods are not suitable for consumption significantly influence folk dietetics and pharmaceutical practices. Foods and changes in diet are thought to predispose and cause illnesses in many cultures. For instance, the eating of sweet foods is thought to cause a local category of illness in Nigeria termed *jedi jedi*, manifested as diarrhea, hemorrhoids, and impotence (Odebiyi 1989).[18] This interferes with oral rehydration programs. The population feared that oral rehydration therapy (ORT; a solution of sugar and salt) would worsen jedi jedi—a conception that challenged local health-education initiatives and demanded considerable cultural sensitivity (Brieger 1990).[19] In northeastern Thailand, fear of consuming inappropriate foods (especially foods locally classified as fruits) while ill with a fever suspected of being "fruit fever" is of greater concern. Contraindicated (*phit*) foods and medicines are commonly held responsible for fever-related deaths including cases found to be malaria (Pylypa 2004, 2007).

Some foods are also thought to enhance health and prevent illness. For example, bitter foods and foods that increase urination and clean the intestines are consumed during the rainy season in southwestern India to avert illness (Nichter 1986, 2003a). In addition to having inherent medicinal qualities, foods are thought to have qualities that may either complement or interfere with the efficacy of medicine. One of the most common questions South Indians ask practitioners is what foods they should avoid eating while taking specific medicines.

Foods are evaluated in many ways, ranging from their physical properties to their effect on the body in different seasons and when one has different health problems. It is worth highlighting three valuable lessons learned by health social scientists studying folk dietetics in developing countries.[20]

First, there is an important difference between cultural representations of appropriate dietary practice and actual dietary practice. Not only do food practices vary from person to person in accordance with individual responses to particular foods (explained by bodily constitution) but also folk dietary rules are commonly broken due to preference or convenience, unless they involve a serious taboo.[21] Key questions include who follows dietary rules, when, and for what reason. Generally, those people deemed most vulnerable in a population are those most likely to follow folk dietetic rules: pregnant and lactating mothers, infants and the elderly, and those who are ill or convalescent. Often, these are the people who remind others in their culture about folk dietetic and preventive health principles (Nichter 1986, 1987b, 2003a).

Second, more than one model of ethnophysiology may coexist within popular health culture. In our study of dietary practice during pregnancy in South India (Nichter and Nichter 1996b), we found that within the same community there existed a divergence of opinion as to whether eating more or less during pregnancy would result in a woman having a bigger or smaller baby.[22] Some women ate more so that they would have a smaller baby at the time of delivery, reflecting the belief that the baby and food shared the same stomach space. Others ate more to have a larger baby, and still others ate less to have a smaller baby.[23] The take-home message is that intracultural diversity in perceptions of ethnophysiology exists and needs to be explored.

Lastly, although illness is often attributed to inappropriate diet, an important determination to make is whether the primary and immediate cause of illness is diet alone or the perception that diet has rendered a person weak and susceptible to illness in conjunction with other causes. In some cases, insufficient food or untimely eating is thought to render one vulnerable to illness, while in other cases, the properties of specific foods or food combinations are thought to give rise to specific illnesses. For example, diarrhea and respiratory illness (as well as a number of tropical diseases) are widely associated with eating the wrong kinds of foods at particular times. Guinea worm in Nigeria (Brieger and Kendall 1992) and schistosomiasis in Egypt (Winch and Mehanna 1995) and Zambia (Kaona et al. 1994) are both attributed entirely or partly to diet. Finally, nearly half of those patients interviewed by Mull and colleagues (1989) in their study of leprosy in Pakistan identified food combinations as a causal agent.

An issue that requires additional attention is how diet-based explanations of illness interface with other notions of causality. Do they deflect attention from explanations involving pathogens or disease vectors, or is diet viewed as a predisposing factor that renders one vulnerable to other causal agents?

PERCEPTIONS OF ETHNOPHYSIOLOGY ARE NOT STATIC

Ideas about how the body functions are dynamic. They change in response to public health messages, medical advertisements, and emergent analogical frameworks related to changing technology (Nichter 1989a; Nichter and Nichter 1996e).[24] Future research on ethnophysiology must document changes and revisions in how local populations respond to new information, whether in the form of overt health messages or in medical and diagnostic practices that a population comes to interpret in one or more ways. Far more research is needed on images of physiological processes used in medical advertising now that far more advertising is targeting consumer populations in urban areas.

NOTES

1. Ethnophysiology is distinct from the term *local biology*. I discuss local biology in chapter 8.
2. Some examples of ethnographies that describe ethnophysiological processes include Bastien 1985 for Bolivia, Good 1980 for Iran, Lambert 1992 for India, Sivin 1987 for China, Sobo 1993a and 1993b and Quinlan 2004 for the Caribbean, Tabor 1981 for India, and Taylor 1988 for Rwanda.
3. In some cases, the qualities of seasons are directly linked to states of illness. In other instances, the kind and/or amount of foods seasonally available and work cycles are associated with states of health and illness.
4. For examples of ethnographies that address the cultural significance of worms, see Booth et al. 1993; Geissler 1998; Kendall et al. 1984a; Quinlan et al. 2002; Sobo 1993a, 1993b.
5. In a somewhat related way, septic wounds in some cultures are related more to blood impurities and diet than to hygiene. For example, in South India, those with wounds or skin diseases are restricted from consuming foods thought to produce pus, increase body heat, cause internal toxins to react, or draw tiny worms to the wound (Nichter 1986). Sepsis is often treated more through diet than through wound cleansing.
6. Differences in male and female perceptions of ethnophysiology are important to document, but most studies have focused on one gender or the other. For an example of a study that attends to both genders, see Victora and Knauth 2001.
7. Women's health is a broad subject area. A burgeoning literature has emerged in the past twenty-five years on women's sexual and reproductive health over the life course as well as on the experience of infertility and reproductive tract infections. More research is needed on how the health of elderly women is interpreted in relation to their reproductive histories and the extent to which they were able to follow cultural prescriptions related to the postpartum experience. Another topical area only recently addressed is the perception of women's bodies as seen in relationship to the reproductive capacity of their male partners. Inhorn (1994, 2003) provides a recent study of infertility that draws attention to the ways in which traditional and changing knowledge of male infertility influences representations of women's fertility.

8. Johnson-Hanks (2005) reports similar behavior in Cameroon and introduces the useful term *judicious opportunism* to describe women's reproductive decision making in contexts of "radical uncertainty." Less attention has been focused on men and their notions of ethnophysiology associated with sexuality, fertility, and the aging process. Van der Geest (2001) provides one of the few good case studies that do so.

9. Procreation is a biosocial process in cultures where babies are perceived as being produced through multiple forms of interaction, conjugal and otherwise, and not just the result of one act of insemination. Strathern (1988) provides an instructive example from Melanesia, where a child is seen as the outcome of interactions of multiple others, and many different types of exchange. In this case, procreation requires a consideration of both ethnophysiology and local biology, a concept introduced by Lock (1993) to describe how bodies and culture mutually constitute each other. The success of a pregnancy may also depend on ritual behavior engaged in by the father. In several societies, the father maintains a metonymic relationship with the mother-to-be pre- and postdelivery, a relationship known as *couvade*. Ritual actions may vary from not sitting in doorways (symbolic of obstruction) to maintaining food restrictions that mimic those of the mother to experiencing sympathetic labor pains (Doja 2005; Middleton 2000).

10. Studies from several parts of the world have also documented the perception that sterilization procedures result in humoral bodily imbalances, weakness, long-standing health problems, and bodily complaints that emerge late in life. Such perceptions are biosocial in nature and reflect the interaction between biological and social states. Biosocial perceptions of ethnogynecology and cultural preferences for dryness and relative wetness during sex also demand investigation before interventions such as microbicides are introduced (Braunstein and van de Wijgert 2005).

11. Several other studies document the fear that temporary methods of family planning may result in permanent states of infertility. See, for example, Castle 2003 in Mali and Bledsoe et al. 1998 in the Gambia.

12. Research is needed on how women interpret reproductive health problems (ranging from vaginal discharge to infertility) related to such diseases as schistosomiasis (Talaat et al. 2004) and tuberculosis (Figueroa-Damian et al. 1996; Namavar Jahromi et al. 2001).

13. According to the Centers for Disease Control (CDC), breast-feeding should not be discouraged for women being treated with first-line antituberculosis drugs because the concentrations of these drugs in breast milk are too small to produce toxicity in the nursing newborn. However, drugs in breast milk are not an effective treatment for TB disease in a nursing infant. Breast-feeding women taking INH should also take pyridoxine (vitamin B6) supplementation (see www.cdc.gov/nchstp/tb/pubs/tbfactsheets/250160.htm).

14. Health staff are often reluctant to offer the ill or vulnerable preventive medications out of fear of being blamed if mothers or their children become ill shortly thereafter. This concern was documented during ethnographic research on missed opportunities for vaccinations in India. Despite guidelines, health staff were reluctant to immunize children sick with minor respiratory illnesses, skin diseases, and diarrhea (Nichter 1991a).

15. Other anthropological studies of women's reproductive health have drawn attention to a wide range of local health concerns related to who gets cervical cancer following public health screening programs (Chavez et al. 2001; Gregg 2003; Wood et al. 1997).

16. Women's understandings of the relationship between ethnogynecology and illness are important to address for more than psychological reasons. Public health researchers need to pay credence to women's empirical observations of their bodies, health concerns, and response to medical procedures, medicines, contraceptives, devices, etc.

17. For other examples of respiratory illnesses perceived to transform from one illness category to another, see Cody et al. 1997; Hudelson et al. 1994; Stewart et al. 1994.

18. The consumption of sweet foods is associated with illness in other areas of Africa as well. In Ghana, sweet foods are associated with fevers that can predispose one to hydrocele, a symptom of filariasis (Gyapong et al. 1996). Curiously, the increased consumption of monosodium glutamate (MSG) in the same region has been linked to a rise in the prevalence of filariasis. In Sierra Leone, sweet foods are thought to cause worm problems and are controlled by the consumption of bitter things (Bledsoe and Goubaud 1985).

19. Another reason that giving a salt-sugar solution appeared odd to mothers was that worms are activated by sugar, and *jedi jedi* may be caused by worms. In other cultures, salt also has cultural significance. Green and colleagues (1994) describe the challenge of encouraging the use of salt in ORT in central Mozambique, where young children are not given salt before their teeth appear, for fear of making them sick.

20. Folk dietetics vary in complexity by culture and among different strata of the same culture. For an example of a fairly complex folk dietetic tradition in South India, see Nichter 1986.

21. Bentley and colleagues (1999) provide a good example of how folk dietetic rules are manipulated in Lese society in the Congo. Pregnant and lactating women are subjected to many food taboos. During hunger season, however, they snack more frequently, are more apt to taste what they cook, cheat on adherence to food taboos (by discounting them or by using prophylactic plants that supposedly prevent the negative consequences of breaking taboos), cooperate with other women more frequently in projects that lead to food sharing, and hide desirable resources from other household members. Bentley suggests that Lese women are able to reduce nutritional constraints that would affect their ability to reproduce by consciously bending the rules in hunger season far more than at other times.

22. In our 1980 study (Nichter and Nichter 1996b) of women's food consumption during pregnancy in rural South India, we found that women's dietary practices were influenced by physical ailments experienced as well as concern about baby size. Subsequent studies elsewhere in South India have suggested that reduction in food consumption is primarily related to women's physical ailments during pregnancy (Andersen et al. 2003; Hutter 1994). In our study, we specifically interviewed women about ethnophysiology and not just diet, a subject that led them to talk about baby space, which led to the observation being made.

23. Perceptions of ethnophysiology affect nutritional advice and medicine-taking behavior during pregnancy. For example, it has been reported in several different cultural contexts that some pregnant women choose not to take the ferrous sulfate tablets given to them by primary health center staff, for fear that the medicine will result in a larger baby and a more difficult delivery. See Galloway et al. 2002 for a review of this concern and behavior pattern. Notably, differing ideas within the same communities present an opportunity for dialogue. See also Tripp et al. 2001 for a consideration of cultural reasons for both under- and overconsumption of micronutrient supplements in Somali and Sudanese refugee camps in Kenya.

24. For a review of analogical reasoning underlying representations of the body as a procedure for engaging in education by appropriate analogy, see Nichter and Nichter 1996d.

2

Representations of Illness Causality and Vectors That Transmit Disease

When one is weak, they are vulnerable to all manner of malevolent forces from wandering hungry *buta* and *preyta* [spirits] to germs. When one is sick they need more than just medicines, they need protection until they become strong. I help them identify what is causing their troubles as well as offer them protection. I help them see when illness is a sign of other troubles, when they need to make offerings to particular spirits and deities, and when they need to block sorcery. I also advise people who are ill to see a *vaidya* or doctor. I do not give a name, but I give the direction where they will find a suitable practitioner. But if a man is weak because he is hungry, what can I do? The biggest cause of sickness here is poverty. The reason vows to ancestor spirits and household deities are not fulfilled, the reason village Buta Kola [yearly rituals] are not performed and sorcery is increasing is poverty, and the politics of land reform.

—Exorcist, South Kannara District,
state of Karnataka, India, 1975

Much of the large ethnomedical literature on illness causality in different cultures describes cultural conceptions of how illnesses are caused and why they occur when they do. Let me highlight a few lessons learned from illness ethnographies and then consider local perceptions of disease vectors and the ways they are thought to be involved in the transmission of "tropical diseases."[1]

Multiple Causality

As noted earlier, one finds both internalizing and externalizing factors associated with ill health (Young 1976) in most cultures.[2] While internalizing factors involve ethnophysiological processes, externalizing forces (such as spirits and ghosts, sorcery and the evil eye, stars and planets) involve agents of misfortune that may or may not intentionally cause harm. Internalizing and externalizing factors are often viewed as interactive. External forces can result in disrupted internal processes, and internal disruptions cause vulnerability that opens one up to external forces. Both externalizing and internalizing causes of illness can also be triggered by emotional states that may be a cause of illness.[3] The afflicted and members of their therapy management groups generate ad hoc explanations for illness experiences that provide models of and models for action. Often, ill health tends to be understood in terms of both narratives and analogies (Kirmayer 2000). What is important is finding some images around which an illness narrative can take shape (Good 1994).

In most cultures, several different internal and external factors are thought to predispose, cause, or contribute to illness. In some cases, a specific type of illness is attributed to a specific etiology. In many other cases, however, any one of several or a combination of causal factors can be thought to cause illness (called multiple causality). Consider, for example, the wide range of factors thought to cause or predispose TB in South India, as illustrated in figure 1.[4]

Survey data are often unable to distinguish between a factor that is thought to predispose one to illness and a factor that directly causes an illness. It is common for one factor to be seen as predisposing a population to a wide variety of illnesses by creating a state of vulnerability. For example, in India, excessive heat resulting from engaging in "heating activities" may either predispose or cause one to experience diarrhea, skin rash, burning urine, or fever, depending on the circumstances.

Let me cite a different example. In the Philippines, a condition known as *pasma*, described either as a shock to the body caused by sudden changes from hot to cold (climatic changes as well as activities) or a shock brought about by hunger (*pasma sa gutom*), renders people weak and vulnerable to respiratory illness, TB, and malaria (Espino and Manderson 2000; Espino et al. 1997; Miguel et al. 1999; Nichter 1997; Palis et al. 2006; Tallo 1999; Tan 1996).[5] Pasma is a major health concern in the Philippines and influences a wide variety of health behavior. For example, agricultural laborers recognize that exposure to pesticides is harmful for health, but many do not wear protective clothing or bathe after spraying fields, for fear of pasma. Pasma related to becoming overheated by wearing gloves or shocking the body by bathing when hot is seen as predisposing workers to chronic illness conditions (such as rheumatoid arthritis). Filipino farmers' concern for the risks of pasma supersedes their concern for the health risks from pesticides (Palis et al. 2006).[6]

FIGURE I. Factors causing or predisposing tuberculosis

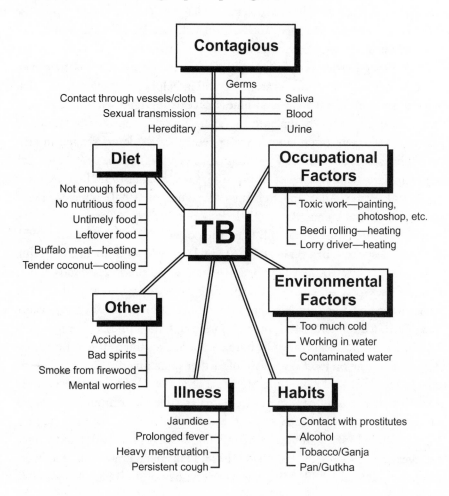

It is also important to recognize that an illness may be viewed as one of a number of possible signs of malevolence caused by external factors such as sorcery, witchcraft, and the wrath of ancestor spirits.[7] In this case, treating an illness requires attending to the deeper cause of misfortune through divination as well as diagnosis. Among the Xhosa-speaking people of South Africa, for example, TB is associated both with a lack of hygiene and with witchcraft, leading people to seek the treatment of a diviner first (de Villiers 1991). Only when traditional treatment fails is Western medicine sought. In other cases, treatment from traditional practitioners may be sought to address the cause of misfortune before Western medicines are used, so that these medicines may be effective. For example, Filipinos reason that bodily dislocations (*pilay hangin*) resulting from a fall or physical mishap may be the underlying cause of lung problems or diarrhea among children. If these dislocations are not rectified, medication will not be effective and scarce resources will be wasted (Nichter and Nichter 1996c).

Another lesson learned from studies of illness causality is that even when health-education efforts are successful in helping people recognize that a vector or "germs" are a cause of illness, preexisting representations of causality are not necessarily replaced or superseded. Rather, interpretations of illness causality are often cumulative or syncretic,[8] as demonstrated in ethnographic studies of dengue (e.g., Kendall et al. 1991), filariasis (Coreil et al. 1998), malaria (e.g., Brieger et al. 1984–85; Gessler et al. 1995; Hausmann et al. 2002; Helitzer-Allen and Kendall 1992; Munguti 1998), schistosomiasis (e.g., Huang and Manderson 1992; Imevbore et al. 1990; Kaona et al. 1994; Winch and Mehanna 1995), TB (e.g., Liefooghe et al. 1997; Nichter 1997), onchocerciasis (e.g., Brieger et al. 1986), and leprosy (e.g., Gerochi 1986; Mull et al. 1989; White 2002). Many people who learned to associate mosquitoes with diseases such as malaria or dengue fever have done so in ways that differ from biomedical thinking. Mosquitoes are thought to spread diseases because they breed in dirty places and spread filth through their bites, either by laying eggs in water that is consumed by humans and makes them sick, or by urinating or defecating on food as a means of further spreading disease (e.g., Espino et al. 1997; Pylypa 2004, 2007; Stephens et al. 1995). However, even after accepting that mosquitoes are a cause of malaria, people continue to attribute malaria to other causes such as weather changes; exposure to the sun, rain, cold, or wind; drinking dirty or contaminated water; or hard work and fatigue (Brieger et al. 1984–85; Gessler et al. 1995; Hausmann et al. 2002; Helitzer-Allen and Kendall 1992; Miguel et al. 1999; Munguti 1998; Ongore et al. 1989; Ramakrishna et al. 1989; Ruebush et al. 1992).[9]

Studies of malaria in Africa (Hausmann et al. 2002) and Southeast Asia (Pylypa 2004), as well as studies of leprosy conducted in Africa (Opala and Boillot 1996) and Southeast Asia (Boonmongkon 1995), have illustrated that rather than being replaced, indigenous notions of causality often interact with biomedical explanatory models, producing hybrid ideas. What results are reinterpretations of biomedical ideas in ways that fit local understandings of cosmology, ethnophysiology, vulnerability, and etiology. I return to this point later in a consideration of hybrid ideas that have spun off from public health campaigns.

The mere existence of indigenous ideas about illness causality does not mean that new ideas about causality will not be accepted.[10] Some researchers have commented that people in other health cultures appear to live with far more cognitive dissonance about illness causality than do people in Western cultures (MacLachlan and Carr 1994). This is debatable.[11] A far more useful way of appreciating how multiple causes of an illness are thought about simultaneously is to recognize that "what if" thinking (Good and Good 1994) is facilitated by recognition of several different levels of causality, ranging from the proximate to the distal.

Anthropologists have long recognized that illness may be conceptualized in terms of multiple levels of causality involving instrumental, efficient, and ultimate causes (e.g., Glick 1967). For example, in a study of Kyasanur forest disease (Nichter 1987a), I found that even when South Indians accepted that this arboviral disease was caused by ticks, they still questioned what it was that rendered one community more vulnerable to the illness than another and why some individuals were more susceptible than others. Although ticks were considered a likely immediate cause of "monkey forest disease," many South Indians suspected that the anger of deities was involved because only isolated villages were affected. By lay epidemiological reasoning, people identified those communities most at risk as those that were both unable to hold annual rituals as a result of disrupted social relationships following land reform and also experiencing deforestation and the destruction of sacred trees. People reasoned that deities had either sent this tick-borne problem or had not protected communities or households against it.

One of the problems with the notion of multiple causality is that people may come to believe that there is no way to avoid or control an illness such as malaria (Oaks et al. 1991). A related challenge is that the illness may be subclassified into many different subtypes. Health messages must then confront multiple types of an illness, an issue I address shortly in a consideration of illness classification.

PERCEPTIONS OF CONTAGIOUS AND HEREDITARY ILLNESS

Understanding a local population's recognition of disease transmission routes (also known as "lay epidemiology")[12] is critical to preventive health interventions.[13] Diverse perceptions of contagion and transmission have been widely documented in developing countries and involve contaminated food, touch, breath, contact with human fluids (e.g., their urine, feces, blood, menstrual blood, spit, sputum, and semen), and physically stepping over such human waste products.[14] We know little about when and for how long the afflicted are considered contagious once ill.

Studies of TB in India, Pakistan, and the Philippines have found a wide range of ideas about when, how, and for how long someone with TB is contagious (Liefooghe et al. 1995; Nichter 1997, 2002b). According to some people in the Philippines, a person afflicted with TB is contagious only after they begin to spit blood. Other Filipinos suggest that even those with "weak lungs," a precursor to TB, are contagious. In this case, contagion is more widely thought to relate to contact with food touched by the afflicted than with inhalation of airborne pathogens. In both the Philippines and India, there is a wide range of ideas and much confusion about how long one remains contagious after taking TB medications—from a few days to a few years. Notably, national TB directly observed therapy short-course (DOTS) programs do not include an education module that addresses such basic health concerns. An ongoing study of TB in India (Nichter 2002b) has shown that health care providers are poorly informed about how to answer patients and their families when they ask questions about contagion following the initiation of treatment.[15]

Another lesson learned is that contagion is often conflated with the notion of hereditary illness; perceptions of vertical and horizontal contagion merge, and illness clustering mimics heredity. Studies of filariasis conducted in Ghana (Ahorlu et al. 1999; Gyapong et al. 1996), India (Bandyopadhyay 1996), and Thailand (Rauyajin et al. 1995) have determined that many people consider this disease to be hereditary because it spreads within households. In India, some women blamed themselves for passing the illness on to a child, linking edema they suffered during pregnancies to the symptoms of the disease. And in the Philippines and India, TB is thought to be a hereditary illness as well as one transmitted by those who are ill (Nichter 1997). In Cameroon, onchocerciasis is recognized to be caused by the bite of the black fly, but a majority also believe it may be transmitted sexually as well as parentally (Hewlett et al. 1996).

Public health messages about contagion need to be critically examined and local response to these messages carefully monitored. Take, for example, messages pointing to the unhygienic habits of particular communities as creating conditions for communicable diseases. Ideas inadvertently introduced in the course of identifying groups at risk can foster a process of blaming and "othering" that stigmatizes groups and reinforces preexisting prejudices and group animosities. For example, a population labeled as a *group at risk* may be seen as unhygienic as a result of cultural practices that set them apart from a dominant group or types of behavior adopted because of poverty but ascribed to the minority group's "character."[16] This process of othering has been widely observed in studies of HIV/AIDS and TB (e.g., Castro and Farmer 2005; Coker 2004; Crawford 1994; Farmer 1992, 1996; Gilman 1988; Rosenberg 1992; Schoeph 2001) as well as cholera (Anderson 1995; Ghosh and Coutinho 2000; Nations and Monte 1996; Briggs 1999, 2001). It is equally true for other stigmatized diseases, especially during an epidemic.[17]

Messages about contagion may also be reinterpreted as messages about hereditary illnesses that could affect family members' social status or marriageability. Unmarried women in India often travel some distance for TB treatment, instead of receiving treatment in a more convenient but less confidential setting. Health education messages that emphasize that TB is not hereditary and clarify that one is not contagious after taking medicine for a fixed amount of time might help allay fears of contagion, increase chances for adherence to treatment, and reduce stigma.

The perception that illness is hereditary has been widely reported in the literature in relation to many different types of disease. Yet little research has been conducted on how people respond to the perception that a particular illness "runs in the family" and whether actions are taken to reduce the chances of this occurring. Future studies of chronic diseases such as diabetes will demand such a consideration.[18]

Perceptions of Vectors Associated with "Tropical Diseases"

Considerable research has been conducted on cultural recognition of transmission vectors associated with tropical diseases.[19] A review of this research reveals that levels of recognition appear to vary widely by class, rural versus urban residence, and education. In several cultural contexts, either vectors are not recognized to cause illness or the wrong vectors are the focus of attention. In Malaysia (Evans et al. 1993; Haliza and Mohd 1986), southern Thailand (Rauyajin et al. 1995), the Sorsogon region of the Philippines (Lu et al. 1988), and parts of South India (Bandyopadhyay 1996; Ramaiah et al. 1996), only a minority of people identified mosquitoes as a causal agent of filariasis. In Andean communities in Bolivia (Bastien 1998), neither triatomine insects nor other vectors are commonly associated with Chagas disease. Many people in the Congo (Leygues and Gouteux 1989) do not associate tsetse fly with African trypanosomiasis. And in Nigeria, few people were found to associate simulium flies with onchocerciasis (Awolola et al. 2000). People interviewed by Arana and colleagues (2000) in their study of leishmaniasis in Guatemala associated the disease with insect bites, but they did not identify the correct insect. In the Colombian rain forest, mosquitoes are not thought to be an agent of malaria transmission, and malarial fevers are viewed as an unavoidable part of rain forest life (Lipowsky et al. 1992). Mosquitoes are only weakly linked by the public to malaria in some parts of Kenya (Mwenesi et al. 1995; Ongore et al. 1989) and Ghana (Agyepong 1992; Atkins et al. 1993). And in areas where both dengue fever and malaria coexist, it is not uncommon for messages about specific vectors to become confused.

In many areas where malaria is endemic and health-education programs have been active, people are now aware that mosquitoes cause malaria. However, lay understanding of how mosquitoes cause malaria transmission is often quite different from that of health staff trained in biomedicine.[20] As noted earlier, in many parts of the world people think mosquitoes cause disease because they breed in dirty water and unclean places. Contact with these places either directly infects mosquitoes with germs or renders them carriers of impurity. Germs or impurities are injected into the bodies of humans from bites as well as being consumed in the form of mosquito eggs or wastes deposited in water sources. For this reason, people associate malaria with drinking contaminated water from ponds or slow-moving streams where mosquitoes congregate. Although they recognize that mosquitoes play a part in malaria transmission, they view malaria transmission as primarily waterborne. People having such a perception commonly say that a good way to prevent disease during malaria season (often the summer season, when fresh water is limited) is to boil drinking water.

The way a community understands mosquitoes can prove important to malaria control (Agyepong 1992). Ethnographic research has revealed not only that many people confuse the species of mosquito that causes malaria with those that cause dengue or filariasis, but also that they often have misguided notions about where one is most at risk from dangerous mosquitoes. For example, mosquitoes that live in one's home are often considered harmless, whereas mosquitoes outside one's home (Kendall et al. 1991) and in forest areas (Pylypa 2004) are believed dangerous. Studies of urban malaria in India have shown that malaria is believed to be caused by mosquitoes that breed in dirty water and uncollected garbage in slum areas of cities, and this is typically blamed on the poor (Kamat 2000; Nandita 1995).[21] In fact, the primary urban malaria vector, *Anopheles stephensi*, breeds in clear water and is often found in open water tanks on the roofs of apartment buildings and the pots of ornamental plants.[22] Mistaken perceptions of where dangerous mosquitoes breed influence disease-control strategies, which are sensitive to political pressure from the wealthy, who are all too willing to blame the poor for public health problems.

People's ideas about when mosquitoes are dangerous are also important to consider (Winch et al. 1994, 1995). They involve not only recognition of peak biting times during the day but also ideas about the seasons in which malaria is caused by mosquitoes. Winch and colleagues (1994) provide an instructive case study from Tanzania, where during the heavy rainy season there is an increase in all fever diseases. People associate fevers at this time with hard work, getting caught in the rain, and an increase in the number of mosquitoes. During the rainy season, people use bed nets and take anti-malarial medications promptly. When rains become lighter, during the rice harvest in June and July, people become much less vigilant about mosquitoes. Notably, during this time, childhood mortality from febrile illness is at its peak. Bed nets are used far less, and people more often suspect supernatural causes of fevers. Because the local population sees fewer mosquitoes, they wrongly assume that mosquitoes are less dangerous during this season. Instead, they attribute fevers to spirits who attack people to satisfy their hunger at a time when food is more abundant and nights are cold, rendering blood thin. As a result, people feel as though they have minimal resistance to malevolent spirits.

An intervention project for schistosomiasis in the Kaele region of Cameroon provides another instructive case study (Cline and Hewlett 1996; Hewlett and Cline 1997). The local population was found to associate schistosomiasis with the hot season, although disease transmission takes place throughout the year. The project team was unable to convince the majority of the local population that snails were linked to the disease and to motivate people to take an active interest in snail control.[23] However, they were able to introduce important behavioral changes that had a positive impact on disease prevalence. They did this by supporting the idea that the hot season was the time when symptoms occurred and treatment should be sought, while the wet season was the time when the disease was transmitted through contact with water.

Do changes in community awareness of vectors responsible for illness have an impact on people's thinking about prevention? A review of previous intervention projects reveals some success stories that suggest that changing representations of illness causality and increased knowledge about vector control may contribute to behavior change. For example, an *Aedes aegypti* breeding-site control project funded by the Rockefeller Foundation in Honduras and Mexico employed a social entomology approach, teaching community members about the biology, life cycle, and breeding sites of mosquitoes responsible for dengue fever. This resulted in measurable behavior change in the control of breeding sites at both the household and neighborhood levels. Social mapping of breeding sites identified different types of both disposable and nondisposable containers that acted as breeding sites and those people (by gender and age) generally responsible for the container or the space in which it was located (e.g., males, tires; children, pet dishes; women, washbasins and flowerpots; see Kendall 1998; Lloyd et al. 1994). Breeding-site control efforts involved a mix of interpersonal communication, mass communication, and social marketing that targeted specific people to engage in the control of specific breeding sites (Nichter, unpublished data, 1996–97). Representations of breeding-site responsibility were established that were attentive to existing gender norms.

Findings such as these are encouraging. However, in many contexts, increased attention to mosquito control, not just control of specific vectors, may be the answer to sustainable vector control programs (Agyepong and Manderson 1999; Macintyre et al. 2002). Where mosquitoes are considered a nuisance, local populations are motivated to control them, even when people are only minimally concerned with preventing dengue or other vector-borne diseases (Samuelsen 2004; Winch et al. 1991). Urban residents in tropical countries spend significant resources on relatively inefficient measures to combat mosquitoes (Lines et al. 1994). Programs that target mosquito control in general may have the advantage of maintaining community interest in breeding-site reduction even at times when the prevalence of vector-borne diseases is low. Community tolerance of all mosquitoes needs to be reduced and effective, and accessible, technologies for controlling breeding sites made available.

VULNERABILITY AND RISK

How a population experiences vulnerability and perceives risk influences how individuals within that population respond to public health interventions and the courses of action they choose to adopt or ignore. In the next chapter, I discuss representations of risk produced by health experts. First, though, let me draw attention to lessons learned about why laypeople feel vulnerable to illness and the efforts they take to reduce harm, especially when they feel as if they cannot control factors rendering them vulnerable.[24] Lupton (1999:104) has referred to this as the study of "risk subjectivities," which may be thought about in relation to (1) whether and to what extent individuals perceive themselves to be at risk for developing a particular health condition, (2) reflexive weighing of health risks against social risks, (3) what it means for the individual to be at risk, and (4) how individuals negotiate such "lived risk" inclusive of the practices they undertake in response to such perceptions. Negotiations of "lived risk" are often expressed in terms of risk avoidance and harm reduction (Nichter 2003a, 2006b). I would also call attention to the concepts of social risk and hierarchies of risk, two valuable concepts for examining social response to illness.

Sources of Risk

In a recent review of the literature, I identified five common sources of health vulnerability (Nichter 2003a). Let me briefly review these sources and add a sixth, a place-based notion of vulnerability.

Trait-Based Vulnerability. Individuals may reason that they have a weak constitution or predisposition to illness (in general or to a specific illness) on the basis of physical signs and symptoms interpreted as traces of some underlying truth about the person, a past history of illness or poor health that leads them to be labeled as weak or susceptible, or some association with a hereditary predisposition that indexes familial (or ethnic group) histories of illness. For example, in some areas of Tanzania, people associate vulnerability to malaria with the strength of one's blood, which is associated with innate constitution as well as state-based (environmental) factors (Hausmann et al. 2002).

Trait-based perceptions of "weak" and "strong" infants and children contribute to patterns of behavior described as "selective neglect" (Scheper-Hughes 1991, 1992) and "selective survival" (Howard 1994).[25] Perceptions of a child's chances of survival and productivity lead to diminished or preferential investment of material and emotional resources in contexts of poverty. Studies of children also suggest that trait-based perceptions of body constitution may also be tied to class identity, with upper-class children seen as more sensitive and vulnerable to fever and the elements (Nichter 1987b).

State-Based Vulnerability. A wide range of climatic and environmental factors is believed to render people vulnerable to health problems. Specific seasons are rightly and wrongly associated with increased vulnerability to specific diseases (malaria, dengue, etc.). Such perceptions influence both lay and practitioner diagnoses of episodes of ill health,[26] as well as the motivation to undertake preventive health measures such as bed-net use.[27]

Sudden changes in climate and particular types of wind are often thought to shock the body or cause humoral or hot-cold imbalances, rendering one vulnerable. Hunger and overwork can also leave one weak and vulnerable to sickness. Other state-based factors widely associated with vulnerability include transitional life stages such as pregnancy, infancy, and old age. These life stages are associated with states of openness, rapidly occurring transformation, and states of weakness. In many cultures, the experience of negative emotional states (anger, sadness, jealousy, shock) is thought to render one vulnerable to ill health. These states may also exacerbate an existing illness by upsetting the afflicted and opening them to malevolent forces that prey upon the weak. Other environmental factors may include supernatural forces within one's cosmology.

Vulnerability to Illness Transformation and Flare-Up. Investigating why a mild illness is thought to transform into a more serious one (whether of the same type or in a different category), why a latent disease flares up, or why a recurrent disease returns can provide insights into not only what people think causes illness but also what renders the afflicted vulnerable and leads to illness exacerbation. Research on "provoking factors" (Hunt et al. 1998) might provide clues to how local populations exposed to vector-borne diseases in endemic areas make sense of why some individuals become ill repeatedly, or more severely, and others do not. Attending to provoking factors instead of just focusing on more immediate causes of illness leads to a better appreciation of local health concerns tied to states of vulnerability (e.g., work load, basic needs such as housing and food availability).

Illnesses may transform and latent illness may flare up for any one of a host of reasons.[28] In the Philippines, many people think that TB can result from poorly treated respiratory illness, while some believe that lung cancer could occur as the result of poorly treated TB (Nichter 1997).[29] In Pakistan, there is a perception that tuberculosis medicines are ineffective during pregnancy and, furthermore, that pregnancy can reactivate tuberculosis even after a woman has been treated (Liefooghe et al. 1995). In Palawan in the Philippines, settlers from other islands who experience recurrent malaria are spoken of as *malariado.* The term has several different connotations, including the sense that one has adjusted to the local environment. A malariado easily suffers from malaria when in a weakened state attributable to hard work or hunger but does not contract severe malaria as newcomers do (Castillo-Carandang and Nichter, unpublished data, 1990).[30] Maintaining and regaining resistance (*resistensiya*) is a health concern central to Filipino perceptions of health promotion and the prevention of disease relapse and flare-up. In several South and Southeast Asian countries where I have conducted research, alcohol and tobacco are thought to cause a latent illness such as TB or sexually transmitted disease to flare up or reoccur.[31]

Cumulative Sources of Negativity. Vulnerability is also associated with the accumulation of some negative entity (e.g., impurities, residues, toxins, germs) within the body through time.[32] A common perception is that one can withstand some level of negative load but that once a threshold level has been surpassed, illness manifests. This perception of vulnerability has been documented in Thailand as an explanation for why some people fall ill after engaging in risky sex and others do not. It is also the basis of harm-reduction practices involving antibiotic use prior to sex (Nichter 2001, 2003a).[33] Cumulative risk reasoning also underlies explanations of why some people are more likely to get malaria in northeastern Thailand and the Philippines. Those who have experienced malaria before are thought to carry latent illness. When mosquitoes bite them, they get ill faster because they reach an illness threshold sooner.[34]

I have encountered a different form of cumulative reasoning in India that links excessive drinking and smoking to TB. Such behavior is seen to not only weaken the body but also cause cumulative damage among those who are not innately strong. We know little about how comorbidity is viewed in relation to perceptions of cumulative risk. For example, is such reasoning, along with local ideas of resistance, used to explain how past experience with malaria might predispose one to HIV, and vice versa, in places where both are prevalent? *Vulnerability Based on Exposure to Risk Information.* Exposure to information about risk can trigger a sense of vulnerability and in some cases lead a person to adopt an "at-risk role" that mimics a "sick role" (Nichter 2003a).[35] For example, a sense of vulnerability may unintentionally be fostered by diagnostic tests at both the individual (Kavanagh and Broom 1998) and the community level (Boonmongkon et al. 1999).[36] The case of cervical cancer in northeastern Thailand presented earlier illustrates how a screening test may contribute to perceptions of disease prevalence that far exceed actual prevalence, resulting in an epidemic of fear. Newspaper headlines may also foster a sense of vulnerability. In the Philippines, I have witnessed a period during which first-page news coverage of HIV temporarily influenced the use of condoms among prostitutes and clients, until coverage waned (Nichter 2001, 2003a). In the state of Kerala, India, in 2003 I observed the dramatic effect that news coverage of dengue had on the local population. A rising sense of vulnerability and fear of death due to dengue resulted in government health facilities being swamped with any patient having fever. Political pressure was placed on doctors to admit all patients with fever, even those not suspected of having dengue. Increases in patient loads at hospitals for relatively minor illnesses meant that there was less time to manage patients who were more seriously ill. Recent public response to news reports of the disease *chickungunya* in South India provoked similar reactions.[37]

The impact of risk communication has also been studied in relation to how different communities respond to epidemics and the contagious nature of epidemic fear (Strong 1989; Van Damme and Van Lerberghe 2000). Social scientists have long studied local response to epidemics (Hsu 1955), investigating such things as emergent interpretations of why epidemics have occurred (e.g., HIV in Haiti; Farmer 1990, 1992),[38] perceptions of why epidemic disease affected some communities more than others (e.g., Kyasanur forest disease in India; Nichter 1987a), who is blamed for epidemics seen in terms of the politics and geography of blame (e.g., cholera in Venezuela; Briggs 2004, Briggs and Mantini-Briggs 2003),[39] and the stigmatization of deviant others (HIV in Thailand and Nepal; Lyttelton 1996; Pigg 2002).[40] More recently, research on severe acute respiratory syndrome (SARS) has focused on how public responses to new diseases tap into social memory, awakening old fears and patterns of stigma in some instances propagated by the media (Kleinman and Lee 2006; Loh et al. 2004; Person et al. 2004).[41] Research on the plague in India (Garrett 2000; Shah 1997) has presented us with a worst-case scenario of epidemic fear. I experienced this firsthand in Maharashtra during 1994 as I watched doctors and the public flee plague-stricken areas of India in an immense overreaction to a health problem blown out of proportion by the press.

Place-Based Vulnerability. Places are often perceived as dangerous. Reasons for feeling vulnerable in a particular place may have to do with perceptions of environmental or religious pollution, the presence of endemic illness (e.g., AIDS, dengue, malaria)[42] or stigmatized groups, sources of danger, embedded memories of violence or tragedy, a breakdown in social order, or mistrust of agents of the state exercising power. For example, several ethnographers have noted that women from indigenous groups find government hospitals to be dangerous places to deliver babies because of the presence of sickness, sadness, fear, and strangers who might bewitch them, as well as places where government health staff may subject them to unwanted medical procedures, including sterilization (e.g., Tibet, Adams et al. 2005; Indonesia, Hay 1999; Mexico, Miller 2003). Perceptions of risk associated with place influence health and health care behavior in a variety of ways.

It is useful to distinguish between risks purely associated with physical spaces, and *place* as a space predisposed to particular types of thinking, doing, and social interaction (Casey 1996; Feld and Basso 1996; Gesler and Kearns 2002; Gieryn 2000). Places are spaces that have a social history and embedded memories that accumulate through time and are experienced temporally, just as senses of behavioral appropriateness and cultural expectations are associated with places and perceptions of what may transpire at different junctures in time. Studies of place and perceived risk must consider the relationship that particular groups have with places, when and how they transverse these places, and who and what they feel govern places.[43] There is also a need to examine perceptions of responsibility for different spaces and places—an examination crucial to our understanding of who is responsible for doing what to avert or manage epidemic disease.[44]

Age, Gender, and Perceptions of Risk and Causality

Gender- and age-specific differences in the prevalence of disease exist as a result of differential exposure to sources of infection, vectors, and toxins (such as smoke), as well as differences in nutritional and pharmaceutical intake (Allotey and Gyapong 2005; Cárdenas et al. 1994; Kaur 1997; Rathgeber and Vlassoff 1993; Vlassoff and Moreno 2002). For example, several studies of schistosomiasis in Africa have found that exposure to *Schistosoma haematobium* and *Schistosoma mansoni* through water contact is greater for women than for men as a result of domestic activities such as washing dishes and clothes and fetching water from the river. In other contexts, however, the opposite is true. Higher rates of infection have been found among men as a result of gendered toilet habits and gendered work patterns where work sites, such as crop fields, lie far from sanitary facilities (Brown and Inhorn 1990; Huang and Manderson 1992). In Egypt, it was also observed that ritual ablutions before prayer have been responsible for much higher schistosomiasis rates among Muslims than among Christians.

How do local populations understand gender-based differences in disease prevalence in terms of vulnerability, risk, or causality? Little research has been carried out on this issue, but ethnographic observations suggest that it is important to pursue.[45] In the Philippines, males are thought to incur filariasis as a result of hard work and exposure to the elements, whereas the disease in women is stigmatized and associated with promiscuity (Evans et al. 1993; Lu et al. 1988). Gender-specific bodily states such as pregnancy have also been reported to be associated with illness causality. In India, pregnancy is thought by some to render women vulnerable to some types of illness and is associated with illness relapse. For example, pregnancy is believed capable of causing TB to recur.[46]

How about differences in the perception of children's and adults' illness? A few studies suggest that children's illnesses and adult illnesses may be thought about as discrete ailments. For example, studies of infant diarrhea and ARI have found that in some places people do not consider children's illnesses to be transmittable to adults.[47] In a study of TB in the Philippines, I specifically examined this issue and found significant differences in opinion as to whether TB was a child's illness or whether a child having "weak lungs" was contagious for adults (Nichter 1997). Recent research among the Shipibo of Peru suggests that this population does not think that young children are vulnerable to either malaria or yellow fever but does think that they are vulnerable to dengue (Doreen Montag, unpublished data). In Uganda, the local term *omusujja* encompasses malaria as well as a wide range of other illnesses. Kengeya-Kayondo and colleagues (1994) have noted that different types of omusujja affect different age groups in distinct ways.

In addition to noting local explanations for gender and age differences, future research needs to consider how local representations of risk and causality affect gender- and age-based patterns of health care seeking and disease diagnosis.[48] For example, it has been reported in several countries (Ghana, South Africa, Nepal, and Vietnam) that women not only consult practitioners later than men when exhibiting symptoms of TB but also are diagnosed later than men after seeking help at clinics (Lawn et al. 1998; Long et al. 1999; Pronyk et al. 2001; Thorson et al. 2000; Yamasaki-Nakagawa et al. 2001). Because women are not perceived to fit high-risk TB profiles, they may be paid less attention by both family members and health care providers, even when presenting the same symptoms as men.

With respect to children, research is urgently needed on health care–seeking behavior for children perceived as vulnerable owing to their past health history (i.e., as weak). Are such children taken to health facilities more rapidly, or are household members more reluctant to spend scarce resources on them if poor? Does this vary by gender, age, or birth order? And how does the experience of one child in the household affect other children (Das Gupta 1990; Nichter and Kendall 1990)?

Acceptable Risk. A representation of risk that demands critical assessment at both the grassroots and the health policy levels is "acceptable risk," or risk tolerated by a population as the price that must be paid for living in a particular location or engaging in a particular occupation or lifestyle. Studies of leishmaniasis in Guatemala (Arana et al. 2000) and onchocerciasis in Nigeria (Bradley 1981) and several studies of schistosomiasis and malaria have suggested that local communities think that these diseases are unavoidable. What demands further investigation is the extent to which such thinking alters a community's willingness to be involved in interventions once a demonstration effect has been recognized. My own observation is that even when risk is seen as part of life, there is considerable interest in risk- and harm-reduction measures. Another issue that demands investigation is the extent to which ideas about acceptable risk are associated with modes of production and forms of employment upon which populations have become dependent for survival. To what extent is it in an employer's best interests to have workers accept risks to keep costs down?[49]

Harm Reduction. How do people respond to feelings of vulnerability associated with the sources of risk highlighted above? One of the most common responses is that people engage in "harm reduction" (Nichter 2003a, 2006b), a behavior and mind-set that is too little studied by social scientists.[50] Harm reduction, as I use the term, encompasses primary, secondary, and tertiary prevention in that it may be engaged in prior to, during, and after illness. For example, workers entering forested areas associated with malaria in the Philippines and northeastern Thailand engage in a variety of harm-reduction behaviors in an effort to prevent or minimize illness (Nichter, unpublished data; Pylypa 2004). They may take an antimalarial medicine as a prophylactic against disease, boil water collected in the forest before using it, drink profuse amounts of water when leaving the area to flush out malaria germs in the urine, and/or drink alcohol and smoke heavily while in the forest. The latter two substances are sometimes thought to deter mosquitoes from biting; alcohol may also be perceived to kill germs in the body.[51]

In cases where illness is thought to be latent or inevitable, harm-reduction measures may be taken to alleviate symptoms or to minimize risk of serious illness. For example, people living in an area where malaria or dengue is endemic often spend more time and resources on measures aimed at preventing mild illnesses from becoming severe than trying to prevent these illnesses from occurring in the first place (Winch et al. 1991).

In the private sector, a booming harm-reduction industry feeds off people's insecurities in places where and at times when they feel that they have little control over environmental or occupational factors causing illness. Medicines are marketed to reduce accumulated impurities in the body, as well as to keep latent illness from flaring up. For example, tetracycline has been subtly marketed to Thai women as a medicine that will enable them to keep latent gynecological problems in check (Boonmongkon et al. 2001). In Thailand as well as the Philippines, antibiotics are consumed as prophylactic medicines by commercial sex workers and their patrons to both prevent sexually transmitted infections and keep weak germs from gaining strength (Nichter 2001). Similar behavior has been reported in Malawi (Bruun 2002). In all three countries, one of the most common drugs used was rifampicin, one of the most important drugs used in the treatment of TB.[52] Note that although health care providers find it challenging to explain the concept of asymptomatic disease to patients, members of the same local populations maintain representations of latent illness.

Many people are more comfortable with the concept of harm reduction than that of total disease prevention, owing in part to the concept of multiple causality and to the fact that many diseases share common symptoms or mimic one another.[53] Measles vaccinations in India and the Philippines provide a good example. Many Indians and Filipinos respond better to the message that the vaccination prevents their children from developing a serious life-threatening case of measles than to a message that the vaccine protects children from ever having the disease (Bisht and Coutinho 2000; Nichter 1996b; Ramos-Jimenez et al. 1999).[54] Other rashes are confused with measles, making total prevention seem unrealistic.

Harm reduction may also be engaged in as a form of promotive health behavior. For example, intravenous saline drips sometimes containing medicine cocktails (ranging from vitamin B-12 to antibiotics) are routinely taken by those engaging in hard or tedious labor in many Asian and Latin American countries. Saline drips are thought to promote strength and health as well as to reduce the harm of illnesses that may lurk within the body. Ten- to fourteen-day courses of the micronutrient zinc are currently being promoted to reduce the severity and lessen the chance of recurrent diarrhea in children (Black 2003). Given that most cases of diarrhea abate in three or four days, social science research has been enlisted to figure out how best to introduce zinc in different cultures as a form of harm reduction as well as a medication for diarrhea (INCLEN IC-ZED Group 2006).[55]

Social Risk. The risk of disturbing social and economic relationships impacts how illness is talked about, diagnosed, and treated (Crandon-Malamud 1991). As a number of ethnographic studies have demonstrated, concern about social risk—that is, risk to valued social relationships—often eclipses physical risk.[56] People continue to risk exposure to diseases such as TB and AIDS rather than risk losing long-standing social relationships (Bujra 2000; Campbell 1995; Heise and Elias 1995) as well as potential social relationships (Connors 1992; Green et al. 2000; Sobo 1995).[57] For example, in the Philippines, TB may be diagnosed and referred to by family members as "weak lungs" to reduce the stigma of TB and to enable household members to interact with the afflicted in a way that psychologically minimizes a sense of threat (Nichter 2003a).[58] In Indonesia, those afflicted with TB may tell others that they have allergies or *flek*, a term used much like "weak lungs" in the Philippines (Padmawati, personal communication, 2005). In many parts of Asia and Africa where I have worked, it is commonplace for wives to have unprotected sex with husbands who are migrant laborers when the men periodically return home. They are well aware that their husbands are likely to have had sex with other women or prostitutes. However, the social risk of losing their husband's emotional and economic support by requesting condom use eclipses concern about the immediate risk of physical disease.[59]

Some practitioners tailor their diagnosis and treatment of patients in ways that minimize social risk and fear. They are afraid of demoralizing patients with stigmatized or frightening diseases.[60] For example, in India, I observed a popular urban doctor tell older, middle-class patients with lung cancer that they had TB as a result of having a weak immune system. He described their TB as being attributable to their exposure to all kinds of people on the street. Patients were offered TB medications and a TB identity. The doctor explained to me that he did so to avert the greater stigma of lung cancer (his perception) and "to offer the patient and their family hope because TB is curable" (Nichter, unpublished data, 2001).[61] Given some chance of hope, he reckoned, the social relations of a family would not be disrupted.

Doctors experience social risk in the form of risk to their reputations. In the 1980s and early 1990s, I observed several private doctors in India treating patients whom they suspected had TB for some time without informing the patients that they might have TB. When asked why they would not confer this diagnosis, they noted that it would be too risky for their reputation to diagnose the patient as having TB or to tell the afflicted that several months' worth of medications would be necessary (Nichter 2002b). One practitioner stated that if he requested that patients take medications for several months, the patients might think he was trying to "milk them" for money for as long as possible. To tell patients they had TB before their symptoms were very serious was deemed risky, as patients were likely to consult another doctor, who would not give them such bad news. A multisite TB study in India (conducted by the IndiaCLEN TB Study Group in 2004) found that some patients who attended government TB clinics following visits to private practitioners were initially reluctant to accept a diagnosis of TB. They had already been told different diagnoses by previous practitioners and given medications that provided temporary relief. Doctors noted that winning the confidence of such patients proved challenging unless they were seriously ill.

Social risk may also affect people's interaction with government health staff. In contexts where programs have targeted diseases such as HIV, sexually transmitted infections (STIs), and TB, community members may be hesitant to visit clinics or interact with health staff for fear that others will think or come to know that they have a stigmatized disease. In such cases, the social risk was described as just too great. In India, unmarried women are often afraid of receiving TB treatment locally for fear that they will not be able to find a marriage partner later. And in both the Philippines and India, I have observed people afraid of being visited by HIV outreach workers for fear that others would think they are infected (Nichter, unpublished data, 1998). In northern Thailand, Ngamvithayapong and colleagues (2000) describe a situation in which HIV programs have led to people being hypersensitive to being labeled AIDS patients. Some people having the symptoms of TB do not attend nearby TB clinics for fear that others would think they have HIV. This study speaks to the importance of confidentiality and leads me to question whether the closest point of treatment for stigmatized diseases (or medical procedure, such as for family planning or domestic violence) is always the best and whether this matters more for women or the unmarried than others.

Hierarchies of Risk. How "risk" is responded to by local populations involves hierarchies; that is, how risk is judged in context as well as in relation to other risks rather than in isolation (Connors 1992).[62] The concept of risk hierarchies may be a productive way to think about how local populations respond to health interventions in contexts where multiple diseases and other health concerns (such as violence, insecurity, stigma, and social risk) coexist.

A hierarchy of risk assessment, for example, might prove insightful when studying local response to interventions in contexts where trust in state government and/or international agencies, and by extension health care workers, is questionable. Negative response to immunization programs offers a case in point. In an overview of studies on vaccination acceptance, Streefland and colleagues (1999) have noted several instances where local populations have been wary of the true intentions of health officials promoting vaccinations.[63] Recently, such vaccination refusal has made the international press. In West Africa (most notably Nigeria), people have refused to be immunized with polio vaccine for fear that it was part of a covert family-planning program (Feldman-Savelsberg et al. 2000; Obadare 2005; Yahya 2005) or, worse yet, that polio vaccine spreads HIV (Raufu 2004a, 2004b).[64] Although people recognize the value of protection from diseases, they fear loss of fertility more. In light of the many new vaccines on the horizon for diseases ranging from hepatitis and pneumonia to malaria and HIV, it is imperative that immunizations be introduced in ways that evoke community confidence and that rumors be dealt with in a culturally sensitive manner.

To do so requires taking stock of competing fears that loom large in the public imagination.[65] Public health officials must anticipate problems and not merely be reactive.

A hierarchies-of-risk approach might further prove useful in assisting us to understand why people do not adopt protective health measures when they recognize occupational risks. As noted earlier, agricultural workers in tropical countries such as the Philippines acknowledge the risk of handling pesticides but commonly do not wear protective clothing. The use of protective equipment in the tropics is viewed by these workers as exposing themselves to additional health risks, such as overheating the body or causing them to perspire too much. Risk from pesticides is superseded by health concerns such as *pasma* that result in ailments perceived to be more debilitating (Palis et al. 2006). This reasoning helps explain why agricultural workers prefer to engage in harm-reduction practices after they have sprayed fields, instead of taking precautions while spraying. No doubt many other examples of this type of concern and practice exist.

NOTES

1. There are multiple dimensions of illness causality, ranging from the predisposing (vulnerability) and instrumental (how) causes of illness to ultimate causes that address questions of "why me?" and "why now?" (Nichter 1987a). Additionally, forces of malevolence are often thought to be omnipresent and to interact with other causes of illness. For example, Sommerfeld and colleagues (2002) note in a study of risk perception in Burkina Faso that illness (*bana*) is a negative force surrounding the individual on a constant basis. Prevention entails more than physical protection because imbalances or breaches in the social and spiritual spheres can also render one vulnerable: illness is a biosocial event.

2. There are many advantages to analyzing illness causality in terms of internalizing and externalizing factors instead of using the common dichotomy of naturalistic and personalistic factors found in early social science and public health literature. See Young's (1976) classic article on perceptions of illness causality in Ethiopia for a review of these reasons.

3. Farmer's (1988) research on *move san* (bad blood), a condition in Haiti that causes breast milk to spoil, illustrates how the physiological and psychological state of a person may be seen as coextensive. The etiology of move san is malignant emotions caused by strife, grief, shock, or emotional abuse. Culturally, the condition move san serves as a warning against the abuse of pregnant or nursing women, and a diagnosis of move san permits criticism of inappropriate behavior on the part of the afflicted person's significant others. Cartwright (2007) provides another instructive case in which toxic emotions literally take on a life of their own as an external cause of illness among the Amuzgos Indians of Oaxaca in southern Mexico: *susto* (fright) and *coraje* (anger) leave the bodies of the afflicted and dwell in places where violence has occurred and rage was experienced. These places are avoided and feared, as one can catch a susto and be affected by coraje just from passing through the place where a bad thing happened in the past. In many cultures, a pregnant or lactating mother's anger is thought to affect her baby.

4. Figure 1 summarizes information collected by the IndiaCLEN (Indian Clinical Epidemiology Network) TB working group, of which I am a member. The data set represents ideas found in six different sites of south-central and northern India.

5. In some areas of the Philippines, weakness related to *pasma* is thought to predispose one to malaria or is held directly responsible for causing malaria. In other areas, pasma is thought to constitute a condition that resembles malaria. When pasma is directly linked to malaria, herbal treatment tends to be used more than in cases when it is not (Miguel et al. 1999).

6. Palis and colleagues (2006) further note that young men are commonly given the job of spraying pesticide because they are thought to have stronger bodies able to withstand the harm of these toxic chemicals. The authors observe that young men who do pesticide spraying experience high rates of cardiac problems, an observation that warrants more rigorous investigation.

7. Illness is also thought to strike people making negative comments about the afflicted. In Haiti, filariasis is thought to afflict people making disparaging remarks about those who are ill (Coreil et al. 1998).

8. Medical anthropologists have documented that interpretations of an illness are often cumulative. This is as common in North America as in Southeast Asia. For example, Hunt and colleagues (1989) found that Americans trying to make sense of illnesses often add new explanations to their prior perceptions, thus combining explanations.

9. Other mosquito-borne diseases are thought to be caused by multiple factors as well. For example, in several different countries, filariasis is associated with stepping over enchanted medicines or polluted substances, consuming contaminated food or water, bathing in stagnant water, carrying heavy loads, foreign objects entering the body, or heredity (Coreil et al. 1998; Eberhard et al. 1996; Evans et al. 1993; Gyapong et al. 1996; Rauyajin et al. 1995).

10. For example, Imevbore and colleagues (1990) note that in southwestern Nigeria, schistosomiasis is strongly associated with drinking polluted water. They suggest that the local population would be receptive to messages describing the role of snails in polluting water. The problem lies in convincing them that human contact with such water poses a greater threat than drinking it.

11. Instead of thinking about people living with multiple perceptions of illness causality as experiencing cognitive dissonance, it is more productive to think of them as experiencing cognitive polyphasia (Moscovici 1981; Wagner et al. 2000). De Rosa (2004) defines cognitive polyphasia as a tendency to employ diverse and even opposite ways of thinking such as scientific and religious, metaphorical and logical, and so forth, as a normal state of affairs in ordinary life and communication. The logical or cognitive unity of our mental life, which is taken for granted by many psychologists, may well be a social construction and expression of our desire to "govern the soul" (Barry et al. 1996).

12. I use the term *lay epidemiology* to refer to how local populations think about the cause and spread of illness (encompassing routes of illness transmission) within popular health culture. Others have used the term *lay epidemiology* in a somewhat broader manner (see Allmark and Tod 2006; Davison et al. 1991, 1992; Rose 1985). In this book I use the terms *lay epidemiology* and *popular epidemiology* in distinct ways, as noted in chapter 8.

13. It is equally important to document contexts where a sense of the randomness and unpredictability of illness eclipses cultural ideas about causality and contagion noted during interviews (Castro 1993). In some instances, this may be related to a more general sense of uncertainty associated with shifting ecological conditions or an oppressive political situation.

14. For example, in South India, it is widely believed that one can get TB by walking on or stepping across the sputum of the afflicted. A similar idea is found in Zambia, where it is thought that stepping over the urine of one suffering from schistosomiasis will cause one to become ill (Frederick and Thomas 1994). In Burkina Faso, it is believed that if people step over the leftover medicine used to treat a particular episode of childhood illness, they will pass the illness on to their own children (Samuelsen 2004).

15. An ongoing INCLEN (International Clinical Epidemiology Network) intervention is exploring a bottom-up approach to TB education that addresses such questions as what the duration of contagion after taking medicines is, and whether taking TB medicines during pregnancy and lactation is safe. Surprisingly few such education packages have been developed to address questions raised by patients and identified by social science research. See Datta and Nichter 2005 (see also www.tnmmu.ac.in/edu.pdf).

16. Turning unhygienic natives into hygienic citizens and a respectable proletariat was a central feature of the colonial project. But as Anderson (2002) points out, reformed natives were often considered unstable hybrids, mere imitators who could revert back to old ways quickly and therefore in need of sustained monitoring.

17. Briggs (2005) has called for critical-discourse analysis of press accounts of epidemic disease that closely examine both narrative and statistical representations used to construct topographies of risk that map onto preexisting racial characterizations. Such accounts naturalize disease distribution and may be used to rationalize racist government policies. Briggs (2004) also calls for research on conspiracy theories as they are used by marginalized groups to counter interpretations of epidemics that suggest that the group's backwardness is what places them at risk for disease. Conspiracy theories often involve social commentary on state politics, globalism, economic exploitation, environmental destruction, and so on.

18. Research on family response to diseases perceived to "run in the family" has been conducted in the West, but I have not encountered much research on the topic in developing countries. For instructive examples in the West, see Frich et al. 2006; Halbert et al. 2006; Hunt et al. 2001; Jacobsen et al. 2004; Walter and Emery 2005, 2006; Walter et al. 2004.

19. See Kendall et al. 1990 for a discussion of ethno-entomology.

20. For research on lay understanding of how mosquitoes transmit malaria, see Agyepong 1992; Ahorlu et al. 1997; Aikins et al. 1994; Espino et al. 1997; Hausmann et al. 2002; Mwenesi et al. 1995; Pylypa 2004; Utarini et al. 2003; Winch et al. 1996.

21. The poor are often blamed for vector-borne diseases. In Manila, the poor are similarly blamed for dengue fever, which is associated with unhygienic living conditions (Nichter, unpublished data, 2000). In Brazil, dengue is also associated with poverty. Upper-class people feel that their neighborhoods are relatively safe. This leads them to be lax in following preventive measures. A recent epidemic in Rio de Janeiro affected all social classes and led the public to rethink this representation of the disease (Jurberg 2002).

22. *Anopheles stephensi* (a vector for urban malaria) shares the same kind of breeding sites as *Aedes aegypti*, the vector responsible for the rise in dengue fever in India's urban localities.

23. In another case, in southeastern Brazil, local populations did come to believe that snails were involved in the transmission of schistosomiasis. However, they imagined the disease to be caused by snails entering the body, a perception that diverted popular attention away from the role played by human feces in disease transmission (Rozemberg 1994).

24. Although many medical anthropologists have commented on local perceptions of vulnerability, harm reduction, and disease prevention, few studies have made a concerted

effort to rigorously study such perceptions in a manner useful to those in international health. Recent studies such as those by Sommerfeld and colleagues (2002) are a step in the right direction.

25. The literature on selective neglect folds into the literature on maternal competence, a very contested area of study (Finerman 1995). Some studies on selective neglect suggest that mothers consciously withdraw resources and emotional attachment (Scheper-Hughes 1991, 1992), while others suggest that what appears to be selective neglect is culturally styled coping behavior that involves the whole community (Nations and Rebhun 1988b).

26. For example, the clinical features of pneumonia and malaria overlap in children. O'Dempsey and colleagues (1993) note that in the Gambia, whereas malaria peaks only once (during the rainy season), pneumonia peaks twice (in rainy and dry seasons), creating times when clinical overlap is common. WHO guidelines used for the two diseases promote overtreatment of both diseases and contribute to mortality because malaria drugs have no impact on pneumonia. It is common in many parts of Africa for people to think that fevers in particular seasons are malaria.

27. Health care seeking may vary by season and the availability of time and money. Sauerborn and colleagues (1996b) describe how financial hardship in particular seasons may influence perceptions of illness severity and result in treatment delay. Far too few studies have looked at the interface between household economics and health perceptions.

28. In some cases, people may intentionally engage in behaviors that are thought to provoke or hasten an illness as a form of diagnosis. For example, in both Thailand and the Philippines, I have come across men who consume foods and alcohol thought to hasten illness a few days after engaging in risky sex. This is done to test whether they have been infected with disease before returning home to have sex with wives or girlfriends.

29. I encountered similar thinking in the Philippines in the mid-1990s. Some informants thought that untreated sexually transmitted disease could transform into AIDS.

30. On the importance of the local concept of resistance in the Philippines, see Espino et al. 1997. Research is urgently needed on migrant groups' perceptions of disease resistance and the preventive behavior they engage in to minimize risk.

31. In the case of TB, the chances of relapse following successful treatment are much higher among those who smoke (Thomas et al. 2005).

32. Lifelong poverty, exposure to the elements, hard work, and marginalization are also recognized to have a cumulative effect resulting in a weak body and illness.

33. Ideas of cumulative risk may well be affected by diagnostic tests and preventive health metrics such as viral loads among those who are HIV positive (Davis et al. 2002).

34. I have come across the opposite reasoning as well: one exposed to malaria for some years may be thought to become resistant to the disease and to not easily become ill.

35. Assuming a "risk role" after receiving a nonconclusive (suggestive) diagnostic test is an example of what Hacking (1983, 1986) has referred to as "dynamic nominalism." Hacking talks of a "kind of person" coming into being at the same time the "kind itself" is being invented. Hacking observes that people classified in a particular way tend to conform to the ways in which they are described. Their understanding and experience of a category evolve so that classifications and descriptions are constantly being revised, something he refers to as a "looping effect" (Hacking 1995). On assuming a risk role, also see Lock's (1998) notion of suffering from "pre-illness" and Clark and colleagues (2003) on the process of biomedicalization.

36. Kavanagh and Broom (1998) have called upon medical and public health practitioners to look beyond environmental risk (something that happens to people) and lifestyle risk (things people do or do not do that expose them to harm) when considering how best

to inform people about disease susceptibility detected through diagnostic tests. They rightly argue that it is important to consider how embodied risk (corporeal risk associated with the bodily states or characteristics of individual people) is interpreted and responded to following an abnormal test result. Community-based screening campaigns are just beginning to be promoted in developing countries. Those that have been initiated have often been implemented in great haste and with little background knowledge of the cultural environments into which they are being introduced. This raises the danger of such tests being misinterpreted.

37. In the early to mid-1990s, reports of HIV sparked public concern about the disease in Kerala, India, and many patients came to clinics demanding to be tested for HIV although their histories were not suggestive of HIV risk. Many suffered from symptoms that turned out to be pseudo AIDS. Pseudo AIDS is a term given to patients who tested negative for HIV and had not engaged in risky sex for more than seven years by my colleague, the late Dr. Suraraj Mani. Patient histories commonly revealed guilt and anxiety over masturbation, sexual fantasies, homosexuality, and sexual contact experienced years prior to HIV being reported in Asia. For a related phenomenon and a detailed discussion of technoneurosis associated with both HIV and HIV tests being introduced to Brazil, see Biehl et al. 2001.

38. See also Strong 1989 concerning epidemics of interpretation and moralization associated with epidemics that may lead to discourse on the social order. During the initial stages of an epidemic, the public searches for possible explanations in the absence of established responses to the disease. Different actions and interpretations are proposed by various parties, which then compete in public discourse for legitimacy.

39. Briggs and Mantini-Briggs (2003) extend Farmer's (1992) concept of the "geography of blame" that occurs when nationalistic discourse places responsibility for a disease on a devalued "other." In the case they present, the racialization of space and spatialization of race occurs. By associating a backward and unhygienic "*indígenas* other" with the cholera epidemic, the majority population distances its own fear as well as social responsibility for the inequality underlying the maldistribution of the disease. The politics of "othering" associated with epidemic disease typically link the group blamed with exotic, unhygienic, or deviant forms of behavior and states of uncontrol (see Gilman 1985; Joffe 2004; Nelkin and Gilman 1988). Xenophobic othering also plays off of preexisting prejudices that vilify foreigners (see, for example, Petros et al. 2006 on the politics of blame for HIV in South Africa).

40. It is reassuring for those in a mainstream group to view those labeled deviant as "reservoirs of infection" and distant from their way of life. See, for example, the demonization of commercial sex workers (CSWs) in public health messages and the media in many countries. The portrayals of CSWs as the source of the illness direct attention to the role they play in transmitting HIV, not as the people who are most at risk of becoming infected from others.

41. See also research on media coverage and response to SARS in the West (Wallis and Nerlich 2005). The media's perception of its role and responsibilities when reporting disease events and pharmaceutical news begs further ethnographic inquiry (Schwitzer et al. 2005).

42. A particularly pernicious form of risk subjectivity has been identified by Barnett and colleagues (2001) in their discussion of "subjective demography." They note that for the young living in countries with high rates of HIV/AIDS, the disease may be seen as inevitable. When this happens, one response is to live for the day and not worry about risk avoidance. For an extreme example of this thinking, which has led to pathological behavior on the part of adolescent Zulu boys, see Leclerc-Madlala 1997.

43. Places may be both collaborative and disputed environments.

44. See, for example, Paley 2001 for an ethnographic account of how the Chilean Ministry of Health distanced itself from infrastructure-related risk factors contributing to a cholera epidemic (e.g., raw sewage in irrigation ditches). The government conducted a publicity campaign informing communities that they, not the government, were responsible for keeping public places clean of trash. The locus of concern for the epidemic was further shifted to self-care (hand washing) and the household (covering trash).

45. Although much research has been carried out on gender bias in health care seeking, far less has considered gendered responses to illness. Gendered differences in illness experience need to be made a research priority. Consider, for example, the research of Dreyer and colleagues (1997), who report in passing that serious social and sexual ramifications result from lymphedema associated with lymphatic filariasis in Brazil. They report that both men and women experience pain during sexual intercourse, leading to marital discord and a propensity to seek out homosexual relationships. What are the ramifications of such dramatic behavioral changes for men and women? How are women and men treated differently at home when they experience the same chronic stigmatized illness? Do age and social status exacerbate or minimize difference?

46. Clinical studies of leprosy in Ethiopia suggest that deterioration of the immune system during pregnancy may be linked to disease relapse (Kaur 1997).

47. Children's illnesses are not always thought to be contagious to adults. Likewise, the bodily wastes of small infants and even young animals (Harvey et al. 2003) are not always thought to be as polluting or dangerous as the wastes of adults or mature animals. Biomedically speaking, children's feces are as likely to spread disease as are adult feces.

48. In need of further research is how the stigma of diseases such as filariasis affects women's lives pre- and postmarriage (Amazigo and Obikeze 1992; Bandyopadhyay 1996).

49. See, for example, the literature on landowners' perceptions of farmworkers' risks for pesticide exposure (Rao et al. 2004). How do the owners of mines, factories, and so forth see the occupational hazards of workers in the short and long term?

50. *Harm reduction* is a term generally used in public health to refer to needle-exchange programs for intravenous drug users. My use of the term is far broader, as described in this book and elsewhere (Nichter 2003a, 2006b).

51. Ideas about preventing mosquito bites abound. One memorable informant in Palawan, Philippines, advocated drinking hard alcohol to make the blood hot as a means of deterring mosquitoes. He stated that cooler-blooded people such as babies and foreigners attracted mosquitoes. Another informant noted that tobacco made an effective insect repellant if boiled and sprayed on plants. He reckoned that if one smoked, the chemicals within tobacco would enter one's bloodstream and deter mosquitoes from biting.

52. Rifampicin-resistant MDR-TB (multidrug-resistant tuberculosis) is a huge global health problem. The taking of a few tablets of this drug in the hope of preventing STIs obviously fosters drug resistance.

53. The concept of harm reduction may prove useful when a vaccine for HIV is introduced in the future. As noted by Streefland (2003), an important factor will be introducing the vaccine along with conveying the message that practicing safe sex is still necessary, as one can still contract AIDS after receiving the vaccine if one engages in at-risk behavior.

54. It would be worth piloting a harm-reduction approach in contexts where measles vaccinations are not yet well received by local populations, such as in northern Nigeria, and where the disease is associated with deities and sorcery (Ambe et al. 2001).

55. Zinc is currently being introduced to mothers as a form of harm reduction for diarrhea, but its efficacy is also being tested for ARI and as a useful supplement-prophylactic for members of households where someone is suffering from TB. The social marketing of zinc will need to take into account its single versus multiple uses when constructing

harm-reduction messages. Zinc messages associated with diarrhea must also stress that zinc does not reduce the need to take oral rehydration fluid. For a manual that spells out in detail how to carry out social science research when introducing a new medicine to a population using zinc as an example, see Nichter et al. 2005.

56. The concept of social risk requires further refinement. I originally used the term *social risk* in the early 1980s to draw attention to risks to one's valued social relationships in the present as well as desired social relations in the future. Prior to that time, I had only heard the term used to describe individuals and groups that placed "society at large" in danger. In the 1990s, I encountered another form of social risk: risk to an individual or group's autonomy. For example, being labeled "at risk" and subjected to involuntary public health regulations can result in one's freedoms being curtailed.

57. A good example of a behavior that risks potential relationships is asking a potential life partner to use condoms during sexual acts. This may signal mistrust, social distance, or the perception that this is a short-term relationship.

58. Other stigmatized diseases (e.g., asthma, epilepsy) may not be referred to directly by name, by both family members and practitioners. This has been pointed out by anthropologists for some time. For example, in the 1970s–80s, some practitioners attempted to avert stigma and fear of leprosy by telling parents that their children were in a "pre-leprous" state. The parents were further told that treatment would prevent the disease from developing (Berreman 1984). In other cases, medical practitioners may attempt to reduce social risk by not informing patients of the cause of the illness if stigma is involved or if they feel it will upset the patient and there is little that can be done about it. Giffin and Lowndes (1999) provide a case of such behavior in Brazil, related to sexually transmitted disease. Clinicians described other causes of STIs experienced by women because they did not feel that the women were in a position to confront their husbands.

59. Risk to social status may reduce the chance that HIV tests will be requested of men prior to marriage in cultures where women are subjected to virginity testing. I have encountered one incidence of virginity testing specifically being associated with HIV in South Africa. This practice focusing on women is troubling because it conveys the impression that the disease can somehow be contained by controlling women (Leclerc-Madlala 2001).

60. Another form of risk that practitioners are concerned about is shocking patients with bad news. In many cultures, practitioners are often instructed by family members not to tell patients that they have cancer, as it is believed that this would cause fear and worsen their prognosis as well as quality of life. See, for example, Gregg 2003. Not informing patients of dread diseases has sparked ethical debates. Is it the moral duty of a practitioner to inform patients of their diagnosis or to respect the wishes of relatives? How far should a practitioner respect cultural perceptions about appropriate behavior in such cases? How much information should be disclosed (Beach et al. 2005; Hack et al. 2005; Pellegrino 1992; Surbone 1992)?

61. This doctor saw his behavior as humanitarian. He alluded to the fact that because TB and lung cancer are sometimes misdiagnosed, there was little harm and perhaps an ounce of hope in his practice. He perceived middle-class patients as viewing cancer as more stigmatized than TB and related to smoking and drinking, while TB was associated with contact with the poor and unwashed. Whether his patients saw the matter in the same way is open to question. Among the poor, smoking and drinking in excess is linked to TB. What is notable about the case is the doctor's concern about patients losing both their social reputation and their hope—a double affliction.

62. In her ethnography of risk among intravenous drug users in New York City, Connors (1992) describes how risk is judged in context and in relation to coexisting risks.

Although sharing needles puts a person at risk for contracting HIV, it also decreases the risk of being arrested and subsequently denied access to heroin in jail.

63. See Greenough 1995 on resistance to large-scale vaccination programs and Waldman 2003 for a report of how mistrust of polio immunizations has led some Muslims in India to reject them, undermining the polio eradication program. For an even more poignant example of mistrust of the intentions of public health programs as well as pharmaceutical companies, see Fassin and Schneider 2003 on the politics of AIDS in South Africa.

64. In Nigeria, fear of polio vaccine prompted a suspension of the global polio eradication initiative. Health officials suspect that poliovirus circulating in northern Nigeria infected people in seven neighboring countries that were previously free of the disease (Pincock 2004).

65. Addressing rumors in a culturally sensitive manner requires an understanding of what they really index. Anthropologists studying family-planning rumors, vaccine rumors, blood- and organ-stealing rumors, and rumors associated with clinical trials and foreign medical aid in Africa have all noted that these rumors are not random events. Rumors are tied to political-economic concerns, collective anxieties, fears of globalization, and explanations for why sudden wealth befalls some but not all people (see Comaroff and Comaroff 1999; Fairhead and Leach 2006; Geissler 2005; Geissler and Pool 2006; Kaler 2004; Kroeger 2003; Moore and Sanders 2002; Weiss 1998; White 2000). Rumor may be used as a social leveling device and a form of resistance as well as a means of calling into question relations of trust and the way knowledge and power are being exercised. Rumor has long been a weapon of the weak as well as a divisive tool wielded by the politically astute. What has changed is the speed at which rumor can currently travel within and across countries as a result of cell phones, text messaging, and the Internet.

3

Why Is Research on Local Illness Categories Important?

You anthropologists go to such lengths to investigate local illness classification. I just don't see what difference it all makes at the end of the day. Give me one example of when this matters. Can't you just help us convince people to accept vaccinations and to use ORS when they have diarrhea?

—HEAD OF PRESTIGIOUS INTERNATIONAL
HEALTH PROGRAM IN THE UNITED STATES, 1988

The investigation of how illness is categorized locally is a core health social science research activity. Some of the principal motivations for studying local representations of illness have been to better understand which symptom sets are accorded cultural significance, identify illnesses perceived to be mundane versus those that are serious, and examine how illness categorization influences patterns of health care seeking and treatment delay.[1] Regardless of their biomedical significance, symptom sets accorded cultural importance flag local health concerns. During the past three decades, we have learned time and again that local health concerns demand serious public health attention.

Understanding the ways in which illnesses are classified provides insights into "differences that make a difference" within local health cultures. Features of illness are recognized as well as ignored during the course of differentiating one type of illness from another. Medical anthropologists investigating the language of illness typically begin with a free-listing exercise that generates lists of illness categories having some core feature in common (e.g., children's illnesses, skin ailments, lung problems, fevers). They then often search for consensus about what constitutes a prototype of a particular illness. Generally, the next step is to construct a local illness taxonomy. In principle, illness taxonomies exhaustively divide up the illness universe into mutually exclusive categories agreed upon by most members of a culture. The assumption is that people within a given culture may disagree on what kind of illness an individual is experiencing but generally subscribe to a common classificatory schema. It is questionable how valid this assumption is in popular health cultures characterized by pluralistic health care arenas where people are exposed to an influx of new ideas about illness.

While such illness taxonomy exercises can be insightful, three things are often left out: an appreciation for the importance of ambiguity in illness categorization; an account of the circular nature of illness naming, which involves multiple ways of thinking about illness in varying contexts (Bibeau 1981); and factors beyond inclusion and exclusion criteria that lead people to classify illnesses in particular ways. The last include both social factors that influence the production of knowledge about (and the description of) illness, and practical issues that lead people to think of illness in terms of resources at hand—taskonomy in addition to taxonomy.[2] Interpretations of illness are simultaneously guided by schema aptly described by Good (1977) as semantic illness networks, and co-constructed during social interactions in a world where illness representations convey meanings beyond the medical.

Lessons Learned

The results of studies of illness classification and semantic illness networks are important to those engaged in international health care. Lessons learned from studies of three health problems—diarrhea, ARI, and malaria—have significantly advanced our understanding of the interface between ethnomedicine and public health. Let me briefly highlight some of the major lessons learned from studies of each.

Diarrheal Disease

One of the earliest foci for research on disease classification within international health was promoting oral rehydration therapy (ORT) as a cheap and effective intervention for diarrheal disease. Research was conducted in several countries on local terms for different categories of diarrhea to be used in ORT messages.[3] It quickly became clear that efforts to encourage people to use ORT with one category of diarrhea-related illness did not carry over to other types of diarrhea. Moreover, to give an accurate picture of ORT use, ORT program evaluation required assessing rates of ORT use across different types of illness categories.

Three projects among the many conducted may be highlighted to demonstrate the importance of ethnosemantic studies of diarrhea classification.

Yoder (1989), in research on diarrheal disease in Zaire, illustrated two major points. First, morbidity surveys that asked informants to report on diarrheal disease only as a general ailment missed more than 50 percent of diarrhea cases in the community. Second, differences in oral rehydration therapy (ORT) use varied as much as 400 percent among local illness categories having diarrhea as a symptom. Mushtague and colleagues (1988), in a study of ORT utilization patterns in Bangladesh, similarly documented that patterns of health care–seeking behavior and ORT use were illness-category-specific. Notably, they illustrated that it was prudent to evaluate the success of ORT programs following the lines of illness categories. Smith and colleagues (1993) echoed the findings of several studies around the world (see Yoder and Hornick 1996), reporting that in Nicaragua, mothers' local classification of diarrhea episodes significantly influenced their self-care and health care–seeking practices.

Other studies of diarrhea found that perceptions of illness severity needed to be examined within and not just between categories of illness. Although people commonly reported to researchers that one type of illness was more dangerous than another, it was misleading for researchers to rank-order categories of illness on the basis of perceived severity. Instead, signs of severity had to be elicited *within* each type of illness. Researchers also learned that illness categorization was often provisional and subject to revision through time if initial treatments failed, even if symptoms changed little. For example, Malik and colleagues (1992:1052) found in their study of childhood diarrhea in Pakistan that "mothers use local illness categories in a flexible manner. As they seek to make sense of a child's symptoms, of an illness episode, or the unfolding of a disorder and the efficacy of treatment, they adjust and reassess what diarrhea and associated symptoms mean, and redefine what may be the cause and category of the disorder." Studies such as this illustrate that within households, deciding from which illness the afflicted is suffering often involves "what if" thinking that leads people to try different therapeutic modalities as well as entertain multiple causal explanations. Further, an illness is commonly identified after the fact on the basis of "diagnosis by treatment"; that is, its identity is confirmed by whatever treatment was perceived to have ultimately cured or assisted the afflicted (Nichter and Nichter 1996c).

A certain tension has surrounded social science research on diarrheal diseases. On the one hand, this research illustrated a clear need to move beyond a one-size-fits-all approach to promoting ORT. Researchers debated the pros and cons of using various local names for illnesses in health messages, as well as the utility of addressing cultural concerns in social marketing campaigns. On the other hand, there was a strong need to coordinate the activities of several international health agencies introducing ORT within the same country. To avoid confusion, it was agreed that the public needed to be exposed to a common set of simple messages. Many public health practitioners argued that key symptoms needed to be targeted, irrespective of what names for diarrhea were used in health messages. Different countries have adopted different approaches to dealing with the issue of what language to use. In each case, an informed decision needed to be made after weighing local data carefully and monitoring the effectiveness of messages developed.

Acute Respiratory Infections

Attention to illness classification was next directed toward acute respiratory infection (ARI). Spearheaded by a World Health Organization initiative that supported focused ethnographic research (Gove and Pelto 1994), and building on lessons learned from ORT, several studies of ARI were conducted over a short period of time.[4] A major goal of ARI research was to document overlap between local categories of respiratory illness and life-threatening cases of pneumonia. Researchers identified local illness terms for the most severe forms of ARI, and an attempt was made to estimate how closely or how often these illnesses classified in different ways were, in fact, pneumonia. In some cases, the sensitivity and specificity of local illness categories to predict pneumonia were calculated (Campbell et al. 1990).[5]

Public health researchers identified a highly predictive set of clinical signs associated with pneumonia. To save lives, they wanted to introduce a simple diagnostic algorithm for ARI that would enable both local practitioners and community health workers to identify pneumonia quickly and treat it appropriately with an inexpensive antibiotic. Two issues needed to be investigated. First, how would people in different cultures respond to the clinical signs in the algorithm, and did they currently recognize these signs as indicative of serious illness? Second, depending on the strength of existing perceptions of illness, was there a need to include culturally meaningful symptoms in ARI messages that were not evidence-based signs for pneumonia?

Researchers learned that although the sensitivity of some illness categories and culturally valued symptoms (such as the sounds of different coughs) for identifying cases of pneumonia was high, the specificity was often low (e.g., there were many false positives). Some illness terms were used very loosely. In addition, researchers found important cultural differences in the interpretation of key signs of pneumonia. For example, although rapid breathing is an important clinical sign of pneumonia, several studies revealed that mothers were far more concerned with difficult or labored breathing than the speed of breathing (Chand and Bhattacharyya 1994; Hudelson et al. 1994; Iyun and Tomson 1996; Kresno et al. 1994; McNee et al. 1995; Nichter and Nichter 1996c; Stewart et al. 1994). Fast breathing became a major health concern only when accompanied by other symptoms such as fever (Kresno et al. 1994; Nichter and Nichter 1996c) or convulsions (Cody et al. 1997; McNee et al. 1995; Nichter and Nichter 1996c). And in some contexts, rapid breathing was perceived as slow breathing and tiredness (Hudelson et al. 1994). Indrawn chest, another important clinical sign of pneumonia, was recognized by mothers in some cultures but not in others where attention was instead drawn to a child's bulging or rising stomach (Bhattacharyya 1997; Nichter and Nichter 1996c). Despite being a poor marker of pneumonia, fever was considered an important sign of severity in many cultures (e.g., Hudelson et al. 1994; Kresno et al. 1994; Nichter and Nichter 1996c).

Studies of ARI made it clear that local terminologies for serious illnesses were not simply approximations of biomedical diseases and that merely calling attention to clinical signs of pneumonia in health messages was insufficient in many cultures. ARI outreach required that both the clinical signs of pneumonia and the cultural signs of illness severity be addressed if local communities were to gain confidence in programs. Another lesson that emerged from social science of ARI (and diarrhea) research was the importance of investigating how local categories of illness were treated before using local names in health messages. In India, Chand and Bhattacharya (1994) caution that although the local term *potat ala* often refers to pneumonia, substituting the name can be dangerous because potat ala is believed to be a stomach-based illness treatable by making the person vomit.

Lessons learned from ARI research may prove useful in other interventions. For example, it may be wise to pay more attention to symptoms that have cultural importance but are not currently addressed by educational programs. Let me cite an example. In Nigeria, skin ailments associated with onchocerciasis such as lizard skin and pruritis that develop soon after infestation are given little attention in disease control programs that focus on blindness. Blindness is a consequence of untreated onchocerciasis that emerges after many years. Skin ailments are important because they are stigmatized and reduce the chances that one will be married or stay married (Amazigo 1993, 1994; Amazigo and Obikeze 1991). If a connection between onchocerciasis and skin ailments were made clear, people would possibly be more motivated to engage in preventive behavior. A pan-African study of the disease (Vlassoff and Moreno 2002) notes that women are more concerned about onchodermatitis and its impact on life chances when compared to men. They might be particularly receptive to such messages.

Malaria

Malaria research provides us with additional lessons about the importance of illness classification. It also presents us with additional challenges related to the different ways in which this disease may manifest, as well as the manner in which chronicity and recurrence are understood.

In contexts where many different types of fevers affect children, it is important to examine the specificity or ambiguity of local terms used to refer to simple malaria. Several studies of uncomplicated malaria in Africa have found that local terms used for malaria fever identify a broad category of mild childhood disease that local populations do not necessarily think requires malaria-specific treatment. Instead, treatment often involves general management of mild fever with whatever medicine is easily accessible (Williams and Jones 2004).[6] In other contexts, where malaria is endemic, it is thought to be a recurrent fever experienced in the rainy season. Any fever or malaise involving body pain experienced in this season is presumed to be malaria (Hausmann et al. 1998; Winch et al. 1994). In this situation, all illness is initially treated with antimalarial drugs, a behavior pattern that may prove dangerous when a child has a disease with overlapping symptoms (such as pneumonia) for which antimalarials have no efficacy.

Social science research on malaria also teaches us that minor and more-severe episodes of the same disease may be classified and seen as discrete illness categories. In several areas of Africa where malaria is endemic, seizures are viewed as a "folk illness" largely unrelated to malaria and are often attributed to supernatural causes.[7] In several different places, convulsions are treated by herbal medicines and rituals prior to seeking biomedical care. In other places, both herbal and biomedical care are sought simultaneously. For example, Baume and colleagues (2000) report that in Zambia, convulsions are treated by indigenous medicines, but such treatment results in little delay in resorting to biomedical clinics.

Severe anemia and splenomegaly are also commonly considered distinct from malaria and not linked by any notions of ethnophysiology (Mwenesi et al. 1995; Winch et al. 1996). Although most studies of health care–seeking behavior for malaria have reported a clear preference for biomedicine in cases of uncomplicated malaria, some have shown that people frequently opt for traditional medicine to treat convulsions.[8] This choice is problematic, as cerebral malaria is life-threatening to children and requires immediate medical intervention.

One of the major challenges malaria presents to both clinicians and health social scientists is the fact that clinical presentations of malaria overlap with other childhood diseases and vary considerably among children (Oaks et al. 1991; O'Dempsey et al. 1993). Symptoms also vary between children and adults.[9] For example, fever combined with cough, rapid breathing, and chest in-drawing may be indicative of pneumonia, malaria, or both (English et al. 1996; Gove 1997; WHO 1995). Malaria symptoms are often confused with the symptoms of pneumonia (Kallander et al. 2004; O'Dempsey et al. 1993), and malaria may present as diarrhea in children as well. More research is needed on differences in local perceptions of adult and child malaria and whether sets of symptoms other than fever (such as diarrhea) are associated with malaria.

Several other issues related to malaria remain to be researched more fully. One major research question has to do with how local populations think about recurrent sickness and malaria fever cycles. Do local populations have a perception of latent or asymptomatic illness, or do they view episodes of fever separated in time as being distinct and unrelated? How do such perceptions influence medication use and health care seeking? A study in Kenya found that if a fever returned within a week after a child sought treatment for malaria, the treatment was deemed to have been ineffective; if the fever returned after two weeks, however, the two episodes were treated as different sicknesses (Marsh and Mutemi 1997, cited in Williams and Jones 2004).

A study by Hausmann and colleagues (1998) on "fake malaria" in Tanzania illustrates just how important it is to study local perceptions of symptom persistence and illness relapse. When illnesses that are treated by a biomedical practitioner persist, unexpectedly flare up, or return soon after a course of medicine is completed, some people interpret the sickness as a sign of witchcraft.[10] In this case, the failure of biomedicine signified witchcraft through a process of diagnosis by treatment. Treatment of such cases requires the services of practitioners of both traditional and modern medicine.

In another insightful study, this one of *degedege*, a folk illness in Tanzania, Langwick (2007) points out that knowledge of malaria does not displace the importance of local illness categories that involve other sources of vulnerability (in this case, *shetani* spirits) that require forms of treatment to ward off potential sources of malevolence. In a population quite familiar with malaria and its link to mosquitoes, concern about degedege remains strong. This concern influences people's willingness to use biomedicine when a child becomes ill with fever. Powerful injections are thought to be capable of shocking the child's body and creating the very conditions under which degedege is likely to occur. Langwick notes that local practitioners are less interested in the diagnosis of specific spirits and more interested in denying such spirits the opportunity to act and become visible. This case leads us to rethink divisions between diagnostic and therapeutic procedures and reminds us that local diagnostic categories involve sets of relationships and actors within local worlds that biomedicine cannot explain away through the use of evidence and specificity.

Winch and his colleagues (1995:1603–5) put together a checklist of five steps to follow when designing a malaria control program sensitive to local categories of illness. These steps have general relevance and are worth summarizing.

1. Identify the local terms currently used by the health system for malaria (etc.) in government health messages.
2. Find out what the term means to the local population and how it fits into the local illness taxonomy of fevers (diarrheas, coughs, etc.).
3. Look for symptoms and manifestations of malaria (etc.) that fall outside the local taxonomy for sorting out fevers: for example, anemia.
4. Examine whether the local taxonomy of fevers (etc.) affects the perceived efficacy of malaria control measures (etc.) by the community.
5. Determine whether there are political and social implications of using certain terms when communicating to different groups of people inhabiting the same area: for example, immigrants versus local people, the affluent, or those with different levels of formal education.

LANGUAGE AND ILLNESS

Illness Categories Are Not Static

Popular health culture is dynamic and ever-changing. Globalization feeds popular health cultures with a steady stream of new health products, ideas, and terminology that may be appropriated or rejected. The language of illness reflects both continuity and change in popular health culture. Old terms are used in new ways, and new terms are added to people's health vocabularies and interpreted in novel ways.[11] Often, new terms adopted from biomedicine do not retain their original meaning but instead are used to express hybrid ideas or long-standing concepts in modern ways. In other cases, new terms are adopted to minimize social stigma. For example, Van Sickle (2004) documented use of the term *eosinophilia* in Chennai, India, to avoid the stigma of both filariasis and asthmalike symptoms. Hybrid forms of health knowledge and the changing meaning of illness terms and categories require ongoing social science research. In addition to investigating local appropriation of illness terminology from the media, public health messages, and the terminology used by medical practitioners, researchers need to be aware of the impact of the pharmaceutical industry. The industry plays an active role in introducing "textually transmitted" illness through the marketing of products to relieve or prevent novel health conditions hyped up by advertising (Nichter and Vuckovic 1994). The industry also fosters bracket creep, the expansion of a diagnostic category and/or the medicines used to treat it as a means of expanding the market for products.[12]

The Language of Illness Affects Risk Perception

In addition to influencing health care seeking and perceptions of illness severity, local illness classification can also influence perceptions of the commonality of various diseases in an area. This in turn can affect interest in prevention activities. For example, Pylypa (2004, 2007) points out that local classification of dengue cases as fruit fever (*khai makmai*) in northeastern Thailand contributes to an underperception of the significance of dengue as a local problem. Also contributing to under-recognition is the perception of dengue as constituting only the more severe hemorrhagic form of the disease associated with secondary infections. When simple and relatively mild dengue fever is considered to be another form of illness, local populations may be less compelled to take breeding-site control measures seriously.

The press also contributes to perceptions that an illness—especially an epidemic illness—is immanent, prevalent, or of concern. This may be done through sensationalism, misleading headlines, or under-reporting a serious illness such as cholera by using vague terms such as *gastroenteritis* (in India) or euphemistically speaking about avian flu as "bird cholera" (in Thailand) to minimize concern.

Message Crossover

Let me note one last issue related to language and perceptions of illness. Communities are exposed to a plethora of health-education messages. In some cases, messages concerning one health problem influence or confound thinking about other health problems.[13] White (2002) provides an example from northeastern Brazil of message drift from general health-education messages that associate unsanitary environments with disease in general to ideas about what causes leprosy, such that leprosy comes to be thought of as being spread by contact with contaminated water sources. Pylypa (2004) provides two other related examples of "message crossover" from northeastern Thailand. She notes that public health messages for diarrhea related to keeping drinking water (largely rainwater) uncontaminated were conflated with mosquito control messages encouraging people to cover their large ceramic water-storage jars. Villagers integrated the two sets of messages and came to think that keeping mosquitoes from laying eggs in and contaminating their drinking sources was necessary to prevent disease. An idea emerged that ingesting mosquito eggs would lead people to develop both malaria and dengue fever. She further observed that people conflated education messages directed toward dengue with those addressing malaria. Some of the villagers she interviewed came to think that both diseases were spread by the same type of mosquito.[14] In one case, an informant stated that an adult bitten by a mosquito would suffer from malaria, while a child bitten by the same mosquito would suffer from dengue.[15]

Another type of crossover occurs when modern interventions come to be interpreted as similar to indigenous interventions. Samuelsen (2001) provides a relevant case in her investigation of why vaccinations are popular for children in Burkina Faso. Indigenous modes of healing and preventing illness by piercing the skin and mixing medicine in the blood have a long history in some parts of Africa. Some people, she reports, see vaccinations as a modern version of an old technique. She notes that local demand for both vaccination and indigenous forms of healing coexist and share many structural similarities in how they are delivered. Samuelsen recommends that public health practitioners make the most of similarities between modern and indigenous notions of prevention and harm reduction. Other social scientists have drawn attention to ways in which local populations understand vaccinations, indigenous medicines, and talismans as complementary (Cassell et al. 2006)[16] and have suggested that vaccinations can be explained to local populations through concepts of protection that they already comprehend (Nichter 1991b, 1995).[17] One method for doing so is "teaching by analogy," a pedagogical technique that Mimi Nichter and I have discussed and experimented with at some length (Nichter and Nichter 1996d). Use of this technique requires a sound and grounded understanding of local culture and communication patterns and encourages participatory research involving creative "thinking within the metaphor." Utilizing this methodology demands rigorous iterations of pretesting and evaluation.

FIGURE 2. Vertical research agenda: each disease studied in isolation

MALARIA	DENGUE	FILARIASIS	TB
Research related to the control of mosquito breeding sites	Research related to the control of mosquito breeding sites	Research related to the control of mosquito breeding sites	How to better identify TB cases, in public and private sector
Mosquito exposure and how to reduce, bednet use and how to increase	Mosquito exposure and how to reduce	Mosquito exposure and how to reduce	How to reduce extreme poverty and overcrowding, how to reduce tobacco use as risk factor
How to improve sentinel surveillance, how to encourage blood testing and clinical use	How to improve sentinel surveillance, how to encourage blood testing and clinical use	How to improve sentinel surveillance, how to encourage blood testing and clinical use	How to encourage people with symptoms to come into government clinic for free sputum test
Research on home treatment of fever and health care–seeking behavior	Research on home treatment of fever and health care–seeking behavior	Research on home treatment of symptoms and health care–seeking behavior	Research on home treatment of persistent cough and health care–seeking behavior
Research on compliance with malarial medications		Response to mass treatment	Research on compliance with DOTS therapy
Pregnancy targeted as risk group		How to overcome stigma, gender sensitivity	How to overcome stigma, gender sensitivity

And so on

Overarching Message: Important Lessons Are to Be Learned from Thinking beyond Single Diseases

What I have attempted to demonstrate thus far is that much is to be learned if we mine the existing social science in international health literature and look for lessons that crosscut individual disease studies. Conceptualized visually in figure 2, most ethnographic studies in international health prior to 2000 tended to be vertical and strictly focused on one disease, such as malaria, dengue fever, TB, and so on. In keeping with the type of analysis

FIGURE 3. Horizontal research agenda: focus on issues that crosscut diseases

HORIZONTAL RESEARCH AGENDA	MALARIA	DENGUE	MEASLES	DIARRHEA	ARI	TB	AIDS
Local perceptions of vulnerability and risk, lay epidemiology, cultural health concerns, social relation of illness, illness representation	⇔	⇔	⇔	⇔	⇔	⇔	⇔
Local behavior related to illness prevention and harm reduction	⇔	⇔	⇔	⇔	⇔	⇔	⇔
Ecological and political-ecological factors affecting environment-vector-host relations, unnatural distribution of disease	⇔	⇔	⇔	⇔	⇔	⇔	⇔
Structural factors affecting health care delivery and health-system adherence to established treatment guidelines	⇔	⇔	⇔	⇔	⇔	⇔	⇔
Pharmaceutical practice as affected by local perceptions of the body, illness, health concerns, interpretation of medicine action, pharmaceutical practice influenced by pharmaceutical industry	⇔	⇔	⇔	⇔	⇔	⇔	⇔
Impact of one health program on health programs, impact of NGO or private-sector activity on public health sector and vice versa	⇔	⇔	⇔	⇔	⇔	⇔	⇔

I have begun in this chapter, it is time to examine illnesses horizontally in terms of the type of research questions outlined in figure 3. Why is this worth doing? Among other things, it will enable us to identify lessons related to how risk perception and lay epidemiology influence health-related practice, as well as how health-related concerns influence the adoption of interventions and pharmaceutical practice (the focus of the next chapter). We also gain insights into how messages about one illness affect thinking and practice about other illnesses (message crossover) and how attention to one problem (the push of linear programs) affects other programs. Further, horizontal thinking might reveal ways in which illness messages or programs might be bundled. For example, might several different programs related to vector control, water availability and management, or fever diagnosis and treatment be interlinked (Molyneux and Nantulya 2004)?

Horizontal thinking requires ethnographers who have a broad under-standing of popular health cultures. It demands thinking in cultural epide-miological as well as conventional epidemiological terms.[18] What I call for in the last chapter of this book is a process of participatory problem solving that interlinks cultural, epidemiological, political-economic, and ecological dimensions of ill health. This participatory process needs to directly involve communities. Such a process has already been embraced by some practitio-ners in the fields of environmental and occupational health and is referred to as "popular epidemiology" (Brown 1987, 1997).

NOTES

1. The relationship between illness classification and treatment delay is an important area of research. It requires rigorous examination of health care–seeking behavior that takes into account taskonomy as well as taxonomy, user fees and the costs of treatment as well as interpretations of illness severity. See Kamat 2006 for a recent example involving the treatment of fever in a malarial zone of Tanzania. Research on health care–seeking delay cannot use traditional therapy as a proxy for treatment delay, because traditional medi-cine is often used at the same time as biomedicine (Baume et al. 2000; Heggenhougen et al. 2003).

2. Another type of behavior that is closely related to taskonomy is strategic symptom reporting, whereby the afflicted present their ailments in ways that gain them a pre-ferred identity or valued resources (Nichter 1989b). For example, Kamat (2006) notes that mothers in Tanzania selectively report symptoms to health workers so the latter will believe that the children are really ill. An appreciation of the social relations of the lan-guage of illness is also essential to understanding how illnesses are and are not discussed in particular settings, as well as levels of specificity when they are.

3. See Bentley et al. 1988; de Zoysa et al. 1984; Frankel and Lehmann 1984; Kendall et al. 1984b; Malik et al. 1992; Mull and Mull 1988; Nations 1986; Nichter 1988, 1991a; Scrimshaw and Hurtado 1988; Smith et al. 1993; Yoder 1995; Yoder and Hornick 1996; Weiss 1988.

4. See Chand and Bhattacharyya 1994; Cody et al. 1997; Hudelson et al. 1994; Kresno et al. 1994; McNee et al. 1995; Mull et al. 1994; Nichter and Nichter 1996c; Stewart et al. 1994.

5. In epidemiology, *sensitivity* refers to the proportion of individuals in a population who will be correctly identified when administered a test designed to detect a particular disease. Sensitivity is calculated as the number of true positive results divided by the number of true positive and false negative results, thus generating the probability that an individual who does not have the particular disease will be correctly identified as negative when tested.

6. As noted by V. Kamat (2004) and Whyte (1997), doctors and nurses in Tanzania and Uganda often do not tell patients whether or not they have malaria. They simply give medicine and use a general term to refer to the illness episode that subsumes many types of fever. Health care providers are often engaging in diagnosis by treatment.

7. See, for example, Aikins et al. 1994; Alilio and Bammek 1998; Comoro et al. 2003; Gessler et al. 1995; Makemba et al. 1996; Mwenesi et al. 1995; Oberlander and Elverdan 2000; Okeke et al. 2005; Ramakrishna et al. 1989; Samuelsen 2004; Tarimo et al. 2000; Williams et al. 1999; Winch et al. 1996.

8. On interpretations of convulsions in Africa, see Agyepong 1992; Makemba et al. 1996; Molyneux et al. 1999; Munguti 1998; Mwenesi et al. 1995; Ongore et al. 1989; Ongore and Nyabola 1996; Ramakrishna et al. 1989; Tarimo et al. 2000; Winch et al. 1996. For comprehensive overviews of social science research on malaria, see Heggenhougen et al. 2003; McCombie 1996, 2002; Williams and Jones 2004.

9. The symptoms of dengue fever also vary between young children and adults (Rigau-Perez et al. 1998).

10. Witchcraft was not thought to cause malaria but was believed to confound or "play" with the disease, cause symptoms that mimic the disease, or use malaria as a way to camouflage itself so that it could not be detected easily.

11. Biomedical terms are often appropriated within popular health culture and given new meaning. In many cases, new terms index preexisting health concerns. A good example is the use and interpretation of the terms *blood pressure* in Tanzania (Strahl 2003) and *hypertension* in the Philippines (Rueda-Baclig and Florencio 2003). For a general discussion of the issue, see Nichter 1989b.

12. In a country such as India where there is already a proclivity to treat mental health problems with psychiatric medications (Ecks 2005; Nunley 1996), it is only a matter of time before antidepressants, antianxiety drugs, and drugs for attention deficit disorder are popularized for emotional problems, ways of coping with stressful social situations, and to enhance mental concentration when studying for hypercompetitive exams and so forth. Valium (under the brand name Calmpose) has been liberally used for nonpsychiatric purposes in India for years.

13. Sometimes interventions are confused because they appear to be similar. For example, Harper (2002) found that in Nepal, polio programs and vitamin A programs were organized in very similar ways. Both programs require giving medicine drops to children and were often confused with one another.

14. Differentiating types of mosquitoes might appear to be a lot to ask of people. However, the habits of these mosquito species and how one has to control and protect against them are quite different.

15. Pylypa (2004) notes that *dengue* was a term this informant associated with dengue hemorrhagic fever (DHF), not simple dengue fever, because public health messages on dengue focus only on the severe form of the illness. DHF affects the young more commonly than adults, leading this informant to see it more as a child's illness caused by mosquitoes.

16. Cassell and colleagues (2006) note that women taking children to urban clinics for valued vaccinations place talismans around their children's necks to ward off sources of malevolence that they might encounter in crowded places where one does not know the people assembled. Women recognize talismans and vaccinations as protecting against different kinds of danger.

17. Recognizing homologies between local and biomedical ideas that can create a space for dialogue about health principles is quite different from the manipulation of local health ideas toward the end of fostering compliance without understanding. Other social scientists have suggested that the more health advice offered to caregivers can tap into everyday knowledge, the more likely it is to be communicated and integrated in the community (Craig 2000).

18. The term *cultural epidemiology* has been used in many different ways. For example, Weiss (2001) uses the term cultural epidemiology to integrate a concern for disease with a concern for "illness" within epidemiology. This is similar to Kleinman's efforts in the 1980s to do the same in clinical medicine through the use of explanatory model interviews. Trostle (2005) uses the term to further designate how diseases are defined and measured as well as patterned. I use *cultural epidemiology* as an umbrella term that covers three overlapping research agendas: (1) the study of lay epidemiology (local perceptions of risk and the spectrum of popular illness categories); (2) the study of etic (biomedical) disease categories, groupings (e.g., constructions such as "tropical disease"), and measurement as influenced by the biotechnical and geo-political-economic contexts in which interventions are mounted; and (3) popular epidemiology, a research agenda that involves community-expert dialogue and problem solving related to proximate and distal causes of ill health (Brown 1987, 1997).

4

Perceptions of Pharmaceuticals and Quality of Care

Every year new medicines come onto the market, new companies spring up, and more pharmaceutical representatives request us to prescribe their products. So many medicines are there now on the shelves of chemist shops. Which ones are good for patients? As doctors, we must try and see. Which ones suit a patient? That is something that the patient must also tell. Diseases may be the same under the microscope in the USA and India, but bodies are different. Combinations of medicines that you see here, you will not see in the USA. You will wonder why we are giving them and you may call us irrational. Our patients demand such things because it matches their complaints and their concerns. And unlike the USA we must diagnose the pocket as well as the problem.

—Allopathic doctor practicing
in a small town in South India, 1990

Research on local perceptions of medicines has also contributed significantly to international health. Indeed, I do not think it an overstatement to say that studies of explanatory models of pharmaceuticals have proven just as important as explanatory models of illness. Of even more importance is the interactivity of explanatory models of illness and medicines. How medicines are thought to function affects ideas about bodily processes related to pathophysiology and vice versa. Moreover, people often come to understand their illnesses through the type, strength, and quantity of medications they consume (Nichter and Vuckovic 1994). It is common for the afflicted not to be told the type (diagnosis, name) of illness they are suffering from by busy practitioners and even more common for them not to be told the cause of their illness. The nature and the severity of their illness are often evaluated in terms of the medications provided or prescribed to manage their ailments.[1]

Medicines may be taken, offered, prescribed, or administered for many reasons. To reflect this multiplicity of reasons, medical anthropologists have examined the social relations of medicine exchange and the meaning of medicines as well as cultural expectations of medications, cultural interpretations of medicine effectiveness, medicine self-regulation, and compliance.[2] In some cases, medicine given to a patient or family member signifies concern or is a fetish of "best care" and modernity. In other cases, medicines may be administered to silence a population, deflect attention from factors rendering a population unhealthy, or medicalize a social or economic problem (Rozemberg and Manderson 1998; Scheper-Hughes and Lock 1991). In still other cases, taking and demanding medicines may function as an idiom of distress (Nichter 1981; Nichter and Vuckovic 1994).

An overview of social science research on pharmaceutical use in developing countries is summarized by Nichter and Vuckovic (1994), Van der Geest and colleagues (1996), Van der Geest and Whyte (1989), and Whyte and colleagues (2002). Here I highlight a few of the major lessons learned from the study of pharmaceutical practice and pharmaceutical marketing. I also draw attention to important research on medicine delivery devices (hypodermic injections) and then briefly consider two other topics: perceptions of the quality of medical care, and the rising importance of diagnostic testing in the developing world.

Perceptions and Expectations of Medications

Many studies have noted that treatment expectations guide health care–seeking as well as compliance behavior. For example, Kamat (2001), in his study of urban malaria in Mumbai, India, documented a widespread perceived need for intravenous glucose drips to treat malaria.[3] Demand for IV drips influenced people's choice of practitioners as well as the routine treatment practices of "doctors" in the slum in which the study took place. IV drips are popular elsewhere as well. For example, while working in the rural Philippines, I observed some mothers who bypassed local clinics where health care providers did not offer IV drips; they traveled to towns when their children suffered from the symptoms of pneumonia. Drips were deemed a measure of "best care" (Nichter and Nichter 1996c).

In the same population, I observed another powerful example of just how crucial it was to research patient expectations of medications. Mothers of children who took medications for primary complex TB classified locally as "weak lungs" expected that this medication would cure other respiratory problems as well (Nichter 1997). In some cases, children treated with the

TB drug INH (termed locally "vitamins for the lungs") were not taken to practitioners when suffering from pneumonia until they were extremely ill. Treatment delay was directly associated with mothers' expectations that INH would take care of the illness, an expectation not addressed by health staff at the time TB medications were provided. In an analogous situation in Sierra Leone, Yumkella (1996) found that women taking medicine for onchocerciasis believed that all other worms would be expelled from their bodies as well. When this did not occur, they were disappointed.

From a review of the literature, I have identified the following six research questions pertaining to expectations of medicines. Answers to these questions provide insights into how perceptions of medicines influence pharmaceutical practice.

1. What do people expect from medications?[4]
2. How quickly do people expect medications to work?
3. How realistic are people's expectations?
4. Do people expect medicines to cure and/or prevent an illness or just manage it?
5. At what point after taking medicines do people think themselves no longer contagious to others?
6. What expectations do people have that a medication found effective for one illness may be effective for other illnesses thought to involve similar causes or disturbed physiological processes by way of cultural reasoning?

Physical Properties

People often evaluate medications based on color, form, and taste. In their study of pharmaceuticals among the Mende in Sierra Leone, Bledsoe and Goubaud (1985) found that people assessed the strength and effects of medications largely by evaluating physical characteristics, such as the size of a pill indicating that it was potent. Numerous studies in Africa, Asia, and Latin America have reported similar findings, with some noting that humoral reasoning guides such evaluation (Ferguson 1988; Haak 1988; Logan 1973). Let me briefly cite two examples from India.

In India, the black color of ferrous sulfate tablets given to women at no cost to prevent anemia has greatly contributed to their unpopularity over the years (Nichter and Nichter 1996b). Pregnant women perceived these "hard and heaty" pills to be difficult to digest and to cause nausea and constipation.[5] The same women who rejected the black pills often purchased a liquid "blood tonic," which turned out to be either an Ayurvedic tonic or a general vitamin tonic (of which there are many) when they had the where-withal to do so. During focus groups that I carried out with Indian colleagues in the 1970s, 1980s, and 1990s in three states of South India, white tablets or red liquid medications were preferred and requested by women as appropriate to take during pregnancy.[6] Yet the government continued to dole out black tablets.[7]

A second case involves directly observed short-course therapy (DOTS) that consists of variously sized and colored tablets contained in blister packs. While conducting research on patients' perceptions of the quality of the medicines they were asked to take, I was often asked what the most important medicine was—the white tablets or the red one, the big one or the small ones? The IndiaCLEN TB Research Group of which I am a member has been recording these types of questions and developing a patient-friendly education guide to address patients' medicine-attribute questions as well as questions about why they need to take so many pills at once, why for a minimum of six months, and why on an empty stomach.[8]

Although the public health sector has not given much thought to how local populations perceive medications having different physical characteristics, the private sector has. The private sector takes medicine color, form, and taste associations seriously when marketing products pitched to particular market sectors. How the industry positions products has a significant effect on how government-issued medicines are perceived.

Injections: Popular but How Safe?

One form of medication is worth special consideration. In many cultures, injections are considered to be more powerful than pills (Birungi 1998; Etkin 1992; Nichter 1989a; Nichter and Nichter 1996e; Reeler 2000; Van der Geest and Whyte 1989).[9] Where supply and demand for injections is particularly high, a set of issues related to hypodermic hygiene arises related to disease transmission.[10]

In developing countries, unhygienic needles and syringes contaminate a significant proportion of injections administered.[11] A recently completed national study of injection use in India carried out by IndiaCLEN (Arora 2004) found that of all the injections administered, two-thirds are unsafe and one-third carry a potential risk of transmitting a blood-borne virus. Notably, the rate of unsafe injection was highest at immunization clinics (74.0 percent; 95 percent CI, range 71.4–76.6), followed by government health facilities (68.7 percent; 95 percent CI, range 66.1–71.3) and private health facilities (59.9 percent; 95 percent CI, range 56.9–62.8). Unhygienic injection practices have contributed to the spread of such blood-borne infections as hepatitis and HIV,[12] as well as African haemorrhagic fever, schistosomiasis, lassa fever, and malaria.[13]

Research has begun to be conducted on local perceptions and practices of syringe and needle hygiene, focusing on what is safe and what is dangerous when it comes to the reuse of needles and syringes for different types of medications and people (Lakshman and Nichter 2000).[14] In India, Lakshman and I found that because children's illness is often considered harmless to adults, multiple children or a child and an adult may be injected with the same needle (be it disposable or not) without sterilization of the hypodermic set. Among practitioners who did attempt to sterilize needles and syringes, most did so by ineffective means such as rinsing them with water or disinfectant. In one memorable case, a practitioner placed his hypodermic set in a refrigerator overnight as a means of sterilization. Not uncommonly, I have observed malaria workers use the same needles to take blood samples from multiple potential malaria patients without sterilizing the needles first. A fresh needle would be used only if the person was deemed to be seriously ill or "known to be an alcoholic," which marked him as a member of a special risk group.[15]

Representations of injection safety may affect public response to government health programs. In an ethnographic study in Uganda, Birungi (1998) found that in the early 1990s the public began to mistrust state health care institutions during a time of political and economic upheaval. At the same time, anti-AIDS education campaigns warned the public against the dangers of sharing unsterilized needles. This reinforced existing mistrust in public health facilities and led the local population to seek health care from people they knew were using injection equipment over which they had personal control.[16] One of the fears of those in the international health community is that studies such as those of Gisselquist (Gisselquist et al. 2002, 2003) on the link between HIV and injection use will be picked up by the press and reported in a sensationalistic way. Representations of HIV as spread through needles and syringes could undermine faith in immunization and contraceptive programs as well as in messages about condom use.

In an earlier passage, I note that the perceived strength of injections made them popular for some people, while at the same time marking them as inappropriate therapy for other groups. Studies of malaria in multiple regions of Africa have found that although injections are frequently considered superior to oral medications for adults, injections are thought to be too strong for young children, especially when the children are seriously ill. Parents avoid seeking treatment for children from health facilities if they suspect that an injection will be administered (Baume et al. 2000; Comoro et al. 2003; Hamel et al. 2001; Makemba et al. 1996; Oberlander and Elverdan 2000; Williams et al. 1999; Winch et al. 1996). Other studies have shown that in places where injections are seen as preferred treatment for children with malaria, tablets are devalued.

Medicine Compatibility

Cultural perceptions of compatibility play an important role in how people determine the suitability of particular types of medication for their personal use. Compatibility—the fit between medication and the bodily constitution of an individual—is used to explain why a medication proves efficacious for one person and not another person, given a similar type of complaint. Described most extensively in research in the Philippines as a concept guiding pharmaceutical use (Hardon 1987, 1991, 1994; Tan 1994, 1996), variations of the concept have been reported elsewhere in Indonesia, Thailand, and Vietnam. The perception of a medicine's being compatible is important for at least four reasons: (1) people may use a drug deemed compatible as self-treatment for a wide variety of complaints (Craig 2002); (2) drug effectiveness may be misjudged after a short time if expectations of a drug are unmet, leading the user to think that the medicine is incompatible; (3) side effects may be seen as a sign of a drug's incompatibility;[17] and (4) noncompliance with medication prescribed may be justified on the basis of a medicine's not being compatible (Nichter 2002a).

Research into how medicines are evaluated at the site of the body that take into account cultural perceptions of compatibility also provide insight into treatment adherence among those having chronic illness. In her study of people's evaluations of leprosy treatment regimens, Boonmongkon (1995) found that patients viewed multidrug therapy positively, reporting that they experienced a sensation of lightness, which is locally associated with good health. In contrast, a monodrug therapy was considered by many people to produce an unhealthy feeling of heaviness. Considerations of which medication regimen is right for a particular person and/or cultural group need to be guided by local perceptions of well-being as much as cost.

Self-Treatment

Self-medication is a common and complex behavior pattern examined by many social scientists through both household and pharmacy studies. It is best looked at as a continuum from self-regulation of drugs previously prescribed to self-trial of medications one has never been prescribed (Okumura et al. 2002). In developing countries, people commonly purchase small quantities of medication from local shops without a practitioner's prescription to see whether their ailments can thereby be managed or cured. In some cases, these medications have previously been prescribed for the illnesses experienced; in other cases, people have used the medication before for illnesses they think are similar, with good results and/or a sense that the medication is compatible. In the former case, medication cost may lead people to purchase a one- or two-day dose of a drug to see whether it works. If it does, more may be purchased or symptoms may have abated to the point that the afflicted person feels as though the illness no longer exists or can be managed without medication and more expense. Expectations of how fast the medication should produce a demonstration effect influences how long it is taken. In the latter case, familiar medications may be taken to manage ailments or in some cases prevent them from occurring or getting worse, an issue I discuss shortly. Sometimes this type of self-treatment is an extension of a practitioner's previous recommended treatment, while in other cases people apply their knowledge of medicines to different ailments thought to be similar in some way (e.g., both caused by heat in the body). In other cases, people simply take what is on hand or easily available (as in the case of antimalarial medications in Africa) or take a medication that has a reputation for being powerful. Self-treatment also entails people taking larger and smaller doses of a medication than what is recommended as a form of self-regulation. This may be influenced by cost and perceptions of body sensitivity and medicine strength. In some cases, fear of a medication's power and side effects influences the dosage and duration of treatment. And in still other cases, social status influences patterns of self-medication.

All of these behavior patterns are documented in a large literature on pharmaceutical practice that Das and Das (2005) encourage us to read critically in relation to how data are gathered and the need to pay attention to contingencies that influence medicine purchase and consumption behavior. Let me draw attention to another aspect of self-treatment that has been less described: diagnosis by self-treatment in the case of stigmatized illness. During an STI prevention project in a North Indian slum, I encountered youths who challenged health messages recommending that they get tested after engaging in risky sex. They asked why it made sense to invest time or money to get a diagnostic test only to learn that you were ill and had to take medicine. One would then have to invest time and money again to get treated. Why not just pay once for treatment that would cure the disease if you had it (Awasthi et al. 2000)? They were mostly interested in learning the names of good medicines for sexually transmitted diseases (not distinguished in terms of multiple illness categories), learning how to determine whether a private doctor was good, and what the cost for treatment was likely to be.

Curative Medicines Used to Prevent Disease

Medications are sometimes used in public health for prophylactic purposes; chemoprophylaxis for TB and malaria are cases in point. An important issue to consider is how local populations understand this medication practice and how they extend and apply the logic of prophylaxis when self-medicating. Little research to date has been conducted on the prophylactic use of medicines as a form of self-styled harm reduction, but existing studies suggest that representations of medicine as capably warding off illness are important. I have already provided three examples of iatrogenic behavior related to the use of medicines for prophylactic and harm-reduction-related practices: the use of TB drugs as "vitamins for the lungs" capable of preventing serious respiratory illnesses in the Philippines (Nichter 1997), the use of tetracycline to prevent culturally identified "uterus" problems from becoming serious in Thailand (Boonmongkon et al. 2001), and the use of antibiotics prior to or following sex to prevent STIs and HIV in the Philippines and Thailand (Abellenosa and Nichter 1996; Kilmarx et al. 1997; Kuntolbutra et al. 1996; Nichter 2001). I suspect that these examples are just the tip of the iceberg. Future studies should address emerging representations of medicine-fixes in a world where both a sense of risk and a demand for harm-reduction measures appear to be growing.[18]

Drug Resistance

How do local populations understand drug resistance? Very little research has been conducted on this important topic by social scientists in developing countries (Orzech and Nichter 2008). Research is needed on what lay populations think are the reasons behind the diminishing power of particular drugs. To what extent is reduced effectiveness viewed as population based and to what extent specific to particular types of people? In India, I have encountered several reasons given for why medicines are no longer considered as effective as they once were: the declining quality of medicines and adulteration are commonly cited. Diminished power is also viewed in terms of how much of a particular allopathic medicine someone has personally used over a given period of time, with some people concerned that overuse of a drug might render it less effective in the future.[19] Others associate diminished effectiveness with the use of other drugs to which the body has become accustomed. And among the better educated, resistance is discussed, but it is conceptualized as an individual- as much as a population-based phenomenon.[20] Judicious use of pharmaceuticals and the reduction of medication resistance are a global health priority. Educating the community about drug resistance is a necessary but insufficient step given the political economic factors that drive medication supply, sale, distribution, and consumption.

How could one educate the lay population about drug resistance using local knowledge? In many societies, medicines, chemical fertilizers, and insecticides are viewed in similar ways. Could lessons learned from experience with antimicrobials and insecticides be generalized? Antibiotic and pesticide resistance do have points in common, and both phenomena are fostered by the inappropriate use of chemical fixes (Orzech and Nichter 2008). Perhaps a well-thought-out "teaching by analogy" approach to non-formal education could be used to engage local communities in problem solving that extends observations in one domain of life and applies them to another (Nichter and Nichter 1996d).

REPRESENTATIONS OF NEW DRUGS

With the rising rates of drug resistance and innovations in pharmaceutical research, public health practitioners are routinely introducing new medicines and revisiting their use of known drugs. How do local populations understand and use new medicines recommended as replacement therapies for drugs they have come to know and trust? Chloroquine (CQ) provides an excellent case in point. Drug resistance has led to the discontinuation of CQ for the treatment of malaria in many parts of Africa. Today, combination-therapy employing drugs such as sulfadoxine-pyremethamine (S/P) and, more recently, artemisinin is preferred or required.[21] How have local populations responded to new-generation drugs being promoted by their governments in locations where CQ supplies continue to be available? Several recent studies have found that local populations continue to value and use CQ, not just because CQ is much cheaper than S/P but also because it has antipyretic and anti-inflammatory properties (which S/P does not exhibit) and its bitter taste has cultural significance. Among populations who associate serious cases of malaria with the rapid progression of fever, CQ's rapid antipyretic properties are a tangible and immediate sign of effectiveness. In contrast, S/P often causes fevers to spike when it is first taken and causes side effects (skin irritation, ulcers) that concern local populations. In some cases, people interpret these side effects as an indication that the medicine is too strong for a child or as a sign of incompatibility. Researchers suggest that local populations must be better prepared to assess new-generation antimalarials, that valued demonstration effects (such as fever) and negative side effects need to be addressed by practitioners, and that treatments need to be made more affordable (Nsimba 2006; Tarimo et al. 2001; Whyte et al. 2002; Williams et al. 1999). Nostalgia for older drugs such as CQ needs to be closely examined, as do the ways in which these familiar drugs are actually used (Djimde 1998) and reported on household surveys.[22] Further research is also needed to investigate how new drugs are marketed. Hsu (2002) provides a most interesting study of artemisinin in Tanzania.[23]

Research is also needed on how people respond to messages telling them that previously contraindicated drugs for young children are now acceptable frontline drugs, as is the case for sulfadoxine-pyremethamine.[24] And what do local doctors make of press that draws attention to rising rates of resistance for sulfadoxine-pyremethamine and the specter of drug resistance to artemisinin when used as monotherapy (Greenwood 2004)?[25] Additionally, how will the presence of fake artemisinin on the Asian and African markets affect local perceptions of its effectiveness (Dondorp et al. 2004; Magnus et al. 2007; Newton et al. 2001, 2003)?

Another important topic worthy of study is how new forms of medication are viewed by local populations, given notions of ethnophysiology and the way drugs act in the body. For example, it would be important to investigate how rectal suppositories are viewed by populations having a long-standing tradition of enema or purgative use. The World Health Organization is in the process of recommending artesunate suppositories for single-dose use in the management of acute malaria. How will different populations respond to this mode of administering medication?

Perceptions of Side Effects

Another important area of research is the way a medicine's effects on the body are experienced and evaluated biosocially. Notions of etiology and how a medication is thought to act in the body influence whether symptoms experienced after taking the medicine are judged in a positive or negative light (Etkin 1992; Nichter 1989a; Nichter and Nichter 1996e). For instance, is the diarrhea, burning sensation, or colored urine experienced after taking a medicine an anticipated part of the healing process associated with the removal of toxins or heat from the body, or is it viewed as an unexpected negative side effect? How about menstruation lapse when taking forms of contraception such as Depo-Provera? How is this interpreted?

Cultural interpretations of medications are an important issue to consider in relation to both nonadherence and a population's propensity to complain or not complain about the side effects of medications. Side effects may involve the disruption of culturally valued physical processes or make visible certain symptoms that some people wish to hide. For example, changes in skin pigmentation from leprosy medication proved to be a barrier to its usage among women in Brazil, who feared that it would reveal their diseased state to others and that such pigmentation changes would be permanent (de Oliveira 1997).[26]

Side effects are valued in at least two instances. In Malawi, women infrequently complain about the side effects of chloroquine because they feel that these symptoms indicate the drug is working (Helitzer-Allen 1989). This is a case of a side effect being interpreted as a demonstration effect. As another instance, in an area of West Africa where spurious drugs are commonly found on the market, informants felt that they knew they were taking the real drug by its telltale signs on the body (Van der Geest 1982). Other social scientists have corroborated this "proof" function of side effects in markets ever more polluted by poor-quality and bogus drugs (Cockburn et al. 2005).[27]

One wonders why so little attention has been focused on lay perceptions of side effects in different cultures. In their investigation of treatment adherence among leprosy patients in Pakistan, Mull and colleagues (1989) found few published reports on the suffering caused by side effects from leprosy medication. Yet in their ethnographic study, more than half of those labeled by clinic staff as "noncompliant" reported distressing side effects ranging from sensations of heat to nausea and pain. As more and more clinical trials are being carried out in developing countries (Bhatt 2004; Borfitz 2003; Lambert et al. 2004; Rai 2005),[28] it will become increasingly important to understand both symptoms deemed important enough to complain about and causing people to leave trials and symptoms not complained about that could be red flags that the medication is doing harm.[29] Stage-four clinical trials involving surveillance of pharmaceuticals released to the market will also demand a cultural assessment of side effects.[30]

PERCEPTIONS OF RATIONAL DRUG USE: WHOSE RATIONALE?

Representations of "rational drug use" in the public health literature are based on "evidence-based medicine" and pharmaco-epidemiological studies that take account of the efficacy and cost-effectiveness of medication, patterns of drug resistance, and the like. These representations are produced and promoted by expert bodies such as the World Health Organization. For some years now, I have argued that what is rational in principle is not always rational in practice when one takes into account the position of all stakeholders involved in medicine distribution and exchange (Nichter and Nichter 1996e; Nichter and Vuckovic 1994).[31] When one examines rationales guiding medicine-taking and medicine-giving behavior in context, one soon appreciates that complex market forces are in play (Fabricant and Hirschhorn 1987; Okeke et al. 1999). Practitioners need to administer and prescribe medications that enable them to maintain a positive reputation in a competitive health care arena where "lay cost reckoning" (reasoning about how much services should cost) influences day-to-day practice. The microeconomics of collecting a fee for health care services affects the range of medications doctors prescribe. If fees are indirectly collected, practitioners must dole out medicines or prescribe diagnostic tests that net them a profit. In India, significant profit makers for dispensing doctors and chemists have long been vitamins and tonics, as well as proprietary drugs that conform to lay cost reckoning and are least subject to price regulation. Where consultations are paid for directly by the patient and practitioner shopping is common, practitioners are more inclined to offer a mix of medicines that produce an impressive, even if temporary, demonstration effect (e.g., the prescribing of steroids). While clinically irrational, such practices are quite economically rational. Doctors are guided by their clinical experience but are also influenced by the economics of the game, topped off by perks from pharmaceutical companies (Kamat and Nichter 1998; Nizami et al. 1997; Pearl and Stecklow 2001). They are also responsive to what they perceive to be consumer demand. Consumer demand for health care resources is in turn responsive to perceptions of what treatments are most effective, their relative cost, and a whole range of social factors beyond the scope of this book but readily found in the medical anthropological literature. As for the pharmaceutical industry, those companies are in business to maximize profits and expand as well as exploit markets for their products. Industry practice with respect to the ethics of marketing products varies substantially by company (Consumers International 2006). The representation and/or misrepresentation of medicines to practitioners and the public constitutes a fertile area for critical social science research in developing countries (Herxheimer et al. 1993; Lexchin 1992, 1995; Moynihan and Cassels 2005; Moynihan et al. 2002; Stryer and Bero 1996; Wilkes et al. 1992).[32]

Social scientists have drawn attention to why it is important to consider professional identity and status when making recommendations about rational drug use. Medicines and diagnostic tests used by practitioners convey prestige and have symbolic importance. The case of oral rehydration is instructive. Nations and Rebhun (1988a) provide a powerful case study from Brazil of how health care providers initially mystified the use of oral rehydration salts (ORS) to maintain their professional identity, rather than promoting home use. Other studies have documented practitioners who fail to recommend homemade oral rehydration therapy (ORT) because there is no profit in doing so; instead, they prescribe commercial ORS preparations that are costly, or ORS in combination with antibiotics (Okeke et al. 1996). Practitioners prescribe medicines for watery diarrhea against clinical guidelines not just to earn a profit but also to meet consumer demand for medicines with an immediate demonstration effect. They also feel that they are responding to a perceived patient desire for polypharmacy. I have been told by many practitioners that patients will question their competence if they advise the afflicted to use only ORS for three days.[33]

In the 1980s and 1990s, I interviewed many doctors in India about why they prescribed so much cotrimethoxazole and fluoroquinolones for complaints that could well have been managed far less aggressively. Most were aware that their practice was overkill, but they had a reputation to keep or establish. These were the most popular drugs in the marketplace and were being marketed irrationally for wide ranges of complaints. As one practitioner noted, "Others are giving on this same street, so I must also give or be seen as behind the times. Then who will come to me? Only my relatives or those with no money to pay for first-rate service."

REPRESENTATIONS OF A MEDICINE'S VALUE

A widespread perception exists that the more expensive the drug, the more efficacious it will be. This representation underlies the commonly encountered perception that free government medication is not as beneficial as medicine available in the private sector. Where this representation of medication occurs, it presents a formidable challenge for primary health care and targeted disease control programs. For example, medicines distributed freely at government clinics in India, especially loose tablets, have a rather poor reputation. Because of the perceived poor quality of medications and an uncertain supply of medicine, people did not consult primary health centers in many parts of India for illnesses suggestive of TB prior to the implementation of the DOTS program. Instead, patients typically consulted a sequence of private practitioners until their resources became depleted (Nair et al. 1997; Nichter and Van Sickle 2002; Pathania 2001; Rangan and Uplekar 1999; Uplekar and Shepard 1991; Van der Veen 1987).[34] In order to win the confidence of the public, India's National TB Program initiated a DOTS strategy that delivers all the medication required to treat a patient for six months at one time into the hands of someone who will help the patient manage his or her therapy. As noted earlier, a large part of the success of the DOTS program is the result of effective marketing. Public confidence in the quality of government TB medications rose dramatically after distribution of the drugs in blister packs began.[35] During interviews I conducted in Karnataka and Tamil Nadu, India, patients identified this new medicine as expensive, in contrast to the cheap and ineffective medicine provided before. This success is a powerful demonstration of effective marketing that might be played up more in DOTS promotion to patients and their families.

A major challenge for those in public health will be to convince local communities that generic drugs are as effective as brand-name drugs. An effective social marketing program will need to address representations of trust and quality as well as cost and clinical efficacy. In a similar manner, cultural representations of the qualities of government-provided versus private-provided medical treatment have also been found to influence health care–seeking decisions.

DIFFERENCES BETWEEN PUBLIC AND PRIVATE CURATIVE CARE

Representations of differences between public and private health care index ideas about the quality and supply of medications, the motivation and attitudes of practitioners toward patients, and the quality of facilities often judged by the availability of modern medical technology. In many developing countries, years of drug shortages have led to representations of government health services as providing unreliable care, even when clinics are adequately stocked to handle diseases such as TB and malaria. Furthermore, when government doctors carry out private practice after hours in which they provide different types of medications,[36] they either intentionally or inadvertently contribute to the impression that the standards of government care are inferior.[37]

The businesslike approach to medicine that characterizes the private sector has given rise to two distinct sets of representations of doctors. One representation characterizes private doctors as more motivated and better equipped to cure patients than government doctors because remuneration is higher and the doctors must build solid reputations if they wish to remain popular. Another representation portrays the private doctor as someone who diagnoses the patients' pocketbooks as much as their ailments and strives to maximize only profit. Little research has been conducted on factors that foster positive and negative representations of health care providers and types of medical service, other than important research on waiting time, cleanliness, cost, and types of medications and tests administered. Other social relational factors may well be involved. Questions may also arise about the extent to which popular opinion about government health services simply mirrors popular opinion about other government programs.

Another question that begs investigation is how representations of government services and generic medications are affected by the impact of structural adjustment and neoliberal reform, which favors growth of the private sector at the expense of the public. I have been closely tracking "health care transition" in India for the past twenty years.[38] One notable aspect of this transition is the increasing popularity and affordability of diagnostic testing for the middle class. Increases in the availability of medical technology (everything from blood work and stool examinations to sonograms, CT scans, and MRIs) have been fostered by liberal bank loans to doctors and entrepreneurs in the private sector.[39] Use of diagnostic tests is certainly driven by the desire to better diagnose patients, but it is also driven by the profitability of administering and interpreting tests, as well as the use of tests to attract patients for other services. Test popularity has also been fostered by private practitioners' need to pay back bank loans on the equipment, kickbacks for test referral in a largely unregulated market (Sharma 2002), and mushrooming medical and nursing schools that make a profit from training practitioners in how to administer tests. The prestige value of recommending modern tests clearly influences their use.

Liberal use of diagnostic tests has dramatically affected representations of what good-quality health care looks like. It has also affected patient expectations of practitioners (Nichter and Van Sickle 2002). In contexts where high-quality care is now measured in terms of tests, procedures, and medications that do not reflect "rational medicine," how will public health practitioners instill a sense of public confidence in government health services? Will public demand for tests influence the direction of health planning? Also in need of further investigation is what motives lie behind state policies that promote the proliferation of pathology labs, high-end scanning centers, and the like. In India, state policy appears to favor representations of India as a modernizing nation despite high levels of dire poverty, as a center for global medical care and a good destination for medical tourism, and as a center of biotechnology and medical training.

1. The afflicted are often told little about their illness by practitioners, who do not have the time or inclination to engage them. For example, Mogensen (2005) notes that in Uganda, cognitive understanding is not the focal point of interactions between health staff and the afflicted; the focus is on getting and giving medicines. The afflicted diagnose (or divine) their own problems, and physical examinations performed by health staff using instruments are thought to help them determine the best treatment to administer. Caring for the patient is demonstrated through filling out a prescription, which is a social and symbolic act (see also van der Geest et al. 1996).

2. Another important area of medical anthropological research has been medicine entitlement both within households and as a form of medical citizenship. This is a topic I turn to in chapter 8.

3. The popularity of IV drips is twofold. First, IV drips are routinely given to patients upon their entering private hospitals, even when not required for effective care, because IV drips have symbolic value. IV drips also exhibit a demonstration effect: saline drips given to dehydrated patients improve their condition and raise their energy level rapidly, and glucose drips give patients a surge of energy.

4. When studying a population's expectations of medications, researchers need to include youth as a sample, particularly in places where youth directly purchase medications for self-treatment. A good case in point is a study in Kenya by Geissler and colleagues (2000) that found that over half of schoolchildren aged 11 to 17 had engaged in self-medication with Western pharmaceuticals.

5. Nausea is a side effect more commonly experienced when women take ferrous sulfate on an empty stomach. During my research, I found that most women given iron tablets had not been told to take the medication following food.

6. White carried a neutral or health-giving association. White tablets were more likely to be seen as less harsh on the body despite the fact that many antibiotics are white and deemed powerful. Red was associated with blood producing or deemed good for the blood.

7. For reviews of cross-cultural research pointing out that iron supplement color and form affect compliance among pregnant women, see Galloway et al. 2002 and Galloway and McGuire 1994.

8. See Datta and Nichter 2005.

9. Capsules are often thought to be more powerful than pills. In one area of India where I have worked, they are referred to as "injection-powered pills." In need of further study are popular perceptions of medicines marketed in different forms that might reduce injection popularity.

10. Other issues related to popular and often inappropriate use of injections, including the occurrence and interpretation of provocation polio (Wyatt 1984, 1996), are also in need of investigation.

11. See WHO 2004.

12. Some controversy exists as to what percentage of HIV cases have been spread by injections, especially in Africa. This is a complex issue requiring a careful weighing of the facts and cautious comparisons of Africa (where rates of sexually transmitted diseases appear to be higher) and Asia (where injection use may be more common).

13. For hepatitis and HIV, see Brewer et al. 2003; Gisselquist 2002; Gisselquist et al. 2002, 2003; Hutin and Chen 1999; Hutin et al. 2003; Kane et al. 1999; Khan et al. 2000; Lakshman and Nichter 2000; Luby et al. 1997; Minkin 1990; Simonsen et al. 1999; Singh et al. 2000; Yerly et al. 2001. For African haemorrhagic fever, see Anonymous 1977; for schistosomiasis, see Frank et al. 2000; for lassa fever, see Fisher-Hoch et al. 1995; and for malaria, see Jule et al. 1997 and Simonsen et al. 1999.

14. Research on representations of safe injection practice is urgently needed. Just as it is important to explore local perceptions of those people with whom it is deemed safe to have intercourse (without a condom), so too is it important to investigate with whom it is deemed safe to share a needle (without sterilization). Notably, in the first instance, potential sexual partners make such decisions, based on issues such as social risk. In the second situation, the health care provider most often makes this decision.

15. I observed malaria workers taking multiple blood samples with the same needle several times in the 1980s–90s. In the late 1990s, Vinay Kamat (unpublished data) observed the same behavior among malaria workers in slum areas of Mumbai, one of India's epicenters of HIV infection.

16. Changing perceptions of trust in the health care system (at large) as well as different types of health personnel in both the public and private sector must be studied (Gilson 2003).

17. A drug's negative effects on a population may go unreported if people feel that it has not worked for them due to incompatibility. The perception is that the drug might be compatible for others.

18. It is equally important to investigate popular representations of what else a medication is useful for, other than the medicine's intended medical indications. For instance, Price (2002) provides an example of TB drugs (Diateben: isoniazid and thiacetasone) in the Congo being purchased over the counter as a weight enhancer. Recognition of this by TB authorities led to the more careful monitoring of the sale of all TB drugs in the private sector.

19. Perceptions of diminished effectiveness must be studied not just in relation to drug resistance but also in relation to medicine adherence among the chronically ill. Self-regulation of medication as a form of reasoned self-care is affected by contingencies. Cost and other enabling factors loom large. But it is also important to examine perceptions of medicine that lead one to both make and rationalize decisions to alter prescribed treatment.

20. This observation is not based on rigorous research but reflects what I have heard in natural settings. Bear in mind that biomedical drugs are not the only medicines that are thought about in terms of diminishing capacity; in India, herbal medicines can likewise be viewed poorer in quality because of soil conditions, how and where they are harvested, how they are prepared, whether they are adulterated, and so on. People are also not thought to respond to herbal medicines as they once did, owing to their consumption of foods laced with pesticides and increased blood impurities, taking allopathic medications (which render herbal medicine less effective), and adopting a more modern lifestyle, leading one to become "hybrid." This comment is a reflection of changes in one's "local biology."

21. Bloland (Bloland 2003; Bloland et al. 2000) discusses both the promise and the challenges of introducing new combination drugs for malaria in developing countries. International debates have taken place over what constitutes the most effective and affordable treatment for malaria in various regions of Africa and Asia (Yamey 2003). These debates trickle down to the local press. Little research has been conducted on how representations of "best therapy" affect the perceptions of local practitioners. For example, recent CQ use in Malawi made international news when chloroquine was found to once again be highly effective treating malaria twelve years after having been withdrawn due to drug resistance (Laufer et al. 2006). How will this news be interpreted by practitioners in Malawi and in nearby countries?

22. A recent study by Patterson and colleagues (2006) points out that drugs reported to be CQ in community surveys may not actually be CQ, but a variety of medicines locally

available in shops doled out for malaria and recognized by familiar colors and shapes. In the 1980s–90s, I made a similar observation in India. I found that the term *antibiotic* was loosely used as a general marker for strong medicine, making validation of the identity of medications on household surveys important. On this point also see Etkin and colleagues (1990) on the Hausa term *farin kapso*, used to refer to chloramphenicol, penicillins, sulphonamides, and vitamins.

23. Hsu (2002) investigates the extent to which local thinking about artemisinin is influenced by local perceptions of Chinese medicine, the reputation of traditional Chinese medicine doctors licensed by the Tanzanian government, and packaging of artemisinin as a traditional modern drug.

24. Another related issue is how populations with chronic illnesses such as HIV/AIDS will respond to public health advice to use drugs having waning popularity, as with prophylactic use of co-trimoxazole (Chintu et al. 2004).

25. With regard to artemisinin, in early 2006 the World Health Organization called upon pharmaceutical companies to stop selling this highly effective drug as a stand-alone therapy for malaria. This was a preemptive action to protect against resistance. In fact, many companies market artemisinin monotherapy in Africa and sell the medicine to drug shops, where it is sold over the counter and in inadequate doses. Research is needed on how shopkeepers and community members understand government rules and regulations involving artemisinin use and sale.

26. Change in skin pigmentation is also a concern that leads some women to reject oral contraceptive use in Chiapas, Mexico (Namino Glanz, unpublished data).

27. Drug counterfeiting has reached epidemic proportions and constitutes a major challenge for global health. The World Health Organization estimates that at least 10 percent of the global drug market consists of counterfeits. A study conducted in the World Health Organization's South-East Asia Region in 2001 revealed that 38 percent of 104 antimalarial drugs on sale in pharmacies did not contain any active ingredients.

28. International drug companies save over 50 percent of costs by conducting clinical trials in developing countries and so prefer outsourcing clinical trials. The growth in trials in the past five years has been exponential. One indication in a country such as India is a rise in the number of Contract Research Organizations (CROs), which are contracted to recruit subjects for trials. The number increased fourfold between 2001 and 2003. By 2010, two million patients are expected to have been recruited for clinical trials in India alone.

29. A much larger issue that encompasses how subjects understand side effects is their understanding of the informed consent process, given unequal power relations and often-unrealistic expectations. This is an area in need of medical anthropological research. See, for example, Petryna 2005 and Petryna et al. 2006.

30. Postmarketing screening of adverse drug reactions (ADRs) is extremely important and poorly carried out until disaster strikes. Before a drug is introduced into the market, it is generally tested in no more than a thousand patients. Adverse reactions that occur in one in one thousand or more cases cannot be detected prior to marketing. Furthermore, drugs that are deemed nearly identical to other drugs on the market may undergo little if any testing.

31. There is a robust literature on factors influencing drug use in developing countries. See, for example, Radyowijali and Haak 2002 on factors that influence antibiotic use. Improving rational drug use requires more than simple knowledge translation as a means of addressing a know-to-do gap.

32. See the Web pages of nongovernmental organizations that monitor drug marketing in developing countries, such as Health Action International and the Medical Lobby for

Appropriate Marketing. Medical anthropological research is needed on how representations of the truth (such as statistics) are used in medicine advertisements and how they are scrutinized by practitioners. Such research also needs to examine the credibility afforded by citations in medical journals, given the close ties of journals to the pharmaceutical industry (Smith 2005).

33. Practitioners further justify their use of antibiotics for watery diarrhea by registering concern for comorbidity. In opposition to clinical guidelines, many practitioners whom I have interviewed state that they know local disease patterns better than do those making blanket recommendations (Howteerakul et al. 2003). In the case of diarrhea, arguing with them is difficult, as diarrhea is often self-limiting. This is why clinical epidemiological research is essential.

34. By providing blister packs of medicine perceived to be high quality, the DOTS program increased patients' willingness to consult government doctors during office hours and not in their private clinics. Previously, they had often sought private treatment in the hope that they would receive better-quality medicine (as well as to save time and for privacy).

35. Blister packs have proven equally popular for antimalarial drugs and have been cited as enhancing compliance in China (Qingjun et al. 1998), Ghana (Yeboah-Antwi 2001), and Burkina Faso (Sirima et al. 2003). Research needs to be conducted into local perceptions of the quality of drugs packaged in this manner, as well as the manner in which blister packs help people remember correct dosage.

36. Patients are asked to see the doctors later, in their private practice, if the patients wish to receive better medications. On the reasons for dual practice, see Ferrinho et al. 2004.

37. In some cases, supplies from government clinics are kept in doctors' or nurses' private clinics or homes, contributing to the impression that government clinics have no stocks but that the practitioners have their own supplies available at a cost.

38. The term *health care transition* refers to changes in the variety, availability, and use of health care services on patterns of health. Health care transition is influenced by political economy, technology, and issues of entitlement associated with medical citizenship.

39. The pathology market in India is estimated to be about 3 percent of the overall health care delivery market and is expanding rapidly as a new form of investment. There are estimated to be more than 40,000 independent pathology labs in India, in addition to labs attached to small private hospitals (nursing homes), hospitals, and medical schools. The industry is highly competitive and price-sensitive, with kickbacks for referrals in the absence of an effective regulatory body (Nichter and Van Sickle 2002).

PART II
RHETORIC MATTERS

The following is an excerpt taken from my field notes following a discussion that I had with a communicable disease expert who was playing a lead role in promoting the International Network of Clinical Epidemiology (INCLEN). The conversation took place in the early 1990s.

INCLEN MEMBER: To grow this network, what we need to do is inject and infect. We need to provide every developing country with a healthy dose of "evidence-based medicine." How do we do it? We create clinical epidemiology units [CEU] in each country. First, you invite bright people to annual meetings where everyone is speaking the same EBM language, and presenting their research in similar ways. Expose them to the bug [clinical epidemiology] in this kind of international environment and they are going to get infected. Fund them for a project or two, invite them to present at a couple of conferences, and they will infect those around them as well. Then support the clinical epidemiology unit in their institution, and replicate CEUs in neighboring institutions through training courses so everyone is on the same page, speaking the same EBM language. That's the plan, that's the ticket.

MARK: What factors do you see as influencing how fast EBM thinking spreads globally and within countries into which it has been introduced?

INCLEN MEMBER: The more high-profile—virulent (smiles)—the research projects being conducted at a CEU are, the more charismatic the people there, the least amount of resistance from local institutions, the faster the transmission. What is needed? A healthy injection of funds into the process, finding the right people to do research and teach, and a way to win over key people in local institutions so they support and do not hinder the process.

In this section I turn my attention to the social science of international health. In chapters 5 through 7, I critically assess some of the representations held by members of an international health "community of practice" encompassing international-, national-, and district-level public health and medical practitioners. Members of this multitiered community are responsive to global flows of information, the influence of health and development agencies, and shifts in political economic environments.[1] I highlight a few of the many representations and constructs that populate public health discourse to illustrate how such representations influence health policy, knowledge production, and the politics of the possible.[2] My aim is to point out how public health rhetoric uses representations to frame problems and populations in ways that render particular types of solutions compelling and worthy of research and funding.[3] The power of such representations is readily apparent when one considers that international health and development agencies contribute only a meager percentage of total health expenditure in most developing countries yet have a remarkable influence on policy that guides the spending of the majority of health expenditures (Michaud and Murray 1994).[4]

NOTES

1. Members of local communities are, of course, just as responsive to these factors.
2. It is beyond the scope of this book to provide a historical overview of changes in public health rhetoric and the rise and fall of particular representations. This is a study waiting to be conducted.
3. Rhetoric is persuasive argumentation accomplished through positioning and framing issues in ways that appeal to the practical logic of particular audiences (discursive communities). It is a definitional practice that shapes, enables, and also limits how we think about things. Rhetorical repackaging simultaneously holds the promise of being a first step toward real change and a smoke screen for the status quo, as when old wine is presented in new bottles with new labels (Uvin 2004). An example of the latter would be the packaging of community health-worker plans in the 1980s by international donors as examples of democratic participation, when in fact they often were implemented as top-down programs that preserved existing power relations and control over participants' activities (Morgan 1990). Statistics are also used as rhetorical devices to frame arguments. See, for example, Porter 1995 for the point that the appearance of quantitative rigor in official discourse often becomes most important when political and social pressures force compromise. Statistics convey a sense of impersonality in the context of problem solving. The term *evidence-based medicine* is often invoked for rhetorical purposes.
4. The influence of international health agency contributions to national health care budgets needs to be examined historically and in terms of specific programs. It is safe to say that in the 1970s–90s, relatively small amounts of money were leveraged in ways that effected significant health policy change. At present, a large surge of spending by private foundations on a limited number of global health problems is influencing national health policies and priority setting. As Garrett (Farmer and Garrett 2006; Garrett 2007) has noted, even though focused.funding leads to impressive gains in HIV, malaria, and TB management, it also diverts attention from equally important and neglected areas of health care need.

5

Representations That Frame Health and Development Policy

Not everything that can be counted counts; and not everything that counts can be counted.

—GEORGE GALLUP

REPRESENTATIONS REDUCING COMPLEX ISSUES TO SIMPLE EQUATIONS

Public health rhetoric is used to mobilize people and marshal resources as well as provide a framework for problem solving and rationalization for policies initiated.[1] This process of framing issues and identifying groups in particular ways facilitates action but at the same time simplifies complex issues and constrains ways of thinking about potential solutions.[2] Let me cite four examples to briefly illustrate this point and then introduce, in this and the following two chapters, core sets of representations that frame international health policy and planning.[3]

Primary Health Care

Beginning in the 1980s, public health programs were represented as vertical versus horizontal, terms often associated with selective versus comprehensive approaches to primary health care (Rifkin and Walt 1986; Walsh and Warren 1979; Warren 1988). In fact, many programs have elements of both types of approaches to primary health care, leading critics to point to public health rhetoric as fostering straw-man debates (Taylor and Jolly 1988) that reflect the interests and ideologies of donors more than recipient countries (Périn and Attaran 2003). The dichotomy between vertical and horizontal approaches limits thinking about health planning because neither representation accurately captures the complexity of forces shaping the way state governments engage in public health problem solving. As Reich (2002) has argued, a more informed discussion might call attention to relationships and

linkages across public health initiatives as well as the activities of government and nongovernment organizations.[4] A more appropriate representation, he suggests, might be a "web" that reflects the complex political and
ecological field in which public health programs are situated. This framing
calls attention to multiple forces acting simultaneously to reshape public
health policy and to the ways programs are implemented in particular contexts. Sepúlveda (Sepúlveda 2006; Sepúlveda et al. 2006) has likewise criticized the false dichotomy between vertical and horizontal approaches in the
Mexican health care context. He notes that both approaches need to coexist and describes the interaction of the two approaches as being diagonal
in practice.

Political Will

A second representation that gained currency in the 1980s was political will,
a construct commonly found in rhetoric about community participation
and national commitment to development. Analysis of local perceptions of
the political will of the state has at once provided insights into community
response to national health campaigns and suggested that a focus on the
state has deflected attention away from a broader politics of responsibility.

Whiteford (1997) provides a case study from the Dominican Republic,
where local perceptions of political will influenced a dengue fever program
launched by the Ministry of Health. Community members recognized the
importance of mosquito control for dengue fever prevention. However,
because of the government's poor track record in assisting the community
and investing resources in community-based projects, they did not cooperate
with public health authorities. Because the motives of the government were
suspect and trust had not been established, participation was poor.

Similarly, Morgan (1989) provides a case study from Costa Rica that
illustrates the limitations of framing problems in relation to political will.
While calling attention to the importance of a government's willingness to
invest in financial, technical, and human resources for health and development, she describes how the image of a monolithic state has deflected attention from competing factions within governments and their bureaucracies.[5]
An emphasis on a coherent political will existing at the national level may
deflect attention from international health policies that contribute to health
inequities and relations of dependency. Political will, she concludes, needs to
be thought of globally and not just nationally.

Talk Represents Action

"Development speak" can be critical in raising public consciousness about an issue and inviting dialogue. However, it can also suggest that more is being done to address an issue than is actually the case. Consciousness-raising activities (e.g., workshops) promote the emergence of locally important issues, often through the use of key words and salient representations. Before long, it may appear that an issue is already being addressed, owing to the sheer amount of talk generated about it. Those distant from the front lines of a particular problem can become anesthetized by a repetitive development narrative. When this happens, one of the only ways of refocusing attention is to reframe the issue using different language so that people believe that something new is being discussed or that an exciting new initiative is afoot. New representations have to be not only invented but also marketed and managed well to attract critical mass.

Branding Public Health Initiatives

Branding at once facilitates and simplifies international health policy transfer. Ogden and colleagues (2003) provide an insightful case study of the importance of framing, branding, and marketing in their analysis of the DOTS program for TB control. The DOTS program for TB control employs a "one size fits all" top-down approach to set a global agenda. On the one hand, this has enabled international agenda setting and the mobilization of resources in the name of efficiency.[6] On the other hand, implementing the directly observed medicine-taking dimension of DOTS (as intended) has been difficult in many places because of what Ogden describes as a massive simplification of policy that carries inherent risks. This policy is staunchly supported (some might argue proselytized) by advocates who are loath to see the details of the program altered in any way. Social scientists have criticized the DOTS program for being represented as an evidence-based package that must be delivered intact (Bukhman 2001; Farmer et al. 1998; Ogden et al. 2003) without considerations of local contingencies.[7] International health donors who have adopted DOTS have been reluctant until recently to conduct research on how best to adapt and implement the principles of DOTS in different social and cultural contexts. The DOTS framework simultaneously enables and restricts problem-solving activities.

REPRESENTATIONS DERIVED FROM EPIDEMIOLOGY

Despite claims to objectivity and a well-developed methodology aimed at attaining validity, reliability, and generalizability by employing statistically sound sampling procedures, epidemiological data are not value-free.[8] Research is guided by decisions about what variables to take into account, how to measure them, and how to lump and split populations or phenomena of public health importance for comparison (Trostle 2005).[9] Such decisions are influenced by disciplinary as well as political and economic interests.[10]

Epidemiological representations of diseases often reflect biomedical constructs of individualism and tend to be reductionistic. Epidemiology often focuses attention on those "risk factors" closest to an outcome, and these are almost inevitably biological causes of disease in individual bodies (Krieger 1994). As a result, epidemiological analyses do not allow differentiation between determinants of disease in populations and determinants of disease in individuals (Rose 1992). Epidemiology also tends to focus on single risk factors and conflates lifestyle risks with life circumstances predisposing particular populations to risk.[11] Of late, social, ecological, and ecosocial approaches to epidemiology have emerged to correct this deficiency.[12] These approaches to epidemiology draw attention to upstream factors that render a population vulnerable to illness transmission, as well as pointing out patterns of health inequity apparent in the (mal)distribution of diseases, health problems, and health care resources.[13] These new approaches to epidemiology lead us to consider the interplay between factors that affect exposure, susceptibility, and resistance to disease.[14] They remind us that the action is in the interaction.

The way in which epidemiological data are routinely collected and analyzed in, across, and between most developing countries glosses over health disparities. Data collection is not typically designed to take into account important in-country differences related to income disparity and access to resources (Braveman and Tarimo 2002; Gwatkin 2003).[15] Recently, there has been a call by social scientists and public health researchers interested in social justice to focus greater attention on health disparity. Reference to health disparity and health inequity has become politically fashionable, and with it debates about the types of representations of disadvantages that should guide health policy. For example, Murray and colleagues (1999, 2000a) contrast two different representations of disparity: one that they label "health disparities across individuals" and another labeled as "social inequalities in health." According to these authors, the first type of disparity considers differences in health across geographical contexts, and the second considers health in relation to social position, class, and material deprivation as well as social discrimination, alienation, and so forth. They vigorously defend the use of "health disparities across individuals" as a guide for health policy and argue that representations of poor health generated by social inequality analyses are presumptive. By contrast, Braveman and colleagues (2000) critique the distinction made between these two approaches to disparity and claim that they are not mutually exclusive and need to be considered as complementary.[16] It is important to recognize that distinct ideological positions underscore representations of health disparity and inequity,[17] and the different ways in which these terms are used in international health discourse greatly impacts health planning.

An important focus for ethnographic study is how terms such as *health inequity, inequality,* and *disparity* are being appropriated and used by local politicians, health officials, activists, and entrepreneurs. These terms may be used to either advance or confront policies related to public investment in primary health care, neoliberal policies, supporting privatization, health care reform, and so on. Of additional import is how such terms are used and/or unpacked by the press.

Epidemiology also contributes to the production of representations that serve as a metric of health and development. Measures commonly used as indicators of how well a country is doing in terms of health and development need to be examined critically and in relation to particular agendas. Different measures of health status communicate different things about how well a government is attending to the basic needs of its population. For example, Millard (1994) has questioned the use of infant mortality as the major yardstick for a country's progress in achieving better health status for its citizens. She advocates the use of child mortality as a better measure, suggesting that keeping a child alive for the first three to five years of life is a better measure of development and government commitment than are live births and an infant's survival for three weeks. Others have argued that TB rates are a good metric for malnutrition, overcrowding, and a government's ability to mobilize its health infrastructure. Still others have recommended that maternal mortality and morbidity be used as a primary indicator of a country's health and development status. Each metric needs to be considered in relation to who and what it does and does not index.

Crude representations of development have also been criticized for not being tied to health as an indicator of a population's capacity to engage in self-determination. For example, Sen (1993, 1999) has argued that health indicators are better representations of development than are economic indicators such as per capita income or per capita gross domestic product (GDP). A rise in economic status, he argues, should not be seen as an end in itself but rather an opportunity to improve health and well-being and to afford populations the freedom to develop human capacity and self-expression.[18]

The identification of "groups at risk" is a routine procedure performed by epidemiologists. Although a useful exercise, the generation of representations of groups at risk can foster victim blaming. Groups at risk are identified through a review of data on intra- and interpopulation differences in rates of disease incidence and prevalence and likelihood of exposure to risk factors. In the course of calculating risk, group-level variables such as ethnicity are often treated as risk factors because of statistical association.[19] Members of groups at risk are assumed to be exposed to important risk factors more often than members of other groups are. The questions of how and why they are exposed are often left unasked—and this can be highly problematic. Simply identifying a group as being at greater risk from an illness is an invitation for others to think that this is due to an inherent genetic or behavioral group trait. This impression all too often plays into preexisting negative stereotypes. A seemingly neutral concept at this point ceases to be benign.

Epidemiology needs to be held accountable for producing representations that are used in a "politics of othering." Identifying a group at risk on the basis of disease prevalence and behaviors that place members at risk is not enough. Environments of risk need to be accounted for (Ellen et al. 2001; Macintyre and Ellaway 2003; Macintyre et al. 1991, 2002; Mullings 1997), as well as factors that place people in these environments and compel them to act in particular ways within these environments.[20] Research on HIV, for example, has demonstrated that migrant work has placed men—and, thus, their wives—at risk from types of high-risk sexual behavior in environments where political economic factors have dictated work options, pay structures, the absence of wives, and the presence of commercial sex workers. Representations of groups at risk must be seen in light of environments of risk if these groups are not to be stigmatized.

In principle, epidemiology pays as much attention to protective factors as to risk factors; in practice, however, this rarely happens. This trend contributes to representations of groups that characterize them negatively. Too rarely is the question asked, what protective factors within the group exist that prevent a problem from being far worse than it is? Paying more attention to the positive might go a long way in identifying valuable local resources and forms of social capital (addressed later) that contribute to a group's resilience. It may also lead us to look for the salutogenic (healthy) aspects of cultural institutions and group interactions instead of how the latter place a group's members at risk.

Given limited resources, tough decisions must be made by those in public health as to how best to spend scarce resources. This decision making requires the identification of priorities based on cultural as well as so-called objective criteria.[21] Not uncommonly, representations of public health priorities are justified by calculations that strictly favor rational choice and pay little attention to local health concerns and cultural reasoning.[22]

Disability-adjusted life years (DALYs) illustrate a case in point. DALYs were the indicator of choice used to measure the impact of illness and disability in the influential *World Development Report* (World Bank 1993). Faced with the need to weigh and represent the impact of different types of diseases and disabilities, mortality and morbidity were rejected because they did not reflect the effect of different disorders on productivity. DALYs were developed as a measure through a process of deliberation that was ostensibly attentive to productivity and quality of life. Its goal was to measure nonfatal outcomes using the same units as life lost due to premature death. DALYs were calculated for 107 disorders experienced among different age and gender cohorts in seven regions of the world. The scheme provided a single measure useful in setting health and treatment priorities based on the relative ranking of DALYs lost to disability and saved by various health interventions.

A review of the many debates that have emerged regarding the appropriateness of DALYs as a summative measure exceeds the scope of this book.[23] However, a few points of contention can be highlighted to illustrate why representations of disability need to be closely examined by social scientists.

1. There is considerable interpersonal and cultural variation in how people experience the same disability. Moreover, their experience changes over time and is not constant. DALYs were not calculated after reviewing subjective accounts of illness in different cultures. Experts grading the outcome of disabilities were not sufferers of those conditions.
2. DALYs are an individual measure masquerading as a household- or community-based measure. They do not address how the disability of one household member affects others in the same household.
3. DALYs do not account for the total impact of a disability. This depends on the complex interplay of economic, social, and cultural factors. The true burden of an illness needs to be calculated in context after considering such things as social support, work substitution, and the status and roles of the afflicted, not just work productivity.

4. In their favor, DALYs pay credence to age cohorts and gender when considering the impact of various disabilities. How important are other differences such as social class or urban versus rural livelihood?
5. DALYs do not take account of comorbidities or of concurrent and competing aims. They are unable to account for links, for example, between infectious disease such as TB and a woman's ability to become pregnant (Krieger and Gruskin 2001), the course of pregnancy, or her mental health in contexts where TB is stigmatized for both the woman and her daughters.
6. Cultural and gender-specific health concerns are not figured into DALYs calculations. For example, Boonmongkon and colleagues (2001) demonstrate that women's concerns about fairly benign forms of reproductive tract infection (endogenous, fungal) progressing into cervical cancer have significant impacts on their health behavior and well-being—something not paid credence in existing DALYs scales.

This last point raises an important issue related to what counts when calculating priority health measures. Currently, evidence-based medicine and DALYs calculations pay little attention to cultural data such as narrative accounts of the life experiences of the afflicted, health care–seeking behavior, or the impact of one person's illness on the household as a unit of analysis. Some researchers on women's health have argued that such information might enhance the specificity of DALYs and provide a women's perspective to evidence-based medicine—a qualitative perspective largely missing from positivistic thinking about disease and loss of productivity (AbouZahr 1999; AbouZahr and Vaughan 2000). Greater appreciation of the impact of illness experiences in real-world contexts is clearly needed. Toward this end, the value of the case study and the power of example need to be appreciated for their "prototypical value" above and beyond statistics (Flyvbjerg 2001).[24]

Additionally, public health practitioners often face an ethical paradox when attempting to raise the consciousness of the public about a health care problem that is clinically significant but not culturally visible or a significant contributor to mortality. Again, take the case of cervical cancer in northeastern Thailand. An aggressive public health campaign to conduct Papanicolaou (PAP) smears ended up causing significant psychological fear in the population at large for a disease that causes fewer than 25 deaths per 100,000 women. Boonmongkon and colleagues (1999) investigated the perceived threat of this new disease. A majority of women interviewed estimated that three out of every ten women were likely to experience this terrifying ailment. Notably, they perceived the risk of cervical cancer to be greater than the risk of HIV, although they lived in an epicenter of HIV transmission. The problem arose because if the correct health statistics were presented to women, they might not take the risk of this cervical cancer seriously and might forgo PAP smears.[25] I see this as the flip side of the prevention paradox described by Rose (1985), whereby "a preventive measure which brings much benefit to the population offers little to each participating individual" (Rose 1985:36). In the Thai case, public health screening benefits a few individuals out of thousands screened and inadvertently fosters epidemic fear because of the way screening is introduced.

A related paradox is that the more successful an infectious or vector-borne disease prevention program is in the short run, the greater the chance that a local population will lose interest in the problem as a priority and fail to sustain the very practices that led to its control. This dilemma threatens the sustainability of prevention programs and has been witnessed in many countries where diseases such as malaria, yellow fever, and immunizable diseases have been only temporarily controlled. An issue that begs further examination is how illnesses may best be represented to sustain public interest in prevention when a health problem becomes less visible and attention to it wanes or when it is chronic and lacks a dramatic acute stage (as with schistosomiasis).

Local interest in and acceptance of public health interventions often hinge on local perceptions of three things: the importance of the problems being addressed, the government's motives in promoting an activity or initiating a campaign, and the immediate relevance of the program for the local population.[26] The public tends to respond poorly to programs aimed at problems they see as low on a local hierarchy of risk when larger problems are neglected. Community buy-in to prevention programs requires consciousness-raising, local leadership, listening to community members, and the interlinking of programs so that public health agendas become congruent with community felt needs.[27]

Notes

1. Roe (1991) points out that development rhetoric and narratives serve to reduce uncertainty and ambiguity, enabling action. For this reason, they retain their popularity even when their validity is questioned by empirical science. The staying power of development stories is directly related to their ability to stabilize and underwrite assumptions required for policy making. Apthorpe (1997) notes that policy statements are justified more by "what is known" and what "stands to reason" than by a weighing of positions

and evidence. Mosse (2003) observes that in order to work, policies must be reproduced as stable representations. More important than their being well implemented is whether enough people believe that they have been. This is largely accomplished through policy discourse.

2. Some social scientists have gone so far as to suggest that the use of rhetoric not only consolidates ideological positions but also saturates the consciousness of those exposed to them as a form of hegemonic practice. Mosse (2004) notes a current tendency to use "development speak" to package products on the basis of how they will advance policy, not immediate tangible change. Development speak can also be a linguistic performance that is all about social positioning and does not involve a shift in consciousnesses.

3. Many other representations could have been chosen to illustrate how international development rhetoric is used to build authority and establish the appearance of a new vision or paradigm. Consider, for example, recent usage of terms such as *North*, *South*, and *local* (Lister 2003) and *collaboration* and *partnership* (Hill 2002; Ogden and Porter 2000); use of the term *public* as a gloss and counterpart to *public authority* (Habermas 1989); use of the term *empowerment* in microcredit projects (Isserles 2003); and growing use of the terms *reform* and *good governance*, of particular importance to this book (Green 2006).

4. Given globalization, structural adjustment, and the growing importance of NGOs, primary health care policy increasingly involves linkages between the public-NGO-private sectors (Bloom and Standing 2001; Buse and Walt 2000a, 2000b, 2002; Walt 2001a). Clearly, the role of private practitioners and the pharmaceutical industry in public health must be paid far more credence (Aljunid 1995; Berman and Rose 1996). See, for example, efforts made to involve the private sector in implementation of the DOTS program (Gupta et al. 2002; Lönnroth et al. 2004; Newell et al. 2004; Rangan et al. 2004; Uplekar 2003). Standing and Bloom (2002) encourage us to think beyond the dualism of public versus private and engage the changing public health landscape.

5. Reification of the state has been widely critiqued. See, for example, Abrams 1988; Corrigan and Sayer 1985; Scott 1998.

6. The DOTS agenda-setting policy is an example of transnational governmentality (Ferguson and Gupta 2002). Another example of a global agenda-setting health policy is the syndromic management of sexually transmitted infections (STIs) as "best practice" (Lush et al. 2003). As in the case of DOTS, global treatment algorithms for STIs have been promoted in the name of efficiency, and context-appropriate refinement of treatment practices has been stalled. In both cases, treatment guidelines have been treated as sacred and not to be questioned. What works in Africa for STIs misses many reproductive tract infections (RTIs) in Southeast Asia, and syndromic approaches to STIs appear to work better for men than for women where laboratory confirmation is not available. One problem with treating algorithms as set in stone is that fewer attempts are made to improve on diagnostics and match procedures to prevalence data derived from local surveillance.

7. Two criticisms have been leveled against the DOTS programs. The first concerns the strict medicine-observation component of the DOTS program, which I draw attention to shortly. The second criticism relates to multidrug-resistant TB (MDR-TB). Paul Farmer was instrumental in pointing out the danger of adhering to a rigid DOTS drug regimen and the need for a separate MDR-TB therapy. The World Health Organization justified its one-treatment-fits-all-cases policy on the basis of the number of cases treatable by DOTS therapy and the possibility that MDR-TB would be adverted by DOTS therapy. Farmer rightly argued that by doing so, DOTS was actually contributing to the spread of MDR-TB by increasing rates of drug resistance.

8. Epidemiology is necessary for the social organization and practical execution of medicine and public health, but it oversimplifies complex social influences on the health of individuals and communities (Berkwits 1998; Porter 1992). Moreover, quantitative sciences such as epidemiology often become their own standard of objectivity (Hacking 1992). Research is needed on what may be seen as evidence-based symbolism. This includes a critical assessment of representations produced by epidemiologists, evidence-based rhetoric that justifies actions as evidence based when rigorous research has not actually been conducted or subjected to systematic review, and the study of *mindlines*—collectively reinforced, tacit guidelines for medical practice assumed to be evidence based (Gabbay and Le May 2004). Apthorpe (1997) has aptly noted that development language not uncommonly presents policy as data driven when in fact it is data driving in the sense of privileging particular types of data. Epidemiological assessments and evaluations may also be ceremonial in the sense of strengthening the organizational legitimacy of donor agencies (Gulrajani 2004; Meyer and Rowan 1977).

9. As noted by Latour (1993:113), all measures "construct a commensurability that did not exist before their calibration." Commensurability entails processes of integration. The dissimilar are aligned into groups, and numbers attached to such groupings take on integrative power. Numbers are effective integrators, as they capture complex events in familiar, reassuring, and standardized forms. For an early example of how numbers are used as a technology of representation, see Appadurai 1993 on representations created by the census in colonial India and their far-reaching consequences.

10. Social science studies of the "hard sciences" have aptly demonstrated that knowledge is at once constituted by and generative of social practices and is subject to politics in subtle and not-so-subtle ways (Jasanoff 2004; Latour 1987, 1999).

11. Epidemiology has been criticized within its own ranks for focusing too much on single risk factors and the tendency to ignore the social, behavioral, and ecological contexts in which risk factors arise. For critiques of risk-factor epidemiology, see Diez-Roux 1998; Krieger 1994, 2000; McMichael 1999; Pearce 1996, 2004; Susser 1998; Susser and Susser 1996a, 1996b.

12. For a sample of writings that advocate for more social and ecosocial approaches to epidemiology and pay attention to inequity as well as relative economic status, see Adler and Ostrove 1999; Berkman and Kawachi 2000; Krieger 1999; Krieger and Zierler 1996; Marmot 1999; McMichael 1999; Pearce 1996; Yen and Syme 1999.

13. Health equity has been well characterized by Whitehead (1991:220) as follows: "Equity in health is not about eliminating all health differences so that everyone has the same level of health, but rather to reduce or eliminate those which result from factors which are considered to be both avoidable and unfair. Equity is therefore concerned with creating equal opportunities for health and with bringing health differentials down to the lowest levels possible."

14. As Agar (1996, 2003) has pointed out, these new approaches to epidemiology are a return to epidemiology's roots and the contextual assessment of complex agent-host-environment relations. He notes that interest in specific disease agents is giving way to greater interest in probabilistic risk factors and causal assemblages, in global and local contexts and trends, and in the ways meaning attributed to risk and illness by hosts affects context-specific behavior.

15. For example, Graham and colleagues (2004) provide us with a powerful example of the need to closely examine maternal mortality within countries. The authors demonstrate across a diverse set of countries that women's poverty status (proxied by educational level, source of water, and type of toilet and floor) predicts maternal mortality. In Indonesia, for example, 32–34 percent of the maternal deaths occurred among women from the

poorest quintile of the population. The risk of maternal death in this country was around three to four times greater in the poorest than the richest group.

16. For more on this health inequity debate, see Murray et al. 2000b and Braveman et al. 2000.

17. Ideological positions also underlie different approaches to looking at health inequalities in terms of income inequality (Coburn 2004).

18. Sen's broad-based theory of development advances the idea that the role of development is to enlarge and enhance the choices—basic freedoms—of all citizens. Freedoms are not only the primary ends of development but also among its principal means of achieving them (Sen 1999). See also Levine 2004 on poverty and development as seen through the lens of human capability and the argument that "we are poor not primarily because we lack goods, but because we lack the ability to be and do things that are essential to human life" (p. 102). On different representations of poverty and how they have been used in development discourse, see Green 2006.

19. Although ethnicity may be a risk marker associated with a whole cluster of interrelated factors, it is too often treated as a risk factor in and of itself.

20. Use of culture or ethnicity as a proxy variable for the plurality of contextual factors that place a population at risk to ill health is as misguided as risk-factor epidemiology.

21. Social scientists also need to examine the rhetoric of rationing as rational choice, as distinct from a claims-making activity that entails power relations (Light and Hughes 2001).

22. We need to do more than "globalize evidence" and "localize decisions" (Eisenberg 2002). A culturally sensitive approach to evidence-based medicine requires a careful consideration of local problem solving that takes lay epidemiology into account.

23. For debate on the calculation and application of DALYs, see AbouZahr and Vaughan 2000; Allotey et al. 2003; Anand and Hanson 1998; Arnesen and Nord 1999; Barker and Green 1996; Barnett et al. 2001; Cohen 2000; Murray and Lopez 1996; Murray et al. 2000a; Musgrove 2000; Paalman et al. 1998; Reidpath et al. 2003.

24. See Flyvbjerg 2001 for a discussion of different types of case studies and the value of case narratives that are paradigmatic.

25. The public health importance of cervical cancer cannot be reduced to mortality statistics, which are no doubt underestimated in developing countries (Hunter 2006). One must also consider the experience of morbidity (which is influenced by culture) and the extent to which having cervical cancer might make a woman susceptible to other diseases (STIs, HIV). My point is that fear of the disease is being used to influence health promotion but is placing women at risk of poor health as much as the disease itself does.

26. People often do not recognize themselves as the intended recipients of specific health promotion messages. In some cases, appropriate recipients are thought to be those people depicted on posters. When people depicted look different from the local population, it is imagined that the message does not apply to locals. Posters of chubby babies in India are popular and even placed on the mud walls of huts, but impoverished mothers often think that the messages conveyed by the posters are meant for the middle class rather than the poor. In other cases, however, images of modern community members are preferred by the poor. In a community-based *Aedes aegypti* control project in Honduras, realistic images of rural women were not favored and were replaced by popular images of modern women signifying progress (Nichter, unpublished data).

27. The history of public health is riddled with examples of programs that have failed because local populations did not perceive the problem focused upon as important and saw the program as too expensive, top-down, and uncreative (e.g., Dunn 1983; Foster 1976; Harrison 1978; Hunter 1985; Inhorn and Brown 1990; Philips 1955).

6

Representations of Health Status
and Social Formations

You are a social scientist whose job it is to dig into social issues, identify trends and patterns, and document change. My job is to provide the public with a sense of security, to convince people that the government is doing what it can to solve problems as they arise or are made visible. I am involved in a confidence-raising game where the stakes are which party stays in power. Other parties will do what they can to discredit this government whenever a major health problem gives them the opportunity to question our actions before or after the problem occurs.
—HIGH-LEVEL INDIAN POLITICIAN, 1990

Governments are concerned with managing their image, which in turn entails managing representations of national health status. Measures of health associated with development take on political significance and for this reason are manipulated and in some cases suppressed. Political posturing, the response of health bureaucracies to international health and development agencies, and the availability of funds for countries having significant disease burdens (or potential burdens or success managing health problems) all influence the production of knowledge about health and disease. To begin, I offer four observations related to the state's vested interest in health representations.

THE POLITICS OF HEALTH
Public Health and State Politics
Often, states try to play down public health shortfalls and events that might lead critics to question a government's performance and ability to provide basic services to its citizens. Outbreaks of disease call attention to a government's failure to maintain various infrastructures, and failure to control epidemics may threaten state legitimacy (Farmer 1992, 1994; Ghosh and

Coutinho 2000). As a result, attempts may be made to suppress information about disease outbreaks or to classify diseases in ways that minimize collective anxiety. Such actions have made implementing international health surveillance systems—agreed upon in principle—challenging (Baker and Fidler 2006).[1] In India, for example, cases of cholera have been reported as cases of gastroenteritis and other nondescript illness categories (Ghosh and Coutinho 2000). In Cuba, outbreaks of dengue fever in the late 1990s were suppressed and later attributed to bioterrorism on the part of the United States in the local media (Sara Avery, unpublished data).[2] Dengue was seen as a national embarrassment, given the country's highly praised *Aedes aegypti* control program implemented in the 1980s following a major dengue epidemic (Van Sickle 1998).[3] In several Caribbean countries, dengue has been glossed over as a nonspecific "viral fever," for fear of affecting the tourist industry. In 2004, the Thai government covered up an initial outbreak of avian flu to give corporate poultry producers time to clear their inventories. Backyard poultry producers were then blamed for the problem by government officials (Chanyapate and Delforge 2004; Davis 2005).[4]

Despite misrepresentations, with increased global communication and disease surveillance has come a shift in the position of the state, at least in relation to epidemic diseases linked to global citizenship.[5] For example, the initial suppression of information about the SARS epidemic in China was met with international condemnation. China regained its international stature only after taking extreme measures to rectify the situation, including the firing of high-level health officials involved in the cover-up that included the health minister and deputy mayor of Beijing (Kaufman 2006). The Chinese government's experience with SARS has resulted in the official handling of avian flu in a more transparent manner.[6]

The collection of public health data and the production of knowledge about disease do not occur in a vacuum. As stated earlier, epidemiological data are not neutral. Representations of diseases are a matter of national as well as international health politics. I return to this issue in the next chapter.

Health Reporting as Strategic

Health statistics are commonly used to judge a country's level of development and modernity. For example, the prevalence of illnesses such as tuberculosis is taken as a marker of political and infrastructure problems as well as a symptom of poverty and underdevelopment. Precisely because disease affects international reputation, tourism, and investment, some governments may prefer not to report outbreaks or may minimize them (Cash and

Narasimhan 2000). For this reason, a disease control program may not always enjoy government support or fanfare, as it advertises that such a disease exists within the country (Foster 1987).

However, there may be an incentive to report the prevalence of diseases for which international aid is available. Governments and NGOs may be put into a position in which attracting global funds depends on showing that a significant health need exists. In such cases, statistics may be manufactured, manipulated, or tailored to draw funding. For example, epidemiological projections may be made on the basis of hospital-based rather than community-based data sets, or estimates may be extrapolated from special, high-risk populations. The political economy of international health is a contested field where different health problems are championed with more or less vigor. Representations of need are produced to attract funding in what often seems like a zero-sum game.

Symbolic Aspects of Public Health Actions

State authorities often respond to public health crises with dramatic acts, even when these acts are only ineffective gestures. These gestures, in turn, foster impressions of appropriate disease-management strategies. For example, during outbreaks of vector-borne illness such as dengue fever or urban malaria, insecticide spraying is often conducted en masse. A highly visible, resource-intensive, militarized campaign is not effective in controlling the vector, but it provides evidence of a committed government.[7] Provision of cholera vaccinations during cholera outbreaks is another example of a government gesture undertaken to contain fear and represent the state as in control of the situation.

The Symbolic Capital of Buzzwords

If you have the fresh words, funders find your proposals delicious, but if you use yesterday's words, who will want to eat them? That is why going to international workshops and conferences is so important. Meeting people and learning what is in fashion and favored is highly desired by my colleagues. It helps us get the money for projects and teaches us how to talk about and package our work. Writing in English—that is the hard part. Catching the idea, we are good at that.

—MEMBER OF A THAI WOMEN'S HEALTH ADVOCACY GROUP,
MID-1990S

Politicians, local health officials, medical researchers, academics, and NGOs value the rhetoric of international health agencies. The latest international health buzzwords, conceptual frameworks, and representations of cutting-edge thinking constitute a form of symbolic capital signifying that one is a global health insider.[8] Indeed, for NGOs, using the right rhetoric can increase the likelihood of securing international funds and being included in international health initiatives. This speaks to the tremendous influence of international health agencies as trendsetters framing the next generation of thinking about health. Yet international "health speak" is often appropriated without the user's accepting the tenets upon which new concepts are based or championing new courses of action (Justice 1987).[9] New paradigms of public health come to take on hybrid meanings as they percolate down through the tiers of long-established health bureaucracies.[10] In many cases, ineffective health programs come to bear the stamp of the latest health rhetoric. "Business as usual" is thus given a new veneer and represented as the new and innovative. Health social science research must clarify shifts in how international health discourse frames problems and solutions, the channels through which "development speak" is propagated, the manner in which it helps constitute "communities of practice," and the way it takes on local meaning when appropriated.

Representations of the Household and Community

Representations of local households and communities influence health policy by suggesting what kinds of interventions are possible within these two social formations. Assumptions about social relations foster expectations and lead those in the health field to assign responsibility for health activities to particular people. Two examples may illustrate this point.

The control of vector-borne diseases, such as dengue fever, requires careful assessment of social spaces and the identification of actors most suitable to accomplish specific tasks related to breeding site control in these spaces (Parks and Lloyd 2004). Different areas of households and containers that serve as breeding sites are often designated as male and female domains. Yet all too often, programs are hampered by naive representations of households as homogenous units engaging in cooperative tasks.

In other cases, the capacity of the household or community may be undervalued. For example, the global DOTS TB program long maintained a representation of the household as poorly suited for directly observed TB therapy or its support. Although this may be the case in some cultural contexts and in the special case of people with alcoholism, in many other cultural contexts the household has been found to be a highly supportive environment for managing TB treatment. Several studies have demonstrated that TB treatment adherence rates are just as high when therapy is supervised by family members as when supervised by non-kin in a position of greater external control (Garner and Volmink 2003, 2006; Newell et al. 2006; Wright et al. 2004). The DOTS program has looked to communities primarily for assistance in program surveillance, while social scientists working to enhance TB programs have looked to communities as sites of local problem solving (Ogden 1999; Ogden et al. 1999; Rangan and Uplekar 1999).[11] This involves thinking beyond the management of cases to getting medicine to individuals having real-world constraints, ensuring confidentiality, and helping provide basic necessities to the afflicted when they cannot work.[12]

Social science research on vector control and TB treatment programs teach us valuable lessons about representations of the household and community and the role they can play in facilitating disease control efforts. Vector control programs illustrate that the household as a general unit may not always be the most relevant target for interventions and that directing specific messages to men, women, and children within households may be more effective. Research on the DOTS program, in contrast, suggests that misrepresentations of the household may preclude the optimal use of households as sites of therapy management.

Representations of the Household Revisited

An understanding of the social, cultural, and economic reality of local populations is often undermined by idealized and inadequate conceptualizations of the household as a static social unit. A narrow focus on the physical space constituted by a house and member counts overlooks the extent to which households are constituted through social processes and projects (Wilk and Netting 1984) as well as the extent to which household boundaries are permeable, membership fluid, and intrahousehold processes variable (Pfeiffer 2003a). Kin are drawn together as household members in different ways at different times for functions that range from production to reproduction, from establishing social status to securing the blessings of ancestor spirits or the gods through appropriate rituals. Several lessons about representations of households may be gleaned from international health and development research.

Addressing the House as an "Environment of Risk." Issues of identity and social status are at stake when the house is treated as an environment of risk. Vector control programs are often faced with the objective of teaching community members that disease originates from within houses and that household members must remain vigilant. Yet in many cultures, the house is seen as a clean and healthy environment—a haven from disease. As noted earlier, dangerous sources of disease such as mosquitoes are often associated by the public with dirty environments, stagnant water, garbage, and bad habits. Public health messages to clean up breeding sites within the house compound imply that the household is an environment of risk, a message that women in many cultures find offensive. Winch and colleagues (1994) suggest that promoters of dengue control programs often underestimate the resentment women feel when their identity as caretakers is challenged and their status undermined.[13] Gender identity is a key factor that needs to be taken into consideration when framing health messages about the house as an environment of risk.

*Levels of Status and Responsibility among Household Members.*Numerous studies have argued that greater sensitivity to gendered dimensions of the household production of health is called for in international health (Berman et al. 1994; Schumann and Mosley 1994).[14] This includes paying more attention to (1) the division of household labor as it affects caring for the young, ill, disabled, and elderly; (2) the management of food, hygiene, water, and waste; (3) access to resources; and (4) roles in decision making in various types of situations (Browner 1989; Caldwell and Caldwell 1993; Chatterjee 1989; Sauerborn et al. 1996a). Researchers have further noted that it is essential to consider how women's work loads and household responsibilities hinder their own health, in turn threatening the well-being of other household members (Caldwell and Caldwell 1993; Castle 1993; Messer 1997; Nichter and Kendall 1990).

Studies have also examined the responsibilities of different family members when a child falls sick. Some have noted that young mothers often feel too powerless or insecure to make decisions about health care seeking, leave the house unaccompanied, or spend scarce resources without permission or without first consulting elders or male family members. In such societies, delays in health care seeking often occur *after* a mother recognizes the severity of an illness.[15] When this is the case, educating the mother about how to recognize the signs of illness severity is not enough; men and elders must also be involved in more proactive behavior.[16]

Many studies have drawn attention to inequities in the power and status between women and men as a factor influencing health care decisions.[17] Other studies have called attention to the importance of examining relationships among women as a factor influencing the household production of health (Olson 1994). For example, Castle (1993) demonstrates that in patrilineal agro-pastoralist societies such as those in rural Mali, health-seeking behavior is best understood by assessing how women differ from each other in terms of their socioeconomic and political power within the household. Child mortality, in the groups she researched, was less associated with differences in household wealth than with variations in women's status within the ranks of female household members and access to resources for children's treatment and care.

Other studies have pointed out that different family members are mobilized in response to illness depending on its severity. For example, in Ghana, Kirby (1997) describes how illness episodes are labeled "white," "red," and "black" in accordance with the stage and severity of an illness. Different social roles and responsibilities are associated with each stage. At the onset, or white stage, of an illness, self-care is encouraged. But when an illness enters the red stage, other actors, resources, and expert knowledge become involved. One's therapy management group kicks into gear; once this occurs, the roles and functions of significant others are proscribed.

As already noted, vector-borne disease-management programs require a close understanding of household responsibilities, to target specific behavioral messages to appropriate members. Research is needed to determine who is responsible for potential breeding sites (e.g., tires, pet dishes, water storage drums, ornamental plants, and so on) for *Aedes aegypti* control, for example.[18]

Misrepresentation of Household Membership as Stable. Household membership among the poor is often fluid and responsive to seasonal work. It may be subject to temporal shifts in work opportunities and resource availability, as well as political-economic processes. Among the poor, work availability often determines patterns of male, female, and child labor. Migratory labor impacts long-term treatment programs for diseases such as TB. Where seasonal migratory labor is common, as it is in northeastern Thailand, special provisions need to be put into place to track TB patients and ensure a continuous, available supply of medicine. Supplying medicine is easier to accomplish when work migration is tied to a particular location for a specified duration. It becomes more difficult when work migration is more fluid and occurs for an unknown duration.

Overemphasis on Cooperation in Representations of the Household. Many social scientists have critiqued simplistic representations of households as consensual and benevolent social units. Households have been more aptly described as sites of negotiation, exchange, and conflict (e.g., Browner 1989; Bruce 1989; Folbre 1986, 1997; Guyer and Peters 1987; Sen 1990). A more grounded appreciation of household dynamics leads us to pay equal attention to cooperation and conflict, changing perceptions of entitlement, and persistent notions of obligation. Ethnographic research has revealed important differences in resource allocation and health care decision-making power along gender, generational, birth order, and kin-based lines (Bledsoe 2001; Das Gupta 1990; Levine 1987; Messer 1997; Miller 1997a, 1997b; Mimi Nichter and Mark Nichter 1998; Wadley 1993). Such research suggests that those designing health interventions need to be sensitive to both how resources flow within different types of households and how interventions that privilege particular members influence the social dynamics of households both positively and negatively.[19] They must also be attentive to oppression and exploitation within households, not just the pooling of resources for common ends (Phillips 1987, 1989) and the ways in which structural inequalities (by gender, birth order, etc.) are fostered by political-economic processes and degrees of poverty (Bruce 1989).

Misrepresentation of Social Relations in Household Surveys. Surveys employing random samples of households can tell us much about such things as disease prevalence, health care utilization, household economics, and food security. However, they also miss important dimensions of the household production of health that require ethnographic research sensitive to social relations not generally reported on surveys. Women may report that their husbands are the primary decision makers within their households, but this tells us little about the influence that women do or do not wield in various circumstances (Mimi Nichter and Mark Nichter 1998).

Representations of Community

Like representations of the household, representations of the community in international health tend to overemphasize collaboration, cooperation, and organization, and they typically leave power relations unspecified (Jewkes and Murcott 1996, 1998; Nichter 1995; Rifkin 1986, 1987; Rifkin et al. 1988; Wayland and Crowder 2002).[20] They also tend to depict community in strictly spatial terms—a limited concept when dealing with urban neighborhoods, displaced and transient populations, and multisited ethnic enclaves in the twenty-first century.[21] A recent TDR report on Community Participation and Tropical Disease Control (Espino et al. 2004) critically examines how rather naive representations of community have underscored international health policies. Notably, it calls attention to social science critiques of the idealistic definitions of community and community participation underlying the Alma Ata Declaration of 1978, which promoted the concept of comprehensive primary health care. An overview of community participation by Botes and van Rensburg (2000) draws attention to ways this term is used in the rhetoric of governments and international organizations to sell preconceived programs and gain legitimacy. For example, in some instances, acceptance of already-assembled packages is obtained through various forms of leverage and "community renting" as a form of "selective participation."[22] Unpacking the substantial literature on community participation in primary health care is beyond the scope of this book.[23] However, we have learned much from studying the social dynamics of communities that are of particular relevance to international health.

First, communities are dynamic. They are not static structures. Enlisting community support entails mobilizing "action sets," groups of people who come together as a result of common goals and specific tasks (such as performing a ritual, digging a well).[24] A community is not a static entity but a project in the making, forged and sustained by mutually appreciated risks and benefits as well as social obligations and patterns of reciprocity and patronage. What this suggests is that those designing interventions need to carefully consider factors that foster cooperation and the mobilization of particular groups of people at specific times and also factors that sustain a sense of collective efficacy.

In this context, it is important to review the lessons of both community-participation success stories and initiatives that have failed. A few recent examples of successful community-participation efforts related to vector-borne and infectious diseases are (1) the formation of "TB clubs" in northern Ethiopia that have resulted in higher rates of medicine adherence and reduced social isolation of the afflicted (Demissie et al. 2003); (2) community ownership of an ivermectin treatment program for onchocerciasis in Uganda (Katabarwa et al. 2000); (3) community recognition of leprosy care management and stigma reduction in India (Arole et al. 2002); and (4) the formation of support groups for lymphatic filariasis in Haiti that have enhanced home-care practices and the quality of life of members (Coreil et al. 2003). Examples of failed community participation include the many community health-worker programs initiated in the 1980s that gave insufficient thought to social factions within communities, the selection of health workers, their expectations from programs, and their acceptability to intended recipients of services (Mburu 1994; Nichter 1999; Paul and Demarest 1984; Sauerborn et al. 1989).[25]

Second, communities are more fluid today than ever before. One would be hard-pressed to find a region in Asia today without significant outmigration or circular migration, or that has not been dramatically affected by global markets, the destabilizing effects of structural adjustment, or flows of remittances from household members who have left. In much of sub-Saharan Africa, one would be hard-pressed to find regions where a breakdown of civil services, family structures, and agricultural production has not occurred as a result of war, drought, and HIV/AIDS. Given this set of circumstances, and a greater movement toward cash transactions instead of reciprocal work exchanges, community participation and donated labor may be harder to marshal today unless in response to a disaster.

Third, communities are not homogeneous; they should not be treated as such. Representations of community that minimize the importance of heterogeneity (class, caste, gender, occupation, generation) result in privileging the position of some stakeholders (oftentimes those identified as spokespeople) and overlooking the perspectives of many others. Community leaders and those who volunteer to represent their communities often have their own agendas and represent particular factions. For this reason, a community diagnosis (Nichter 1999) of stakeholder positions related to any intervention initiated in the name of the "community" is required.[26] Such analysis needs to consider both who stands to gain or lose from particular types of collective action and how such a threat may be minimized. The latter assessment necessitates attention to the transfer of different types of capital, an issue to which I turn in the following chapter.

NOTES

1. See Manderson 1995 for an early (1925–42) history of the international politics of disease surveillance.

2. A possible link between bioterrorism and dengue was also suspected by some political factions in India at the time of an unprecedented outbreak in Delhi in 1996 (Sharma 2001). Yang (2004) provides an insightful study of how the Chinese government used fear of American bioterrorism in 1952 to mobilize nationalist sentiment and create a patriotic health campaign that played a pivotal role in China's public health movement.

3. In 1981, a dengue epidemic swept through Cuba's population and infected more than 300,000 people. Ten thousand serious cases of dengue hemorrhagic fever were reported, resulting in 158 deaths. From 1982 to 1996, no dengue transmission was reported. The 1981 dengue outbreak in Cuba and outbreaks since 1996 have been attributed to bioterrorism on the part of the United States. The United States has harbored similar suspicions about Cuba, fostering a war of representations that continues today.

4. In 2003, Thailand was the fourth-largest poultry exporter in the world, selling 540,000 tons abroad for an estimated 1.2 billion dollars. Up to 90 percent of Thailand's chicken production is exported, mainly to the European Union and Japan. Bird flu caused a political crisis. Prime Minister Thaksin Shinawatra, one of the richest businessmen in the country, supported the national poultry industry so blatantly that Thai consumers

started doubting everything he was saying about bird flu. On the crisis of confidence, see Chanyapate and Delforge 2004 and Davis 2005.

5. A Global Public Health Information Network was set up in 1997 to inform the World Health Organization of disease outbreaks (Grein et al. 2000). Notably, the network monitors the media, government institutions, and NGO reports. The Internet has facilitated types of surveillance today that were never possible before. However, the proliferation of information and rumor requires careful screening.

6. Contrast this with China's lack of transparency about numbers of HIV/AIDS cases and drug addicts. These numbers would devalue China's reputation and so are suppressed.

7. Insecticide spraying has a remarkable demonstration effect although it does little to control the breeding sites of many disease vectors. It may in fact worsen a vector problem through time by encouraging the development of insecticide resistance (Brogden and McAllister 1998; Spiegel et al. 2005).

8. Cultural capital is also traded in the health and development market in the form of testimonials and photographs that provide people and organizations the legitimacy of being close to the people they are representing. Knowing how to use testimonials and photographs and the right vocabulary is essential to image management.

9. Terms such as *civil society*, *community collaboration*, and *empowerment* have been described as "hurrah words" (Macdonald and Schwartz 2002), that is, ambiguous terms used and supported by everyone because they are politically correct and associated with progress, if not reform.

10. In addition to international programs being reinterpreted within bureaucratic structures, rhetoric is more broadly fit to culture. Orlandini (2003) provides an illustrative case study of the "consumption of discourse on good governance" in Thailand and its re-elaboration. Citing the theorist de Certeau, Orlandini points out that the "space of creativity" increases as the technocratic expansion of institutions that control it declines.

11. I have found the World Health Organization's hard stance on DOTS rather puzzling given all the social science research encouraged by the TDR program. A disjuncture between the findings of social science studies and DOTS policy is evident (Nichter 2006d). Recently, there have been some signs that the DOTS program might be loosening up and taking stock of the particularities of communities (Garner and Volmink 2006).

12. The emphasis here is not on merely tailoring programs to individuals but tailoring programs to groups of individuals subject to common structural problems such as labor availability. Many laborers afflicted with TB need to respond to labor availability with little notice for unspecified amounts of time; transferring a DOTS medicine box with their name on it thus becomes difficult.

13. On a slightly different note, women often feel demeaned when presented over and over again with health-education messages that they grasp but cannot implement because of household power relations. Montgomery and colleagues (2006) describe a case in which women are targeted by educational programs that attribute delays in health care–seeking for children's malaria to ignorance. These researchers found that the women have good knowledge of malaria and its danger signs. Power relations, not "cultural beliefs," were most commonly the reason for delay.

14. Berman and colleagues define "the household production of health" (HHPH) model as "a dynamic behavioral process through which households combine their (internal) knowledge, resources, and behavioral norms and patterns with available (external) technologies, services, information, and skills to restore, maintain, and promote the health of their members" (Berman et al. 1994:206). Far from idealistic, the model acknowledges the embeddedness of health production in diverse spaces; addresses the influences of macro-level structural factors on health at the micro-level; and pays credence to intrahousehold

competition, collaboration, and unequal distribution of resources and responsibilities. For further discussion of the HHPH, see Schumann and Mosley 1994.

15. The term *delay* needs to be carefully conceptualized and defined. At issue is who gets to define a delay. To public health researchers or health practitioners, *delay* may refer to the amount of time that has expired from the onset of a problem to when biomedical services are engaged. But delay also needs to be thought about in terms of when severity is first recognized and when actions are taken to address the problem. These actions may include being actively engaged in obtaining the resources necessary for further health care–seeking. A processual analysis is in order.

16. Beyond education, we need to consider what other factors would speed health care–seeking, such as access to emergency funds, transportation, culturally appropriate chaperons to accompany women to clinics, and so on.

17. Other studies have drawn attention to birth order or age as eclipsing the importance of gender in differentials in resource allocation or time investment. See, for example, Sauerborn et al. 1996a.

18. Research is also needed on perceptions of public and private responsibility for spaces that serve as breeding sites where ownership of the space is not clear (e.g., vacant lots, abandoned construction sites).

19. Careful attention needs to be paid to gender ideologies that reinforce the division of labor, gender-based responsibility for and access to particular resources, and political-economic contexts that influence gender relations.

20. It is beyond the scope of this book to examine the many representations of community that one finds in the social sciences. Common representations of community emphasize shared locality, shared norms, shared identity associated with common interests, and a shared sense of meaning and belonging captured by Putnam's (2000) somewhat idealistic writing on social capital. Rose (1999) and Li (2006, 2007) note that investment in representations of community is motivated. Governance is facilitated by bringing communities into existence so that social forces can be mobilized and enrolled in projects that involve active practices of self-management and identity construction.

21. As Cohen (1985) has noted, while some boundaries of community may be marked on a map as administrative areas by physical features or by religious or linguistic affiliation, not all boundaries are so obvious and exist in the minds of the beholders. Appadurai (1991, 1995) has argued for considering locality as primarily relational and contextual, and neighborhoods as both spatial and virtual in a world in which new technologies of interactivity are becoming ever more commonplace. Gupta and Ferguson (1997) argue that global restructuring has resulted in the reterritorialization of spatial and social connections that force us to reconsider ideas of community, especially when considering migrant and refugee populations. Anderson (1991) invites us to consider the social and political agendas underlying the construction of imagined communities.

22. On the tyranny of how the concept of participation is used in the field of development, see Cooke and Kothari 2001.

23. See for example, critical commentary on community participation in primary health care by Berman and colleagues (1987), Stone (1992), Woelk (1992), and Zakus and Lysack (1998). Also see parallels between the rhetoric used to promote community participation and gender awareness (Cornwall 2003).

24. As Lee and Newby (1983) have pointed out, the fact that people live close to one another does not necessarily mean that they have much to do with each other. What needs to be studied is what brings particular groups of people together, for how long, and whether social networks constituted for one purpose serve other functions. For example, Bossart (2003) points out that in urban Abidjan, social networks play an important but

very restricted role in everyday life. Mutual assistance in the time of illness is rare, and the afflicted have a difficult time obtaining resources in times of need from relatives and friends. One cannot assume that social networks form generalized safety nets for members.

25. For a useful examination of community health-worker incentives and disincentives, see Bhattacharyya et al. 2001.

26. On the importance of evaluating stakeholders' positions as part of formative research, see my model of the eight stages of formative research in Nichter 2006a (see also http:// medanthro.net/academic/tools/nichter_formative_research.pdf).

7

NGOs, Social Capital, and the Politics of the Possible

NGOs must lead where governments are reluctant to go, until others praise the country for having gone there. Once praised, governments and development agencies rush in, but with their own agenda. That is where the real risk lies. It is easy to be seduced by the sweet talk of good intentions and a bag of money when you need resources bad, and you are running on hope.
— NGO MEMBER, PHILIPPINES, MID-1990S

Pioneers get the arrows, settlers get the land.
— PROVERB

Throughout the past decade, reference to social capital in international health and development discourse has escalated and is now commonplace. Although the concept of social capital has been defined in a number of different ways by various social scientists (Bourdieu 1986; Coleman 1988, 1990; Fukuyama 1996, 1999, 2001; Putnam 1993, 1995; Woolcock 1998; Woolcock and Narayan 2000), the term is often used in a very general and highly ambiguous manner in public health (Moore et al. 2006),[1] as well as by policy makers.[2] Social capital has been variously described as a process and reified as a thing, considered to be a property of individuals as well as a collective asset. It has been viewed as primarily cognitive, involving subjective norms, values, attitudes, and beliefs (Putnam 1993, 1995), as well as fundamentally structural and involving features of social networks and aspects of social structure that shape social relations and benefit particular stakeholders (Bourdieu 1986; Coleman 1988; Fukuyama 1999).[3] The term *social capital* has also been used as a gloss to describe social support, social reciprocity, and positive features of social organization that facilitate collective action and cooperation. Some health and development publications have gone so far as to suggest that social capital is the "glue that holds social institutions together" and the "missing link" in sustainable economic development (Grootaert 1998; World Bank 1997). When social capital is spoken about in such terms, it appears to be a panacea for all that ails the development process, a point not missed by critics wary of how the term has recently been used in support of neoliberal reform.[4]

Repeated reference to social capital in "development speak" implies consensus about the meaning, relevance, and importance of this representation of social cohesion. Concerns about negative aspects of social capital are left unaddressed,[5] as are ramifications of targeting particular social groups (such as women) for interventions to promote social capital and questions about how different types of social capital can be strengthened. Let me speak to each of these points in the course of highlighting issues that health social scientists need to bear in mind when conducting research on social capital and how this representation is being used in international health and development.

Negative aspects of social capital coexist with positive social attributes. Interventions that foster the social capital of a particular group without considering that group's relations with other groups may unintentionally facilitate the reproduction of social inequality (Pearce and Davey Smith 2003). Stated more bluntly, enhancing one group's social capital can lead to another group's oppression.[6] Bourdieu (1986) aptly reminds us that social capital is a resource that is used in social struggles carried out in different social arenas or fields.[7] In some instances, interventions introduced in the name of social capital may help enhance both inter- and intragroup cooperation for change. But in other instances, increasing the social capital of one group may lead its members to resist interacting with others in their community. This might be the case, for example, if members of one group feel that such interaction reduces their competitive advantage or, worse yet, places them at a distinct disadvantage.

A second issue returns us to a point raised earlier: communities are not homogeneous and may exhibit rather rigid hierarchical structures. When thinking of enhancing the social capital of communities, those designing interventions must be sensitive to important class, ethnic, and gender divisions and patterns of resource allocation (Mohan and Stokke 2000; Shields et al. 1996; Snyder 2002). How, one might ask, is providing resources to women through microfinancing viewed by men? And how does one design an intervention to increase cooperation between women and men, instead of exacerbating gender tensions?

A third issue in need of consideration is the "politics of responsibility" as it pertains to social capital. Speaking of the need to increase social capital in the "community" as the ticket to development may serve to depoliticize interventions, divert attention away from macro-level factors affecting communities, unintentionally foster victim blaming, and overburden existing social networks (Fine 1999, 2002; Harriss 2002). As noted by Pearce and Davey Smith, "Intervening in communities to increase their levels of social capital may be ineffective, create resentment, and overload community resources, and to take such an approach may be to 'blame the victim' at the community level while ignoring the health effects of macro-level social and economic policies" (Pearce and Davey Smith 2003:122).

A fourth important area for social science investigation is the convertibility of material (economic) and nonmaterial (social and cultural) forms of capital. Bourdieu encourages us to view capital through the lens of whatever is valued in a given society and to consider those strategies available for achieving or maintaining social distinction. For example, we should examine those circumstances under which economic capital (e.g., land, money, resources) is converted into either social capital (i.e., the ability to mobilize interpersonal relationships toward desired ends) or cultural capital (i.e., the ability to mobilize valued social institutions and culturally valued resources).

An example from Sri Lanka illustrates the kind of lesson that may be learned from social science research attentive to power relations and the convertibility of capital. In the mid-1980s, I observed members of the Sri Lankan NGO Sarvodaya tactfully deal with powerful people capable of obstructing community-participation projects that the NGO was attempting to promote. The NGO provided these people with an opportunity to gain social prestige by publicly endorsing projects that would otherwise threaten their economic interests or power base in some way. Sarvodaya applied the principles of convertible capital and made what would have been a loss of physical capital (e.g., money, labor) to potential obstructionists an investment in a more highly valued cultural capital: prestige. For example, they were asked to participate in a public event organized to initiate the building of a new road, clinic, cooperative society, or the like—an event that would be well covered by the local press. Association with religious leaders, politicians, and even foreign consultants at the event would raise the prestige of these community members both among the local community and beyond. We know far too little about the role played by conversions of capital in advancing community projects, how such conversions are accomplished, in what contexts they are successful, and when they fail or backfire.

A fifth area in need of study is the ways in which social capital may be generated within and between different social groups. Such investigation requires that social scientists pay attention to existing social networks as well as the formation of new ones, structural factors that foster and deter network formation and participation, and distinct types of social capital. Social networks are established through exchange relations involving some form(s) of reciprocity. The formation of social networks is influenced positively as well as negatively by macro-level factors. For example, state policies fostering the decentralization of rule (e.g., in Indonesia) may foster social dialogue and the formation of new social groups active in civil society. Increased state surveillance, in contrast, may foster a sense of distrust—precluding open discussion and group formation—or may foster the formation of secretive groups that have restricted membership. Structural adjustment policies can influence resource allocation in ways that at once encourage cooperation (e.g., the formation of women's groups around microcredit schemes) and foster gender tension, resulting in escalations of violence, and ways that expand social safety nets as well as place existing ones in jeopardy.[8]

Three types of social capital coexist. *Bonding social capital* describes the strengthening of already-existing social ties within a group, thereby reaffirming and contributing to a shared sense of identity. *Bridging social capital* enables people to forge new relationships with others outside their immediate social network. *Linking social capital* facilitates connections that span even larger social divides associated with power differentials, religious or ethnic identity, social class, and so on.[9] Throughout the past decade, NGOs have been increasingly identified as vehicles for fostering these three different types of social capital and facilitating broader and more socially conscious forms of interaction. Let me turn to a brief consideration of how NGOs are represented and whose interests they have come to serve.

Nongovernment Organizations: Whose Interests Do They Represent?

Several different types of NGOs coexist, and various typologies have been used to characterize them (Boli and Thomas 1999; Clark 1991; Fisher 1997; Kamat 2002, 2003a, 2003b; Padron 1997). Ostensibly, all are nonprofit organizations that maintain some degree of autonomy from the formal political sector. In this sense, they are social formations that embrace and contribute to civil society, a public sphere that "in theory exists between the state, family and market, though in practice, the boundaries between state, civil society, family and market are often complex, blurred and negotiated" (London

School of Economics and Political Science 2004: www.lse.ac.uk/).[10] The following three types of NGOs are commonly differentiated:

1. Community-based organizations (CBOs) are typically represented as grassroots organizations (GROs) that have their fingers on the pulse of the community and work to strengthen civil society as well as build social capital.[11] CBOs are represented as legitimate spokesmen for marginalized and disempowered groups. Historically, these NGOs have been associated with participatory research, critical thinking, consciousness-raising, and innovative demonstration projects that rarely go to scale but sometimes prove sustainable. At times, CBOs may be directly supported by international NGOs (INGOs) and coalitions of NGOs that have transnational agendas such as human rights, women's rights, and so on.

2. National nongovernmental development organizations (NGDOs) support the efforts of CBOs and sometimes organize and support local CBO networks. Their strength lies in the ability to respond to the needs of diverse populations in a manner more flexible and efficient than overburdened state bureaucracies.

3. International development cooperation institutions (IDCIs) are large donors generally located in the North that channel significant resources to NGDOs and CBOs, often in the South, according to their own mandates, priorities, and ideologies.[12]

For the past two decades, NGOs have proliferated in developing countries in response to transnational health, development, human rights, and women's movements,[13] and to neoliberal reform initiatives that support groups that represent and expand civil society.[14] Transnational NGO networks have sought partners in developing countries and have offered them a broader sense of identity and purpose as well as social and material support (Keck and Sikkink 1998). These transnational NGOs tend to have agendas geared toward social change. Large international development cooperation institutions (IDCIs), including lender institutions such as the World Bank, have injected a major influx of funds into a second set of NGOs seen as "operational"—that is, capable of promoting a structural adjustment agenda (World Bank 1995) tied to a hegemonic perception of democratization (Ayers 2006).[15] These NGOs provide technical and managerial expertise to large international health projects and often serve as subcontractors for government agencies encouraged to outsource services (Kamat 2003a, 2003b).[16]

NGOs have come to represent civil society in the eyes of donors, but the question remains: whose interests do they actually serve? This question is increasingly posed by social scientists.[17] At present, NGOs of all stripes operating in developing countries are adapting their operations to the guidelines and assessment procedures of donor agencies and becoming subject to audit culture (governance through accountability; Strathern 1996)[18] and transnational governmentality (governance on a global scale; Ferguson and Gupta 2002).[19] One ramification of NGOs' dependency upon donor dollars and collaboration with state agencies is that they have become less likely to risk being critical of those who stand to be their potential benefactors or collaborators.[20] When this happens, NGOs unintentionally contribute to the depoliticizing of development (Basok and Ilcan 2003; Ferguson 1990; Fisher 1997; Harriss 2002; Kamat 2002, 2003b; Miraftab 1997) and the representation of poverty and disease as technical problems that NGOs can fix, rather than larger structural problems that call for more-systemic social changes (White 1999).[21]

The NGO accountability debate is complicated. Some critics have gone so far as to argue that most NGOs have become so co-opted that they are more the representatives of donors than representatives of the populations they purport to serve. Others have argued that the distinction between civil society and state has been rendered artificial, a distinction that S. Kamat (2004) notes has always been simplistic and misleading.[22] Those supporting NGO collaboration counter these criticisms, noting that NGOs are in a better position to foster "linking capital" between those in the community and those further up the power chain.[23] Still others articulate concerns about jealousy between civil servants and NGOs.[24]

In some cases, NGO success undermines the very principles upon which the NGO was constituted.[25] Successful NGOs face donor pressure to take on more projects than they can handle (often projects outside their immediate interest) and to accept more funds than they can manage effectively. In addition to "mission creep," they are also pushed to represent themselves or stretch the truth in the media in ways that serve their own purposes more than those of the communities they serve. Heads of NGOs are often quite aware that donors need success stories to justify their programs, and this means visible examples of community participation, social capital, and so forth.

What have health social scientists contributed to the study of NGO impact on the health systems of developing countries, beyond documenting demonstration projects? Two important issues that social scientists have examined are the role of NGOs as agents of development and the impact of

NGO service provision on the reputation of state institutions (Kamat 2002; White 1999). Does increased NGO activity contribute to the strengthening of a resource-deficient government health sector by providing adjunct services, or does it result in a deterioration of the government sector and health workers leaving government service to join higher-paying NGOs?

Pfeiffer (2004) has provided us with an excellent case study from Mozambique that addresses these questions. His ethnography found that health workers in Mozambique often leave government service for greener pastures and float between NGOs that offer better benefits.[26] In principle, NGOs complement and strengthen the existing health care system. In practice, NGOs often contribute to the undoing of government services. Based on his research, Pfeiffer calls for dialogue on how salaries can be normalized across NGOs and efforts taken to protect government services from manpower losses that result in chaos. Pfeiffer challenges international donors to find a way of promoting civil society that strengthens rather than diverts resources from the public sector, thereby casting NGOs in a support function that will increase their local credibility.[27] His analysis joins the ranks of others, such as Bond (2000), who have pointed out that NGO activity in the health sector of Mozambique is far from cost-effective.

This is a poignant example of the kind of practical problem solving that critical health social science research can contribute to the field of health policy.[28] Yet there are relatively few examples in the international health literature of social scientists being asked to engage in health-systems research or critical assessments of health programs as they affect local populations and health systems (Castro and Singer 2004).[29] I cannot help but wonder whether the failure to be involved in this type of research is symptomatic of a larger identity problem facing health social scientists—at least medical anthropologists.[30] Have our colleagues in international health come to think of us as conducting research on a very limited set of issues such as the exotic health beliefs and practices of the natives, focused illness ethnographies, and the like? If so, we need to expand their appreciation of what we can contribute to a study of the multilevel impact of evolving global health policy (Janes 2004) and to the generation of new ideas leading to other possible futures. This task strikes me as urgent.

THE POLITICS OF THE POSSIBLE

"Imagination is more important than knowledge" (Albert Einstein).[31]

Clearly, the growing interdependency between NGOs, the state, and international donors has both positive and negative features that beg for further examination by social scientists. What is needed at this juncture is a hard look at the trajectories of different types of NGOs given the roles they are being asked to assume, the types of support they receive and with what provisions, their internal decision-making processes, and their own identity, as well as how they are representing themselves to funding agencies and policy makers. Here it strikes me as important to take stock of three broad, overlapping motivations driving NGOs: humanitarianism, human rights, and social justice. *Humanitarianism* is motivated by charity, compassion, and the imperative to respond to human suffering, which once witnessed becomes shared with the observer. Humanitarian engagement is often crisis driven and represented as apolitical. *Human rights* emphasizes the universal and inalienable nature of human dignity regardless of the policies of state governments or issues of citizenship and entitlement. The right to health and access to basic health services was central to the World Health Organization's Declaration of Alma Ata (1978). A third motivation is *social justice*, which calls attention to structural inequalities within and across states that result in human suffering; advocates of social justice adopt a more proactive agenda of social change.

It is important for social scientists to study the representations of "the possible" and "the just," not merely engage in the critique of that which currently exists. Such inquiry entails studying how past experiments in public health influence future thinking about what is possible, highlighting lessons from innovative programs sponsored by NGOs of different persuasions, and bringing the stories of real people into the policy arena to inform, evoke compassion, and render transparent the results of inaction.

Tesler (2005) provides a good example of ways in which past experience with public health programs can lead to both a critique of present programs and perceptions of an imagined future. In a study of primary health care in Nicaragua, Tesler documents how social memory is a resource for the future. Residual "structures of feeling" (Williams 1977) carried over from the Sandinista era that valorized an ethos of solidarity, cooperation, and service inspire people to look for an alternative to the contemporary ethos of individual competition and self-preservation.[32] Villagers imagine a possible future that is not the same as the past but incorporates an ethic of community service not currently promoted.

The public-policy activism of the international NGO Partners in Health (PIH) provides an apt example of a group of scholar-activists committed to the politics of the future. Representatives of this NGO employ the perspectives of critical public health and medical anthropology to accomplish four objectives. First, they demonstrate that quality health care can serve as an effective leverage point to inspire hope, improve social conditions, and foster a sense of individual as well as collective efficacy among impoverished HIV- and TB-afflicted populations. Second, they identify what it will take to deliver such health care in terms of both resources and policies governing the cost and availability of medicines such as antiretroviral drugs and second-line antituberculosis drugs. Third, they use stories of the afflicted to relate the larger importance of the pathogenic effects of poverty perpetuated by local as well as global power brokers, political-economic forces, racism, and prejudice. Finally, their fourth objective has been to bring home the message that to be complacent in the face of health inequity is to be complicit in its perpetuation (Castro 2004; Farmer and Castro 2004).

Members of this NGO group have sharply critiqued "cultural barrier"-type arguments used to explain away failures in health programs as well as the slow progress of global health strategies. This type of misguided reasoning, they stress, has resulted in victim blaming as well as an apolitical stance toward problem solving. They draw attention to "structural violence," structural inequalities affecting access to resources and social services, as the major factor contributing to human suffering among the poor (Castro and Farmer 2005; Farmer 1999, 2003, 2004; Kim et al. 2000). Social science research focusing on "health beliefs," they argue, has deflected attention away from the material and social structural conditions that have contributed to the misdistribution of illness in society and poor health care provision. I view this critique not as dismissive of social science in international health research but as a much-needed corrective to an imbalance in the scope of research funded by health and development agencies. This imbalance is being addressed by an increasing number of social scientists, but we can do better.

It is beyond the scope of this book to summarize the many lessons that one might glean from an ethnography of Partners in Health and other NGOs engaged in health as human rights activism. Of relevance to this book are lessons related to (1) how representations of those subjected to structural violence are being employed to broaden the horizons of present-day thinking about global health policy and state health initiatives and (2) how these representations are being responded to by different audiences. Real-life stories of people afflicted with infectious diseases such as TB and AIDS are a powerful rhetorical device, because such stories are evocative and provocative and hail our humanity (Flyvbjerg 2001). They call out to us in ways that body counts cannot. They unsettle us and force us to look at the afflicted as more than faceless "casualties of poverty" written off as beyond our means to help.

The health care that NGOs such as PIH deliver to the poor is inexpensive by Western standards, although expensive by international standards, especially when considered in relation to the total health budgets of developing countries and the vast number of problems in need of being addressed. Critics have been quick to point out that it would be unrealistic to provide such care globally at today's prices. This is precisely the debate that PIH wants to foster as part of an effort to imagine a "politics of the possible." Such a debate highlights a fundamental moral question—are the medical resources that are desperately needed by those who are poor and afflicted a commodity subject to market forces or a human right to which the state and its citizens are entitled? If the latter is the case, then the only way developing countries can afford such resources is for the costs of essential drugs to be lowered, patent regulations relaxed to increase the availability of generic drugs, and global responsibility for treating the afflicted recognized and acted upon in good faith.

By giving faces and stories to the afflicted and by calling attention to what is possible, one becomes cognizant of a form of violence in the act of withholding health care from the poor to protect the profit margins of the pharmaceutical industry (Farmer 2003).[33] Should human rights not be adequate to motivate global action, a further motivation may be salient: the global threat of diseases such as multidrug-resistant TB associated with inadequate care.[34] Some argue that if we do not tend to the afflicted with appropriate medicines in adequate supply, then they will become the source for drug-resistant strains of disease that will affect us all (Barry 2003; Heymann et al. 1999).[35] Others, however, oppose the free provision of drugs such as antiretrovirals to the poor in developing (and developed) countries on the grounds that poor compliance and unregulated prescribing of medicine regimens in poorly monitored health care arenas will contribute to drug resistance.[36] PIH experience counters representations of the poor as unreliable custodians of their own health care, illustrating instead that the poor are motivated to use medical resources effectively once therapy is stabilized and they come to understand what is at stake for themselves and their community. Representations of the poor as unreliable and backward are challenged by research that combines the strengths of both evidence-based and narrative-based medicine.

What success have NGOs such as PIH had in reframing such debates in international health? Ethnographic studies of the impact of NGOs (and NGO networks) on the health-policy arena need to be conducted. PIH appears to have had some measure of success in attracting the attention of politicians and international donors (for example, the Bill and Melinda Gates Foundation) interested in innovative health programs. More important is that this NGO has been successful in rekindling moral discourse about the politics of responsibility in the international health community through the use of human rights language populated with stories of the afflicted.

Human rights discourse has also breathed new life into health social sciences such as medical anthropology. A new generation of social scientists is currently emerging, attentive to health inequity and new ways of framing and positioning research. Research on structural violence has greater appeal to many members of this generation of scholars than research labeled "critical" or "political-economic," perhaps because the latter has become abstract and encumbered.[37] The language of human rights and the stories of "organic intellectuals" (Gramsci 1971) such as Paul Farmer have charismatic appeal (Kidder 2003).[38]

Yet we must be wary of the appeal and easy appropriation of concepts such as "social capital" and "structural violence." This brings me to a final point. To ensure that structural violence remains a robust analytic tool, we must engage in research that illustrates the multifarious ways in which oppression manifests and plays out in nested social contexts. If we fail to do so, the concept may end up "generating more moral heat than analytic light" (Wacquant 2004:322) and inadvertently serving a liberal agenda by reducing the impact of poverty and the solution of problems to familiar scenario.[39]

NOTES

1. As noted by Moore (Moore et al. 2005, 2006), public health has tended to adopt a strictly communitarian definition of social capital advocated by Putnam. Social epidemiological research has largely employed social capital as an ecological construct and has treated social contexts as bounded places. Social epidemiologists have treated social capital as a psychosocial mechanism that helps explain the effect of income inequality on population health (e.g., Kawachi et al. 1997; Wilkinson 1996). What is particularly problematic is that the measurement of social capital commonly adopted by those in public health relies on aggregated individual data (e.g., related to levels of trust, civil participation, reciprocity). It assumes that members of communities have the same "stocks" of social capital, ignoring intracommunity dynamics and the possibility that social aggregates do not function as communities. Too little attention is also paid to network dimensions of social capital captured by the more nuanced concepts of bridging and linking social capital.

2. For critical reviews of the ways in which the term *social capital* has been used, see Dasgupta 1999; Fine 2002; Moore et al. 2006; Portes 1998; Sobel 2002.

3. Some descriptions of social capital are very general and index both cognitive and embodied norms that one picks up as habitus. For example, Fukuyama (1999) describes social capital as an instantiated informal norm that promotes cooperation between two or more individuals.

4. Strong criticism has been leveled against the use of social capital in rhetoric that insinuates that a lack of social capital is the reason neoliberal reform has faltered in many countries (Fine 1999, 2002; Harriss 2002).

5. Advocates of social capital as social support tend to downplay coercive aspects of interlocking networks of obligations and forced conformity associated with group membership. They also play down inequities in access to resources, which is at the heart of a social-justice agenda that endorses the importance of transformative social engagement (Wakefield and Poland 2005).

6. Network membership is complex and layered, with overlapping arenas of rules, norms, and opportunities, and with each person's social capital processes touching upon the social capital processes of others (Fukuyama 2001). Strengthening or weakening one relationship has a symbiotic effect on others. The term *negative social capital* refers to situations in which strong networks produce positive short-term impacts on members but long-term negative impacts on nonmembers and the community at large. Coercive aspects of social capital are inherent in networks of obligations, forced conformity, obligatory voluntarism, inhibition of individual expression, and downward-leveling pressures (Fukuyama 2001; Harriss 2002; Keck and Sikkink 1998; Kunitz 2001; Pearce and Davey Smith 2003; Portes 1998; Portes and Landolt 1996; Shields et al. 1996; Snyder 2002; Woolcock 2002).

7. According to Bourdieu (1986), membership in a group provides each of its members with the backing of collectively owned capital that enables them to maintain durable relationships that are of mutual benefit.

8. For example, structural adjustment policies have fostered cooperation through microcredit schemes to women's groups, but they have also threatened preexisting safety nets to escalating rates of poverty. When the poor have so few resources that they are no longer able to honor reciprocal exchange relationships, they suffer loss of social capital, identity, and self-respect as victims of structural violence. As I see it, there are different types of structural violence. In one case, the implementation of political ideology or social policy can discriminate against particular social groups, resulting in suffering of one type or another. In another case, poverty is so extreme that social bonds weaken, such that reciprocity and mutual assistance become impossible and a group's "social immunity" against disaster such as food shortage wanes (Mtika 2001). In a third case, poverty, disaster, disease, or war weakens social structure to the point that social institutions are rendered dysfunctional. De Waal (2003) provides us with a good case of the last type of structural violence by describing the impact of HIV/AIDS on governments in sub-Saharan Africa.

9. Putnam (2000) describes "bonding social capital" as mutually supportive relations within relatively homogeneous groups that tend to be exclusive. "Bridging (inclusive) social capital" refers to relations with more-distant friends, associates, and colleagues. Examples of these are co-members of civil rights movements and religious organizations. These weaker ties (Granovetter 1973) are important resources enabling one to expand and realize mobility opportunities. So while *bonding* social capital is crucial for "getting by," *bridging* social capital is especially important for "getting ahead" (de Souza Briggs 1998). "Linking social capital" (a subtype of bridging capital) involves relations between individuals, groups, and institutions occupying different social strata in a hierarchy. Woolcock (2001) speaks of this as a capacity to leverage resources, ideas, and information from formal institutions beyond the community (see also Szreter and Woolcock 2004). An example of linking social capital would be a marginal group securing ties to a government official or an international health agency through an NGO.

10. The representation of NGOs as apolitical, although popular, has been widely critiqued (e.g., Carothers and Ottoway 2000; Cruikshank 1999; Dean 1999, 2002; Edkins 2000;

Ferguson 1990; Fisher 1997; Pfeiffer 2003b; Rose 1999; Uvin 2004). For example, critics have pointed to the manner in which NGOs are involved in the exercise of governmentality through mobilizing community formations to act in particular programmatic ways in the name of empowerment. The concept of governmentality used here involves forms of governance that extend beyond the formal apparatus and institutions of state government to programs that direct the actions of others even when they are framed as "bottom up." Fisher has called the representation of NGOs as apolitical (antipolitics) and value neutral an obfuscation of their political positioning and an example of ideology at work.

11. Other terms used to describe such groups are *civil society organizations* (CSOs), *community-based organizations* (CBOs), *grassroots organizations* (GROs), *people's organizations* (POs), *private voluntary associations* (PVAs), and *local development associations* (LDAs).

12. International NGOs range from secular agencies such as CARE (Cooperative for Assistance and Relief Everywhere), Oxfam, Save the Children, and the Ford and Rockefeller Foundations to religiously motivated groups. Their activities vary from mainly funding local NGOs, institutions, and projects to implementing the projects themselves.

13. Many transnational NGOs and coalitions (coalitions against child labor, violence against women, and so forth) have been formed in the North to address global humanitarian issues. Through an infusion of resources, they have empowered local groups in developing countries by providing these groups with new forms of global legitimacy and acknowledgment and a greater sense of purpose and order. However, adoption of the language and ways of framing problems advocated by these groups can limit creative approaches to local problem solving. Transnational advocacy networks have also emerged in the South as "communities of practice" inspired by local groups reaching out to kindred groups in other countries as part of a process of internationalization. Appadurai (2001a, 2001b) has described such groups as the crucibles in which "globalization from below" is occurring. These groups are currently making use of rapid communication technologies to share experience, challenge ineffective or unjust state or international policies and programs, and discuss innovative ways of solving problems. Appadurai believes that the destablization of nations provides opportunities for the empowerment of previously marginalized groups that form grassroots alliances. Appadurai's conception of grassroots globalization as the true expression of civil society and an effective buffer against misguided or poorly implemented neoliberal policy fails to pay enough attention to the impact that funding sources have on NGO operation, leadership, and accountability. The work of Kamat (2003a, 2003b) provides a necessary corrective.

14. Some social scientists have pointed to the relationship between neoliberal policy and NGOs as one of mutual reinforcement. Neoliberal policy encourages the growth of NGOs, and the successes of NGOs justify the continuation of neoliberal reform.

15. The "democratization project" of neoliberalism urges "the liberation of civil society from the suffocating grip of the state" and has been described as the hegemonic ideology project of our time (Ayers 2006:330). This project seeks to establish democracy in one sense of the term, while blocking it in others (Ayers 2006). Divergent transnational organizations ranging from NGOs to multinational corporations and international treaty agreements constitute an emergent political field that challenges state sovereignty in more and more domains (Keohane and Nye 2001). At the same time, like many NGOs and CBOs, IDCIs are often funded by state governments that require that their activities comply with state law governing the use of the funding. For example, CARE's use of funding from the President's Emergency Plan for AIDS Relief (PEPFAR) must be compliant with its terms, such as emphasizing the "ABCs," into which an abstinence agenda figures prominently.

16. In keeping with structural adjustment policies, national governments in developing countries have been forced to cut back on their social service budgets, thus paving the way for increased NGO involvement to fulfill this shortfall (Pfeiffer 2003b). The proportion of projects involving NGOs funded by the World Bank rose from 20 percent in 1989 to 52 percent in 1999 (World Bank 2000).

17. On the impact of external funding on NGO activity and dependency, see Vincent 2006.

18. The term *audit culture* (Shore and Wright 1999; Strathern 1996) describes institutional governance exercised through the use of templates that measure accountability, efficiency, quality assurance, and so on. Although generally applied to the public sector by those calling for neoliberal reform, audit culture also influences NGO activity (Najam 1996). NGOs learn to adapt to the organizational demands of donors, resulting in the professionalization of NGOs (Kamat 2003b) and the standardization of problems and solutions (Arce and Long 2000; Ferguson 1990; Green 2003). This constitutes a form of governmentality exercised through the public services sector (Rose 1999). A notable strategy of transnational governance is to construct an image of scientific or managerial neutrality and to hide the tension between agency and compliance, ownership, and conditionality. As noted by Anders (2005) in an assessment of World Bank strategies, this is done through the language of technical assistance, performance criteria, and structural benchmarks. External audits to meet standards of competence have a delocalizing effect on decision making in contexts where state health infrastructures are subject to programs designed by organizations at a distance (Whiteford and Manderson 2000).

19. The term *transnational governmentality* refers to modes of government set up on a global scale that "include not only new strategies of discipline and regulation, as exemplified by the World Trade Organization and the structural adjustment programs implemented by the International Monetary Fund, but also transnational alliances forged by activists and grassroots organizations and the proliferation of voluntary organizations supported by complex networks of international and transnational funding and personnel" (Ferguson and Gupta 2002:989). Ferguson and Gupta invite us to reconsider common spatial images of how governance takes place—states (above) exercising authority on regions and locales (below) through bureaucratic structures. Today, in many parts of the world, the authority of global institutions and alliances supersedes that of nation-states, and the functions of the state have been taken over by NGOs and transnational institutions. Governance is being carried out through new modalities that propagate their own means of evaluation and audit. This, like audit culture (see note 18), has a delocalizing effect on health care decision making in contexts where state health infrastructures are subject to programs designed by organizations at a distance (Whiteford and Manderson 2000) and subject to audit.

20. Kamat (2003b) has drawn a useful distinction between "struggle-based NGOs" and "operational NGOs," that is, NGOs for whom empowerment is central and NGOs more closely tied to the state and the market. This begs the question of NGO accountability, an issue that Lister (2003) argues needs to be part of any discussion of NGO legitimacy. On NGO dependency on donor dollars and how this constrains what they do, see Hudock 1999.

21. Kamat (2003b:90) also notes that a shift to a "functionalist problem-solving approach" to social issues of inequality and poverty fosters a sense of paternalism toward the target group.

22. As argued by the social theorist Antonio Gramsci, the hegemony of the state is located not only in the formal apparatus of government and representations of public order but also in civil society and spaces seen as private and sites of the expression of agency. Hegemony is a project that is never complete. Sangeeta Kamat (2004) notes how NGOs

play an instrumental role in the remaking of the state, just as the state plays an important role in reconfiguring civil society. She rightly warns us not to reify either state or civil society. Neither has rigid boundaries.

23. Key research questions concern the extent to which the idealism of NGOs subscribing to social-justice agendas has been co-opted and the extent to which NGO members have adapted and continued to keep their eye on the prize (empowerment) once the basic needs of the poor are attended to, placing them in a position to take the next steps. Case studies of the social life of NGOs and the social relations of NGO engagement in response to competing agendas and contingencies need examination. The resulting ethnographies must document transitions and turning points in group activities and the life histories and motivation of members.

24. Jealousies between civil servants and NGOs have been reported in the case of NGOs that keep a low profile as well as NGOs that have joint programs with the state yet are given resources above and beyond those received by civil servants (Clark 1991).

25. Just as some donor agencies worry about NGOs becoming dependent upon them and not developing sustainable programs, so too do some successful NGOs worry about donors taking advantage of them by pushing agendas that deflect attention from their primary objectives and fostering dependency relationships on them. See Uvin 2004 for a useful discussion of a human rights approach to development that acknowledges the pitfalls of large funding agencies that remove local leaders from their social bases and turn them into "aid parrots" in the international aid circuit.

26. Garrett (2007) provides other examples of how foreign NGOs funded by North American or European governments, and the Gates Foundation, have hired away health care professionals from government services. The case of Malawi is particularly striking. According to Garrett, the government lost 53 percent of its administrators, 64 percent of its nurses, and 85 percent of its physicians to foreign NGOs.

27. An emergent rhetoric now speaks to the importance of "harmonizing" aid policy (Agg 2006). On the need to think in terms of state–civil society synergy, see Evans 1996 and Radcliffe 2004.

28. For another example of how anthropology can be applied in health systems research, see Nichter 1996c on the need to examine the social relations of primary health care teamwork in developing countries.

29. Social scientists' participation in international health has a long history. What I am calling attention to here is an expanded role that both guides and addresses the impact of health policy at the local community and midlevel of health infrastructure. Others have called for such an expanded role to address the issue of social accountability (e.g., Sadana et al. 2004).

30. Napolitano and Jones (2006) note that most of those in the field of international health have a very limited idea of the scope of work performed by medical anthropologists. General impressions of anthropologists are that they study health beliefs and folk illnesses. Those in international health who have worked with anthropologists have a far broader view of the scope of their work and what they bring to public health policy (Porter 2005).

31. Knowledge is productive and enlists imagination in its service. Imagination holds the promise of moving us beyond the power that knowledge holds over us at any given moment.

32. One of Raymond Williams's key contributions to an understanding of hegemony is his identification of the role of its affective dimensions. As he observes, the meanings and values imparted through the institutions of civil society are often contradictory and subject to the individual's interpretations and selective incorporation. The relationship

between "'structures of feeling,' meanings and values as they are actively felt, and formal or systematic beliefs are in practice variable" (Williams 1977:132). Hence, consent may not necessarily be a positive affirmation of the existing social order so much as a resignation to it or a public performance of conformity. One way in which resistance may be exercised is through the imagination of other futures.

33. On this same point, one is reminded of Mahatma Gandhi, who wrote that the deadliest form of violence is poverty.

34. Adequate care of TB patients may require more than providing an ample supply of medications and securing high rates of treatment adherence. A recent study from China (Li et al. 2007) that employed genetic typing of MDR-TB strains suggests that the lion's share of drug resistance may be the result of primary and not acquired resistance: most cases of MDR-TB investigated were the result of reinfection with different strains of TB transmitted in clinics or communities. If study results are found to be generalizable, then reducing reinfection will require more-comprehensive community-based TB strategies and surveillance, not just individual-based treatment strategies. It will also mean that more resources are needed to enhance the resistance and reduce the susceptibility of those most vulnerable to TB.

35. As Heymann and colleagues (1999) have noted, although treatment of MDR-TB is expensive, not to treat it is even more expensive. Given globalization, TB control in low-incidence countries is dependent on control in high-incidence countries. As Barry (2003) has noted, the same conditions that lead to poor health in distant tropical countries lead to political and social pathologies, all of which affect First World countries.

36. Significant concern has been raised about introducing antiretroviral drug therapy into contexts of poverty and social disorder, because resistance to these drugs can occur when compliance dips below 85–90 percent. Intermittent medication use among the poor is typically associated with medicine cost and availability and with poor communication by practitioners about side effects and why adherence is necessary. PIH has addressed each of these factors and reached high adherence rates among TB and AIDS patients in clinics in countries such as Haiti (see Farmer et al. 2001a, 2001b; see also Coetzee et al. 2004 and Severe et al. 2005). Critics commend these efforts and applaud the fall in TB and HIV drug prices but still point to other sets of conditions that may lead to a state of antiretroviral drug anarchy (Horton 2000) should these drugs be made available in countries with weak health infrastructures and unregulated health care arenas. See Kovsted 2005 for a review of arguments against going to scale with antiretroviral drug distribution, including the presence of too few physicians to monitor drug use and attend to side effects and coinfection, poor drug procurement and distribution systems (making drug interruptions likely), and theft of drugs from health institutions for sale in markets across national borders. Strategies have been advanced to address some of these challenges through the use of community health workers to monitor compliance with drug therapy (Farmer and Garrett 2006; Farmer et al. 2001a, 2001b), combining TB and AIDS treatment programs (Harries et al. 2001), working with private practitioners to coordinate treatment programs (Brugha 2003), and creating an international Peace Corps for Health (Mullan 2007). Only time will tell what resources are needed to sustain community health-worker motivation and what it will take to regulate pharmaceutical markets in places where there is a market for antiretroviral drugs within and/or across borders.

37. Structural violence is generally thought about in relation to political, economic, cultural, and religious institutions that result in the perpetuation of inequality resulting in social suffering among groups marked by ethnicity, gender, age, and so on. As a rubric, structural violence at once draws attention to inequality at large and glosses over the particu-

larities of inequality. As noted by both Wacquant (2004) and Kirmayer (2004), the structural violence concept as used by anthropologists such as Farmer conflates different types of violence and coexisting structures of domination. This complicates the identification of which social forces and actors are responsible for specific forms of oppression. A better understanding of such oppression often demands a deeper historical and broader-ranging multisided ethnography.

38. Gramsci spoke of "organic intellectuals" as working-class intellectuals actively participating in practical life and helping to create a counterhegemony that would lead to a rethinking of existing social relations. He described their role of active participation in practical life as "constructor, organiser, 'permanent persuader' and not just a simple orator" (Gramsci 1971:10). He believed in the innate capacity of human beings to understand their world and to change it.

39. Several social scientists sympathetic to Farmer's research agenda have called for the concept of structural violence to be unpacked and taken even further than it has been to date (Bourgois and Scheper-Hughes 2004; Green 2004; Wacquant 2004).

PART III
FUTURE RESEARCH

Some have lamented that our rudderless, post–cold war society appears to have lost its bearings. Global health (now an achievable imperative for our survival) may well provide the missing compass. . . . We may now see the dawning of an era when, perhaps for the first time in human evolution, we can begin to perceive the survival advantage of caring about the other person, the poor in the tropics. We have seen how emerging and re-emerging infections threaten us all . . . how growing disparity threatens us all.

—RICHARD GUERRANT, PRESIDENTIAL ADDRESS TO THE 46TH ANNUAL MEETING OF THE AMERICAN SOCIETY OF TROPICAL MEDICINE AND HYGIENE, 1998

Up to this point, I have largely extracted lessons from a rather-disparate health social science literature. Let me now turn from lessons learned to issues that social scientists will need to address in the immediate future. In this section of the book, I suggest several directions for future health social science research that serves a global health agenda attentive to biopolitics.[1] Global health is a biopolitical agenda that involves the politics of an unnatural distribution of diseases and health care resources, as well as the politics of transnational governance related to the control of emerging diseases and threats to global biosecurity and health as a human right.[2]

I begin chapter 8 with one representation that I think we should dispense with entirely: tropical diseases. It is high time we think of afflictions currently associated with this term as diseases of poverty, development, and political ecology—not climatic happenstance.[3] Next, I introduce "global health" as a representation that enables thinking about linkages and interconnections that extend beyond nation-states in a changing global landscape. In so doing, a space is created for new partnerships and cooperative agreements to exist, even under conditions of heightened political tension.[4]

Finally, I introduce a set of social science concepts that will prove useful in addressing some of the compelling issues that demand attention now.

NOTES

1. Foucault used the term *biopolitics* to refer to the regulation of populations through an exercise of biopower (the productive power of knowledge) in a way that was distinct from sovereign power (power to take life). Biopolitics involved the governing of ways of living through normative practice. Public health was identified as one important mechanism for extending administrative and regulatory control and for conferring a sense of order at the level of population or collectivity. Life processes involved in the production and the maintaining of health (from birth to death) at the individual and collective level were recognized to have a political dimension. My use of the term *biopolitics* in this book is informed by this theoretical perspective. It refers to a politics of health, public health, medicine, and medical research that involves the exercise of governance through the administration of life and death in the name of global health. Global health is a biopolitical project of "empire" (Hardt and Negri 2000) that supersedes nation-states. My use of the term *biopolitics* also encompasses the politics of health and medical citizenship (defined in chapter 8) and the politics of emerging assemblages in a world increasingly being defined by distributed networks of people who join together and effect change within and beyond nation-states in a new information-technology environment (see Barabasi 2003; Castells 1996; Poster 1995; Rosenau and Singh 2002; Schuler and Day 2004).

2. In an insightful article, King (2002) compares an "emerging diseases worldview" to colonial-era ideologies of medicine and public health. He notes similarities and differences in the mapping and thinking about space-territoriality and the importance of promoting commodity- and information-exchange networks. He draws attention to a transition from metaphors of conversion as a "civilizing mission" to metaphors of integration and international development. Both involve biopolitical agendas; moreover, as King notes, both lead to forms of colonialization with moral agendas that are resisted.

3. The suggestion of treating these afflictions as diseases of poverty or development is not a new idea (Hunter et al. 1982; Shiva 1997; Stock 1986; Turshen 1984). Doing so calls attention to a range of issues having to do with the distribution of the disease(s) in focus, routes of transmission, treatment, prognosis, and mortality. In the case of different diseases, one dimension of the affliction may be more clearly influenced by poverty than others. For example, see Worrall and colleagues' 2005 study of malaria as a disease of poverty.

4. New partnerships may be motivated by different agendas encompassing humanitarianism, commercialism, and enlightened self-interest. Global health provides a rationale for scientists of opposing political regimes to cooperate when confronted by pandemic diseases and for countries at war to suspend hostilities long enough to participate in global vaccination programs. A global health agenda keeps lines of communication open and provides a space (one space) for diplomacy to take place.

8

Toward a Next Generation of Social Science Research in Global Health

> Medicine is a social science, and politics is nothing else but medicine on a large scale. Medicine, as a social science, as the science of human beings, has the obligation to point out problems and to attempt their theoretical solution: the politician, the practical anthropologist, must find the means for their actual solution.
> —RUDOLF VIRCHOW, QUOTED IN ACKERKNECHT 1953

"TROPICAL DISEASES" AS A REPRESENTATION OF THE PAST, NOT THE FUTURE

For the past three decades, much health social science research in international health has investigated "tropical diseases" as distinct phenomena. Although we have learned many valuable lessons from this research, thinking of these diseases as "tropical" has also constrained important avenues of research related to health inequality.[1] To begin with, the very representation of "tropical diseases" is problematic.[2] It is a carryover from colonial medicine, when diseases common to the tropics were responded to by military-style campaigns enabling economic and military expansion. But many of the diseases covered by the TDR program—such as TB, malaria, and dengue—were not and still are not limited to tropical countries.[3] They are associated with poverty and are health phenomena best viewed though a political-ecological lens that, as a cardinal rule, pays attention to the interaction between macro and micro factors impacting disease transmission. As such, diseases such as urban malaria, dengue, and TB serve as barometers for declining socioeconomic conditions, poor urban planning, and the state's inability to maintain essential services.

Labeling these health problems as "tropical diseases" naturalizes them as problems of the tropics and thereby depoliticizes them. They become associated with climate, as do other "tropical" diseases that reemerge as a result of dam projects, irrigation systems, deforestation, water scarcity, and the like. Calling these diseases "tropical" diverts attention from important ecosocial and political ecological dimensions of their transmission and distribution. Farmer (1999) has raised a similar point when drawing attention to the liberal use of the term *emergent disease* to describe diseases long present in the global South.[4] Labeling diseases as "emergent" or "reemergent" discounts the experience of populations who continue to suffer from these diseases.[5] Describing a disease as "emergent" often means that it currently affects populations that are more visible and valued. However, Farmer points out that this representation has helped marshal a sense of urgency in large bureaucracies and has served to refocus attention on old as well as newly identified diseases.

Morse's introduction of the term *emergent disease* in the 1990s was also part of a larger discourse advocating transdisciplinary programs for the study of factors that contribute to global "viral traffic" (King 2004).[6] Such research encompassed a "cell to society" perspective that examined urbanization, environmental degradation, war, migration, and so on in terms of their effect on the evolution and distribution of microorganisms (King 2004). The concept of emerging diseases contributed to a meeting of minds around topics promoting the study of political ecology and global health.

GLOBAL HEALTH VERSUS INTERNATIONAL HEALTH

What is a global health agenda, and how does it differ from an international health agenda? I have seen the term *international health* defined in many different ways, some of which tie international health to a rather narrow, linear, and highly medicalized agenda involving either the export of technical fixes from the global North to the South or medical missionary work. This is certainly not my understanding of the term, nor does it capture the intentions of most of the people I know who have entered this field. My own history is instructive. When I underwent training in international health in 1980 at Johns Hopkins School of Hygiene and Public Health, my fellow students and I certainly did not view the practice of international health as "tropical medicine." Trained in an era when community participation was a buzzword, our late-night discussions turned on how community health workers, drugstore attendants, and the like might deliver primary health care. We discussed the extent to which innovative programs in one place in the South might be applicable in the North among impoverished populations. We read Paolo Freire (e.g., 1970a, 1970b, 1973) and were inspired by experiments in community-based health programs conducted by the Bangladesh Rural

Advancement Committee (Rohde 2005) and by charismatic figures such as Rajnikant and Mabelle Arole in Jamkhed, India (Arole and Arole 1975, 1994). We crammed for exams in epidemiology and biostatistics but also thought about the social and political factors that threatened child survival. We discussed China's Barefoot Doctor program, Cuba's radically different health system, and whether the success of the smallpox campaign could be replicated. However, the purview of our thinking about global health responsibility and our future roles in international health was largely limited to programs funded by bilateral aid, a few foundations, and the World Health Organization (WHO). Moreover, we primarily focused our attention on the first epidemiological transition marked by communicable diseases in developing countries and child survival. Noncommunicable diseases were largely seen as problems of the second epidemiological transition, which affected middle- and high-income countries.

The world changed a lot in the next twenty-five years as a result of a confluence of factors. Neoliberal reform and structural adjustment policies were implemented, giving rise to the proliferation of NGOs. Greater attention was directed to the role of civil society in health and development. Improved telecommunications, the Internet, and the World Wide Web enabled rapid information sharing. The pandemic spread and dramatic impact of HIV/AIDS on households, communities, and nations demanded a global response and calls for accessible antiretroviral drugs and exceptions to patent laws. Widespread pesticide and drug resistance began to be documented, including the emergence of multidrug-resistant strains of TB. New partnerships, alliances, and networks were formed to address global health problems, and the role of philanthropic foundations and entrepreneurs focusing on high-profile problems grew. Better information about the burden of chronic diseases in developing countries became available, as well as the huge public health toll of tobacco. There was a marked increase in the offshore movement of clinical trials to developing countries, medical tourism, and transnational flows of medical personnel from the Third World to meet First World health care needs. A new era emerged that was characterized by a deeper, more expansive, and complicated biopolitics of global health,[7] as well as renewed thinking about the meaning of a "global community" that shares (among other things) common disease threats and a "pharmaceutical commons." The specter of pandemic diseases and bioterrorism drove home the message that nations must learn to cooperate or we all face grave consequences. And the maxim "disease respects no borders" was uttered so many times that it became a cliché. Paradoxically, fears of pandemics turned out to have a positive side. At a time of escalating global conflicts captured by prime-time television, concerns about global health appeared to be one of the few things that brought us together—other than global response to dramatic natural disasters.[8]

The term *global health* has come into favor for a number of reasons.[9] Three attempts at definition shed light on different aspects of global health. The Institute of Medicine, in its landmark publication *America's Vital Interest in Global Health* (IOM 1997), defines global health as "health problems, issues, and concerns that transcend national boundaries, may be influenced by circumstances or experiences in other countries, and are best addressed by cooperative actions and solutions" (p. 1). The report then draws attention to the fact that health problems and risk behaviors, as well as solutions to problems, cross borders. Lessons learned in one place may inform problem solving in other places for better or worse. The report also argues in no uncertain terms that it is in the United States' enlightened self-interest to support a global health agenda that contributes to citizen safety at home. This directly links global health to biosecurity. Another definition of global health is offered in a recent World Health Organization publication (Smith et al. 2006, based on Lee 2003). Global health is defined as "transnational impacts of globalization upon health determinants and health problems which are beyond the control of individual nations. Issues placed on the global health agenda include the inequities caused by patterns of international trade and investment, the effects of global climate change, the vulnerability of refugee populations, the marketing of harmful products by transnational corporations and the transmission of diseases resulting from travel between countries" (Smith et al. 2006:342). Brown and colleagues (2006) describe global health as taking into consideration the health needs of all peoples beyond the concerns of particular nations and note that the term acknowledges the growing importance of actors beyond governmental or intergovernmental organizations and agencies. For example, the media, internationally influential foundations, nongovernmental organizations, and transnational corporations have as much import as do nation-states.

Several key issues related to global health call for social science research attentive to biopolitics. They include the following seven high-priority research needs.

1. The need to better understand positive and negative outcomes of globalization on communicable and noncommunicable health problems, flows of health care resources, and health care personnel.[10]

2. The need to better appreciate the linkages between the global and the local, and the impact of political ecology at both the macro and micro levels.[11]

3. The need for better upstream as well as downstream (distal and proximal) surveillance of factors that contribute to global health problems and controversies and that demand forms of transnational debate, governance, and oversight.[12]

4. The need to address increased fragmentation in the global health landscape as a result of the lack of coordination between nation-states and an increasing number of nonstate participants in global health, requiring new forms of networking and governance.[13]

5. The need to critically assess the local impact of transnational techniques of governance associated with agenda-setting policies and programs, audit, and evaluation.[14]

6. The need to appreciate the role of new and emerging assemblages of people (networks, coalitions, social movements, etc.) drawn together around issues related to global health (and crosscutting issues like the environment, women and children's rights, etc.). These assemblages call attention to both the politics of responsibility and the politics of possibility.

7. A need for translational research (knowledge translation) to facilitate communication across interest groups and the expert-lay divide that is attentive to power relations and the power of social representations to frame thinking.

Let me suggest a few ways in which social science can contribute to an emerging global health agenda through research, as well as a few concepts that may serve as useful lenses to bring issues in need of investigation into better focus.

RECOGNIZE SYNDEMICS

Syndemics are synergistic, intertwined, and/or mutual, and reinforce health, environmental, social, and economic problems facing a population (Singer and Clair 2003).[15] As such, syndemics provide a useful conceptual framework for social science investigations into global health inequity that are sensitive to environments of risk and agents promoting risk, not just groups at risk and risky behaviors. In addition to marking disease clustering and interaction, the term *syndemic* also "points to the importance of social conditions in disease concentrations, interactions and consequences. In syndemics, the interaction of diseases or other health problems (e.g., malnutrition) commonly arises because of adverse social conditions (e.g., poverty, stigma-tization, oppressive social relationships) that put socially devalued groups at heightened risk" (Singer et al. 2006:2011). Attention is drawn to not just causal but also reciprocal relationships that prove decisive in determin-ing the patterns of distribution of disease (Jing 2006).

The concept of "syndemic" is best grasped through example. For one thing, there is a mutually reinforcing relationship between poverty, unem-ployment, HIV, and MDR-TB. A syndemic set of relationships related to TB might look like the following: (1) poverty leads to work migration far from home; (2) loneliness, the drudgery of the job, and being paid every few weeks lends itself to binge drinking and risky sex in an environment where prostitution flourishes; (3) this leads to sexually transmitted infections such as HIV; (4) rising rates of HIV lead to corresponding rising rates of TB; (5) poor adherence to TB medications occurs after a few months of home-based treatment (when symptoms abate) among patients who return to migrant labor far from medicine distribution sites; (6) poor management of those seeking treatment for HIV and TB leads to increases in drug-resistant TB; and so on.

Another set of syndemic relationships might occur in a periurban slum where water supply and waste disposal are less than adequate. The relationship might look like this: (1) poor water supply leads to both a high prevalence of diarrheal diseases and the need to store water in containers; (2) these containers become breeding grounds for vectors of urban malaria and dengue fever; (3) poor trash removal and the accumulation of trash in vacant urban lots foster additional mosquito breeding sites and poor neigh-borhood hygiene; (4) poor neighborhood hygiene increases the prevalence of both vector-borne diseases and diarrheal disease; (5) poor health facili-ties and the presence of practitioners with questionable training lead to diarrhea and fever being treated symptomatically, contributing to further infection; and so on.

Singer and colleagues (2006) provide several other examples of syn-demics gleaned from the literature that result from interactive sets of envi-ronmental risk factors and/or risky behaviors that predispose the poor to illnesses and exposure to diseases of poverty or sources of embodied risk at one point in time, influencing the health status of individuals or communi-ties in different ways sometime in the future.[16]

A third type of syndemic involves multiple sites of harm and depen-dency. A good example of this type of syndemic would be the propaga-tion (engineering) of tobacco use in developing (and developed) countries.

Dependency on tobacco is experienced at the site of (1) individual bodies, where consumers are harmed when the product is used as directed; (2) the land, where pesticide and fertilizer render the land dependent on tobacco cultivation; and (3) the state, where governments become dependent on tobacco tax dollars, lobbying, and contributions (Nichter 2003b).

The tobacco syndemic is informative for two other reasons. First, tobacco not only causes illness but also exacerbates existing illnesses and causes diseases once treated to relapse. I am currently involved in tobacco-related research projects in India and Indonesia (Nichter 2006b) that focus on TB and diabetes patients. In both cases, smoking is common among men, and both patients and ex-patients are not forewarned about how dangerous tobacco is for their health. In the case of diabetes, tobacco use results in serious complications and a much higher risk of mortality.[17] In the case of TB, tobacco use is related to a significantly higher risk of relapse.[18]

Tobacco is instructive for a second reason. Tobacco use is not just a lifestyle choice, it is a behavior aggressively promoted by a global industry that profits off the poor with little concern about the damage it causes. Tobacco marketing is the first global health issue that has resulted in a global effort to govern an industry through the Framework Convention, an intervention to which health social scientists contributed (Kaufman and Nichter 2001).[19]

What is appealing about a syndemic approach to health social science research is both its explicit emphasis on examining connections between health and development and its attention to routes of transmission that affect clusters of interrelated health problems.[20] Prevention and treatment of syndemics require control of component afflictions as well as recognition of the relationships that tie those afflictions together and synergistically amplify their negative consequences. Addressing syndemics requires a systems approach to problem solving. It demands that one look beyond the characteristics of individuals engaging in risky behavior and the identification of cultural barriers to the role of structural violence in the forms that poverty has taken.[21] These demands entail a close examination of problems the state faces in attending to the basic needs of its citizens while trying to break out of a cycle of poverty, global processes fostering inequity, and health system failure and the shortsightedness of existing health interventions (Paluzzi and Farmer 2005).

A syndemic approach to thinking about health inequity is promising but in need of further elaboration. We must consider under what conditions using a syndemic orientation is appropriate and inappropriate, as well as what advantages and limitations are associated with doing so. To study syndemics, one must coordinate the efforts of scholars from different disciplines and activists and learn to think in a transdisciplinary manner. This is a formidable challenge, but I believe we are ready to embrace it. Additionally, we must consider ways of involving community members in participatory problem solving so that they recognize syndemic connections and find solutions.

New Approaches to Epidemiology

Let me draw attention to three promising approaches to epidemiology that call for social science research: ecosocial epidemiology, life-span epidemiology, and popular epidemiology. I briefly describe each, and then introduce social science concepts that may contribute to their implementation. In the case of life-span epidemiology, I introduce the concepts of local biology and life-course studies, and in the case of popular epidemiology, I discuss how participatory GIS may prove useful in fostering participatory research.

Ecosocial Epidemiology

Ecosocial epidemiology studies the unnatural distribution of disease; like syndemic analysis, it looks beyond proximal risk factors to more-distal social and political economic factors that predispose sections of a population to ill health. Krieger (2001) describes ecosocial epidemiology as adding two core research questions to the discipline. First, who (not just what) is responsible for disease distribution and health inequity in a population? Second, in what ways are population-based patterns of health and disease biological expressions of social relations experienced in multiple contexts?[22]

Ecosocial epidemiology calls for a biosocial assessment of health problems that examines both spatial and temporal connections. Four core concepts underlie an ecosocial epidemiology assessment (Krieger 2001). First, material conditions and social relations come to be embodied throughout the course of our lives.[23] Second, pathways of embodiment involve the interplay between the "constraints and possibilities of our biology, as shaped by our species evolutionary history, our ecological context, and individual histories" and "societal arrangements of power and property and contingent patterns of production, consumption, and reproduction" that shape individual and community biosocial trajectories (Krieger 2001:672). Third, the interplay among exposure, susceptibility, and resistance is cumulative and occurs in nested contexts (individual, neighborhood, regional, national, and international settings) seen as ecological niches. Lastly, an ecosocial epidemiology assessment calls for examination of what theoretical frameworks (assumptions, representations, etc.) epidemiologists and other scientists have used (and ignored) thus far to explain social inequalities in health. Issues related to accountability, governmentality, and agency are to be rendered visible.

These concepts are useful lenses for health social scientists investigating the types of syndemic relations described above by Singer and colleagues (2006). Krieger's research has focused on health disparity in North America, but her model has wide applicability in global health. I see it as particularly useful in the study of health trajectories related to cumulative risk from both material conditions (poverty, environmental, and occupational risks) and social relations (racism, uncertainty, fear of violence, and so on). Two other social science concepts provide useful lenses in the study of syndemics: local biology and life-course biology.

Life-Span Perspective

Local biology is a term coined by Lock (1993) to refer to the manner in which one's bodily experience is mutually constituted by biology and culture. This concept is distinct from the concept of ethnophysiology introduced in chapter 2. The concept of local biology invites us to consider the mindful-body of those inhabiting other life worlds, as distinct from how universal biological states are interpreted in different "cultures." Culture and biology exist in an ongoing feedback relationship (Lock and Kaufert 2001). As such, Lock argues, biology cannot be understood separately from culture, and cultural responses to illness cannot be understood without consideration of how biology molds and contains the subjective experience of individuals and the creation of cultural interpretations (Lock 1993).[24] The latter point is important, as it acknowledges that the body is an active agent that persists as a localized site of individuality responsive to environments and history. As Worthman notes, there is a dual or reciprocal nature of embodiment that is driven by developmental processes that by design rely on environmental inputs to shape the course of development from the molecular level upward. In this sense, "all biology is 'local' and ontogeny is to some degree indeterminate, contingent on proximal interactions of individual and environment" (Worthman 1999:52).

Lock primarily employs the concept of local biology to investigate aging and the embodied experience of menopause in different societies. I see broader contributions of this concept in the study of dietary habits and their health and development sequellae, the experience and management of pain, childbirth practices, circadian rhythms related to patterns of work, and the biocultural response to pharmaceuticals.[25] The concept of local biology complements Krieger's conception of embodiment and leads us to rethink the relationship between biology and culture as mediated in place and time by the material conditions of life and social relations that cumulatively affect a person over the course of one's life.

Global health research needs to adopt a life-span perspective that is attentive to "local biology" and is at once biocultural and biopolitical. Where present writing on local biology falls short is in describing what actually happens within the site of the body, beyond vague reference to the way in which culture affects the endocrine system. This is where biocultural anthropology can assist us. A life-span approach to the study of human biology (adopted by biocultural anthropologists) and a complementary life course (adopted by chronic-disease epidemiologists) add another layer to the analysis of embodiment and trajectories of health and illness. Life-span biology investigates the cumulative effects of environmental, sociocultural, and psychosocial influences on individual biology over a person's entire life span (Leidy 1996; Worthman and Kohrt 2005).[26] Proponents of life-span biology examine how experiences at one time of life (and one's developmental cycle) carry over and affect one's health at other stages of life. Notably, this approach takes into account differential periods of growth and developmental cycles, including critical periods for development; biological trade-offs, compensation, and catching up; processes of recuperation and resilience; and the consequences of intermittent and sustained biological insults and psychosocial stress. "Embodiment" in Krieger's sense of the term is brought into sharper focus by viewing the impact of stressors at particular stages of life as well as cumulatively across a life span. Such long-term consequences of acute insults studied by biocultural anthropologists include shorter gestation and poor weight gain among pregnant women, low birth weight among babies, loss of bone density, and high blood pressure, to name a few. Life-span studies also lead us to consider the agency of populations exposed to cyclical challenges to existence. They demonstrate, for example, how seasonal patterns of illness, fluctuations in food availability, and exposure to danger (such as violence or warfare) can influence reproductive decision making.[27]

Life-span–life-course research suggests that states of malnutrition and communicable diseases experienced early in life predispose populations to chronic illness later in life (Godfrey and Barker 2000; Henry and Ulijaszek 1996; Kuh and Ben-Shlomo 2004; O'Connor et al. 2006).[28] This adds an important dimension to public health thinking about a third epidemiological transition generally characterized by emerging and reemerging diseases related to accelerated globalization and antibiotic resistance (Barrett et al.

1998).[29] By demonstrating the need to consider communicable diseases as factors influencing noncommunicable disease trajectories, life-span studies find themselves at the center of a heated policy debate involving how best to expend limited funds to reduce health inequity (Gwatkin et al. 1999; Reddy 1999).[30] Let me suggest how social scientists adopting life-span and household production of health perspectives might inform this debate through their research.[31]

Longitudinal data finding a relationship between previous communicable disease and chronic illness suggest that unless governments do a better job of preventing and managing communicable diseases (and addressing undernutrition), they will bear the fruits of their inaction for decades, not just years. With increased chronic illness comes more, and longer-term, financial burden for the state health care system. This in turn leaves less time and fewer resources for other public health initiatives. For families, the chronic disease of a parent has far-reaching consequences. It may well mean trade-offs between expenditures on the chronically ill and the investment in children. This in turn translates into more communicable disease in children. Studies of the impact of chronic disease on the household production of health might further drive home the point that for every adult breadwinner who becomes ill, many others suffer. Their illness reduces their carrying capacity (their ability to support others young and old).[32] Instead of conducting body counts on the afflicted or assessing DALYs lost, we need better ways of accounting for the impact of the ill on household units. Such data will allow us to see syndemic relationships that involve the chronic illness or disability of a family member predisposing children to acute and later chronic illness, reproducing a vicious cycle of ill health. The chronically ill also have compromised immune systems, which render them more vulnerable to infection and communicable diseases.

One further contribution of life-span studies will be to measure the impact of public health interventions not just in terms of what they were immediately intended to do but in terms of emergent positive and negative effects. For example, Aaby (1995) has demonstrated that children given measles vaccinations are not only protected against measles but also, because of a more generalized immune response, appear to have higher rates of overall survival. Life-span studies might also reveal negative outcomes that emerge from public health interventions or from patterns of medicine-taking behavior through time.

Popular Epidemiology

The aim of popular epidemiology is to engage the public in problem solving through public participation in epidemiology (Brown 1987, 1997). Engagement here refers to something more than public participation in conventional epidemiology. What is emphasized is the critical assessment of social and structural factors that directly and indirectly predispose populations to disease and disability. As described by Brown (1997), popular epidemiology encourages a critical approach to problem solving that involves social movements and utilizes political and judicial approaches to remedy and challenge basic assumptions of traditional epidemiology, risk assessment, and public health regulation. To date, most studies adopting the term *popular epidemiology* have focused on environmental degradation and public responses to toxic waste contamination, but the concept has broad application and encompasses a fair amount of community activism already engaged in by social scientists. The hallmark of popular epidemiology, at least as I have been attempting to practice it, involves providing community representatives with enough basic knowledge of scientific investigation to enable them to participate in dialogue about what research needs to be conducted to solve community problems. This includes a consideration of key variables, outcome measures, and samples selected for comparison (Nichter 2006a). In so doing, science is demystified, democratized, and made more "community near." Involving the community in a process of participatory research is being advocated within the field of epidemiology (Leung et al. 2004; Schwab and Syme 1997) and involves sharing power as well as promoting an exchange of ideas and a weighing of alternatives.

For community-based participatory research to work, many issues need to be addressed and the process of research needs to be facilitated by cultural brokers. Calnan (2004) has identified some of the key issues: how does one choose community representatives; to what extent are those chosen attentive to the views of both mainstream and disadvantaged groups; what are the most effective ways of canvassing community views and engaging the public in dialogue; to what extent are community representatives willing and able to be involved in decision making? Social scientists have a track record in investigating such issues.[33] In addition, they are in a position to facilitate dialogue between four parties: conventional public health and medical researchers, members of the lay community and its different factions, members of communities of practitioners (biomedical, indigenous-complementary),[34] and policy makers. Let me next suggest one promising method for engaging community members in problem solving.

One promising way of engaging local communities in the assessment of syndemic relationships and raising their consciousness is through the use of participatory mapping, an activity that brings community members together to view problems in new ways by testing out possible linkages.[35] This is a visual exercise that may vary in sophistication from "low-tech" paper maps used to solicit community perspectives and commentary to "high-tech" spatial analyses designed to reveal patterns and layers of inequality demonstrated through data overlays. For example, participatory global information systems research (PGIS)[36] might use mapping to facilitate the visualization of possible risk factors contributing to a problem (or syndemic) by displaying areas with higher and lower prevalence along with overlays of data that draw attention to such things as

- The populations inhabiting these spatial grids (e.g., by class, ethnic group, caste)[37]
- The clustering of several types of illness or health problems
- The presence or absence of risk factors that scientists and/or the community associate with the problem
- The presence or absence of resources, such as the availability of clean water
- Common routes of disease transmission or conditions that favor the proliferation of breeding sites of disease vectors
- Resource distribution pathways and hindrances
- The availability of government services (such as trash collection) and health services
- Behavioral patterns that expose particular types of people to risk factors at particular times of the day, such as types of work[38]
- Barriers to effective health care (material or political)

Health disparities become readily apparent when maps are used as tools to view interrelated sets of problems. In concert with the principles of popular epidemiology, community members contribute to (if not drive) the selection of information to be collected and displayed on maps in keeping with local perceptions of proximate and more-distal factors contributing to the problem. Problems associated with the presence or absence of factors that the community has asked to be mapped may prompt community discussion of mappable syndemic relationships. Exposure to spatially and temporally mapped data has the capacity to move thinking about risk and vulnerability from questions about "why me" to "why here" (Monmonier 1997) and to visualize bigger-picture issues that may be contributing to health disparities and/or patterns of acute and chronic illnesses.

Two other uses of maps that may enable biosocial problem solving are worth highlighting. First, maps may be used to display perceived risk factors that have an impact on risk judgments and behavior (Slovic 2000; Slovic et al. 2002). Oaks and Herr-Harthorn (2003) have pointed out that risk perceptions may prove to be a better indicator of behavior or behavior change than are risk factors identified by experts, because laypersons act on perceived risks—at least the ones they realistically think they can easily reduce. Possible impacts of risk perceptions that might be examined would include behaviors associated with increased risk vigilance, risk amplification, stigma, or indifference. A second use of maps might be to track exposure to waves of risk messages and their impacts on populations (Freudenburg 2003; Pidgeon et al. 2003). Such research might examine the impact of health-education messages, newspaper coverage, and advertising campaigns (for such things as vector control–related products) on health and health care–seeking behavior. This might enable a better understanding of not only whether exposure to messages translates into behavior change but also how and for how long, and whether messages directed toward one health problem increase vigilance for other health problems. Further, if spatial representations of local data are treated as in process, then local responses and perspectives to map iterations can be included in a dynamic mapping process (Merrick 2003; Weiner and Harris 2003).

For example, two of my graduate students recently created maps of elder-health survey results (conducted in Comitan, Chiapas, Mexico) that were used to engage locals (researchers, nurses, etc.) in a dialogue about health problems in the community (Glantz and McMahan 2007). The maps were presented as incomplete snapshots that triggered discussion of the conditions on the ground, with discussion generating other factors that needed to be taken into account and issues that extended far beyond the scope of the maps. For the NGO that brought together the participants, presentation examples of the capacity for a spatial perspective catalyzed a productive discussion of how global information systems might be employed to look at a number of other problems important to community members.

What does it take to engage in participatory mapping? To begin with, health social scientists must ensure that the full range of local and expert representations of health problems, resources, and solutions are transferred to the map. Local knowledge is by definition spatially located (within the community), and incorporation of local ideas as a sort of locally available database (Carver 2003) can help transcend the boundaries between expert and locally derived information (as local knowledge is incorporated into regional or even national maps). Those creating maps must in turn be aware of the politics and social relations involved with data presentation (Pickles 1995).[39] A key challenge will be to employ both qualitative and quantitative data judiciously to address local and expert lines of reasoning relating health disparity and locality to perceptions of disease transmission generated by studies of lay epidemiology, the political ecology of health, health care resource distribution, and so on. Those engaged in this research exercise will need to go beyond the easily mapped routine data sets that tend to promote instrumental rationalism by framing issues in predictable ways. They will need to do more than think outside the box: they will need to question the very boxes, those representations and conceptual frameworks that they have become accustomed to thinking within (Nichter 2007).

Transnational Governance

Ethnographies of the "technologies of governance" are a much-needed part of an anthropology of emerging health policy (Castro and Singer 2004) central to global health. Five types of governance projects related to global health demand serious social science attention. First, health social scientists need to work along with their colleagues in allied disciplines (international relations, political science and international law, etc.) and examine both the persuasive arguments for and the contexts in which transnational agreements and treaties related to global health are supported. What sets of issues, stakeholders, and social processes have been involved in successful and unsuccessful attempts at diplomacy and governance? And how far have global health agreements been implemented on the ground once signed? Second, social scientists need to assist in the collection of data documenting the necessity for better coordination, governance, and oversight in global health given shifts in global health participation and leadership. Third, social scientists need to play a critical role in assessing the positive and negative ramifications of agenda setting policy and programs that involve audit and demand compliance. Fourth, they need to become more actively involved in surveillance and monitoring activities as researchers who have their boots on the ground and their fingers on the pulse of local communities. And fifth, they need to provide insights into how best to work on preparedness in contexts of decentralized government.

Identify Lessons from Present-Day Global Governance Projects

There are important lessons to be learned about social and political processes that enable and obstruct transnational cooperative agreements involving both immediate threats to biosecurity and slower-acting global health threats that loom large but do not have the fanfare of an immediate crisis. Two recent cases of cooperative agreement stand out as particularly instructive. First, the growing threat of emerging microbial illnesses has given rise to new transnational agreements that far exceed former efforts of global health governance. In response to a possible SARS pandemic, the World Health Assembly (the policy-making branch of the World Health Organization) adopted a set of International Health Regulations (IHR) in 2005 that significantly surpassed previous IHRs (Aginam 2002, 2005; Fidler 2003, 2004b, 2005; Gostin 2004; Hardiman 2003; Taylor 2002; Tucker 2005).[40] Indeed, Fidler (2005:326) has described these new regulations as "one of the most radical and far reaching changes in international law on public health since the beginning of international health cooperation in the mid-nineteenth century." The regulations reshaped the boundaries of global governance and redefined the World Health Organization's role in global health surveillance and global threat response (Gostin 2005).[41] Notably, the regulations were approved unanimously despite the fact that issues of national sovereignty were clearly at stake.

A second extraordinary case of transnational cooperation is the World Health Organization's Framework Convention on Tobacco Control (WHO 2003; see also www.who.int/tobacco/framework/en), signed thus far by 168 nations and ratified by 145 nations. The treaty provides the basic tools for countries to enact comprehensive tobacco control legislation, including a ban on advertising, sponsorship, and promotion; the placement of large graphic warning labels on cigarette packs; and the regulation of the content of tobacco products. This landmark global health treaty was the result of the combined efforts of many parties beyond the World Health Organization (committed government diplomats, NGOs and advocacy groups, tobacco control and international health experts, etc.) that joined forces and prevailed against a strong tobacco lobby (Roemer et al. 2005). It is an explicit attempt to counter the globalization of the tobacco epidemic through a reconfiguration of health governance that addresses corporate greed (Collin et al. 2002).

Social science lessons of value to health diplomacy and future global health efforts are to be learned from both of these, as well as from other cases of successful and unsuccessful efforts to promote cooperative action, build coalitions, and get important global health issues on the table (Novotny and

Carlin 2005).[42] Important to study will be ways in which states and international organizations enlist the assistance of advocacy groups, NGOs, professional groups, and so forth, to achieve the critical mass needed to carry forward global health agendas. Equally important to examine will be the way in which nonstate actors (foundations, NGOs, advocacy and professional groups, and the like) advance an agenda that is acted on nationally and by global health bodies.

Document the Need for Governance

Social scientists need to document the real-world ramifications of fragmentation in the way global health initiatives are implemented (Walt and Buse 2000). While laudatory, many initiatives promoted by nonstate participants in global health are poorly coordinated and affect national health programs in a negative or unpredictable fashion. Fidler (2007) has aptly referred to this situation as a kind of global health anarchy in need of governance, with many of the players preferring to remain independent actors. At this point in time, a few large private foundations and many small private donors are contributing impressive resources to global health efforts. In most cases, these new world participants in global health are allocating funds for particular high-visibility health problems (HIV/AIDS, malaria, TB, etc.) and the pursuit of much-needed medical technologies. These funds can inadvertently divert attention away from other important health priorities by siphoning off manpower from government programs to build new infrastructures necessary to execute vertical programs. Such programs may also take up the time of key personnel in ministries of health.

The impact of temporary surges of financial support for vertical programs on the broader primary health care agendas of host countries needs to be carefully assessed. Health-systems analysis could inform policies to enhance private-public coordination and ensure that one problem (or population) is not addressed at the expense of others. One can only hope that foundations have the foresight to employ social scientists to carry out health-systems ethnographies such as that called for by Pfeiffer (2003b) following his assessment of NGO employment impact on national health care systems (described in chapter 7).

Audit: Critical Assessment Required

Among the most effective technologies of governance are forms of audit and evaluation that demand particular ways of representing and solving problems.[43] The term *audit culture* (Hopwood and Miller 1997; Shore and

Wright 1999; Strathern 1996) describes institutional governance exercised through the use of templates that ensure accountability and measure efficiency, quality assurance, and compliance. Audits serve the needs of management and can result in the smooth running of complex programs. They can also foster bogus accounting, reduce the opportunity for creative problem solving (thinking out of the box), and decrease teamwork when individual targets are introduced. I have observed all of this in India, where I have worked alongside primary health workers who spent more than one-third of their time on paperwork. The numbers they were required to produce were of little use in health care planning, the primary purpose of the exercise being to keep everyone in line.

Programs that adopt many layers of audit can stifle creativity. The global DOTS Stop TB program is an example of one such "branded" global health program (Ogden et al. 2003). The program became so rigid in its implementation that it invited criticism from many quarters. Justified on the basis of efficiency, a network of audits and auditors that paid little attention to local input hindered the program. In need of study by social scientists are how audits are used, by whom, and with what ramifications. How can standardization (where needed) be balanced with innovation such that programs are open to tailoring?[44] Also in need of study are ways of ensuring accountability while rewarding local creativity.

Surveillance

Surveillance is a cornerstone of global health and a practice that needs to be conducted reflexively. Surveillance of diseases and resistance to medications are fundamental to global health. So too, I would argue, is surveillance of clinical trials carried out across borders, as well as the monitoring of industries such as tobacco, infant formula, and pharmaceuticals. All of these industries have been regulated, yet they have a history of finding ways to promote products in a less-than-ethical manner and to engage in misrepresentation (Consumers International 2006).[45] Social scientists who monitor behavior on the ground and those who "study up" (industry, organizations, policy) can inform advocacy groups and join networks that monitor the marketing activities of national and multinational companies selling products that contribute to the global burden of ill health. Global tobacco and pharmaceutical oversight networks already exist on the World Wide Web (Global Link and E-Drug) and invite participation from social scientists. Social scientists monitoring these industries either by intent or by serendipity need to have clear lines of communication to professional or advocacy groups that can pass on sensitive information to watchdog groups and oversight committees while protecting sources.[46]

Beyond monitoring shifting trends in health-related consumer behavior, social scientists can also assist their colleagues in public health by monitoring public response to health messages and interventions. Such monitoring can serve as a check against misperception, rumor, and in extreme cases, epidemic fear. They might also assist colleagues in the field of infectious disease ecology by monitoring political-economic factors and policies having ecological consequences fostering zoonotic diseases (Wilcox and Gubler 2005).[47]

*Implementing Global Health Programs in Contexts
of Decentralized Government*

Another major challenge for global health governance is the implementation of global health programs in countries currently experiencing decentralized political rule.[48] I am currently involved in an H5N1 avian flu study in Indonesia that speaks to this point (Padmawati and Nichter 2008). Indonesia has experienced a dramatic process of devolution of power over the past eight years, moving from highly centralized to very decentralized governance.[49] Irrespective of national avian flu control guidelines agreed upon by Indonesia's national government in consultation with the World Health Organization, district-level officials decide whether and when to implement avian flu control procedures. Actions are based on what priority they assign to avian flu given the presence or absence of human death in their district, funds available, other pressing problems (such as earthquakes), public opinion, and the influence of the poultry industry. Given Indonesia's vast human and poultry populations, spread out across more than seven thousand islands, it would be virtually impossible for the national government to coordinate a sustained bird and human monitoring program without the direct assistance of local authorities. Therefore, how does one coordinate local preparedness programs for emergent diseases such as avian flu that are poorly understood locally and not of immediate concern when people are not dying in their location? Can avian flu programs be linked to other preparedness programs or be taken up by local organizations that already exist?[50] Social science research into issues such as these will demand an assessment of popular representations of the disease in focus, local trust in national programs and the press,[51] political issues involved with local decision making and power sharing, and the politics of who controls funds and how they are allocated for disease control. Accurate assessments call for ethnographic studies of social organization as well as illness ethnographies.[52]

Health social scientists from the North also have an important global health research agenda at home. Health care policies involving "medical citizenship" (policies of entitlement and deservedness) define us as a society.[53] They articulate what we deem to be the basic rights of citizens, what human rights are recognized for undocumented immigrants, and who gets excluded or sacrificed when health resources are rationed or restricted.[54] Critiques that address the ramifications of exclusionary policies are called for so that policies can better address both extant humanitarian ideals and "enlightened self-interest," which entails serving one's own long-term self-interests by attending to the immediate needs of others (Yach and Bettcher 1998a, 1998b).[55] I end this book with a few reflections on types of social science research that could contribute to both.

Humanitarian groups are already presenting to us images of human suffering. Visual representations of the poor appear routinely on television and in the press at home and in the world. These have at once raised the consciousness of the public and desensitized the public. Health social scientists need to contribute to efforts that make suffering personal and to promote a deeper sense of how we as global citizens can assist others in need. But we need to do more than document suffering. Another important job is rendering visible how social institutions, industry, powerful leaders, and ordinary citizens contribute to human suffering and global ill health through their actions and inactions. At issue here is more than just a call for social scientists to play a more proactive role in policy; we must look beyond occupational and environmental health investigations into exploitive and disease-producing practices that are related to the extraction of resources and manufacturing of goods. The complicity of ordinary consumer citizens in transnational processes leading to global ill health needs to be made more apparent. Further, "ordinary citizens" need to better understand how their purchase of goods, investment in companies, and support of government policies set up the conditions for global ill health. They need to visualize how suffering at a distance in Russian prisons, the slums of Haiti, and Ugandan refugee camps leads to global health problems that will affect them in their lifetime.

Better-informed citizens may vote more responsibly. They also have a choice and a way of engaging in subpolitics through everyday actions (Beck 1996; Holzer and Sørensen 2003). Subpolitics entails political engagement outside and beyond the institutions of the political system of nation-states. It involves, for example, conscientious consumption (e.g., support of free trade coffee) that holds companies accountable for their international trade policies, labor practices (e.g., in relation to child labor), and investment practices (Gereffi et al. 2001).[56] Consumer activism can be mobilized through the exercise of purchasing power.[57] Toward that end, research is needed that renders global commodity chains (Gereffi and Korzeniewicz 1994; Hartwick 2000; Hughes and Reimer 2004) visible and is attentive to the health and well-being of all parties involved in complex global production—consumption feedback loops.[58] Research is also needed on "global health care chains,"[59] that is, transnational flows of doctors, nurses, and medical technicians from developing to developed countries, resulting in health care crises in home countries and brain drain.[60] The global ramifications of reducing predicted shortfalls in health personnel in the North by the importation of health care providers from developing countries needs to be made transparent and the subject of policy debates (Cooper and Aiken 2006; Garrett 2007).[61]

Health social scientists can bring a global health perspective to medical citizenship debates and help clarify why it is in a country's enlightened self-interest to provide health care to impoverished populations at home and abroad. Compelling data that link globalization (global flows of people, goods, etc.) to disease transmission and the recent threats of SARS and avian flu has made it increasingly clear that what happens in the "tropics" affects what happens in Boston, New York, Des Moines, Los Angeles, and Tucson (Guerrant 1998). The very forces of globalization that expand markets bring populations into greater contact with microbial threats while accelerating social and economic processes, such as urbanization and environmental degradation, which provide microbes with fertile conditions for human-to-human transmission (Fidler 2004a, 2004b).[62] Who better than social scientists working in concert with their public health colleagues to raise the consciousness of the public about global patterns of ill health and to challenge rhetoric that makes it appear that we are doing more to solve global health problems than we currently are?[63] Social scientists need to be on the front line of global health research examining the socioeconomic and political-ecological conditions favoring emergent diseases and syndemics. We (they) also need to monitor social representations guiding global health interventions, the metrics used to evaluate development and public health success, and the impact of development dollars and global policies on the ground.

How may we (social scientists) engage the public other than through ethnographies? We also have a role to play in knowledge management and advancing translational research on how best to explain science in clear and understandable ways to lay populations overseas as well as at home so that dialogue is possible.[64] For example, research on factors leading to drug-resistant strains of disease needs to be translated for the public (drug-store owners, private practitioners, etc.) in such a way that the "tragedy of the pharmaceutical commons" (Baquero and Campos 2003; Foster and Grundmann 2006) is understood and made relevant.[65] Drug unavailability for the poor in India or the Philippines, Haiti or Peru, Detroit or Los Angeles needs to be tied to the likelihood that drug-resistant pathogens will circulate around the globe. Translational research engages conceptual translation involving the identification (and pretesting) of appropriate imagery, of appropriate ways to present statistics to local populations, of what comparisons do and do not matter to local populations, and of what facts the public finds evocative. Translational research need not only be directed to the lay population but should also be directed to policy makers. If humanitarian appeals fall on deaf ears, then the translation of human suffering into dollar costs (and other costs) needs to be calculated and projected through time, bearing in mind both a life-span perspective and a household production of health perspective.

Human rights and enlightened self-interest must start at home and be directed to the provision of basic medical care to underserved populations, be they the working poor who cannot afford health insurance or undocumented migrant workers. Debates about extending rights to such populations need to be reframed from "how much this will cost the nation now" to "how much will *not* providing basic care *now* cost the nation in the future, given chronic- and infectious-disease projections." By helping frame national health care priorities in global health terms, health social scientists can play a role in promoting a global sense of biosociality.[66] Such a biosociality should be based on a recognition of common risks, as well as an enlightened appreciation that the bodies and experiences of "others" may hold the key to a better understanding of health problems that potentially affect us all.

This brings me to my last point, an acknowledgment of two types of biovalue. Biovalue is a concept that has largely been used in the social sciences to refer to the commodification of bodies, body parts (from genes to organs), and distinct strains of disease in a global market where new technologies have given them new exchange value.[67] Lessons learned at the site of the body also have a biosocial value that needs to be more fully appreciated.[68] Those living in other societies have much to teach us about local biology; resilience, immune function, and susceptibility (McDade 2005); ecology, migration, and evolutionary biology;[69] poverty, adaptability, and the life-span consequences of biological trade-offs;[70] and the far-reaching effects of defective modernization, from dietary change to global warming

(Epstein 2000).[71] In a similar manner, our own experiences have biosocial value. As social scientists, we have a role to play in rendering visible to those in developing countries the positive and negative outcomes of adopting a more Western lifestyle at this time of rapid globalization. My point is that a two-way exchange of information is fundamental to global health, and social scientists have a central role to play in facilitating this process of exchange and the critical thinking that will inevitably accompany it.[72] Global health must be built on mutual respect for different types of knowledge, a common desire for discovery, an exchange of ideas about possible futures, and a sense of health as a global public good.[73] It demands cooperation that comes not just from fear but from hope and a common sense of purpose.

NOTES

1. For example, the research agenda of the Special Programme for Research and Training in Tropical Diseases (TDR) has become far more biosocial and attentive to the study of "tropical disease" as a product of poverty in the last five years (Farmer and Becerra 2001). In 2000, TDR formed a Social, Economic, and Behavioral Committee (SEB). One of the main objectives of the SEB has been to fund a new generation of projects that look at the impact of social forces on inequality and the distribution of disease.

2. On the history of tropical medicine and its relation to colonization and governance, see Arnold 1988, 1996, 1997; Harrison 2005; Marks 1996; Stepan 1998, 2001; Worboys 1976, 1993, 1996. For an even broader historical consideration of the "tropical" as imaginative geography related to aesthetic, scientific, and political projects, see collections of essays edited by Driver and Yeoh (2000), Driver and Martins (2005), and Stepan (2001).

3. The ecology of tropical countries is conducive to the life cycle of particular disease vectors (Sattenspiel 2000) and presents unique development challenges (Sachs 2001). What I am calling attention to is the way in which portraying infectious and vector-borne disease as tropical naturalizes the problem and deflects attention away from human factors that foster environmental conditions favoring the spread of these diseases. It neglects the history of medicine and lessons learned about the control of malaria in Europe (see *Parassitologia* 1999) and diverts attention from the potential for diseases such as dengue to become epidemic in the West. Indeed, the emergence of vector-borne diseases such as West Nile virus and dengue in the United States illustrate the shortcomings of grouping vector-borne diseases under the rubric of "tropical." In the future, diseases currently considered tropical and emergent diseases associated with developing countries (such as avian flu) are likely to spread globally. Global transmission will be fostered by patterns of migration, increasing long-distance mobility and trade, the social disruption of war and conflict, human-induced global changes, and so forth (Weiss and McMichael 2004).

4. The U.S. Centers for Disease Control and Prevention (CDC 1994) defines emerging infectious diseases as "diseases of infectious origin whose incidence in humans has increased within the past two decades or threatens to increase in the near future."

5. I would argue that we should use the term *emergent* with greater specificity. For diseases that reappear in a cyclical manner, I am partial to using the term *cyclical* to describe them and to call attention to those factors that influence cycles. I prefer the term *resurgent* to describe diseases that are being reported more frequently but are not nascent. The term

resurgent refers to the revival of that which had remained latent. I reserve the term *emergent* for diseases (or strains of disease) that are nascent, such as avian flu H5N1.

6. Morse, a virologist and immunologist, followed a line of research established by disease ecologists dating back to Lederberg (Anderson 2004) and argued that most new or emerging viruses were the result of traffic patterns that gave viruses new highways. He advocated for a science of new traffic patterns, part biology and part social science (Morse 1991, 1993).

7. Describing global or world health as biopolitical is not new (Aginam 2005; Bashford 2006; Fidler 2001). Global health is biopolitical whether it is envisioned as an end worked toward in the name of human rights or a means toward larger diplomatic ends such as biosecurity, protecting trade relations, and so on.

8. However, global threats of disease also render visible the pharmaceutical divide that exists between those states and populations that do and do not have access to stocks of lifesaving drugs (such as Tamiflu in the case of H5N1 avian flu).

9. See Brown et al. 2006 for a history of how the term *global health* has been used by different interest groups and came to be favored by the World Health Organization (WHO) for political reasons having to do with a repositioning of its role. The term *global* was occasionally used before the 1990s by the WHO to describe such initiatives as the "global malaria eradication program" (mid-1950s) and in international health documents describing the global population problem (1970s). In the 1990s, the term began being used differently. As noted by Brown and colleagues, the WHO attempted to use emerging concern with "global health" as an organizational strategy that placed the organization in a coordinating and leadership position at a time when its leadership role was being challenged. A coordinating oversight and governance role for the WHO has been called for by scholar-activists given the changing global health landscape, emerging health problems that demand global solutions, and new sets of actors, networks, and partnerships involved in transnational health initiatives. See, for example, compelling arguments put forward by Kickbusch (Kickbusch 2000; Kickbusch and de Leeuw 1999; Kickbusch and Quick 1998) and Buse and Waxman (2001).

10. A burgeoning literature on globalization and health exists. See, for example, Baris and McLeod 2000; Barnett and Whiteside 2002; Benatar 2003; Berlinguer 1999; Crush 2002; Dollar 2001; Gutiérrez and Kendall 1999; Kawachi and Wamala 2006; Lee and Yach 2006; Lee et al. 2002; McMichael and Beaglehole 2000; McMurray and Smith 2001; Walt 2001b; Woodward et al. 2001; Yach 2005; Yach et al. 2006. For a sense of debates about how political the biopolitical agenda of global health should be, see Yach and Bettcher's (1998a, 1998b) widely cited overview of the globalization of public health as a convergence of altruism and self-interest and Navarro's (1998) critical commentary that invites further political-economic analysis. Kickbusch reminds us that globalization involves both interdependence and interconnectedness and challenges the internal sovereignty of nation-states (Kickbusch 2000; Kickbusch and de Leeuw 1999). There is a tension between globalization and global health governance, global public good, and the self-interests of nations and the interest groups that influence them.

11. Greenberg and Park (1994:1) describe political ecology as "expanding ecological concepts to respond to the inclusion of cultural and political activity within an analysis of ecosystems that are significantly but not always entirely socially constructed." Political ecology demands coparticipation of the social and biological sciences to pursue questions of ecological change within a framework that combines history, demography, and political economy. The discipline "unites the traditional concerns for the environment-technology-social-organization nexus with the emphasis of political economy on power and inequality seen historically, the evaluation and critique of development programs,

and the analysis of environmental degradation." Fundamental to the study of global health is a consideration of how politics directly and indirectly contributes to the spread of infectious disease (Whitman 2000).

12. An example of a transnational controversy would be who gets to set global ethical standards (e.g., related to informed consent for clinical trials, definitions of child labor), and on what basis.

13. Nonstate participants in global health would include advocacy groups and NGOs, philanthropic foundations, public-private partnerships, individual entrepreneurs, celebrity activists championing specific issues, and so on. These groups add an unstructured plurality to global health (Fidler 2007).

14. New partnerships and increased fragmentation in the international health landscape demand new forms of networking, governance, and oversight (Walt and Buse 2000).

15. For a more extensive description of syndemics, see www.cdc.gov/syndemics/overview-definition.htm. Prior to use of the term *syndemics*, Wallace (1988, 1990) called for research on a "synergism of plagues" through which disparities in health developed and were reproduced. Singer (1996) argued that the concept of "concurrent epidemics" was inadequate for describing the dynamic relationship between violence, substance abuse, and AIDS among the urban poor because these health problems interacted synergistically to the extent that they could not be analyzed individually or in parallel. They were, rather, indivisible elements of a single phenomenon, which he termed the "SAVA [substance abuse–violence–AIDS] Syndemic." Syndemics arise in conditions of health and social disparity that predispose populations for multiple, coterminus, and interacting epidemics (Singer et al. 2006).

16. Other types of syndemic relationship exist. Addressing the discipline of anthropology, Jing (2006) calls for an "anthropological epidemiology" that takes into account inequality, structural violence, and political economy as they are related to the distribution of disease in particular historically, socially, and culturally specific contexts. Jing's description of the political economy of the blood-product market in central China and how it led to the distribution of HIV is another type of syndemic assessment that calls attention to the commodification of the body. See also Erwin 2006; Mastro and Yip 2006; Wu et al. 2001.

17. Diabetic smokers have twice the risk of premature death compared to nonsmokers, and the combined cardiovascular disease risks from smoking and diabetes are nearly fourteen times higher than the risk of either smoking or diabetes alone (Foy et al. 2000). Smoking impairs metabolic control and increases the risk of both macrovascular and microvascular complications, including coronary artery disease, stroke, peripheral artery disease, proteinuria, renal failure, and neuropathy (Eliasson 2003).

18. Researchers in India have demonstrated important links between smoking and TB. Smokers are at once at greater risk of getting TB (odds ratio of 1.8 for light smokers, 3.7 for heavy smokers) and dying from TB (odds ration of 4.5) (Kolappan and Gopi 2002). Ex-patients are more than three times more likely to relapse if they smoke following short-course TB treatment (Thomas et al. 2005). For a useful review of studies on the association of TB and smoking, see Hassmiller 2006.

19. See the Framework Convention Alliance for Tobacco Control Web site (www.fctc.org); see also World Health Organization Web pages on the Framework Convention (www.who.int/tobacco/framework/en).

20. An understanding of syndemics is crucial to implementation of the United Nations Millennium Declaration, which calls for multisectoral action to address health and development challenges.

21. An excellent example of the difference between a public health behaviorist and syndemic assessment of health problems is provided by Basu (2004) in a discussion of AIDS

interventions, although he does not use the term *syndemic*. Basu also provides a useful critique of the way in which "culture" is misused in interventions.

22. This is a rather simplistic account of ecosocial epidemiology. For a more complete account, see Krieger 1994, 1999, 2001; Krieger and Gruskin 2001; Krieger and Zierler 1996. For a comparison with social epidemiology, see Berkman and Kawachi 2000; Blane et al. 1997; McMichael 1999; Susser 1996a, 1996b.

23. The term *embodiment* has been used in many different ways in the social science literature. Krieger defines embodiment as "the way we literally incorporate biologically the world in which we live, including our societal and ecological circumstances" (2005:351).

24. Kirmayer (1992) makes a similar argument when he draws attention to "the body's insistence on meaning." He notes that "any theory of meaning that hopes to address the experience of illness must give due weight to the primacy of the body not only as an object of thought, but as itself a vehicle for thinking, feeling and acting" (1992:325).

25. Let me provide two examples that illustrate the utility of the local biology concept: the study of diet and the study of child delivery. Bodies that become accustomed to different diets have their own local biologies. This is particularly the case in contexts where foods are embodied along with strong perceptions of how these foods will affect the body-mind. In such contexts, foods are the vehicle of expectations and may be fetishized. Infant and child feeding patterns create local biologies through the content of foods provided for the child to eat, the child's body becoming habituated to the properties of these foods (feelings of fullness, food transit time, etc.), the timing and social relations of different modes of feeding, and expectations of how foods will affect them. In India, local theories of transubstantiation further posit that local biologies (caste habitus) are created through the consumption of particular types of foods having particular qualities (*guna*). Ethnosociologists have described the Indian caste system as being built upon the idea that humans are "dividuals" defined as unique composites of diverse subtle and gross substances (Marriott and Inden 1977). In urban China, my colleague Terry Woronov has observed that the bodies and minds of middle-class children are being developed to participate in the global market through the appropriate consumption of foods such as milk, McDonalds hamburgers, and Kentucky Fried Chicken. Food consumption is being used to create a new type of citizen with a new local biology to create a new economy and future for China (Woronov 2007). A second example of why local biology matters involves preferred childbirth practices. Women living more modern or urban lifestyles see their local biologies as different from those of their mothers or grandmothers, who toiled in the fields. This has affected the type of childbirth experience they seek out, perceptions of how much pain they can safely tolerate, and demand for pharmaceuticals. Van Hollen (2003) provides a good case study of childbirth that addresses these issues in South India.

26. Life-span biologists study cumulative events during development and aging as a continuous process (Leidy 1994, 1996).

27. For example, hunger seasons appear to drive not only Turkana women's fecundity (Leslie et al. 1999) but also reproductive decision making among poorer Turkana households (Pike 1996, 1999). See Pike 2004 for an example of how reproductive decision making is influenced by danger and being on the run in a conflict-ridden terrain.

28. For example, low birth weight increases the risk for cardiovascular and metabolic disorders later in life (Barker 1997; Godfrey and Barker 2000; Stein et al. 1996), and human papillomavirus (HPV) infection increases the chance of developing cervical cancer (Hunter 2006). For an overview of chronic disease epidemiology that takes a life-course perspective, see the edited volume by Kuh and Ben-Shlomo (2004).

29. For example, in an otherwise excellent review of (re)emerging infectious diseases and the third epidemiological transition, Barrett and colleagues (1998) call no attention to how infectious disease predisposes one to chronic ailments later.

30. On the importance of noncommunicable diseases for global health and how little money is allocated to prevent and manage these diseases by international donors, see Yach 2005 and Yach et al. 2006.

31. Another contribution to this debate would be drawing attention to risk factors that predispose both communicable and noncommunicable disease. For example, smoking is associated with both a wide range of noncommunicable diseases and TB. If we were to just focus on vaccinating children against communicable diseases, it could be argued that we are simply "saving the children for the tobacco industry" (Nichter and Cartwright 1991) and possible affliction with either cancer or TB.

32. All members of impoverished households with chronically ill members suffer. First, all bear witness to the suffering of the afflicted. Second, household members have to expend scarce resources in caring for the afflicted. Even if this is just time, opportunity costs are there for care providers. Third, if the afflicted is a former breadwinner living on the margin, his or her inability to provide resources for others jeopardizes household health.

33. For example, medical anthropologists investigated who became community health workers in the 1970s–90s, the extent to which they represented different community factions, and the scope of their participation in carrying out public health mandates. See, for example, Nichter 1999 and Paul and Demarest 1984.

34. Participatory research may also involve communities of practitioners that join together to form "practice-based networks" (Lindbloom et al. 2004; Nutting et al. 1999; Thomas et al. 2001). This is a model of participatory research that I am currently attempting to facilitate in tobacco cessation research in India and Indonesia.

35. Maps can enable data typically displayed in a series of tables or through statistics to be read more easily by the layperson (e.g., through color coding). Depending on its use, mapping can be used as either a democratizing technology or an elitist, antidemocratic technology. At issue is not just complexity and cost but also efforts made to present or suppress particular types of data. Participatory mapping involves thinking critically about what information is (and should be) mapped, how it was collected, by whom, and for what purpose.

36. There has been some debate surrounding the use of participatory GIS (PGIS) and public participation GIS (PPGIS)—explained in greater detail in Elwood 2006. The debate centers on similar concerns that have confronted participatory researchers, namely, who constitutes a public and what constitutes participation, compounded by a concern for power relations embedded within GIS because of its strong reliance on knowledge and technical expertise. Participatory approaches seek to transcend these limitations and better include community perspectives in research design, data collection, and spatial analysis.

37. See Krieger et al. 2003a and 2003b for an example of a geocoding project in the United States that looks at area-based socioeconomic measures and race/ethnicity in an analysis of public health disparities.

38. The field of health geography can play a valuable role in creating visual representations that illustrate how location, place, and access to goods and services both promote health and foster ill health (Gatrell 2002; Gatrell and Rigby 2004). To do so, geographers should be working in concert with medical anthropologists and epidemiologists who are actually collecting data and not just mining existing data sets. The motivations for both collecting particular types of data and representing them in particular ways require critical examination.

39. Maps can both clarify and distort, as well as affirm and challenge, intentionally as well as unintentionally (Cromley and McLafferty 2002; Monmonier 1996). There is a well-established literature in the social sciences that speaks to the motivated use of maps as a means of constructing a sense of nation and community (e.g., Anderson 1991), as well as for purposes of governance. Foucault (1984, 1991) has drawn our attention to how discourses (ways of constituting knowledge that entail power relations), maps, and other favored representations have shaped and created meaning systems by gaining truth status and widespread currency at particular times. Alternative discourses, maps, and representations can also be used as sites to explore new sets of possibilities and can provide the opportunity for new generative discourses to emerge.

40. Previous IHRs (previously referred to as International Sanitary Regulations) were approved in 1951 and required WHO member states to report outbreaks of cholera, plague, and yellow fever. The revised IHR (WHO 2005) covers a range of global health emergencies and sets in place procedures to both detect and respond.

41. Notably, brokering global agreements such as the IHR and the Framework Convention on Tobacco Control regained for the WHO some of the prestige it had lost to the World Bank in the 1990s as a policy maker.

42. Important lessons are also to be learned from colleagues who have studied other international agreements and treaties (for example, the regulation of breast milk substitutes, establishing voluntary guidelines for the human right to food, treaties on land mines, child labor agreements) and global social movements (for example, the environmental movement). As Marchione (2007) has noted, we need to "unearth the political, economic, and cultural factors influencing the stance a country assumes toward global (human rights) treaties, answering questions such as why a treaty might have been ratified, rejected, or is being contested." We also need to closely examine the extent to which such treaties are being upheld once ratified and how specific countries deal with blatant attempts to nullify the intent of global agreements.

43. For studies of "audit culture," see Miller and Rose 1992; Power 1997; Rose 1999; Strathern 2000. Audits often produce decontextualized information of questionable validity that takes on truth value, especially when presented quantitatively. On the power of quantitative representations that appear objective, see Porter 1995.

44. There needs to be flexibility to develop culturally tailored programs, which can then be evaluated against standard programs. Outcome measures used in evaluations also need to be the subject of scrutiny from cultural and social-process vantage points.

45. Sociocultural anthropologists are very sensitive to calls for increased surveillance, as many associate surveillance with governance, disciplinary and normalizing practices, and Foucault's writing on the panopticon and the "conduct of conduct." I argue for monitoring and rendering visible the marketing (and clinical trial) practices of industries such as big pharmaceuticals, tobacco, and infant formula. These industries already have extensive surveillance networks that inform their marketing activities. A monitoring of the marketing and surveillance activities of these industries is called for, as is a monitoring of consumer trends that affect global health positively and negatively. Consider, for example, the extensive surveillance system maintained by the pharmaceutical industry in India, which has kept track of the monthly drug prescription and purchasing behavior of medical practitioners for at least the past thirty years. While the government (state and national offices) has a very poor database of where practitioners are located and what medicines they are using, pharmaceutical companies have been using data on specific practitioners (and drugstores) to engage in aggressive marketing activities. Recently, public health activists and pharmacists established the India-Drug Communication Network (india-drug@healthnet.org) as a watchdog organization to

monitor the drug promotion activities of the pharmaceutical industry as well as to discuss what can be done to increase rational drug use in the country. Social scientists could add a much-needed dimension by monitoring the pharmaceutical practice of patients, self-medicators, practitioners, and pharmaceutical representatives. See, for example, Kamat and Nichter 1998.

46. While president of the Society for Medical Anthropology, I set up a "Takes a Stand" task force to educate members on how to monitor clinical trials as well as assist local groups of scientists to improve informed consent procedures, and the like. What I failed to do was establish clear lines of communication to oversight and advocacy groups and procedures for reporting confidential information. This placed colleagues in the uncomfortable, if not dangerous, position of not knowing who to trust with sensitive information gathered. Other professional groups should learn from this experience and establish safe protocols for passing on information.

47. The vast majority of emerging infectious diseases are zoonotic in origin (Murphy 1999), and the significance of zoonoses in the emergence of human infections cannot be overstated (Lederberg et al. 1992; WHO 2004; Woolhouse et al. 2005). The occurrence and spread of zoonotic diseases needs to be better monitored in relation to political economic factors that alter and intensify man–animal and animal–animal contact, such as deforestation; intensive factory farming of cattle, pigs, and poultry; the creation of new breeding sites associated with dams, irrigation systems, urbanization, and so on. Social scientists can bring a much-needed political-ecological perspective to infectious disease epidemiology.

48. Other contexts beg social science investigation as well. Beyond contexts of decentralization, research is needed in places with little government at all (e.g., Somalia) or where governments exist with little jurisdiction (e.g., Iraq) and places where the private rules the public.

49. Soeharto's highly centralized "New Order" political regime remained in control of Indonesia from 1966 to 1998 and was replaced by the Habibie regime, which instituted decentralized governance (Bourchier and Hadiz 2003). The passing of Law 22 (in 1999) and Law 25 (in 2001) moved Indonesia from a centralized state to a partially decentralized state managed by provincial government offices and to further devolution and decision making at local levels of government (Alm et al. 2001; Antolöv 2003; Booth 2003; Fane 2003).

50. For example, Padmawati and I have argued (2008) that the control of avian flu and dengue fever involve a common set of challenges. Both require sustained community participation to control and monitor breeding sites (for mosquito vectors, for sick poultry) at the household, neighborhood, and local industry level. Both involve the threat of a disease that may intermittently appear, and the two diseases have symptoms that overlap with many other diseases. Indonesia has already made some headway in organizing local communities around dengue control and coordinating national and local dengue control activities (Kusriastuti and Sutomo 2005). Efforts to combat avian flu might borrow from or piggyback on dengue control efforts or other community-based disaster or disease control efforts. Given the need to maintain a ready state of local biopreparedness, it might be best to organize groups around more than one threat so as to sustain interest and maintain clear lines of communication and command.

51. Public interpretation of the motivation of the press when reporting about illness, especially epidemic illness, is an important avenue for future research. See Peterson 1998 for an insightful examination of public response to news coverage of AIDS in India.

52. Indonesia provides a good case study of why ethnographic studies of social organization are needed before considering community-based efforts to control avian flu. In the past,

the Indonesian government has often used the Family Guidance Welfare Movement, or PKK (Pembinaan Kesejahteraan Keluarga), as an infrastructure to carry out health work at the local level. During the New Order era, the group was also used by the government to establish hegemonic rule through mothers, a phenomenon that Suryakusuma (1996) has termed "state Ibuism." Women's groups were used to establish social and political control through promoting and implementing official development plans such as family planning. In the new era of decentralized rule, care needs to be taken to invite participation of local organizations such as the PKK, as distinct from efforts to impose programs on them from above. The PKK in the past served the interests of government servants and their wives more than community members (Wolf 1992). Its infrastructure still exists. Around what issues can this group be mobilized? International groups must exercise some measure of caution when engaging groups such as the PKK in this new political environment.

53. Different social scientists have used the terms *health*, *therapeutic*, *medical*, and *pharmaceutical citizenship* to discuss the politics of health care and medicine entitlement. For example, anthropologists have used the concepts of health citizenship (Robins 2006) and medical citizenship (Nguyen 2005) in close examinations of antiretroviral drug distribution policies, state responsibility, the rights and obligations of "responsibilized patient-citizens," and emergent assemblages of people mobilized around ethical claims to essential medicines (Collier and Lakoff 2005; Ong and Collier 2005). For the sake of simplicity in this book, I use the term *medical citizenship* to broadly address health care entitlement as a right of citizenship, a right that is often qualified. For other anthropologists who use the term *medical citizenship* in this more general sense, see Wailoo et al. 2006.

54. Providing health care to undocumented immigrants is a subject of contention on both sides of the Atlantic. Castañeda (on Germany: 2007) and Fassin (on France: 2001, 2004) provide two very different case studies illustrating the paradoxical situation in which state governments find themselves with respect to providing medical care to undocumented immigrants. On the one hand, states wish to maintain their moral identity by providing care as a measure of humanity. On the other hand, they are subject to the political economics of providing such care, especially during times of heightened nationalism and rising taxes. In the case of Germany, medical aid is criminalized. Doctors are required to report patients to the government, which can lead to their deportation. This complicates the control of infectious diseases. The government solves the paradox by allowing NGOs to serve this population and not prosecuting doctors practicing under the banner of humanitarianism or human rights. In France, accidents and illness are two of the only sources of legitimacy to which undocumented immigrants can lay claim, by requesting asylum in the name of humanity.

55. Enlightened self-interest, a principle examined by such social philosophers as Alexis de Tocqueville and Adam Smith, involves more than short-term sacrifice and the postponement of immediate gratification as a means of securing long-term gains or a sense of security enabling business as usual; it also involves what Bourdieu has described as convertible capital. One may convert monetary capital into cultural or social capital through acts that promote community or assist those in need. This helps explain acts of corporate responsibility and generosity as a means of securing a good public image.

56. NGOs have played an important role in rendering industries accountable by both serving as watchdogs and reporting egregious practices to the press, as well as by proactively lobbying for certification of fair practices. On the importance and politics of certification, see Gereffi et al. 2001.

57. Raising the consciousness of the public may promote forms of subpolitics that involve consumerism with a conscience. Such acts of subpolitics, however, may be undermined

by marketing campaigns that misuse or overstate "green" and fair-trade representations to sell products. For research on product representation and trust in labeling, see Barham 2002; Bryant 2004; Bryant and Goodman 2004; Jackson 1999; Lyon 2006. Subpolitics may also involve shaming corporations into being more ethical, as they stand to lose considerable symbolic capital when unethical practices are made public. Recovering such capital often requires an expensive public relations campaign.

58. A commodity chain refers to the entire range of activities involved in the design, production, distribution, and marketing of a product (Gereffi and Korzeniewicz 1994). Different types of commodity chains exist. Producer-driven commodity chains typically involve large transnational manufacturers that coordinate all aspects of global production networks. Buyer-driven commodity chains are set up by large retailers and branded manufacturers and involve more-decentralized production networks in developing countries. The critical assessment of commodity chains called for here would require multisited ethnographies (Marcus 1995) that closely examine policies that influence the health and welfare of all participants involved in different types of commodity chains and agricultural-based global commodity systems (Mintz 1985). Such research needs to identify best-case as well as worst-case scenarios.

59. Global health care chain analysis involves an assessment of changes in host-country doctor/nurse–patient ratios, country capacity to produce health care providers, state and private investment in the medical education of those health professionals leaving, and overseas work-migration trends among health personnel having different levels of training and competency. It also examines the market value of migrant health personnel in developed countries, efforts to recruit and credential foreign-trained health personnel, and factors affecting market demand for particular types of health professionals in the North (e.g., demographic shifts, retirement trends).

60. On flows of health care professionals from developing countries to developed countries see Brush et al. 2004; Garrett 2007; Hochschild 2000; Paral 2004; Ross et al. 2005; WHO 2006a; Yeates 2004.

61. Global health care chain analysis also needs to be conducted on flows of health personnel within countries from the public to the private and NGO sectors, and from clinical practice to the overseeing of clinical trials. The effect of South–South flows of medical personnel also demands serious consideration. What is the social and political impact, for example, of the 30,000–40,000 doctors being sent by Cuba to work in community health in more than sixty-eight developing countries as part of its strategy of medical diplomacy and a means of generating much-needed foreign revenue? In addition to supplying countries such as Venezuela, Haiti, Yemen, and South Africa with doctors, Cuba is setting itself up as a hub for medical education suitable for developing world health care practice (there are currently 25,000–30,000 foreign medical students in Cuba; see Frank and Reed 2005), and as a destination for medical tourism. How are Cuban doctors greeted by the communities in which they work and by the medical community in host countries? In what ways does their presence serve biopolitical agendas and change local populations' opinion of government health services? Similarly, what has been the social impact on the state of Kerala, India, of sending 40,000 to 60,000 nurses to the Middle East (Percot 2006)? Medical tourism and the outsourcing of diagnostic tests and medical procedures are other emerging global health phenomena that demand research. How well established are medical tourism routes between Middle Eastern countries and between these countries and India? And how is India positioning itself to become a center of medical tourism for India's growing population living abroad?

62. Given current demographic projections, poverty will continue to drive populations into periurban slums with little if any infrastructure (Davis 2006; United Nations

Human Settlements Programme 2003), creating the ideal conditions for resurgent and emergent diseases. Likewise, unprecedented concentrations of animals are being raised on industrialized farms where animal "health" has to be maintained by routine doses of antibiotics, creating ideal niches for emergent and drug-resistant diseases (Davis 2005; Greger 2006).

63. There is a need to monitor political rhetoric about U.S. contributions to global health, as well as public opinion about what our commitment should be. For example, opinion polls conducted in the United States in the mid-1990s found that U.S. citizens were under the impression that our government spent 15 percent of the national budget on foreign aid when in fact the figure was closer to 1 percent, with only a fraction of this going to health (IOM 1997; Kull 1995). The public was predisposed to spend 5–6 percent of gross national product on foreign aid.

64. Translational research also plays a role in what has been referred to as the "democratic turn" in the public understanding of science movement (Durrant 1999), which encourages scientific citizenship (Elam and Bertilsson 2003; Irwin 2001) and recognizes the role of laypeople in producing and disseminating scientific knowledge (Callon 1999). Scientific citizenship calls for public engagement of science and technology such that innovation and the direction of science are subject to critical review (see, for example, Epstein 1996 on AIDS activism). A forum is established in which public confidence in science can be either affirmed or challenged. I view this as complementary to a popular epidemiology agenda. Knowledge translation and the role of social science in addressing the "know-do gap" are being accorded more importance of late in global health discourse. See Birn 2005; Lavis et al. 2006; Pablos-Mendez and Shademani 2006; Pablos-Mendez et al. 2005; Pang 2003; Pang et al. 2006; WHO 2006b. Knowledge translation and knowledge management are called for to reduce what Pang and colleagues (2006) have referred to as the fifteenth grand challenge for global health: keeping flows of knowledge open and unpolluted. This requires both the effective filtering and the translation of information in a timely manner. Knowledge translation requires participatory translational research.

65. My use of the term *pharmaceutical commons* indexes Hardin's (1968, 1998) neoclassical economic analysis of the difference between behavior associated with private and communal ownership. Writing on the "tragedy of the commons," Hardin argued that private ownership gives individual owners an incentive to conserve and use resources wisely so as not to diminish their future value. By comparison, resources owned communally are much less likely to be conserved or used appropriately, because it is in an individual's best interest to derive as much personal benefit from commonly owned resources as possible, given a supply that appears unlimited. Individuals who primarily think of themselves would overuse resources. In the case of medicines, such as antibiotics, individuals given access to a pharmaceutical commons (poorly regulated drugstores and medical practice) would use medicines inappropriately for immediate relief, without worrying about the ramifications of population-based drug resistance. This argument, while compelling, is limited. It requires a biopolitical perspective. In the case of pharmaceuticals, industry is as much to blame for the misuse of antibiotics as are individual practitioners, patients, or those using antibiotics for animal husbandry or agriculture. Patterns of prescribing and use are influenced by marketing strategies as well as government policy. Further, the commons described by Hardin poorly captures communally owned space. Communities were often custodians of the commons because they were seen as a resource passed down from one generation to the next. In the case of medicines, community stakeholders need to be educated to better understand the population-based effect of drug misuse.

66. The term *biosociality* (Rabinow 1996) has generally been used to refer to groups that come to share a common biologically understood identity because of some illness or health-related condition. In some instances, shared biological affiliation has led members of a community of affliction to make demands on institutions, governments, and scientists as a form of biopolitics (Fassin 2001, 2004; Novas 2006; Robins 2006). For example, Petryna (2002) develops the notion of biological citizenship (associated with the Chernobyl disaster) to illustrate how assaults on health become the medium through which people stake claims for resources from the state. Members of communities of affliction also play a role in negotiating how science will be conducted and how the fruits of science will be distributed; they thus drive a political economy of hope (Novas 2006). I extend the use of the term *biosociality* to include groups of people who come to share a common sense of risk for either a particular disease (avian flu, for example) or a set of conditions predisposing them to many forms of ill health (food security, for example). A sense of risk can draw people together within a country or globally and can inspire social movements that render visible biopolitical dimensions of public health and inspire new forms of scientific citizenship (Irwin 2001), a phenomenon much in line with Ong's writings on emergent forms of "flexible citizenship" (Ong 1999; Ong and Collier 2005). Global biosociality is facilitated by rapid communication technologies that can link geographically distant individuals, enabling the creation of digital communities (Rose and Novas 2005) that share global health agendas. In addition to sharing information about risks, members of such communities may exchange strategies for political action and critically assess media coverage and industry hype (Brown 2003). Consider, for example, the groundswell of NGO support for the Framework Convention that contributed to its success, as well as the expansion of the tobacco control community through such digital online communities as Global Link. See Castells 1996 for an introduction to the social science of emerging assemblages fostered by recent advances in communication technology (from computers to cell phones) enabling global connectivity and making possible a new network society.

67. *Biovalue* is a term introduced by Waldby (2002) to draw attention to how body parts and products (DNA, blood, tissue, organs) have productive value for advancing health research and augmenting human health, giving them value on the market as a form of wealth. Social scientists, especially medical anthropologists (see, for example, Cohen 2003; Scheper-Hughes 2000, 2003a, 2003b), have played an important role in monitoring and raising ethical questions about the commodification of body parts and forms of exploitation associated with their harvesting and sale. The concept of biovalue needs to be extended to cover strains of bacteria and viruses identified in particular populations. For example, in early February 2007, the Indonesian government announced that it would not share samples of the avian flu H5N1 virus with the rest of the world and began sending samples just to a U.S. drug manufacturer. In return, the company allowed Indonesia to retain intellectual property rights over virus strains in the country and promised that any vaccines produced would be affordable. A week later, a deal was brokered with the World Health Organization to share samples of viruses with the stipulation that this "free sharing of viruses" would guarantee an affordable vaccine for developing countries.

68. The biosocial value of local experience is underappreciated in biomedicine, being largely left to biocultural anthropologists to study. For example, pharmaceutical companies are increasingly exploiting Third World bodies (especially bodies with untreated illnesses) as a cheap resource for stage three clinical trials. Many such trials recruit subjects from several different countries who share a common disease but whose lives, past experiences, and local biologies differ in profound ways. In the future, sample selection may change

as more-sophisticated genetic assessments of both populations and strains of illness are required for pharmacogenetic studies (Roses 2000), but these studies will most likely pay attention only to genetic differences even though other aspects of local biology, life world, and life course need to be taken into account.

69. For example, recent research suggests that the evolutionary consequences of long-standing human-pathogen associations may affect disease susceptibility and the spread of mycobacterial lineages (genetic strains) of diseases such as *M. tuberculosis* (Gagneux et al. 2006).

70. Critical studies of adaptability raise two questions: adaptive for whom, and adaptable at what cost? When populations have been forced to adapt to harsh living or work conditions as a result of political-economic forces, adaptability needs to be viewed through the lens of exploitation (Singer 1989), and the cost of adaptability needs to be seen in terms of embodiment, as proposed by Krieger (2005).

71. Epstein (2000) calls for an ecological epidemiology attentive to climate change and the way this affects vector-borne and water-borne diseases; Moore (2006) calls for better surveillance of mortality and morbidity trends by climate in developing countries. Social scientists need to work in conjunction with epidemiologists studying human response to changes in climate and ecology that include but go beyond the emergence of communicable diseases. They need to consider climate change as it affects a wide range of human behavior, from changes in diet (related to agriculture, hunting, fishing, etc.) to the availability of medicinal plants (related to drought and a falling water table), and so on. Those not living in thermostat-regulated environments are far more attentive to changes in nature that affect us all. Their experience needs to be seen as an early warning system to which we need to pay close attention. Climate change also needs to be considered in terms of a widening of health inequalities within as well as between countries (Sunyer and Grimalt 2006).

72. Cross-cultural exchange of experience and forms of knowledge invites forms of engagement similar to those described by Nowotny (1993) in an examination of contexts in which science meets the public in the West. During such engagement, there is often a blurring of boundaries between expert and lay knowledge, a questioning of the idea that bioscience has a monopoly on all truth, and acknowledgment of different types of knowledge and counterexpertise. Contests of meaning will arise, as will novel forms of problem solving and scientific endeavor.

73. Chen and colleagues (1999) note that health as a global public good requires the international community to adopt a collective responsibility for the creation and dissemination of knowledge advancing a global health agenda. This presents a dilemma: the need to balance business interests, intellectual property rights, and monopoly rents with a need for sharing a common pool of knowledge toward the ends of collective survival and health equity. On the concept of global public good, see Kaul et al. 1999.

REFERENCES

Aaby P. Assumptions and contradictions in measles and measles immunization research: is measles good for something? *Social Science and Medicine*, 1995, 41 (5): 673–686.

Abellanosa I, Nichter M. Antibiotic prophylaxis among commercial sex workers in Cebu City, Philippines. *Sexually Transmitted Diseases*, 1996, 23:407–412.

AbouZahr C. Disability adjusted life years (DALYs) and reproductive health: a critical analysis. *Reproductive Health Matters*, 1999, 7:118–129.

AbouZahr C, Vaughan JP. Assessing the burden of sexual and reproductive ill-health: questions regarding the use of disability-adjusted life years. *Bulletin of the World Health Organization*, 2000, 78 (5): 655–666.

Abrams P. Notes on the difficulty of studying the state. *Journal of Historical Sociology*, 1988, 1:58–89.

Ackerknecht E. *Rudolph Virchow: doctor, statesman, anthropologist.* Madison, University of Wisconsin Press, 1953.

Adams V et al. Having a "safe delivery": conflicting views from Tibet. *Health Care for Women International*, 2005, 26:821–851.

Adamson J. Review of *Epidemiology and culture* (Trostle, JA, Cambridge University Press). *International Journal of Epidemiology*, 2006, doi:10.1093/ije/dy1028.

Adler NE, Ostrove JM. Socioeconomic status and health: what we know and what we don't. *Annals of the New York Academy of Sciences*, 1999, 896:3–15.

Agar M. Recasting the "ethno" in "epidemiology." *Medical Anthropology*, 1996, 16 (4): 391–403.

Agar M. How the drug field turned my beard grey. *International Journal of Drug Policy*, 2002, 13:249–258.

Agar M. Toward a qualitative epidemiology. *Qualitative Health Research*, 2003, 13 (7): 974–986.

Agg C. Winners or losers? NGOs in the current aid paradigm. *Development*, 2006, 49 (2): 15–21.

Aginam O. International law and communicable diseases. *Bulletin of the World Health Organization*, 2002, 80 (12): 946–951.

Aginam O. *Global health governance: international law and public health in a divided world.* Toronto, University of Toronto Press, 2005.

Agyepong IA. Malaria: Ethnomedical perceptions and practice in an Adangbe farming community and implications for control. *Social Science and Medicine*, 1992, 35 (2): 131–137.

Agyepong IA, Manderson L. Mosquito avoidance and bed net use in the greater Accra region, Ghana. *Journal of Biosocial Science*, 1999, 31:79–92.

Ahorlu CK et al. Malaria-related beliefs and behaviour in southern Ghana. *Tropical Medicine and International Health*, 1997, 2:488–499.

Ahorlu CK et al. Lymphatic filariasis-related perceptions and practices on the coast of Ghana: implications for prevention and control. *Acta Tropica*, 1999, 73:251–261.

Aikins MK et al. Attitudes to malaria, traditional practices and bednets (mosquito nets) as vector control measures: a comparative study in five West African countries. *Journal of Tropical Medicine and Hygiene*, 1994, 97:81–86.

Aldarazi FA. Bahraini women's health practices. *Journal of Tropical Paediatrics*, 1987, 33 (suppl. 4): 14–16.

Alilio M, Bammek J. A KAP study on malaria in Zanzibar: implications for prevention and control. A study conducted for UNICEF Sub-Office Zanzibar. *Evaluation and Programming Planning*, 1998, 21:409–413.

Aljunid S. The role of private medical practitioners and their interactions with public health services in Asian countries. *Health Policy and Planning*, 1995, 10 (4): 333–349.

Allmark P, Tod A. How should public health professionals engage with lay epidemiology? *Journal of Medical Ethics*, 2006, 32:460–463.

Allotey P, Gyapong M. *The gender agenda in the control of tropical diseases: a review of current evidence.* Social, Economic and Behavioural Research, Special Topics No. 4, TDR/STR/SEB/ST/05.01. Geneva, World Health Organization TDR, 2005.

Allotey P et al. The DALY, context and the determinants of the severity of disease: an exploratory comparison of paraplegia in Australia and Cameroon. *Social Science and Medicine*, 2003, 57 (5): 949–958.

Alm J, Aten RH, Bahl R. Can Indonesia decentralize successfully? Plans, problems, prospects. *Bulletin of Indonesian Economic Studies*, 2001, 37(1): 83–102.

Alonzo F et al. The concepts, attributes and beliefs of the Filipino on lung cancer. *Journal of Internal Medicine*, 1991, 29:255–271.

Amazigo UO. Traditional and Western attitudes towards the care of tropical diseases: the case of onchocerciasis. *Journal of Seizon and Life Science*, 1993, 4:239–251.

Amazigo UO. Detrimental effects of onchocerciasis on marriage age and breast feeding. *Tropical and Geographical Medicine*, 1994, 46:322–325.

Amazigo UO, Obikeze DS. *Socio-cultural factors associated with prevalence and intensity of onchocerciasis and onchodermatitis among adolescent girls in rural Nigeria.* Unpublished WHO/TDR final project report, 1991.

Amazigo UO, Obikeze DS. Social consequences of onchocercal skin lesions on adolescent girls in rural Nigeria. World Health Organization/TDR Discussion Paper. Geneva, World Health Organization, 1992.

Amazigo UO et al. Urinary schistosomiasis among school children in Nigeria: consequences of indigenous beliefs and water contact activities. *Journal of Biological Science*, 1997, 29 (1): 9–18.

Ambe J et al. Perceptions, beliefs and practices of mothers in sub-urban and rural areas towards measles and measles vaccination in northern Nigeria. *Tropical Doctor*, 2001, 31:89–90.

American Academy of Pediatrics, Committee on Drugs. The transfer of drugs and other chemicals in breast milk. *Pediatrics*, 2001, 108:776–789.

Anand S, Hanson K. DALYs: efficiency versus equity. *World Development*, 1998, 26 (2): 307–310.

Anders G. Good governance as technology: towards an ethnography of the Bretton Woods Institutions. In: Mosse D, Lewis D, eds. *The aid effect: giving and governing in international development.* London and Ann Arbor, MI, Pluto Press, 2005:37–60.

Andersen LT et al. Food and nutrient intakes among pregnant women in rural Tamil Nadu, South India. *Public Health Nutrition*, 2003, 6 (2): 131–137.

Anderson B. *Imagined communities: reflections on the origin and spread of nationalism*, rev. ed. London, Verso, 1991.

Anderson W. Excremental colonialism: public health and the poetics of pollution. *Critical Inquiry*, 1995, 21:640–699.

Anderson W. Going through the motions: American public health and colonial "mimicry." *American Literary History*, 2002, 14 (4): 686–719.

Anderson W. Natural histories of infectious disease: ecological vision in twentieth-century biomedical science. In: Mitman G et al., eds. *Landscapes of exposure: knowledge and illness in modern environments.* OSIRIS, 2004, 19:39–61. Chicago, University of Chicago Press.

Anonymous. African hemorrhagic fever. *WHO Weekly Epidemiological Record*, 1977, 52:177–184.

Antolöv H. Village government and rural development in Indonesia: a new democratic framework. *Bulletin of Indonesian Economic Studies*, 2003, 39: 193–214.

Appadurai A. Global ethnoscapes: notes and queries for a transnational anthropology. In: Fox RG, ed. *Recapturing anthropology: working in the present.* Santa Fe, NM, School of American Research Press, 1991.

Appadurai A. Number in the colonial imagination. In: Breckenridge C, Van der Veer P, eds. *Orientalism and the postcolonial predicament: perspectives on South Asia.* Philadelphia, University of Pennsylvania Press, 1993:314–339.

Appadurai A. The production of locality. In: Fardon R, ed. *Counterworks: managing the diversity of knowledge.* London, Routledge, 1995:204–225.

Appadurai A. Grassroots globalization and the research imagination. In: Appadurai A, ed. *Globalization.* Durham, NC, Duke University Press, 2001a:1–21.

Appadurai A. Deep democracy: urban governmentality and the horizon of politics. *Environment and Urbanization,* 2001b, 13 (2): 23–43.

Apthorpe R. Writing development policy and policy analysis plain or clear: on language, genre and power. In: Shore C, Wright S, eds. *Anthropology of policy: critical perspectives on governance and power.* London, Routledge, 1997.

Arana BA et al. Cutaneous leishmaniasis in Guatemala: people's knowledge, concepts and practices. *Annals of Tropical Medicine and Parasitology,* 2000, 94 (8): 779–786.

Arce A, Long N. *Anthropology, development and modernities.* London, Routledge, 2000.

Arnesen T, Nord E. The value of DALY life: problems with ethics and validity of disability adjusted life years. *British Medical Journal,* 1999, 319: 1423–1425.

Arnold D, ed. *Imperial medicine and indigenous societies.* Manchester, UK, Manchester University Press, 1988.

Arnold D, ed. *Warm climates and Western medicine: the emergence of tropical medicine, 1500–1900.* Clio Medica/The Wellcome Series in the History of Medicine 35. Amsterdam and Atlanta, GA, Rodopi, 1996.

Arnold D. The place of the tropics in Western medical ideas since 1750. *Tropical Medicine and International Health,* 1997, 24:303–313.

Arole M, Arole R. A comprehensive rural health project in Jamkhed (India). In: Newell K, ed. *Health by the people.* Geneva, World Health Organization, 1975:70–90.

Arole M, Arole R. *Jamkhed: a comprehensive rural health project.* London, Macmillan Press, 1994.

Arole S et al. Social stigma: a comparative qualitative study of integrated and vertical care approaches to leprosy. *Leprosy Review,* 2002, 73:180–196.

Arora NK. *Assessment of injection practices in India, part 1: quantitative*. Central Coordinating Team on Behalf of IndiaCLEN Program Evaluation Network, 2004.

Atkins MK et al. A malaria control trial using insecticide-treated bed nets and targeted chemoprophylaxis in a rural area of the Gambia, West Africa. *Transactions of the Royal Society of Tropical Medicine and Hygiene*, 1993, 87 (suppl. 2): 25–30.

Awasthi S et al. Developing an interactive STD-prevention program for youth: lessons from a North Indian slum. *Studies in Family Planning*, 2000, 31 (2): 138–150.

Awolola TS et al. Knowledge and beliefs about causes, transmission, treatment and control of human onchocerciasis in rural communities in southwestern Nigeria. *Acta Tropica*, 2000, 76:247–251.

Ayers AJ. Demystifying democratization: the global constitution of (neo)liberal polities in Africa. *Third World Quarterly*, 2006, 27 (2): 321–338.

Baker MG, Fidler DP. Global public health surveillance under new international health regulations. *Emerging Infectious Diseases*, 2006, 12 (7): 1058–1065.

Bakhtin M. In: Holquist M, ed., Emerson C and Holquist M, trans., *The dialogic imagination: four essays*. Austin, University of Texas Press, 1981 [1935].

Bandyopadhyay L. Lymphatic filariasis and the women of India. *Social Science and Medicine*, 1996, 42 (10): 1401–1410.

Baquero F, Campos J. The tragedy of the commons in antimicrobial chemotherapy. *Revista española de quimioterapia*, 2003, 16 (1): 11–13.

Barabasi A-L. *Linked: how everything is connected to everything else and what it means*. New York, Plume/Penguin Group, 2003.

Barham E. Towards a theory of values-based labeling. *Agriculture and Human Values*, 2002, 19:349–360.

Baris E, McLeod K. Globalization and international trade in the twenty-first century: opportunities for and threats to the health sector in the South. *International Journal of Health Services*, 2000, 30 (1): 187–210.

Barker C, Green A. Opening the debate on DALYs. *Health Policy and Planning*, 1996, 11:179–183.

Barker DJP. Maternal nutrition, fetal nutrition, and disease in later life. *Nutrition*, 1997, 13 (9): 807–813.

Barnett T, Whiteside A. *AIDS in the twenty-first century: disease and globalization*. Houndmills, Basingstoke, UK, Palgrave, 2002.

Barnett T et al. The social and economic impact of HIV/AIDS in poor countries: a review of studies and lessons. *Progress in Development Studies*, 2001, 1 (2): 151–170.

Barnhoorn F, van der Geest S. Letter to the editor. *Social Science and Medicine*, 1997, 45 (10): 1597–1599.

Barrett R et al. Emerging and re-emerging infectious diseases: the third epidemiologic transition. *Annual Review of Anthropology*, 1998, 27:247–271.

Barry A et al, eds. *Foucault and political reason*. Chicago, University of Chicago Press, 1996.

Barry M. Diseases without borders: globalization's challenge to the American Society of Tropical Medicine and Hygiene. A call for public advocacy and activism. *American Journal of Tropical Medicine and Hygiene*, 2003, 69 (1): 3–7.

Bashford A. Global biopolitics and the history of world health. *History of the Human Sciences*, 2006, 19 (1): 67–88.

Basok T, Ilcan S. The voluntary sector and the depoliticization of civil society: implications for social justice. *International Journal of Canadian Studies*, 2003, 28:113–131.

Bastien JW. Qollahuaya-Andean body concepts: a topographical-hydraulic model of physiology. *American Anthropologist*, 1985, 8:595–611.

Bastien JW. *The kiss of death: Chagas' disease in the Americas*. Salt Lake City, University of Utah Press, 1998.

Basu S. AIDS, empire, and public health behaviorism. *International Journal of Health Services*, 2004, 34 (1): 155–167.

Bauman R, Briggs C. Poetics and performance as critical perspectives on language and social life. *Annual Review of Anthropology*, 1990, 19:59–88.

Baume C et al. Patterns of care for childhood malaria in Zambia. *Social Science and Medicine*, 2000, 51:1491–1503.

Beach WA et al. Disclosing and responding to cancer "fears" during oncology interviews. *Social Science and Medicine*, 2005, 60 (4): 893–910.

Beals AR. Strategies of resort to curers in South India. In: Leslie C, ed. *Asian medical systems: a comparative study*. Berkeley, University of California Press, 1976: 184–200.

Beard VA. Individual determinants of participation in community development in Indonesia. *Environment and Planning C: Government and Policy*, 2005, 23 (1): 21–39.

Beck U. World risk society as cosmopolitan society? Ecological questions in a framework of manufactured uncertainties. *Theory, Culture and Society*, 1996, 13 (4): 1–32.

Beck U. The cosmopolitan society and its enemies. *Theory, Culture and Society*, 2002, 19 (1–2): 17–44.

Bello CS, Idiong DU. Schistosoma urethritis: pseudo-gonorrhoeal disease in northern Nigeria. *Tropical Doctor*, 1982, 12 (3): 141–142.

Benatar S et al. Global health ethics: the rationale for mutual caring. *International Affairs*, 2003, 79 (1): 107–113.

Bentley GR et al. Women's strategies to alleviate nutritional stress in a rural African society. *Social Science and Medicine*, 1999, 48 (2): 149–162.

Bentley ME et al. Rapid ethnographic assessment: applications in a diarrhea management program. *Social Science and Medicine*, 1988, 27 (1): 107–116.

Berkman LF, Kawachi I, eds. *Social epidemiology*. Oxford, Oxford University Press, 2000.

Berkwits M. From practice to research: the case for criticism in an age of evidence. *Social Science and Medicine*, 1998, 47 (10): 1539–1545.

Berlinguer G. Globalization and global health. *International Journal of Health Services*, 1999, 29 (3): 579–595.

Berman P, Rose L. The role of private providers in maternal and child health and family planning services in developing countries. *Health Policy and Planning*, 1996, 11 (2): 142–155.

Berman P et al. Community based health workers: head start or false start towards health for all? *Social Science and Medicine*, 1987, 25:443–459.

Berman P et al. The household production of health: integrating social science perspectives on micro-level health determinants. *Social Science and Medicine*, 1994, 38 (2): 205–215.

Berreman JM. Childhood leprosy and social response in South India. *Social Science and Medicine*, 1984, 19 (8): 853–865.

Bexell A. The use of iron tablets in thirteen rural health centers in Western Province, Zambia. *Essential Drugs Programme*. Lusaka, Zambia, Ministry of Health, 1990.

Bhatt A. Clinical trials in India: pangs of globalization. *Indian Journal of Pharmacology*, 2004, 36 (4): 207–208.

Bhattacharyya K. Key informants, pile sorts, or surveys? Comparing behavioral research methods for the study of acute respiratory infections in West Bengal. In: Inhorn MC, Brown PJ, eds. *Anthropology of infectious disease: international health perspectives*. Amsterdam, Gordon and Breach, 1997:211–238.

Bhattacharyya K et al. *Community health worker incentives and disincentives: how they affect motivation, retention, and sustainability*. Arlington, VA, Basic Support for Institutionalizing Child Survival Project (BASICS II) for the U.S. Agency for International Development, 2001.

Bibeau G. The circular semantic network in Ngbandi disease nosology. *Social Science and Medicine*, 1981, 158:295–307.

Biehl J et al. Technology and affect: HIV/AIDS testing in Brazil. *Culture, Medicine and Psychiatry*, 2001, 25:87–129.

Bierlich B. Notions and treatment of guinea worm in northern Ghana. *Social Science and Medicine*, 1995, 41 (4): 501–509.

Bierlich B. Injections and the fear of death: an essay on the limits of biomedicine among the Dagomba of northern Ghana. *Social Science and Medicine*, 2000, 50:703–713.

Birn A-E. Gates's grandest challenge: transcending technology as public health ideology. *Lancet*, 2005, 366:514–519.

Birungi H. Injections and self-help: risk and trust in Ugandan health care. *Social Science and Medicine*, 1998, 47 (10): 1455–1462.

Bisht S, Coutinho L. When cure is better than prevention: immunity and preventive care of measles. *Economic and Political Weekly*, 2000, 2:19–26.

Black RE. Zinc deficiency, infectious disease and mortality in the developing world. *Journal of Nutrition*, 2003, 14 (suppl.): 1485S–1489S.

Blane D et al. Disease aetiology and materialist explanations of socioeconomic mortality differentials. *European Journal of Public Health*, 1997, 7:385–391.

Bledsoe C. Differential care of children of previous unions within Mende households in Sierra Leone. In: Caldwell J et al., eds. *What we know about health transition: the cultural, social and behavioural determinants of health*, vol. 2. Canberra, Australian National University, 2001:561–583.

Bledsoe CH. *Contingent lives: fertility, time, and aging in West Africa.* Chicago, University of Chicago Press, 2002.

Bledsoe CH, Goubaud MF. The reinterpretation of Western pharmaceuticals among the Mende of Sierra Leone. *Social Science and Medicine*, 1985, 21 (3): 275–282.

Bledsoe C et al. Constructing natural fertility: the use of Western contraceptive technologies in rural Gambia. *Population and Development Review*, 1994, 20 (1): 81–113.

Bledsoe C et al. Reproductive mishaps and Western contraception: an African challenge to fertility theory. *Population and Development Review*, 1998, 24 (1): 15–57.

Bloland PB. A contrarian view of malaria therapy policy in Africa. *American Journal of Tropical Medicine and Hygiene*, 2003, 68:125–126.

Bloland PB et al. Combination therapy for malaria in Africa: hype or hope. *Bulletin of the World Health Organization*, 2000, 78:1378–1388.

Bloom G, Standing H. *Pluralism and marketisation in the health sector: meeting health needs in contexts of social change in low and middle income countries.* IDS Working Paper 136. Brighton, Sussex, UK, Institute of Development Studies, 2001.

Boli J, Thomas GM. *Constructing world culture: international nongovernmental organizations since 1875*. Stanford, CA, Stanford University Press, 1999.

Bond M. The backlash against NGOs. *Prospect Magazine*, 2000, 51 (April): 52–55.

Boonmongkon P. *Khi thut*, "the disease of social loathing": an anthropological study of the stigma of leprosy in rural north-east Thailand. *Social and Economic Research Project Reports*, 1995, 16:1–50.

Boonmongkon P et al. Emerging fears of cervical cancer in northeast Thailand. *Anthropology and Medicine*, 1999, 16 (4): 359–380.

Boonmongkon P et al. Women's "mot luuk" problems in northeast Thailand: why women's own health concerns matter as much as disease rates. *Social Science and Medicine*, 2001, 53:1095–1112.

Booth A. Decentralisation and poverty alleviation in Indonesia. *Environment and Planning C: Government and Policy*, 2003, 21:181–202.

Booth S et al. Factors influencing self-diagnosis and treatment of perceived helminthic infection in a rural Guatemalan community. *Social Science and Medicine*, 1993, 37:531–539.

Borfitz D. Lifting India's barriers to clinical trials. *Center Watch*, 2003, 10 (8): 1–9.

Bossart R. "In the city, everybody only cares for himself": social relations and illness in Abidjan, Côte d'Ivoire. *Anthropology and Medicine*, 2003, 10 (3): 343–359.

Botes L, van Rensburg D. Community participation in development: nine plagues and twelve commandments. *Community Development Journal*, 2000, 35 (1): 41–58.

Bourchier D, Hadiz VR, eds. *Indonesian politics and society: a reader*. London, RoutledgeCurzon, 2003.

Bourdieu P. The forms of capital. In: Richardson JG, ed. *Handbook of theory and research for the sociology of education*. New York, Greenwood Press, 1986:241–258.

Bourdieu P. *The logic of practice*. Nice R, trans. Stanford, CA, Stanford University Press, 1990.

Bourgois P, Scheper-Hughes N. Comments (response to Farmer P, "An anthropology of structural violence"). *Current Anthropology*, 2004, 45 (3): 317–318.

Bradley AK. Local perceptions of onchocerciasis in the Hawal Valley, Nigeria. *GeoJournal*, 1981, 5 (4): 357–362.

Braunstein S, van de Wijgert J. Preferences and practices related to vaginal lubrication: implications for microbicide acceptability. *Journal of Women's Health*, 2005, 14 (5): 424–433.

Braveman P, Tarimo E. Social inequalities in health within countries: not only an issue for affluent nations. *Social Science and Medicine*, 2002, 54:1621–1635.

Braveman P et al. Health inequalities and social inequalities in health. *Bulletin of the World Health Organization*, 2000, 78 (2): 232–233.

Brewer DD et al. Mounting anomalies in the epidemiology of HIV in Africa: cry the beloved paradigm. *International Journal of STD and AIDS*, 2003, 14:144–147.

Brieger WR. Jedi jedi, a Yoruba cultural disease with implications for home management of diarrhea. *Health Education Research*, 1990, 5 (3): 337–342.

Brieger WR, Kendall C. Learning from local knowledge to improve disease surveillance: perceptions of the guinea worm illness experience. *Health Education Research*, 1992, 7 (4): 471–485.

Brieger WR et al. Issues in collaborative research between health educators and medical scientists: a case study. *International Quarterly of Community Health Education*, 1984–85, 5:229–237.

Brieger WR et al. Improving recognition of onchocerciasis in primary care-2: learning from a cultural perspective. *Tropical Doctor*, 1986, 16:9–13.

Brieger WR et al. Guineaworm control case study: planning a multi-strategy approach. *Social Science and Medicine*, 1991, 32 (12): 1319–1326.

Briggs C. Lessons in the time of cholera. In: Briggs C. *Infectious diseases and social inequality in Latin America: from hemispheric insecurity to global cooperation*. Woodrow Wilson Center Working Paper Series #239. Washington, DC, 1999.

Briggs C. Modernity, cultural reasoning, and the institutionalization of social inequality: racializing death in a Venezuelan cholera epidemic. *Comparative Studies in Society and History*, 2001, 43:665–700.

Briggs CL. Theorizing modernity conspiratorially: science, scale, and the political economy of public discourse in explanations of a cholera epidemic. *American Ethnologist*, 2004, 31:164–187.

Briggs CL. Communicability, racial discourse, and disease. *Annual Review of Anthropology*, 2005, 34:269–291.

Briggs C, Mantini-Briggs C. *Stories in the time of cholera: racial profiling during a medical nightmare*. Berkeley, University of California Press, 2003.

Brogden WG, McAllister JC. Insecticide resistance and vector control. *Emerging Infectious Diseases*, 1998, 4 (4): 605–613.

Brown N. Hope against hype—accountability in biopasts, presents and futures. *Science Studies*, 2003, 16 (2): 3–21.

Brown P. Popular epidemiology: community response to toxic waste induced disease in Woburn, Massachusetts, and other sites. *Science, Technology, and Human Values*, 1987, 12:76–85.

Brown P. Popular epidemiology revisited. *Current Sociology*, 1997, 45 (3): 137–156.

Brown PJ, Inhorn MC. Disease, ecology, and human behavior. In: Johnson TM, Sargent CF, eds. *Medical anthropology: a handbook of theory and method*. New York, Greenwood Press, 1990:187–214.

Brown TM et al. Public health then and now: the World Health Organization and the transition from "international" to "global" public health. *American Journal of Public Health*, 2006, 96 (1): 62–72.

Browner CH. Women, household and health in Latin America. *Social Science and Medicine*, 1989, 28 (5): 461–473.

Bruce J. Homes divided. *World Development*, 1989, 17 (7): 979–991.

Brugha R. Antiretroviral treatment in developing countries: the peril of neglecting private providers. *British Medical Journal*, 2003, 326:1382–1384.

Bruner J. The narrative construction of reality. *Critical Inquiry*, 1991, 18:1–21.

Brush BL et al. Imported care: recruiting foreign nurses to US health care facilities. *Health Affairs*, 2004, 23 (3): 78–87.

Bruun B. *Service of the engine: pharmaceuticals, moralities, and sex in a Malawian fishing village*. Amsterdam, Aksant Academic Publishers, 2002.

Bryant RL. *Making moral capital: non-governmental organizations in environmental struggles*. New Haven, CT, Yale University Press, 2004.

Bryant RL, Goodman MK. Consuming narratives: the political ecology of "alternative" consumption. *Transactions of the Institute of British Geographers*, 2004, 29 (3): 344–366.

Buckley TCT, Gottlieb A, eds. *Blood magic: the anthropology of menstruation*. Berkeley, University of California Press, 1988.

Bujra J. Risk and trust: unsafe sex, gender and AIDS in Tanzania. In: Caplan P, ed. *Risk revisited*. London and Sterling, VA, Pluto Press, 2000:59–84.

Bukhman G. Reform and resistance in post-Soviet tuberculosis control [dissertation]. Tucson, University of Arizona, 2001.

Buse K, Walt G. Global public-private partnerships: part I—a new development in health? *Bulletin of the World Health Organization*, 2000a, 78:549–561.

Buse K, Walt G. Global public-private partnerships: part II—what are the health issues for global governance? *Bulletin of the World Health Organization*, 2000b, 78:699–709.

Buse K, Walt G. Globalisation and multilateral public-private health partnerships: issues for health policy. In: Lee K et al., eds. *Health policy in a globalizing world*. Cambridge, Cambridge University Press, 2002:41–62.

Buse K, Waxman A. Public-private health partnerships: a strategy for WHO. *Bulletin of the World Health Organization*, 2001, 79 (8): 748–754.

Caldwell J, Caldwell P. Roles of women, families, and communities in preventing illness and providing health services in developing countries. In: Gribble JN, Preston SH, eds. *The epidemiological transition: policy and planning implications for developing countries*. Washington, DC, National Academy Press, 1993:252–271.

Callon M. The role of lay people in the production and dissemination of scientific knowledge. *Science, Technology, and Society*, 1999, 4 (1): 81–94.

Calnan M. The people know best. *International Journal of Epidemiology*, 2004, 33:506–507.

Campbell C. Male gender roles and sexuality: implications for women's AIDS risk and prevention. *Social Science and Medicine*, 1995, 41:197–201.

Campbell H et al. Acute respiratory infections in Gambian children: maternal perception of illness. *Annals of Tropical Pediatrics*, 1990, 10:45–51.

Canales M. Othering: towards an understanding of difference. *Advances in Nursing Science*, 2000, 22 (4): 16–31.

Cárdenas Timoteo C et al. Diferencia de genero en la adquisición de la leishmaniasis selvática: caso del valle de Kosñipata, Cusco, Perú. *Amazonia Peruana*, 1994, 12 (24): 269–286.

Carothers T, Ottaway M, eds. *Funding virtue: civil society aid and democracy promotion*. Washington, DC, Carnegie Endowment for International Peace, 2000.

Cartwright E. Bodily remembering: Memory, place and understanding Latino folk illnesses among the Amuzgos Indians of Oaxaca, Mexico. *Culture, Medicine and Psychiatry*, 2007, doi:10.1007/sl1013-007-9063-1.

Carver S. The future of participatory approaches using geographic information: developing a research agenda for the 21st century. *Urisa Journal*, 2003, 15 (1): 61–72.

Casey ES. How to get from space to place in a fairly short stretch of time: phenomenological prolegomena. In Feld S, Basso KH, eds. *Senses of Place*. Santa Fe, NM, School of American Research Press, 1996:13–52.

Cash RA, Narasimhan V. Impediments to global surveillance of infectious diseases: consequences of open reporting in a global economy. *Bulletin of the World Health Organization*, 2000, 78 (11): 1358–1367.

Cassell JA et al. The social shaping of childhood vaccination practice in rural and urban Gambia. *Health Policy and Planning*, 2006, 21 (5): 373–391.

Castañeda H. Paradoxes of providing aid: NGOs, medicine, and undocumented migration in Berlin, Germany [dissertation]. Tucson, University of Arizona, 2007.

Castaneda X et al. Ethnography of fertility and menstruation in rural Mexico. *Social Science and Medicine*, 1996, 42 (1): 133–140.

Castel R. From dangerousness to risk. In: Burchell G et al., eds. *The Foucault effect: studies in governmentality*. Chicago, University of Chicago Press, 1991:281–298.

Castells M. *The information age: economy, society and culture*, vol. 1, *The rise of the network society*. Oxford, UK, Blackwell, 1996.

Castle SE. Intra-household differentials in women's status: household function and focus as determinants of children's illness management and care in rural Mali. *Health Transition Review*, 1993, 3 (2): 137–156.

Castle S. Factors influencing young Malians' reluctance to use hormonal contraceptives. *Studies in Family Planning*, 2003, 34 (3): 186–199.

Castro A. Anthropologists as advocates: power, suffering and AIDS. *Anthropology News*, 2004, 45 (7): 9, 11.

Castro A, Farmer P. Understanding and addressing AIDS-related stigma: from anthropological theory to clinical practice in Haiti. *American Journal of Public Health*, 2005, 95:1.

Castro A, Singer M, eds. *Unhealthy health policy: a critical anthropological examination*. Walnut Creek, CA, Altamira Press, 2004.

Castro R. The subjective experience of health and illness in Ocuituco: a case study. *Social Science and Medicine*, 1993, 41 (7): 1005–1021.

CDC (U.S. Centers for Disease Control and Prevention). *Addressing emerging infectious disease threats: a prevention strategy for the United States*. Atlanta, GA, CDC, 1994.

Chand AK, Bhattacharyya K. The Marathi "taskonomy" of respiratory illnesses in children. *Medical Anthropology*, 1994, 15 (4): 395–408.

Chanyapate C, Delforge I. The politics of bird flu in Thailand. *Focus on Trade* no. 98, April 2004 (http://focusweb.org/publications/FOT%20pdf/fot98.pdf).

Chatterjee M. Competence and care for women: health policy perspectives in the household context. In: Maithreyi K, Chananna K, eds. *Gender and the household domain: social and cultural dimensions*. New Delhi, Sage, 1989.

Chavez LR et al. Beliefs matter: cultural beliefs and the use of cervical cancer-screening tests. *American Anthropologist*, 2001, 103:1114–1129.

Chen LC et al. Health as a global public good. In: Kaul I et al., eds. *Global public goods: international cooperation in the 21st century*. New York, Oxford University Press, 1999:284–306.

Chintu C et al. Co-trimoxazole as prophylaxis against opportunistic infections in HIV-infected Zambian children (CHAP): a double-blind randomized placebo-controlled trial. *Lancet*, 2004, 364:1865–1871.

Chrisman NJ, Kleinman A. Popular health care, social networks, and cultural meanings: the orientation of medical anthropology. In: Mechanic D, ed. *Handbook of health, health care, and the health professions*. New York, Free Press, 1983:569–590.

Christian P et al. An ethnographic study of night blindness "ratauni" among women in the Terai of Nepal. *Social Science and Medicine*, 1998, 46 (7): 879–889.

Clark A et al. Biomedicalization: technoscientific transformations of health, illness, and US biomedicine. *American Sociological Review*, 2003, 68:161–194.

Clark J. *Democratizing development—the role of voluntary organizations*. London, Earthscan Publications, 1991.

Cline BL, Hewlett BS. Community-based approach to schistosomiasis control. *Acta Tropica*, 1996, 61 (2): 107–119.

Coburn D. Beyond the income inequality hypothesis: class, neo-liberalism, and health inequalities. *Social Science and Medicine*, 2004, 58:41–56.

Cockburn R et al. The global threat of counterfeit drugs: why industry and governments must communicate the dangers. *PLoS Medicine*, 2005, 2 (4): 100–106.

Cody SH et al. Knowing pneumonia: mothers, doctors, and sick children in Pakistan. In: Inhorn MC et al., eds. *Anthropology and infectious disease: international health perspectives*. Amsterdam, Gordon and Breach, 1997.

Coetzee D et al. Outcomes after two years of providing antiretroviral treatment in Khayelitsha, South Africa. *AIDS*, 2004, 18:887–895.

Cohen AP. *The symbolic construction of community*. London, Tavistock, 1985.

Cohen J. The global burden of disease study: a useful projection of future global health? *Journal of Public Health Medicine*, 2000, 22:518–524.

Cohen L. Where it hurts: Indian material for an ethic of organ transplant. *Zygon*, 2003, 38 (3): 663–688.

Coker R. Compulsory screening of immigrants for tuberculosis and HIV: is not based on adequate evidence, has practical and ethical problems. *British Medical Journal*, 2004, 328:298–299.

Coleman JS. Social capital in the creation of human capital. *American Journal of Sociology*, 1988, 94 (suppl.): S95–S120.

Coleman JS. *Foundations of social theory*. Cambridge, MA, Harvard University Press, 1990.

Collier SJ, Lakoff A. Regimes of living. In: Ong A, Collier SJ, eds. *Global assemblages: technology, politics, and ethics as anthropological problems*. Malden, MA, Blackwell, 2005:22–39.

Collin J et al. The framework convention on tobacco control: the politics of global health governance. *Third World Quarterly*, 2002, 23 (2): 265–282.

Comaroff J, Comaroff JL. Occult economies and the violence of abstraction: notes from the South African postcolony. *American Ethnologist*, 1999, 26 (2): 279–303.

Comoro C et al. Local understanding, perceptions and reported practices of mothers/guardians and health workers on childhood malaria in a Tanzania district—implications for malaria control. *Acta Tropica*, 2003, 87:305–313.

Conanan EC, Valeza FS. Factors affecting completion rate in tuberculosis short-course chemotherapy. *Journal of Philippines Medical Association*, 1988, 64 (1): 11–14.

Connors M. Risk perception, risk taking, and risk management among intra-venous drug users: implications for AIDS prevention. *Social Science and Medicine*, 1992, 34 (6): 591–601.

Consumers International. *Branding the cure: a consumer perspective on corporate social responsibility, drug promotion and the pharmaceutical industry in Europe.* London, Consumers International, 2006.

Cooke B, Kothari U. The case of participation as tyranny. In: Cooke B, Kothari U, eds. *Participation: the new tyranny?* London, Zed Books, 2001.

Cooper F, Packard R, eds. *International development and the social sciences: essays on the history and politics of knowledge.* Berkeley, University of California Press, 1997.

Cooper RA, Aiken LH. Health services delivery: reframing policies for global migration of nurses and physicians, a US perspective. *Policy, Politics, and Practice*, 2006, 7 (3): 66S–70S.

Coreil J et al. Filarial elephantiasis among Haitian women: social context and behavioural factors in treatment. *Tropical Medicine and International Health*, 1998, 3:467–473.

Coreil J et al. *Support groups for women with lymphatic filariasis in Haiti. Final Report.* Geneva, World Health Organization, 2003.

Cornwall A. Whose voices? Whose choices? Reflections on gender and partici-patory development. *World Development*, 2003, 31 (8): 1325–1342.

Corrigan P, Sayer D. *The great arch: English state formation as cultural revolution.* Oxford, UK, Blackwell, 1985.

Craig D. Practical logics: the shapes and lessons of popular medical knowledge and practice—examples from Vietnam and indigenous Australia. *Social Science and Medicine*, 2000, 51:703–711.

Craig D. *Familiar medicine: everyday health knowledge and practice in today's Vietnam.* Honolulu, University of Hawai'i Press, 2002.

Crandon-Malamud L. *From the fat of our souls: social change, political process, and medical pluralism in Bolivia*. Berkeley, University of California Press, 1991.

Crawford R. The boundaries of the self and the unhealthy other: reflections on health, culture and AIDS. *Social Science and Medicine*, 1994, 38 (10): 1347–1365.

Cromley EK, McLafferty S. *GIS and public health*. New York, Guilford Press, 2002.

Cruikshank B. *The will to empower: democratic citizens and other subjects*. Ithaca, NY, Cornell University Press, 1999.

Crush J. The global raiders: nationalism, globalization, and the South African brain drain. *Journal of International Affairs*, 2002, 56 (1): 147–172.

Das V, Das RK. Urban health and pharmaceutical consumption in Delhi, India. *Journal of Biosocial Science*, 2005, 38 (1): 69–82.

Das Gupta M. Death clustering, mothers' education and the determinants of child mortality in rural Punjab, India. *Population Studies*, 1990, 44:489–505.

Dasgupta P. Economic progress and the idea of social capital. In: Dasgupta P, Serageldin I, eds. *Social capital: a multifaceted perspective*. Washington, DC, World Bank, 1999:325–424.

Datta M, Nichter M. Towards introducing culturally sensitive tuberculosis education and context specific patient screening. IndiaCLEN Tuberculosis Study Group, Chennai, India, 2005 (www.tnmu.ac.in/edu.pdf).

Davis M. *The monster at our door: the global threat of avian flu*. New York, New Press, 2005.

Davis M. *A planet of slums*. London, Verso, 2006.

Davis MDM et al. "HIV is HIV to me": the meanings of treatment, viral load and reinfection for gay men living with HIV. *Health, Risk and Society*, 2002, 4 (1): 31–43.

Davison C et al. Lay epidemiology and the prevention paradox: the implications of coronary candidacy for health education. *Sociology of Health and Illness*, 1991, 13 (1): 1–19.

Davison C et al. The limits of lifestyle—reassessing fatalism in the popular culture of illness prevention. *Social Science and Medicine*, 1992, 34:675–685.

Dean M. *Governmentality: power and rule in modern society*. London, Sage, 1999.

Dean M. Liberal government and authoritarianism. *Economy and Society*, 2002, 31 (1): 37–61.

de Bessa GH. Ethnophysiology and contraceptive use among low-income women in urban Brazil. *Health Care for Women International*, 2006, 27:428–452.

Demissie M et al. Community tuberculosis care through "TB clubs" in rural north Ethiopia. *Social Science and Medicine*, 2003, 56 (10): 2009–2018.

de Oliveira MH. The effects of leprosy on men and women: a gender study. *Gender and Tropical Diseases*, 1997, 4:1–10.

de Rosa AS. Why does it matter? Notes inspired by a reflexive view of the social representations theory. Invited lecture, 7th International Conference on Social Representations. Social Representations and Forms of Interaction: Individuals, Groups and Social Movements. University of Guadalajara, Mexico, September 10–14, 2004.

de Souza Briggs X. Doing democracy up-close: culture, power, and communication in community building. *Journal of Planning Education and Research*, 1998, 18:1–13.

de Villiers S. Tuberculosis in anthropological perspective. *South African Journal of Ethnology*, 1991, 14 (3): 69–72.

de Waal A. How will HIV/AIDS transform African governance? *African Affairs*, 2003, 102:1–23.

de Zoysa I et al. Perceptions of childhood diarrhoea and its treatment in rural Zimbabwe. *Social Science and Medicine*, 1984, 19 (7): 727–734.

Diez-Roux AV. On genes, individuals, society, and epidemiology. *American Journal of Epidemiology*, 1998, 148:1027–1032.

Djimde A et al. Use of antimalarial drugs in Mali: policy versus reality. *American Journal of Tropical Medicine Hygiene*, 1998, 59:376–379.

Doja A. Rethinking the *couvade*. *Anthropological Quarterly*, 2005, 78 (4): 917–950.

Dollar D. Is globalization good for your health? *Bulletin of the World Health Organization*, 2001, 79 (9): 827–833.

Dondorp AM et al. Fake antimalarials in Southeast Asia are a major impediment to malaria control: multinational cross-sectional survey on the prevalence of fake antimalarials. *Tropical Medicine and International Health*, 2004, 9 (12): 1241–1246.

Dressler WW. Modeling biocultural interactions: examples from studies of stress and cardiovascular disease. *Yearbook of Physical Anthropology*, 1995, 38:27–56.

Dressler WW. Modernization, stress and blood pressure: new directions in research. *Human Biology*, 1999, 71:538–605.

Dressler WW. Culture and the risk of disease. *British Medical Bulletin*, 2004, 69:21–31.

Dressler WW. What's cultural about biocultural research? *Ethos*, 2005, 33:20–45.

Dressler WW. Taking culture seriously in health research. *International Journal of Epidemiology*, 2006, 35:258–259.

Dressler WW, Bindon JR. The health consequences of cultural consonance: cultural dimensions of lifestyle, social support and arterial blood pressure in an African American community. *American Anthropologist*, 2000, 102:244–260.

Dreyer G et al. The silent burden of sexual disability associated with lymphatic filariasis. *Acta Tropica*, 1997, 63:57–60.

Driver F, Martins L, eds. *Tropical visions in an age of empire*. Chicago, University of Chicago Press, 2005.

Driver F, Yeoh B. Constructing the tropics: introduction. *Singapore Journal of Tropical Geography*, 2000, 21 (1): 1–5.

Dunn FL. Human behavioural factors in mosquito vector control. *South East Asian Journal of Tropical Medicine and Public Health*, 1983, 14:86–94.

Durkheim E. Individual and collective representations. In: Durkheim E. *Sociology and philosophy*. Pocock DF, trans. New York, New Press, 1974 [1896]: 1–34.

Durrant J. Participatory technology assessment and the democratic model of the public understanding of science. *Science and Public Policy*, 1999, 26:313–319.

Eberhard MJ et al. A survey of knowledge, attitudes and perceptions (KAPs) of lymphatic filariasis, elephantiasis, and hydrocele among residents in an endemic area of Haiti. *American Journal of Tropical Medicine and Hygiene*, 1996, 54:299–303.

Ecks S. Pharmaceutical citizenship: antidepressant marketing and the promise of demarginalization in India. *Anthropology and Medicine*, 2005, 12 (3): 239–254.

Edkins J. *Whose hunger? Concepts of famine, practices of aid*. Minneapolis, University of Minnesota Press, 2000.

Eisenberg JM. Globalize the evidence, localize the decision: evidence-based medicine and international diversity. *Health Affairs*, 2002, 21:166–168.

Elam M, Bertilsson M. Consuming, engaging and confronting science: emerging dimensions of scientific citizenship. *European Journal of Social Theory*, 2003, 6 (2): 233–252.

Eliasson B. Cigarette smoking and diabetes. *Progress in Cardiovascular Diseases*, 2003, 45 (5): 405–413.

Ellen IG et al. Neighborhood effects on health: exploring the links and assessing the evidence. *Journal of Urban Affairs*, 2001, 23 (3–4): 391–408.

Elwood S. Critical issues in participatory GIS: deconstructions, reconstructions, and new research directions. *Transactions in GIS*, 2006, 10 (5): 693–708.

Ember CR, Ember M, eds. *Encyclopedia of medical anthropology: health and illness in the world's cultures*. New York, Kluwer Academic/Plenum, 2004.

English M et al. Clinical overlap between malaria and severe pneumonia in African children in hospital. *Transactions of the Royal Society of Tropical Medicine and Hygiene*, 1996, 90 (6): 658–662.

Epstein PR. Is global warming harmful to health? *Scientific American*, 2000 (August 20): 50–57.

Epstein S. *Impure science: AIDS, activisim, and the politics of knowledge*. Berkeley, University of California Press, 1996.

Erwin K. The circulatory system: blood procurement, AIDS, and the social body in China. *Medical Anthropology Quarterly*, 2006, 20 (2): 139–159.

Espino F, Manderson L. Treatment seeking for malaria in Morong, Bataan, the Philippines. *Social Science and Medicine*, 2000, 50:1309–1316.

Espino F et al. Perceptions of malaria in a low endemic area in the Philippines: transmission and prevention of disease. *Acta Tropica*, 1997, 63:221–239.

Espino F et al. *Community participation and tropical disease control in resource-poor settings*. Geneva, World Health Organization, 2004.

Etkin N. "Side effects": cultural constructions and reinterpretations of Western pharmaceuticals. *Medical Anthropology Quarterly*, 1992, 6 (2): 99–113.

Etkin N et al. The indigenization of pharmaceuticals: therapeutic transitions in rural Hausaland. *Social Science and Medicine*, 1990, 30 (8): 919–928.

Evans DB et al. Social and economic factors and the control of lymphatic filariasis: a review. *Acta Tropica*, 1993, 53:1–26.

Evans P. Government action, social capital and development: reviewing the evidence on synergy. *World Development*, 1996, 24 (6): 1119–1132.

Evans-Pritchard EE. Social anthropology: past and present. *Man*, 1950, 1:118–124.

Fabricant SJ, Hirschhorn N. Deranged distribution, perverse prescription, unprotected use: the irrationality of pharmaceuticals in the developing world. *Health Policy and Planning*, 1987, 2 (3): 204–213.

Fairhead J, Leach M. Where technoscience meets poverty: medical research and the economy of blood in the Gambia, West Africa. *Social Science and Medicine*, 2006, 63 (4): 1109–1120.

Fane G. Change and continuity in Indonesia's new fiscal decentralization arrangements. *Bulletin of Indonesian Economic Studies*, 2003, 39:159–176.

Farmer P. Bad blood, spoiled milk: bodily fluids as moral barometers in rural Haiti. *American Ethnologist*, 1988, 15 (1): 63–83.

Farmer P. Sending sickness: sorcery, politics and changing concepts of AIDS in rural Haiti. *Medical Anthropology Quarterly*, 1990:6–27.

Farmer P. *AIDS and accusation: Haiti and the geography of blame*. Berkeley, University of California Press, 1992.

Farmer P. AIDS—talk and the constitution of cultural models. *Social Science and Medicine*, 1994, 38:801–809.

Farmer P. Social inequalities and emerging infectious diseases. *Emerging Infectious Diseases*, 1996, 2 (4): 259–69.

Farmer P. Social scientists and the new tuberculosis. *Social Science and Medicine*, 1997, 44 (3): 347–358.

Farmer P. *Infections and inequalities: the modern plagues*. Berkeley, University of California Press, 1999.

Farmer P. *Pathologies of power: health, human rights, and the new war on the poor*. Berkeley, University of California Press, 2003.

Farmer P. An anthropology of structural violence. *Current Anthropology*, 2004, 45 (3): 305–317.

Farmer P, Becerra M. Biosocial research and the TDR agenda. *TDR News*, 2001, 66:5–7.

Farmer P, Castro A. Pearls of the Antilles? Public health in Haiti and Cuba. In: Castro A, Singer M, eds. *Unhealthy health policy: a critical anthropological examination*. Walnut Creek, CA, Altamira Press, 2004:3–28.

Farmer P, Garrett L. From "marvelous momentum" to health care for all: success is possible with the right programs. *Foreign Affairs*, July/August 2006 (http://www.foreignaffairs.org).

Farmer P et al. The dilemma of MDR-TB in the global era. *International Journal of Tuberculosis and Lung Disease*, 1998, 2 (11): 869–876.

Farmer P et al. Community-based approaches to HIV treatment in resource-poor settings. *Lancet*, 2001a, 358:404–409.

Farmer P et al. Community-based treatment of advanced HIV disease: introducing DOT-HAART (directly observed therapy with highly active antiretroviral therapy). *Bulletin of the World Health Organization*, 2001b, 79:1145–1151.

Fassin D. The biopolitics of otherness: undocumented foreigners and racial discrimination in French public debate. *Anthropology Today*, 2001, 17 (1): 3–7.

Fassin D. Social illegitimacy as a foundation of health inequality: how the political treatment of immigrants illuminates a French paradox. In: Castro A, Singer M, eds. *Unhealthy health policy: a critical anthropological examination*. Walnut Creek, CA, Altamira, 2004:203–214.

Fassin D, Schneider H. The politics of AIDS in South Africa: beyond the controversies. *British Medical Journal*, 2003, 326:495–497.

Feld S, Basso KH, eds. *Senses of place*. Santa Fe, NM, School of American Research Press, 1996.

Feldman-Savelsberg P et al. Sterilizing vaccines or the politics of the womb: ret-rospective study of rumor in Cameroon. *Medical Anthropology Quarterly*, 2000, 14:159–179.

Ferguson A. Commercial pharmaceutical medicine and medicalization: a case study from El Salvador. In: Van der Geest S, Whyte SR, eds. *The context of medicines in developing countries*. Dordrecht, Kluwer Academic Publishers, 1988:19–46.

Ferguson J. *The anti-politics machine: "development," depoliticization, and bureau-cratic power in Lesotho*. Cambridge, Cambridge University Press, 1990.

Ferguson J, Gupta A. Spatializing states: toward an ethnography of neoliberal governmentality. *American Ethnologist*, 2002, 29 (4): 981–1002.

Ferrinho P et al. Dual practice in the health sector: review of the evidence. *Human Resources for Health*, 2004, 2:14.

Fidler D. The globalization of public health: the first 100 years of international health diplomacy. *Bulletin of the World Health Organization*, 2001, 79 (9): 842–849.

Fidler DP. SARS: political pathology of the first post-Westphalian pathogen. *Journal of Law, Medicine and Ethics*, 2003, 31:485–505.

Fidler D. Germs, norms and power: global health's political revolution. *Law, Social Justice and Global Development Journal*, 2004a (www2.warwick.ac.uk/fac/soc/law/elj/lgd/2004_1/fidler/).

Fidler D. *SARS, governance and the globalization of disease*. New York, Palgrave Macmillan, 2004b.

Fidler DP. From international sanitary conventions to global health security: the new international health regulations. *Chinese Journal of International Law*, 2005, 4 (2): 325–392.

Fidler DP. Architecture amidst anarchy: global health's quest for governance. *Journal of Global Health Governance*, 2007, 1 (1): 1–17.

Figueroa-Damian R et al. Tuberculosis of the female reproductive tract: effect on function. *International Journal of Fertility and Menopausal Studies*, 1996, 41:430–436.

Fine B. The developmental state is dead—long live social capital? *Development and Change*, 1999, 30:1–19.

Fine B. The World Bank's speculation on social capital. In: Pincus JR, Winters JA, eds. *Reinventing the World Bank*. Ithaca, NY, Cornell University Press, 2002:203–221.

Finerman R. "Parental incompetence" and "selective neglect": blaming the vic-tim in child survival. *Social Science and Medicine*, 1995, 40 (1): 5–13.

Fisher WF. Doing good? The politics and antipolitics of NGO practices. *Annual Review of Anthropology*, 1997, 26:439–464.

Fisher-Hoch SP et al. Review of cases of nosocomial Lassa fever in Nigeria: the high price of poor medical practice. *British Medical Journal*, 1995, 311:857–859.

Flyvbjerg B. The power of example. In: Flyvbjerg B. *Making social science matter: why social inquiry fails and how it can succeed again*. Sampson S, trans. Cambridge, Cambridge University Press, 2001:66–87.

Folbre N. Hearts and spades: paradigms of household economics. *World Development*, 1986, 14 (2): 245–255.

Folbre N. Gender coalitions: extrafamily influences on intrafamily inequality. In: Haddad L et al., eds. *Intrahousehold resource allocation in developing countries*. Baltimore, MD, Johns Hopkins University Press, 1997:263–274.

Foster G. Medical anthropology and international health planning. *Medical Anthropology Newsletter*, 1976, 7 (3): 12–18.

Foster G. Bureaucratic aspects of international health agencies. *Social Science and Medicine*, 1987, 25 (9): 1039–1048.

Foster KR, Grundmann H. Do we need to put society first? The potential for tragedy in antimicrobial resistance. *PLoS Medicine*, 2006, 3 (2): e29, doi:10.1371/journal.pmed.0030029.

Foucault M. *The history of sexuality*, vol. 1, *An introduction*. Hurley R, trans. Allen Lane, 1979.

Foucault M. Truth and method. In: Rabinow P, ed. *The Foucault reader*. New York, Pantheon Books, 1984:31–120.

Foucault M. Governmentality. In: Burchell G et al., eds. *The Foucault effect: studies in governmentality*. London, Harvester Wheatsheaf, 1991:87–104.

Foy CG et al. Findings from the Insulin Resistance Atherosclerosis Study. *American Journal of Medicine*, 2000, 109 (7): 538–542.

Frank C et al. The role of parenteral antischistosomal therapy in the spread of hepatitis C virus in Egypt. *Lancet*, 2000, 355:887–891.

Frank M, Reed GA. Doctors for the (developing) world. *MEDICC Review*, 2005, 7 (8): 2–4.

Frankel SJ, Lehmann D. Oral rehydration therapy: combining anthropological and epidemiological approaches in the evaluation of a Papua New Guinea programme. *Journal of Tropical Medicine and Hygiene*, 1984, 87:137–142.

Frederick K, Thomas S. *A KAP study to determine perception of schistosomiasis in Kampumbu area—Isoka District of Zambia*. Department of Epidemiology Tropical Diseases Research Center, 1994.

Freire P. *Cultural action for freedom*. Cambridge, MA, Harvard Educational Review and Center for the Study of Development and Social Change, 1970a.

Freire P. *Pedagogy of the oppressed*. Ramos MB, trans. New York, Continuum, 1970b. Reprint, 1998.

Freire P. *Extension or communication*. New York, Seabury Press, 1973.

Freudenburg WR. Institutional failure and the organization amplification of risks: the need for a closer look. In: Pidgeon NF et al., eds. *The social amplification of risk*. Cambridge, Cambridge University Press, 2003:102–120.

Frich J et al. Perceived vulnerability to heart disease in patients with familial hyper-cholesterolemia: a qualitative interview study. *Annals of Family Medicine*, 2006, 4:198–204.

Fukuyama F. *Trust: the social virtues and the creation of prosperity*. New York, Free Press, 1996.

Fukuyama F. Social capital and civil society. Conference on Second Generation Reforms. IMF Headquarters, Washington, DC, IMF Institute and the Fiscal Affairs Department, November 8–9, 1999 (www.imf.org/external/pubs/ft/seminar/1999/reforms/index.htm).

Fukuyama F. Social capital, civil society and development. *Third World Quarterly*, 2001, 22 (1): 7–20.

Gabbay J, Le May A. Evidence based guidelines or collectively constructed "mindlines"? Ethnographic study of knowledge management in primary care. *British Medical Journal*, 2004, 329:1013.

Gagneux S et al. Variable host-pathogen compatibility in *Mycobacterium tuberculosis*. *Proceedings of the National Academy of Sciences*, 2006, 103 (8): 2869–2873.

Galloway R, McGuire J. Determinants of compliance with iron supplementation: supplies, side effects, or psychology. *Social Science and Medicine*, 1994, 39 (3): 381–390.

Galloway R et al. Women's perceptions of iron deficiency and anemia prevention and control in eight developing countries. *Social Science and Medicine*, 2002, 55:529–544.

Garner P, Volmink J. Directly observed treatment for tuberculosis. *British Medical Journal*, 2003, 327:823–824.

Garner P, Volmink J. Families help cure tuberculosis. *Lancet*, 2006, 367 (March 18): 878–879.

Garrett L. *Betrayal of trust: the collapse of global public health*. New York, Hyperion, 2000.

Garrett L. The challenge of global health. *Foreign Affairs*, 2007, 86 (1).

Garro LC. Cultural knowledge as a resource in illness narratives: remembering through accounts of illness. In: Garro LC, Mattingly C, eds. *Narrative and the cultural construction of illness and healing*. Berkeley, University of California Press, 2000:70–87.

Garro LC, Mattingly C. Narrative turns. In: Garro LC, Mattingly C, eds. *Narrative and the cultural construction of illness and healing*. Berkeley, University of California Press, 2000:259–269.

Gatrell AC. *Geographies of health*. Oxford, UK, Blackwell, 2002.

Gatrell AC, Rigby JE. Spatial perspectives in public health. In: Goodchild MF, Janell DG, eds. *Spatially integrated social science*. Oxford, Oxford University Press, 2004:366–380.

Geissler PW. "Worms are our life," part I: Understandings of worms and the body among the Luo of western Kenya. *Anthropology and Medicine*, 1998, 5:63–79.

Geissler PW. Kachinja are coming: encounters around a medical research project in a Kenyan village. *Africa*, 2005, 75 (2): 173–202.

Geissler PW, Pool R. Popular concerns about medical research projects in sub-Saharan Africa—a critical voice in debates about medical research ethics. *Tropical Medicine and International Health*, 2006, 11 (7): 975–982.

Geissler PW et al. Children and medicines: self-treatment of common illnesses among Luo schoolchildren in western Kenya. *Social Science and Medicine*, 2000, 50:1771–1783.

Gereffi G, Korzeniewicz M, eds. *Commodity chains and global capitalism*. Westport, CT, Praeger, 1994.

Gereffi G et al. The NGO-industrial complex. *Foreign Policy*, 2001, 125:56–65.

Gerochi LN. Knowledge, beliefs and attitudes on leprosy in Iloilo City proper, Philippines. *Southeast Asian Journal of Tropical Medicine and Public Health*, 1986, 17:433–436.

Gesler WM, Kearns RA. *Culture/Place/Health*. New York, Routledge, 2002.

Gessler MC et al. Traditional healers in Tanzania: the perception of malaria and its causes. *Journal of Ethnopharmocology*, 1995, 48 (3): 119–130.

Ghosh I, Coutinho L. Normalcy and crises in time of cholera: an ethnography of cholera in Calcutta. *Economic and Political Weekly*, 2000 (February 19–26): 684–696.

Gieryn TF. A space for place in sociology. *Annual Review of Sociology*, 2000, 26:463–496.

Giffin K, Lowndes CM. Gender, sexuality, and the prevention of sexually transmissible diseases: a Brazilian study of clinical practice. *Social Science and Medicine*, 1999, 48:282–292.

Gilman S. *Difference and pathology: stereotypes of sexuality, race and madness*. Ithaca, NY, Cornell University Press, 1985.

Gilman SL. Seeing the AIDS patient. In: Gilman SL. *Disease and representation: images of illness from madness to AIDS*. Ithaca, NY, Cornell University Press, 1988:245–272.

Gilson L. Trust and the development of health care as a social institution. *Social Science and Medicine*, 2003, 56:1453–1468.

Gisselquist DP. Estimating HIV-1 transmission efficiency through unsafe medical injections. *International Journal of STD and AIDS*, 2002, 13:152–159.

Gisselquist DP et al. HIV infections in sub-Saharan Africa not explained by sexual or vertical transmission. *International Journal of STD and AIDS*, 2002, 13:657–666.

Gisselquist DP et al. Let it be sexual: how health care transmission of AIDS in Africa was ignored. *International Journal of STD and AIDS*, 2003, 14:148–161.

Glantz N, McMahan B. Merging formative research with GIS mapping to address elder health in Chiapas, Mexico. *Practicing Anthropology*, 2007. Forthcoming.

Glick L. Medicine as an ethnographic category: the Gimi of the New Guinea Highlands. *Ethnology*, 1967, 6:31–56.

Glik DC, et al. Malaria treatment practices among mothers in Guinea. *Journal of Health and Social Behavior*, 1987, 30 (4): 421–435.

Godfrey KM, Barker DJP. Fetal nutrition and adult disease. *American Journal of Clinical Nutrition*, 2000, 71 (5): 1344S–1352S.

Goffman E. *The presentation of self in everyday life*. New York, Doubleday, 1959.

Goffman E. *Stigma: notes on the management of spoiled identity*. Englewood Cliffs, NJ, Prentice Hall, 1963.

Good BJ. The heart of what's the matter: the semantics of illness in Iran. *Culture, Medicine and Psychiatry*, 1977, 1:25–58.

Good BJ. *Medicine, rationality, and experience: an anthropological perspective*. Cambridge, Cambridge University Press, 1994.

Good BJ, Good MJ DelVecchio. In the subjunctive mode: epilepsy narratives in Turkey. *Social Science and Medicine*, 1994, 38 (6): 835–842.

Good MJ DelVecchio. Of blood and babies: the relationship of popular Islamic physiology to fertility. *Social Science and Medicine*, 1980, 14 B:147–156.

Goodman AH, Leatherman TL, eds. *Building a new biocultural synthesis*. Ann Arbor, University of Michigan Press, 1998.

Gostin LO. International infectious disease law: revision of the World Health Organization's International Health Regulations. *Journal of the American Medical Association*, 2004, 291 (21): 2623–2627.

Gostin LO. World health law: toward a new conception of global health governance for the 21st century. *Yale Journal of Health Policy, Law, and Ethics*, 2005, 5 (1): 413–424.

Gove S. Integrated management of childhood illness by outpatient health workers: technical basis and overview. *Bulletin of the World Health Organization*, 1997, 75 (suppl. 1): 7–24.

Gove S, Pelto GH. Focused ethnographic studies in the WHO programme for the control of acute respiratory infections. *Medical Anthropology*, 1994, 15 (4): 409–424.

Graham WJ et al. The familial technique for linking maternal death with poverty. *Lancet*, 2004, 363:23–27.

Gramsci A. The intellectuals. In: Hoare Q, Smith GN, trans. and eds. *Selections from the prison notebooks*. New York, International Publishers, 1971:3–23.

Granovetter M. The strength of weak ties. *American Journal of Sociology*, 1973, 78 (6): 1360–1380.

Green EC et al. The snake in the stomach: child diarrhea in central Mozambique. *Medical Anthropology Quarterly*, 1994, 8 (1): 4–24.

Green G et al. *The endangered self: managing the social risks of HIV*. New York, Routledge/Taylor and Francis, 2000.

Green L. Comments (response to Farmer P, "An anthropology of structural violence"). *Current Anthropology*, 2004, 45 (3): 319–320.

Green M. Globalizing development in Tanzania: policy franchising through participatory project management. *Critique of Anthropology*, 2003, 23 (2): 123–143.

Green M. Representing poverty and attacking representations: perspectives on poverty from social anthropology. *Journal of Development Studies*, 2006, 42 (7): 1108–1129.

Greenberg JB, Park TK. Political ecology. *Journal of Political Ecology*, 1994, 1:1–12.

Greenough P. Global immunization and culture: compliance and resistance in large-scale public health campaigns. *Social Science and Medicine*, 1995, 41:605–607.

Greenwood B. Treating malaria in Africa: sulfadoxine-pyrimethamine may still have a future despite reports of resistance. *British Medical Journal*, 2004, 328:534–535.

Greger M. *Bird flu: a virus of our own hatching*. New York, Lantern Books, 2006.

Gregg JL. *Virtually virgins: sexual strategies and cervical cancer in Recife, Brazil*. Stanford, CA, Stanford University Press, 2003.

Grein TW et al. Rumors of disease in the global village: outbreak verification. *Emerging Infectious Diseases*, 2000, 6 (2): 97–102.

Grootaert C. Social capital: the missing link? The World Bank Social Development Family Environmental and Socially Sustainable Development Network, April 1998 (www.worldbank.org/socialdevelopment).

Guerrant RL. Why America *must* care about tropical medicine: threats to global health and security from tropical infectious diseases. *American Journal of Tropical Medicine and Hygiene*, 1998, 59 (1): 3–16.

Gulrajani N. World Bank pseudoscience? *Lancet*, 2004, 364 (9448): 1852–1853.

Gupta A. *Postcolonial developments: agriculture in the making of modern India.* Durham, NC, Duke University Press, 1998.

Gupta A, Ferguson J. Beyond "culture": space, identity, and the politics of difference. In: Gupta A, Ferguson J, eds. *Culture, power, place: explorations in critical anthropology.* Durham, NC, Duke University Press, 1997:33–51.

Gupta R et al. Increasing transparency in partnerships for health—introducing the Green Light Committee. *Tropical Medicine and International Health*, 2002, 7 (11): 970–976.

Gutiérrez ECZ, Kendall C. The globalization of health and disease: the health transition and global change. In: Albrecht GL et al., eds. *The handbook of social studies in health and medicine.* London, Sage Publications, 1999:84–99.

Guyatt G et al. Evidence based medicine has come a long way. *British Medical Journal*, 2004, 329:990–991.

Guyer JI, Peters PE. Introduction. In: Conceptualizing the household—issues of theory and policy in Africa. *Development and Change*, 1987, 18 (20): 197–214.

Gwatkin DR. How well do health programmes reach the poor? *Lancet*, 2003, 361:540–541.

Gwatkin DR et al. The burden of disease among the global poor. *Lancet*, 1999, 354:586–589.

Gyapong M et al. Filariasis in northern Ghana: some cultural beliefs and practices and their implications for disease control. *Social Science and Medicine*, 1996, 43 (2): 235–242.

Haak H. Pharmaceuticals in two Brazilian villages: lay practices and perceptions. *Social Science and Medicine*, 1988, 27 (12): 1415–1427.

Habermas J. *The structural transformation of the public sphere: an inquiry into a category of bourgeois society.* Cambridge, MA, MIT Press, 1989.

Hack T et al. The communication goals and needs of cancer patients: a review. *Psycho-Oncology*, 2005, 14:831–845.

Hacking I. *Representing and intervening: introductory topics in the philosophy of natural science.* Cambridge, Cambridge University Press, 1983.

Hacking I. Making up people. In: Heller TC et al., eds. *Reconstructing individualism: autonomy, individuality, and the self in Western thought.* Stanford, CA, Stanford University Press, 1986:222–236.

Hacking I. Statistical language, statistical truth and statistical reason: the self-authentication of a style of scientific reasoning. In: McMullin E., ed. *The social dimensions of science*. Notre Dame, IN, University of Notre Dame Press, 1992.

Hacking I. The looping effects of human kinds. In: Sperber D et al., eds. *Casual cognition*. New York, Clarendon Press, 1995.

Hahn R. Rethinking "illness" and "disease." *Contributions to Asian Studies*, 1983, 18:1–23.

Halbert CH et al. Breast cancer screening behaviors among African American women with a strong family history of breast cancer. *Preventive Medicine*, 2006, 43 (5): 385–388.

Haliza B, Mohd R. Comparison of knowledge on filariasis and epidemiological factors between infected and uninfected respondents in a Malay community. *Southeast Asian Journal of Tropical Medicine and Public Health*, 1986, 17:457–463.

Hamel MJ et al. Malaria control in Bungoma District, Kenya: a survey of home treatment of children with fever, bed net use and attendance at antenatal clinics. *Bulletin of the World Health Organization*, 2001, 79:1014–1023.

Hardiman M. The revised International Health Regulations: a framework for global health security. *International Journal of Antimicrobial Agents*, 2003, 21 (2): 207–211.

Hardin G. The tragedy of the commons. *Science*, 1968, 162:1243–1248.

Hardin G. Extensions of the "tragedy of the commons." *Science*, 1998, 280:682–683.

Hardon AP. The use of modern pharmaceuticals in a Filipino village: doctors' prescription and self-medication. *Social Science and Medicine*, 1987, 25 (3): 277–292.

Hardon AP. *Confronting ill health: medicines, self care and the poor in Manila*. Quezon City, Health Action Information Network, 1991.

Hardon AP. People's understanding of efficacy for cough and cold medicines in Manila, the Philippines. In: Etkin NL, Tan ML, eds. *Medicines: meaning and contexts*. Quezon City, Hain, 1994:47–67.

Hardon A. Women's views and experiences of hormonal contraceptives: what we know and what we need to find out. In: Cottinham J, ed. *Beyond acceptability: users' perspectives on contraception*. London, Reproductive Health Matters and the World Health Organization, 1997:68–77.

Hardt M, Negri A. *Empire*. Cambridge, MA, Harvard University Press, 2000.

Harper I. Capsular promise as pubic health: a critique of the Nepal national vitamin A programme. *Studies in Nepali History and Society*, 2002, 7 (1): 137–173.

Harries A et al. Preventing antiretroviral anarchy in sub-Saharan Africa. *Lancet*, 2001, 358 (9279): 410–414.

Harrison GA. *Mosquitoes, malaria and man: a history of the hostilities since 1880.* New York, Dutton, 1978.

Harrison M. Science and the British empire. *Isis*, 2005, 96:56–63.

Harriss J. *Depoliticizing development: the World Bank and social capital.* London, Anthem Press, 2002.

Hartwick E. Towards a geographical politics of consumption. *Environment and Planning A*, 2000, 32:1177–1192.

Harvey SA et al. Domestic poultry raising practices in a Peruvian shantytown: implications for control of *Campylobacter jejuni*–associated diarrhea. *Acta Tropica*, 2003, 86 (1): 41–54.

Hassmiller KM. The association between smoking and tuberculosis. *Salud pública de méxico*, 2006, 48 (suppl. 1): S201–S216.

Hausmann Muela S, Ribera JM. Recipe knowledge: a tool for understanding some apparently irrational behaviour. *Anthropology and Medicine*, 2003, 10 (1): 87–103.

Hausmann Muela S et al. Fake malaria and hidden parasites—the ambiguity of malaria. *Anthropology and Medicine*, 1998, 5 (1): 43–61.

Hausmann Muela S et al. Medical syncretism with reference to malaria in a Tanzanian community. *Social Science and Medicine*, 2002, 55:403–413.

Hay MC. Dying mothers: maternal mortality in rural Indonesia. *Medical Anthropology*, 1999, 18:243–279.

Heggenhougen K et al. *The behavioral and social aspects of malaria and its control: An introduction and annotated bibliography.* TDR/STR/SEB/VOL/03.1. Geneva, UNCP/World Bank/WHO Special Programme for Research and Training in Tropical Diseases, 2003.

Heise L, Elias C. Transforming AIDS prevention to meet women's needs: a focus on developing countries. *Social Science and Medicine*, 1995, 40:931–943.

Helitzer-Allen D. Examination of the factors influencing the utilization of the antenatal malaria chemoprophylasis program, Malawi, central Africa [dissertation]. Baltimore, MD, John Hopkins University School of Hygiene and Public Health, 1989.

Helitzer-Allen D, Kendall C. Explaining differences between qualitative and quantitative data: a study of chemoprophylaxis during pregnancy. *Health Education Quarterly*, 1992, 19 (1): 41–54.

Helitzer-Allen D et al. The role of ethnographic research in malaria control: an example from Malawi. *Research in the Sociology of Health Care*, 1993, 10:269–286.

Henry CJK, Ulijaszek SJ. *Long-term consequences of early environment: growth, development and the lifespan developmental perspective.* Cambridge, Cambridge University Press, 1996.

Herman E, Bentley ME. Manuals for ethnographic data collection: experience and issues. *Social Science and Medicine*, 1992, 35 (11): 1369–1378.

Herxheimer A et al. Advertisements for medicines in leading medical journals in 18 countries: a 12-month survey of information content and standards. *International Journal of Health Services*, 1993, 23:161–172.

Hewlett BS, Cline BL. Anthropological contributions to a community-based schistosomiasis control project in northern Cameroon. *Tropical Medicine and International Health*, 1997, 2 (11): A25–36.

Hewlett BS et al. Ivermectin distribution and the cultural context of forest onchocerciasis in South Province, Cameroon. *American Journal of Tropical Medicine*, 1996, 54 (5): 517–522.

Heymann S et al. The need for global action against multidrug-resistant tuberculosis. *Journal of the American Medical Association*, 1999, 281 (22): 2138–2140.

Hill PS. The rhetoric of sector-wide approaches for health development. *Social Science and Medicine*, 2002, 54:1725–1737.

Hochschild AR. Global care chains and emotional surplus value. In: Hutton W, Giddens A, eds. *On the edge: living with global capitalism.* London, Jonathan Cape, 2000:130–146.

Holzer B, Sørensen MP. Rethinking subpolitics: beyond the "iron cage" of modern politics? *Theory, Culture and Society*, 2003, 20 (2): 79–102.

Hopwood A, Miller P, eds. *Accounting as social and institutional practice.* Cambridge, Cambridge University Press, 1997.

Horton R. African AIDS beyond Mbeki: tripping into anarchy. *Lancet*, 2000, 356:1541–1542.

Howard M. Socio-economic causes and cultural explanations of childhood malnutrition among the Chaggu of Tanzania. *Social Science and Medicine*, 1994, 38 (2): 239–251.

Howarth C et al. Exploring the potential of the theory of social representations in community-based health research—and vice versa? *Journal of Health Psychology*, 2004, 9 (2): 229–243.

Howteerakul N et al. ORS is never enough: physicians' rationales for altering standard treatment guidelines when managing childhood diarrhea in Thailand. *Social Science and Medicine*, 2003, 57 (6): 1031–1044.

Hsu E. "The medicine from China has rapid effects": Chinese medicine patients in Tanzania. *Anthropology and Medicine*, 2002, 9 (3): 291–313.

Hsu FLK. A cholera epidemic in a Chinese town. In: Paul BD, ed. *Health, culture and community*. New York, Russell Sage Foundation, 1955:135–153.

Huang Y, Manderson L. Schistosomiasis and the social patterning of infection. *Acta Tropica*, 1992, 51:175–194.

Hudelson P et al. Ethnographic studies of ARI in Bolivia and their use by the national ARI programme. *Social Science and Medicine*, 1994, 42 (3): 437–445.

Hudock AC. *NGOs and civil society: democracy by proxy?* Cambridge, UK, Polity Press, 1999.

Hughes A, Reimer S, eds. *Geographies of commodity chains*. London, Routledge, 2004.

Hunt K, Emslie C. The prevention paradox in lay epidemiology—Rose revisited. *International Journal of Epidemiology*, 2001, 30:442–446.

Hunt K et al. Lay constructions of a family history of heart disease: potential for misunderstandings in the clinical encounter? *Lancet*, 2001, 357 (9263): 1168–1171.

Hunt L, Mattingly C. Diverse rationalities and multiple realities in illness and healing. *Medical Anthropology Quarterly*, 1998, 12 (3): 267–272.

Hunt LM et al. Views of what's wrong: diagnosis and patients' concepts of illness. *Social Science and Medicine*, 1989, 28 (9): 945–956.

Hunt LM et al. *Porque me toco a mi?* Mexican American diabetes patients' causal stories and their relationship to treatment behaviors. *Social Science and Medicine*, 1998, 46 (8): 959–969.

Hunter JL. Better late than never: reflections on the delayed prioritization of cervical cancer in international health. *Health Care for Women International*, 2006, 27:2–17.

Hunter JM. Inherited burden of disease: agricultural dams and the persistence of bloody urine (*Schistosomiasis hematobium*) in the upper east region of Ghana, 1959–1997. *Social Science and Medicine*, 2003, 56:219–234.

Hunter JM et al. Man-made lakes and man-made diseases: towards a policy resolution. *Social Science and Medicine*, 1982, 16:1127–1145.

Hunter SS. Historical perspectives on the development of health systems modeling in medical anthropology. *Social Science and Medicine*, 1985, 21:1297–1307.

Hutin Y, Chen RT. Injection safety: a global challenge. *Bulletin of the World Health Organization*, 1999, 77:787–788.

Hutin YJF et al. Use of injections in healthcare settings worldwide, 2000: literature review and regional estimates. *British Medical Journal*, 2003, 327:1075–1078.

Hutter I. *Being pregnant in rural South India: nutrition of women and well-being of children*. Amsterdam, Thesis Publishers, 1994.

Imevbore AMA et al. *The perception of schistosomiasis in four communitites in south-western Nigeria*. Geneva, World Health Organization, Project ID 880631, August 1990.

INCLEN Childnet Zinc Effectiveness for Diarrhea (IC-ZED) Group. Zinc supplementation in acute diarrhea is acceptable, does not interfere with oral rehydration, and reduces the use of other medications: a randomized trial in five countries. *Journal of Pediatric Gastroenterology and Nutrition*, 2006, 42:300–305.

Inhorn MC. Kabsa (a.k.a. mushahara) and threatened fertility in Egypt. *Social Science and Medicine*, 1994, 39 (4): 487–505.

Inhorn M. The worms are weak. *Men and Masculinities*, 2003, 5 (3): 236–256.

Inhorn M. Defining women's health: a dozen messages from more than 150 ethnographies. *Medical Anthropology Quarterly*, 2006, 20 (3): 345–378.

Inhorn MC, Brown PJ. The anthropology of infectious disease. *Annual Review of Anthropology*, 1990, 19:89–117.

IOM (Institute of Medicine). *America's vital interest in global health: protecting our people, enhancing our economy, and advancing our international interests*. Washington, DC, National Academy Press, 1997.

Irwin A. Constructing the scientific citizen: science and democracy in biosciences. *Public Understanding of Science*, 2001, 10:1–18.

Isserles RG. Microcredit: the rhetoric of empowerment, the reality of "development as usual." *Women's Studies Quarterly*, 2003, 31 (34): 38–57.

Iyun BF, Tomson G. Acute respiratory infections—mothers' perceptions of etiology and treatment in south-western Nigeria. *Social Science and Medicine*, 1996, 42 (3): 437–45.

Jackson P. Commodity cultures: the traffic in things. *Transactions of the Institute of British Geographers*, 1999, 24:95–108.

Jacobsen PB et al. Relation of family history of prostate cancer to perceived vulnerability and screening behavior. *Psycho-Oncology*, 2004, 13:80–85.

Jacoby S, Ochs E. Co-construction: an introduction. *Research on Language and Social Interaction*, 1995, 28 (3): 171–183.

Janes CR. Criticizing with impunity? Bridging the widening gulf between academic discourse and action anthropology in global health. *Social Analysis*, 2003, 47 (1): 90–95.

Janes CR. Going global in century XXI: medical anthropology and the new primary health care. *Human Organization*, 2004, 63 (4): 457–471.

Janes CR. "Culture," cultural explanations, and causality. *International Journal of Epidemiology*, 2006, 35:261–263.

Janzen JM. *The quest for therapy: medical pluralism in lower Zaire.* Berkeley, University of California Press, 1978.

Janzen JM. Therapy management: concept, reality, process. *Medical Anthropology Quarterly*, 1987, 10:68–84.

Jasanoff S, ed. *States of knowledge: the co-production of science and the social order.* London, Routledge, 2004.

Jewkes R, Murcott A. Meanings of community. *Social Science and Medicine*, 1996, 43:555–563.

Jewkes R, Murcott A. Community representatives: representing the "community"? *Social Science and Medicine*, 1998, 46 (7): 843–858.

Jing S. Fluid labor and blood money: the economy of HIV/AIDS in rural central China. *Cultural Anthropology*, 2006, 21 (4): 535–569.

Joffe H. *Risk and the other.* Cambridge, Cambridge University Press, 2004.

Johnson-Hanks J. On the modernity of traditional contraception: time and the social context of fertility. *Population and Development Review*, 2002, 28 (2): 229–249.

Johnson-Hanks J. When the future decides: uncertainty and intentional action in contemporary Cameroon. *Current Anthropology*, 2005, 46 (3): 363–385.

Jule WA et al. The intravenous injection of illicit drugs and needle sharing: a historical perspective. *Psychoactive Drugs*, 1997, 29 (2): 199–204.

Jurberg C. Dengue epidemic strikes Rio de Janeiro—as expected. *Bulletin of the World Health Organization*, 2002, 80 (7): 606–607.

Justice J. The bureaucratic context of international health: a social scientist's view. *Social Science and Medicine*, 1987, 25 (12): 1301–1306.

Kaler A. The moral lens of population control: condoms and controversies in southern Malawi. *Studies in Family Planning*, 2004, 35 (2): 105–115.

Källander K et al. Symptom overlap for malaria and pneumonia—policy implications for home management strategies. *Acta Tropica*, 2004, 90:211–214.

Kamat S. *Development hegemony: NGOs and the state in India.* New Delhi, Oxford University Press, 2002.

Kamat S. NGOs and the new democracy: the false saviors of international development. *Harvard International Review*, 2003a, 25 (1): 65–29.

Kamat S. The NGO phenomenon and political culture in the Third World. *Development*, 2003b, 46 (1): 88–93.

Kamat S. The privatization of public interest: theorizing NGO discourse in a neoliberal era. *Review of International Political Economy*, 2004, 11 (1): 155–176.

Kamat V. Resurgence of malaria in Bombay (Mumbai) in the 1990s: a historical perspective. *Parasitologia*, 2000, 42:135–148.

Kamat VR. Private practitioners and their role in the resurgence of malaria in Mumbai (Bombay) and Navi Mumbai (New Bombay), India: serving the affected or aiding an epidemic? *Social Science and Medicine*, 2001, 52:885–909.

Kamat V. Negotiating illness and misfortune in post-socialist Tanzania: an ethnographic study in Temeke District, Dar Es Salaam [dissertation]. Atlanta, GA, Emory University, 2004.

Kamat VR. "I thought it was only ordinary fever!" Cultural knowledge and the micropolitics of therapy seeking for childhood febrile illness in Tanzania. *Social Science and Medicine*, 2006, 62 (12): 2945–2959.

Kamat VR, Nichter M. Pharmacies, self-medication and pharmaceutical marketing in Bombay, India. *Social Science and Medicine*, 1998, 47 (6): 779–794.

Kane A et al. Transmission of hepatitis B, hepatitis C and human immunodeficiency viruses through unsafe injections in the developing world: model-based regional estimates. *Bulletin of the World Health Organization*, 1999, 77 (10): 801–807.

Kaona FAD et al. *A KAP study to determine perception of schistosomiasis in Kampumbu area—Iska District of Zambia.* Geneva, World Health Organization, Project ID 930774, February 1994.

Katabarwa NM et al. Controlling onchocerciasis by community-directed, ivermectin-treatment programmes in Uganda: why do some communities succeed and others fail? *Annals of Tropical Medicine and Parasitology*, 2000, 94 (4): 343–352.

Kaufman J. SARS and China's health-care response: better to be both red and expert! In: Kleinman A, Watson JL, eds. *SARS in China: prelude to a pandemic?* Stanford, CA, Stanford University Press, 2006:53–68.

Kaufman N, Nichter Mimi. The marketing of tobacco to women: global perspectives. In: Samet JM, Soon SY, eds. *Women and the tobacco epidemic: challenges for the 21st century.* Geneva, World Health Organization, 2001.

Kaul I et al., eds. *Global public goods: international cooperation in the 21st century.* New York, Oxford University Press, 1999.

Kaur V. General considerations: tropical diseases and women. *Clinics in Dermatology*, 1997, 15:171–178.

Kavanagh AM, Broom DH. Embodied risk: my body, myself? *Social Science and Medicine*, 1998, 46 (3): 437–444.

Kawachi I, Kennedy BP. Socioeconomic determinants of health: health and social cohesion: why care about income inequality? *British Medical Journal*, 1997, 314:1037.

Kawachi I, Wamala S, eds. *Globalization and health*. Oxford, Oxford University Press, 2006.

Kawachi I et al. Social capital, income inequality, and mortality. *American Journal of Public Health*, 1997, 87 (9): 1491–1498.

Keck ME, Sikkink K. *Activists beyond borders: advocacy networks in international politics*. Ithaca, NY, Cornell University Press, 1998.

Kendall C. The role of formal qualitative research in negotiating community acceptance: the case of dengue control in El Progreso, Honduras. *Human Organization*, 1998, 57 (2): 217–221.

Kendall C et al. Ethnomedicine and oral rehydration therapy: a case study of ethnomedical investigation and program planning. *Social Science and Medicine*, 1984a, 19 (3): 253–260.

Kendall C et al. Anthropology, communications, and health: the mass media and health practices program in Honduras. *Human Organization*, 1984b, 42:353–360.

Kendall C et al. Exploratory ethnoentomology: using ANTHROPAC to design a dengue fever control program. *Cultural Anthropology Methods Newsletter*, 1990, 2 (2): 11–12.

Kendall C et al. Urbanization, dengue, and the health transition: anthropological contributions to international health. *Medical Anthropology Quarterly*, 1991, 5:257–268.

Kengeya-Kayondo J et al. Recognition, treatment seeking behavior and perception of cause of malaria among rural women in Uganda. *Acta Tropica*, 1994, 58:267–273.

Keohane RO, Nye JS Jr. *Power and interdependence*, 3rd ed. New York, Addison-Wesley Longman, 2001.

Khan AJ et al. Unsafe injections and the transmission of hepatitis B and C in a peri-urban community in Pakistan. *Bulletin of the World Health Organization*, 2000, 78:956–963.

Kickbusch I. The development of international health policies—accountability intact? *Social Science and Medicine*, 2000, 51:979–989.

Kickbusch I, de Leeuw E. Global public health: revisiting healthy public policy at the global level. *Health Promotion International*, 1999, 14 (4): 285–288.

Kickbusch I, Quick J. Partnerships for health in the 21st century. *World Statistics Quarterly*, 1998, 51:68–74.

Kidder T. *Mountains beyond mountains: the quest of Dr. Paul Farmer, a man who would cure the world*. New York, Random House, 2003.

Kilmarx PH et al. Medication use by female sex workers for treatment and prevention of sexually transmitted diseases, Chiang Rai, Thailand. *Sexually Transmitted Diseases*, 1997, 24 (10): 593–598.

Kim JY et al. *Dying for growth: global inequality and the health of the poor*. Monroe, ME, Common Courage Press, 2000.

King NB. Security, disease, commerce: ideologies of postcolonial global health. *Social Studies of Science*, 2002, 32 (5–6): 763–789.

King NB. The scale politics of emerging diseases. *OSIRIS*, 2004, 19:62–76.

Kirby JP. White, red and black: colour classification and illness management in northern Ghana. *Social Science and Medicine*, 1997, 44 (2): 215–230.

Kirmayer LJ. The body's insistence on meaning: metaphor as presentation and representation in illness experience. *Medical Anthropology Quarterly*, 1992, 6 (4): 323–346.

Kirmayer LJ. Broken narratives: clinical encounters and the poetics of illness experience. In: Mattingly C, Garro LC, eds. *Narrative and the cultural construction of illness and healing*. Berkeley, University of California Press, 2000:153–180.

Kirmayer L. Commentary on Farmer P, "An anthropology of structural violence." *Current Anthropology*, 2004, 45 (3): 321–322.

Kleinman A. *Patients and healers in the context of culture*. Berkeley, University of California Press, 1980.

Kleinman A. The cultural meanings and social uses of illness. *Journal of Family Practice*, 1983, 16 (3): 539–545.

Kleinman A. Illness meanings and illness behaviour. In: McHugh S, Vallis T, eds. *Illness behavior: a multidisciplinary model*. New York, Plenum Press, 1986.

Kleinman A. *The illness narratives: suffering, healing, and the human condition*. New York, Basic Books, 1988.

Kleinman A. Anthropology of bioethics. In: Kleinman A. *Writing at the margin*. Berkeley, University of California Press, 1995:41–67.

Kleinman A, Kleinman J. Suffering and its professional transformation: toward an ethnography of interpersonal experience. *Culture, Medicine and Psychiatry*, 1991, 15 (3): 275–301.

Kleinman A, Lee S. SARS and the problem of social stigma. In: Kleinman A, Watson JL, eds. *SARS in China: prelude to a pandemic?* Stanford, CA, Stanford University Press, 2006:173–195.

Kloos H. Human behavior, health education and schistosomiasis control: a review. *Social Science and Medicine*, 1995, 40 (11): 1497–1511.

Kolappan C, Gopi PG. Tobacco smoking and pulmonary tuberculosis. *Thorax*, 2002, 57:964–966.

Kovsted J. Scaling up AIDS treatment in developing countries: a review of current and future arguments. *Development Policy Review*, 2005, 23 (4): 465–482.

Kresno SG et al. Acute respiratory illness in children under five years in Indramayu, West Java, Indonesia: a rapid ethnographic assessment. *Medical Anthropology*, 1994, 15 (4): 425–434.

Krieger N. Epidemiology and the web of causation: has anyone seen the spider? *Social Science and Medicine*, 1994, 39 (7): 887–903.

Krieger N. Sticky webs, hungry spiders, buzzing flies, and fractal metaphors: on the misleading juxtaposition of "risk factor" versus "social" epidemiology. *Journal of Epidemiological Community Health*, 1999, 53:678–680.

Krieger N. Epidemiology and social sciences: towards a critical reengagement in the 21st century. *Epidemiologic Reviews*, 2000, 22:155–163.

Krieger N. Theories for social epidemiology in the 21st century: an ecosocial perspective. *International Journal of Epidemiology*, 2001, 30 (4): 668–77.

Krieger N. Embodiment: a conceptual glossary for epidemiology. *Journal of Epidemiology and Community Health*, 2005, 59:350–355.

Krieger N, Gruskin S. Frameworks matter: ecosocial and health and human rights perspectives on disparities in women's health—the case of tuberculosis. *Journal of the American Medical Women's Association*, 2001, 56 (4): 137–142.

Krieger N, Zierler S. What explains the public's health?—A call for epidemiologic theory. *Epidemiology*, 1996, 7 (1): 107–109.

Krieger N et al. Race/ethnicity, gender, and monitoring socioeconomic gradients in health: a comparison of area-based socioeconomic measures—the Public Health Disparities Geocoding Project. *American Journal of Public Health*, 2003a, 93 (10): 1655–1671.

Krieger N et al. Monitoring socioeconomic inequalities in sexually transmitted infections, tuberculosis, and violence: geocoding and choice of area-based socioeconomic measures—the Public Health Disparities Geocoding Project (US). *Public Health Reports*, 2003b, 118:240–260.

Kroeger, KA. AIDS rumors, imaginary enemies, and the body politic in Indonesia. *American Ethnologist*, 2003, 30 (2): 243–257.

Kuh D, Ben-Shlomo Y, eds. *A life course approach to chronic diseases epidemiology*. Oxford, Oxford University Press, 2004.

Kull S. *Americans and foreign aid: a study of American public attitudes*. College Park, MD, Program on International Policy Attitudes, Center for the Study of Policy Attitudes, and the Center for International and Security Studies, School of Public Affairs at the University of Maryland, 1995.

Kunitz SJ. Accounts of social capital: the mixed health effects of personal communities and voluntary groups. In: Leon DA, Walt G, *Poverty, inequality, and health*. Oxford, Oxford University Press, 2001:159–174.

Kuntolbutra S et al. Factors related to inconsistent condom use with commercial sex workers in northern Thailand. *AIDS*, 1996, 10:556–558.

Kusriastuti R, Sutomo S. Evolution of dengue prevention and control programme in Indonesia. *Dengue Bulletin*, 2005, 29:1–7.

Lakshman M, Nichter Mark. Contamination of medicine injection paraphernalia used by registered medical practitioners in South India: an ethnographic study. *Social Science and Medicine*, 2000, 51:11–28.

Lambert H. The cultural logic of Indian medicine: prognosis and etiology in Rajasthani popular therapeutics. *Social Science and Medicine*, 1992, 34 (10): 1069–1076.

Lambert H. Methods and meanings in anthropological, epidemiological and clinical encounters: the case of sexually transmitted disease and human immunodeficiency virus control and prevention in India. *Tropical Medicine and International Health*, 1998, 3 (12): 1002–1010.

Lambert MJ et al. Going global. *Applied Clinical Trials*, 2004, 13 (6): 84–92.

Langwick S. Devils, parasites and fierce needles: healing and the politics of translation in southern Tanzania. *Science, Technology and Human Values*, 2007, 32:88–117.

Latour B. *Science in action: how to follow scientists and engineers through society*. Cambridge, MA, Harvard University Press, 1987.

Latour B. *We have never been modern*. Porter C, trans. New York, Harvester Wheatsheaf, 1993.

Latour B. *Pandora's hope: essays on the reality of science studies*. Cambridge, MA, Harvard University Press, 1999.

Laufer MK et al. Return of chloroquine antimalarial efficacy in Malawi. *New England Journal of Medicine*, 2006, 355 (19): 1959–1966.

Lavis JN et al. Country-level efforts to link research to action. *Bulletin of the World Health Organization*, 2006, 84 (8): 620–628.

Lawn SD et al. Pulmonary tuberculosis: diagnostic delay in Ghanaian adults. *International Journal of Tuberculosis and Lung Disease*, 1998, 2 (8): 635–640.

Lawrence RM, Lawrence RA. Breast milk and infection. *Clinics in Perinatology*, 2004, 31:501–528.

Leclerc-Madlala S. Infect one, infect all: Zulu youth response to the AIDS epidemic in South Africa. *Medical Anthropology*, 1997, 17:363–380.

Leclerc-Madlala S. Virginity testing: managing sexuality in a maturing HIV/AIDS epidemic. *Medical Anthropology Quarterly*, 2001, 15 (4): 533–552.

Lederberg J et al. *Emerging infections: microbial threats to health in the United States*. Washington, DC, National Academy Press, 1992.

Lee D, Newby H. *The problem of sociology: an introduction to the discipline.* London, Unwin Hyman, 1983.

Lee K. *Globalization and health: an introduction.* New York, Palgrave Macmillan, 2003.

Lee K, Yach D. Globalization and health. In: Merson MH et al., eds. *International public health: diseases, programs, systems, and policies,* 2nd ed. Sudbury, MA, Jones and Bartlett, 2006:681–708.

Lee K et al. Global change and health—the good, the bad and the evidence. *Global Change and Human Health,* 2002, 3 (1): 16–19.

Leidy LE. Biological aspects of menopause—across the life-span. *Annual Review of Anthropology,* 1994, 23:231–253.

Leidy LE. Lifespan approach to the study of human biology: an introductory overview. *American Journal of Human Biology,* 1996, 8 (6): 699–702.

Leslie P et al. Synthesis and lessons. In: Little M, Leslie P, eds. *Turkana herders of the dry savanna: ecology and biobehavioral response of nomads to an uncertain environment.* Oxford, Oxford University Press, 1999.

Leung MW et al. Community-based participatory research: a promising approach for increasing epidemiology's relevance in the 21st century. *International Journal of Epidemiology,* 2004, 33 (3): 499–506.

Levine DP. Poverty, capabilities and freedom. *Review of Political Economy,* 2004, 16:101–115.

Levine N. Differential child care in three Tibetan communities: beyond son preference. *Population and Development Review,* 1987, 13 (2): 281–304.

Lexchin J. Pharmaceutical promotion in the Third World. *Journal of Drug Issues,* 1992, 22 (2): 417–422.

Lexchin J. *Deception by design: pharmaceutical promotion in the Third World.* Penang, Malaysia, Consumers International Regional Office for Asia and the Pacific, 1995.

Leygues M, Gouteux JP. La lutte communitaire contre une endemie tropical. *Social Science and Medicine,* 1989, 28 (12): 1255–1267.

Li HZ et al. Increase in cigarette smoking and decline of anti-smoking counseling among Chinese physicians, 1987–1996. *Health Promotion International,* 1999, 14 (2): 123–131.

Li TM. *Neo-liberal strategies of government through community: the social development program of the World Bank in Indonesia.* IILJ Working Paper 2006/2, Global Administrative Law Series. New York, Institute for International Law and Justice, 2006.

Li T. *The will to improve: governmentaliy, development, and the practice of politics.* Durham, NC, Duke University Press, 2007.

Li X et al. Transmission of drug-resistant tuberculosis among treated patients in Shanghai, China. *Journal of Infectious Diseases*, 2007, 195:864–869.

Liefooghe R et al. Perception and social consequences of tuberculosis: a focus group study of tuberculosis patients in Sialkot, Pakistan. *Social Science and Medicine*, 1995, 41 (12): 1685–1692.

Liefooghe R et al. From their own perspective: a Kenyan community's perception of tuberculosis. *Tropical Medicine and International Health*, 1997, 2 (8): 809–821.

Light DW, Hughes D. Introduction: a sociological perspective on rationing: power, rhetoric and situated practices. *Sociology of Health and Illness*, 2001, 23 (5): 551–569.

Lindbloom E et al. Practice-based research networks: the laboratories of primary health care research. *Medical Care*, 2004, 42:45–49.

Lines J et al. Trends, priorities and policy directions in the control of vector-borne diseases in urban environments. *Health Policy and Planning*, 1994, 9 (2): 113–129.

Lipowsky R et al. Sociomedical aspects of malaria control in Colombia. *Social Science and Medicine*, 1992, 34 (6): 625–637.

Lister S. NGO legitimacy: technical issue or social construct? *Critique of Anthropology*, 2003, 23 (2): 175–192.

Lloyd L et al. The design of a community-based health education intervention for the control of *Aedes aegypti*. *American Journal of Tropical Medicine and Hygiene*, 1994, 50 (4): 401–411.

Lock M. *Encounters with aging: mythologies of menopause in Japan and North America*. Berkeley, University of California Press, 1993.

Lock M. Breast cancer: reading the omens. *Anthropology Today*, 1998, 14 (4): 7–16.

Lock M, Kaufert P. Menopause, local biologies, and cultures of aging. *American Journal of Human Biology*, 2001, 13 (4): 494–504.

Lock M, Nichter Mark. From documenting medical pluralism to critical inter-pretations of globalized health knowledge, polices and practices. In: Nichter Mark, Lock M, eds. *New horizons in medical anthropology: essays in honour of Charles Leslie*. London, Routledge, 2002:1–34.

Lock M, Scheper-Hughes N. The mindful body. *Medical Anthropology Quarterly*, 1987, 1:6–41.

Logan M. Humoral medicine in Guatemala and peasant acceptance of modern medicine. *Human Organization*, 1973, 32:385–395.

Loh C et al. The media and SARS. In: Loh C, Civic Exchange, eds. *At the epicen-tre: Hong Kong and the SARS outbreak*. Hong Kong, Hong Kong University Press, 2004:195–214.

Long NH et al. Longer delays in tuberculosis diagnosis among women in Vietnam. *International Journal of Tuberculosis and Lung Disease*, 1999, 3:388–393.

Lönnroth K et al. Public-private mix for DOTS implementation: what makes it work? *Bulletin of the World Health Organization*, 2004, 82 (8): 580–586.

Lu AG et al. *Filariasis: a study of knowledge, attitudes and practices of the people of Sorsogon*. Social and Economic Research Project Reports. Geneva, World Health Organization, 1988.

Luby SP et al. The relationship between therapeutic injections and high prevalence of hepatitis C infection in Hafizabad, Pakistan. *Epidemiology and Infection*, 1997, 119:349–356.

Lupton D. *Risk*. New York, Routledge, 1999.

Lush L et al. Transferring policies for treating sexually transmitted infections: what's wrong with global guidelines? *Health Policy and Planning*, 2003, 18 (1): 18–30.

Lyon S. Evaluating fair trade consumption: politics, defetishization and producer participation. *International Journal of Consumer Studies*, 2006, 30 (5): 452–464.

Lyttleton C. Messages of distinction: the HIV/AIDS media campaign in Thailand. *Medical Anthropology*, 1996, 16 (4): 363–89.

MacDonald L, Schwartz MA. Political parties and NGOs in the creation of new trading blocs in the Americas. *International Political Science Review*, 2002, 23 (2): 135–158.

Macintyre K et al. Examining the determinants of mosquito-avoidance practices in two Kenyan cities. *Malaria Journal*, 2002, 1:14–23.

Macintyre S, Ellaway A. Neighbourhoods and health: an overview. In Kawachi I, Berkman LF, eds. *Neighborhoods and health*. Oxford, Oxford University Press, 2003:20–42.

Macintyre S et al. Area, class and health: should we be focusing on places or people? *Journal of Social Policy*, 1991, 22 (2): 213–234.

Macintyre S et al. Place effects on health: how can we conceptualise, operationalise and measure them? *Social Science and Medicine*, 2002, 55:125–139.

MacLachlan M, Carr S. From dissonance to tolerance: toward managing health in tropical cultures. *Psychology and Developing Societies*, 1994, 6 (2): 119–129.

Macq J et al. Assessing the stigma of tuberculosis. *Psychology, Health and Medicine*, 2006, 11 (3): 346–352.

Magnus AA et al. Quality control of active ingredients in artemisinin-derivative antimalarials within Kenya and DR Congo. *Tropical Medicine and International Health*, 2007, 12 (1): 68–74.

Makemba AM et al. Treatment practices for dege-dege, a locally recognized febrile illness, and implications for strategies to decrease mortality from severe malaria in Bagamoyo District, Tanzania. *Tropical Medicine and International Health*, 1996, 1 (3): 305–313.

Malik IA et al. Mothers' fear of child death due to acute diarrhea: a study in urban and rural communities in northern Punjab, Pakistan. *Social Science and Medicine*, 1992, 35 (8): 1043–1053.

Manderson L. Wireless wars in the Eastern arena: epidemiological surveillance, disease prevention, and the work of the Eastern Bureau of the League of Nations Health Organization, 1925–1942. In: Weindling P, ed. *International Health Organisations and Movements, 1918–1939.* Cambridge, Cambridge University Press, 1995:109–133.

Manderson L, Aaby P. An epidemic in the field? Rapid assessment procedures and health research. *Social Science and Medicine*, 1992a, 35 (7): 839–850.

Manderson L, Aaby P. Can rapid anthropological procedures be applied to tropical diseases? *Health Policy and Planning*, 1992b, 7 (1): 46–55.

Marchione TJ. Filling the anthropologist's chair in the food and human rights in development debate. In: Eide WB, Kracht E, eds. *Food and human rights in development*, vol. 2, *Evolving issues and emerging applications*. Oxford, Intersentia, 2007. Forthcoming.

Marcus GE. Ethnography in/of the world system: the emergence of multi-sited ethnography. *Annual Review of Anthropology*, 1995, 24:95–117.

Marks S. What is colonial about colonial medicine? *Social History of Medicine*, 1996, 10 (2): 207–219.

Marmot MG. Epidemiology of socioeconomic status and health: are determinants within countries the same as between countries? *Annals of the New York Academy of Science*, 1999, 896:16–29.

Marriott M, Inden R. Towards an ethnosociology of South Asian caste systems. In: David K, ed. *The new wind: changing identities in South Asia.* The Hague, Mouton, 1977:227–238.

Marsh V, Mutemi W. A community educational intervention to optimize the home use of shop-bought antimalarial drugs in the management of uncomplicated childhood fevers. Technical report prepared for the KEMRI/CRC/DVBD, 1997.

Martin E. Toward an anthropology of immunology: the body as nation state. *Medical Anthropology Quarterly*, 1990, 4 (4): 410–426.

Martin E. The end of the body? *American Ethnologist*, 1992, 19 (1): 120–138.

Martin E. *Flexible bodies: tracking immunity in American culture—from days of polio to the age of AIDS.* Boston, Beacon Press, 1994.

Mastro TD, Yip R. The legacy of unhygienic plasma collection in China. *AIDS*, 2006, 20 (10): 1451–1452.

Mathew JL. Effect of maternal antibiotics on breast feeding infants. *Postgraduate Medical Journal*, 2004, 80:196–200.

Maynard-Tucker G. Knowledge of reproductive physiology and modern contraceptives in rural Peru. *Studies in Family Planning*, 1989, 20 (4): 215–224.

Mburu FM. Whither community health workers in the age of structural adjustment? *Social Science and Medicine*, 1994, 28 (10): 1081–1084.

McCombie S. Treatment seeking for malaria: A review of recent research. *Social Science and Medicine*, 1996, 43 (6): 933–945.

McCombie SC. Self-treatment for malaria: the evidence and methodological issues. *Health Policy and Planning*, 2002, 17 (4): 333–344.

McDade TW. The ecologies of human immune function. *Annual Review of Anthropology*, 2005, 34:495–521.

McMichael AJ. Prisoners of the proximate: loosening the constraints on epidemiology in an age of change. *American Journal of Epidemiology*, 1999, 149 (10): 887–897.

McMichael AJ, Beaglehole R. The changing global context of public health. *Lancet*, 2000, 356 (9228): 495–499.

McMurray C, Smith R. *Diseases of globalization: socioeconomic transitions and health.* Sterling, VA, Earthscan Publications, 2001.

McNee A et al. Responding to cough: Boholano illness classification and resort to care in response to childhood ARI. *Social Science and Medicine*, 1995, 40 (9): 1279–1289.

Meigs A. *Food, sex, and pollution: a New Guinea religion.* New Brunswick, NJ, Rutgers University Press, 1986.

Merrick M. Reflections PPGIS: a view from the trenches. *Urisa Journal*, 2003, 15 (2): 33–40.

Messer E. Intra-household allocations of food and health care: current findings and understanding—introduction. *Social Science and Medicine*, 1997, 44 (11): 1675–1684.

Meyer JW, Rowan B. Institutionalized organizations: formal structure as myth and ceremony. *American Journal of Sociology*, 1977, 83:340–363.

Michaud C, Murray CJL. External assistance to the health sector in developing countries: a detailed analysis, 1972–90. *Bulletin of the World Health Organization*, 1994, 72 (4): 639–651.

Middleton K. How Karembola men become mothers. In: Carsten J, ed. *Cultures of relatedness: new approaches to the study of kinship.* Cambridge, Cambridge University Press, 2000:104–127.

Miguel CA et al. Local knowledge and treatment of malaria in Agusan del Sur, the Philippines. *Social Science and Medicine*, 1999, 48:607–618.

Millard AV. A causal model of high rates of child mortality. *Social Science and Medicine*, 1994, 38 (2): 253–268.

Miller B. *The endangered sex: neglect of female children in North India*. Oxford, Oxford University Press, 1997a.

Miller B. Social class, gender and intrahousehold food allocations to children in South Asia. *Social Science and Medicine*, 1997b, 44 (11): 1685–1693.

Miller J. Birthing practices of the Rarámuri of northern Mexico [dissertation]. Tucson, University of Arizona, 2003.

Miller P, Rose N. Political power beyond the state. *British Journal of Sociology*, 1992, 43 (2): 172–205.

Minkin SF. Medical research on AIDS in Africa. *Social Science and Medicine*, 1990, 33 (7): 786–790.

Mintz SW. *Sweetness and power*. New York, Penguin, 1985.

Miraftab F. Flirting with the enemy: challenges faced by NGOs in development and empowerment. *Habitat International*, 1997, 21 (4): 361–375.

Mogensen HO. Finding a path through the health unit: practical experience of Ugandan patients. *Medical Anthropology*, 2005, 24:209–236.

Mohan G, Stokke K. Participatory development and empowerment: the dangers of localism. *Third World Quarterly*, 2000, 21 (2): 247–268.

Molyneux CS et al. Maternal responses to childhood fevers: a comparison of rural and urban residents in coastal Kenya. *Tropical Medicine and International Health*, 1999, 4 (12): 836–845.

Molyneux DH, Nantulya VM. Linking disease control programmes in rural Africa: a pro-poor strategy to reach Abuja targets and millennium development goals. *British Medical Journal*, 2004, 328:1129–1132.

Monmonier MS. *How to lie with maps*, 2nd ed. Chicago, University of Chicago Press, 1996.

Monmonier MS. *Cartographies of danger: mapping hazards in America*. Chicago, University of Chicago Press, 1997.

Montgomery CM et al. "To help them is to educate them": power and pedagogy in the prevention and treatment of malaria in Tanzania. *Tropical Medicine and International Health*, 2006, 11 (11): 1661–1669.

Moore H, Sanders T, eds. *Magical interpretations, material realities: modernity, witchcraft and the occult in postcolonial Africa*. London, Routledge, 2002.

Moore SE. Patterns in mortality governed by the seasons. *International Journal of Epidemiology*, 2006, 35:435–437.

Moore S et al. The privileging of communitarian ideas: citation practices and the translation of social capital into public health research. *American Journal of Public Health*, 2005, 95 (8): 1330–1337.

Moore S et al. Lost in translation: a genealogy of the "social capital" concept in pubic health. *Journal of Epidemiology and Community Health*, 2006, 60:729–734.

Morgan L. "Political will" and community participation in Costa Rican primary health care. *Medical Anthropology Quarterly*, 1989, 3 (3): 232–245.

Morgan L. International politics and primary health care in Costa Rica. *Social Science and Medicine*, 1990, 30:211–219.

Morse SS. Emerging viruses: defining the rules of viral traffic. *Perspectives in Biology and Medicine*, 1991, 34 (3): 387–409.

Morse SS, ed. *Emerging Viruses*. New York, Oxford University Press, 1993.

Moscovici S. On social representations. In: Forgas J, ed. *Social cognition—perspectives on everyday knowledge*. London, Academic Press, 1981:181–210.

Moscovici S. The phenomenon of social representations. In: Farr RM, Moscovici S, eds. *Social representations*. Cambridge, Cambridge University Press, 1984:3–69.

Moscovici S. *Social representations: explorations in social psychology*. Cambridge, UK, Polity Press, 2000.

Mosse D. The making and marketing of participatory development. In: Van Ufford PQ, Giri AK, eds. *A moral critique of development: in search of global responsibilities*. London, Routledge, 2003:43–75.

Mosse D. *Cultivating development: an ethnography of aid policy and practice*. London, Pluto Press, 2004.

Moynihan R, Cassels A. *Selling sickness: how the world's biggest pharmaceutical companies are turning us all into patients*. New York: Nation Books, 2005.

Moynihan R et al. Selling sickness: the pharmaceutical industry and disease mongering. *British Medical Journal*, 2002, 324 (April 13): 886–891.

Mtika MM. The AIDS epidemic in Malawi and its threat to household food security. *Human Organization*, 2001, 60 (2): 178–188.

Mull DS et al. Mothers' perception of severe pneumonia in their own children: a controlled study in Pakistan. *Social Science and Medicine*, 1994, 38 (7): 973–987.

Mull JD, Mull DS. Mothers' concepts of childhood diarrhea in rural Pakistan: what ORT program planners should know. *Social Science and Medicine*, 1988, 27 (1): 53–67.

Mull JD et al. Culture and compliance among leprosy patients in Pakistan. *Social Science and Medicine*, 1989, 29 (7): 799–811.

Mullan F. Responding to the global HIV/AIDS crisis: a Peace Corps for health. *Journal of the American Medical Association*, 2007, 297 (7): 744–746.

Mullings L. *On our own terms: race, class, and gender in the lives of African American women*. New York, Routledge, 1997.

Munguti KJ. Community perceptions and treatment seeking for malaria in Baringo District, Kenya: implications for disease control. *East African Medical Journal*, 1998, 75 (12): 687–691.

Murphy FA. Emerging zoonoses. *Emerging Infectious Diseases*, 1999, 4 (3): 429–435.

Murray CJL, Lopez AD, eds. *The global burden of disease*. Cambridge, MA, World Health Organization, 1996.

Murray CJL et al. Health inequalities and social group differences: what should we measure. *Bulletin of the World Health Organization*, 1999, 77 (7): 537–543.

Murray CJL et al. A critical examination of summary measures of population health. *Bulletin of the World Health Organization*, 2000a, 78 (8): 981–994.

Murray CJL et al. Response to P. Braveman et al. (on health inequalities). *Bulletin of the World Health Organization*, 2000b, 78 (2): 234–235.

Musgrove P. A critical review of "a critical review": the methodology of the 1993 World Development Report, "Investing in health." *Health Policy and Planning*, 2000, 15 (1): 110–115.

Mushtague R et al. Perception of diarrhoea and the use of a homemade oral rehydration solution in rural Bangladesh. *Journal of Diarrhoeal Disease Research*, 1988, 6 (1): 6–14.

Mwenesi HA. Social science research in malaria prevention, management and control in the last two decades: an overview. *Acta Tropica*, 2005, 95:292–297.

Mwenesi H et al. Child malaria treatment practices among mothers in Kenya. *Social Science and Medicine*, 1995, 40 (9): 1271–1277.

Nair D et al. Tuberculosis in Bombay: new insights from poor urban patients. *Health Policy and Planning*, 1997, 12 (1): 77–85.

Najam A. NGO accountability: a conceptual framework. *Development Policy Review*, 1996, 14:339–353.

Namavar Jahromi B et al. Female genital tuberculosis and infertility. *International Journal of Gynaecology and Obstetrics*, 2001, 75:269–272.

Nandita J. The sting returns. *Business India*, 1995 (October 9–22): 181–184.

Napolitano D, Jones COH. Who needs "pukka anthropologists"? A study of the perceptions of the use of anthropology in tropical public health research. *Tropical Medicine and International Health*, 2006, 11 (8): 1264–1275.

Nash TE et al. Schistosome infections in humans: perspectives and recent findings. NIH Conference. *Annals of Internal Medicine*, 1982, 97 (5): 740–54.

Nations M. Epidemiological research on infectious disease: quantitative rigor or rigor mortis? Insights from ethnomedicine. In: Janes CR et al., eds. *Anthropology and epidemiology: interdisciplinary approaches to the study of health and disease.* Dordrecht, D. Reidel, 1986:97–123.

Nations MK, Monte CM. "I'm not dog, no!" Cries of resistance against cholera control campaigns. *Social Science and Medicine*, 1996, 43 (6): 1007–1024.

Nations MK, Rebhun LA. Mystification of a simple solution. *Social Science and Medicine*, 1988a, 27 (1): 25–38.

Nations MK, Rebhun LA. Angels with wet wings won't fly: maternal sentiment in Brazil and the image of neglect. *Culture, Medicine and Psychiatry*, 1988b, 12:141–200.

Navarro V. Whose globalization? *American Journal of Public Health*, 1998, 88 (5): 742–743.

Ndyomugyenyi R et al. The use of formal and informal services for antenatal care and malaria treatment in rural Uganda. *Health Policy and Planning*, 1998, 13 (1): 94–102.

Nelkin D, Gilman S. Placing the blame for devastating disease. *Social Research*, 1988, 55:361–378.

Newell JN et al. Control of tuberculosis in an urban setting in Nepal: public-private partnership. *Bulletin of the World Health Organization*, 2004, 82:92–98.

Newell JN et al. Family-member DOTS and community DOTS for tuberculosis control in Nepal: cluster-randomized control trial. *Lancet*, 2006, 387 (March 18): 903–909.

Newton PN et al. Fake artesunate in Southeast Asia. *Lancet*, 2001, 357:1948–1950.

Newton PN et al. Counterfeit artesunate antimalarials in SE Asia. *Lancet*, 2003, 362:169.

Ngamvithayapong J et al. High AIDS awareness may cause tuberculosis patient delay: results from an HIV epidemic area, Thailand. *AIDS*, 2000, 14 (10): 1413–1419.

Nguyen V-K. Antiretroviral globalism, biopolitics, and therapeutic citizenship. In: Ong A, Collier SJ, eds. *Global assemblages: technology, politics, and ethics as anthropological problems.* Malden, MA, Blackwell, 2005:124–144.

Nichter, Mark. Idioms of distress: alternatives in the expression of psychosocial distress: a case study from South India. *Culture, Medicine and Psychiatry*, 1981, 5:379–408.

Nichter, Mark. Modes of food classification and the diet-health contingency: a South Indian case study. In: Khare RS, Rao MSA, eds. *Food, society, and culture: aspects in South Asian food systems.* Durham, NC, Carolina Academic Press, 1986:185–221.

Nichter, Mark. Kyasanur forest disease: an ethnography of a disease of development. *Medical Anthropology Quarterly*, 1987a, 12:406–423.

Nichter, Mark. Cultural dimensions of hot, cold and sema in Sinhalese health culture. *Social Science and Medicine*, 1987b, 25 (4): 377–387.

Nichter, Mark. From Aralu to ORS: Sinhalese perceptions of digestion, diarrhea and dehydration. *Social Science and Medicine*, 1988, 27 (1): 39–52.

Nichter, Mark, ed. *Anthropology and international health: South Asian case studies.* Dordrecht, the Netherlands, Kluwer Academic Publishers, 1989a.

Nichter, Mark. The language of illness, contagion and symptom reporting. In: Nichter Mark, Nichter Mimi, eds. *Anthropology and international health: South Asian case studies.* Dordrecht, the Netherlands, 1989b:85–123.

Nichter, Mark. Diarrhea and dysentery: using social science research to improve the quality of epidemiological studies, interventions and evaluations of impact. *Reviews of Infectious Diseases,* 1991a, 13 (S4): 265–271.

Nichter, Mark. Vaccinations in South Asia: false expectations and commanding metaphors. In: Coreil J, Mull D, eds. *Anthropology and primary health care.* Boulder, CO, Westview Press, 1991b:196–221.

Nichter, Mark. Rethinking the household and community in the context of international health. Invited paper for American Anthropological Association Annual Meeting, Washington, DC, 1995.

Nichter, Mark. Social science lessons from diarrhea research and their application for ARI. In: Nichter Mark, Nichter Mimi, eds. *Anthropology and international health: Asian case studies.* Amsterdam, Gordon and Breach, 1996a:135–171.

Nichter, Mark. Vaccinations in the Third World: a consideration of community demand. In: Nichter Mark, Nichter Mimi, eds. *Anthropology and international health: Asian case studies.* Amsterdam, Gordon and Breach, 1996b:329–365.

Nichter, Mark. The primary health center as a social system: PHC, social status, and the issue of teamwork in South Asia. In: Nichter Mark, Nichter Mimi, eds. *Anthropology and international health: Asian case studies.* Amsterdam, Gordon and Breach, 1996c:367–391.

Nichter, Mark. Illness semantics and international health: the weak lungs/TB complex in the Philippines. In: Inhorn M, Brown P, eds. *Anthropology and infectious disease.* New York, Gordon and Breach, 1997:267–298.

Nichter, Mark. Project community diagnosis: participatory research as a first step toward community involvement in primary health care. In: Hahn R, ed. *Anthropology in public health: bridging differences in culture and society*. New York, Oxford University Press, 1999:300–324.

Nichter, Mark. Vulnerability, prophylactic antibiotic use, harm reduction and the misguided appropriation of medical resources: the case of STDs in Southeast Asia. In: Obermeyer C, ed. *Cultural perspectives on reproductive health*. Oxford, Oxford University Press, 2001:101–127.

Nichter, Mark. Social relations of therapy management. In: Nichter Mark, Lock M, eds. *New horizons in medical anthropology: essays in honour of Charles Leslie*. New York, Routledge, 2002a:81–110.

Nichter, Mark. TB in India: overview and issues meriting anthropological assessment. Paper presented at the Society for Applied Anthropology, annual meeting, Atlanta, 2002b.

Nichter, Mark. Harm reduction: a core concern for medical anthropology. In: Herr-Harthorn B, Oaks L, eds. *Risk, culture, and health inequality: shifting perceptions of danger and blame*. Westport, CT, Praeger, 2003a:13–33.

Nichter, Mark. Smoking: what does culture have to do with it? *Addiction*, 2003b, 98 (suppl 1): 139–146.

Nichter, Mark. Anthropology and global health: reflections of a scholar-activist. *India Review*, 2006a, 5 (3–4): 1–29.

Nichter, Mark. Reducción del daño: una preocupación central para la antropologia médica. *Desacatos*, 2006b, 20:109–132.

Nichter, Mark. Introducing tobacco cessation in developing countries: an overview of Project Quit Tobacco International. *Tobacco Control*, 2006c, 15 (suppl. 1): 12–17.

Nichter, Mark. Talking cultural sensitivity while staunchly defending a one-size-fits-all DOTS policy: how national and international health policy undermines local problem solving. Paper presented at the American Anthropological Association Meeting, San Jose, CA, November 2006d.

Nichter, Mark. Foreword. In: Mapping communities: strengthening research through participatory GIS. *Practicing Anthropology*, 2007, 29 (4): 2–3.

Nichter, Mark. Coming to our senses: appreciating the sensorial in medical anthropology. *Transcultural Psychiatry*, 2008. Forthcoming.

Nichter, Mark, Cartwright E. Saving the children for the tobacco industry. *Medical Anthropology Quarterly*, 1991, 5 (3): 236–256.

Nichter, Mark, Kendall C. Beyond child survival: anthropology and international health in the 1990s. *Medical Anthropology Quarterly*, 1990, 5:195–203.

Nichter, Mark, Nichter, Mimi. *An anthropological approach to nutrition education*. Newton, MA, International Nutrition Communication Service Publications, Education Development Center, 1981.

Nichter, Mark, Nichter, Mimi. Cultural notions of fertility in South Asia and their impact on Sri Lankan family planning practices. *Human Organization*, 1987, 46 (1): 18–28.

Nichter, Mark, Nichter, Mimi. Modern methods of fertility regulation: when and for whom are they appropriate? In: Nichter Mark, Nichter Mimi, eds. *Anthropology and international health: Asian case studies*. Amsterdam, Gordon and Breach, 1996a:71–108.

Nichter, Mark, Nichter, Mimi. The ethnophysiology and folk dietetics of pregnancy: a case study from South India. In: Nichter Mark, Nichter Mimi, eds. *Anthropology and international health: Asian case studies*. Amsterdam, Gordon and Breach, 1996b:35–69.

Nichter, Mark, Nichter, Mimi. Acute respiratory illness: popular health culture and mothers' knowledge in the Philippines. In: Nichter Mark, Nichter Mimi, eds. *Anthropology and international health: Asian case studies*. Amsterdam, Gordon and Breach, 1996c:173–200.

Nichter, Mark, Nichter, Mimi. Education by appropriate analogy. In: Nichter Mark, Nichter Mimi, eds. *Anthropology and international health: Asian case studies*. Amsterdam, Gordon and Breach, 1996d:401–425.

Nichter, Mark, Nichter, Mimi, eds. *Anthropology and international health: Asian case studies*. Amsterdam, Gordon and Breach, 1996e.

Nichter, Mark, Thompson JJ. For my wellness, not just my illness: North Americans' use of dietary supplements. *Culture, Medicine and Psychiatry*, 2006, 30:175–222.

Nichter, Mark, Van Sickle D. The challenges of India's health and health care transitions. In: Ayres A, Oldenburg P, eds. *India briefing: quickening the pace of change*. New York, Asia Society, 2002.

Nichter, Mark, Vuckovic N. Agenda for an anthropology of pharmaceutical practice. *Social Science and Medicine*, 1994, 39 (11): 1509–1525.

Nichter, Mark, et al., eds. Acute respiratory infection. Special issue of *Medical Anthropology*, 1994, 15 (4): 319–446.

Nichter, Mark et al. Introducing zinc in a diarrheal control program: a manual for conducting formative research. INCLEN Web site, 2005 (www.inclentrust.org/downloads/zinc_manual_02_21_05.doc).

Nichter, Mimi, Nichter, Mark. *Women, work, and child welfare: case studies from India*. Ford Foundation Project Report. New Delhi, India, 1998.

Nizami SQ et al. Paediatric prescribing in Karachi. *Journal of the Pakistan Medical Association*, 1997, 47 (1): 29–35.

Novas C. The political economy of hope: patients' organizations, science and biovalue. *BioSocieties*, 2006, 1:289–305.

Novotny TE, Carlin D. Ethical and legal aspects of global tobacco control. *Tobacco Control*, 2005, 14 (suppl. II): ii26–ii30.

Nowotny H. Socially distributed knowledge: five spaces for science to meet the public. *Public Understanding of Science*, 1993, 2 (4): 307–319.

Nsimba SED. How sulfadoxine-pyrimethamine (SP) was perceived in some rural communities after phasing out chloroquine (CQ) as a first-line drug for uncomplicated malaria in Tanzania: lessons to learn towards moving from monotherapy to fixed combination therapy. *Journal of Ethnobiology and Ethnomedicine*, 2006, 2 (5) (www.ethnobiomed.com/content/pdf/1746-4269-2-5.pdf).

Nunley M. Why psychiatrists in India prescribe so many drugs. *Culture, Medicine and Psychiatry*, 1996, 20:165–197.

Nutting PA et al. Practice-based research networks answer primary care questions. *Journal of the American Medical Association*, 1999, 281:686–688.

Oaks L, Herr-Harthorn B. Introduction: health and the social and cultural construction of risk. In: Herr-Harthorn BH, Oaks L, eds. *Risk, culture, and health inequality: shifting perceptions of danger and blame.* Westport, CT, Praeger, 2003:3–11.

Oaks S et al., eds. *Malaria: obstacles and opportunities.* A report of the Committee for the Study on Malaria Prevention and Control: status review and alternative strategies. Washington, DC, National Academy Press, 1991.

Obadare E. A crisis of trust: history, politics, religion and the polio controversy in northern Nigeria. *Patterns of Prejudice*, 2005, 39 (3): 265–284.

Oberlander L, Elverdan B. Malaria in the United Republic of Tanzania: Cultural considerations and health-seeking behavior. *Bulletin of the World Health Organization*, 2000, 78 (11): 1352–1357.

O'Connor SM et al. Emerging infectious determinants of chronic disease. *Emerging Infectious Diseases*, 2006, 12 (7): 1051–1057.

Odebiyi AI. Food taboos in maternal and child health: the views of traditional healers in Ile-Ife, Nigeria. *Social Science and Medicine*, 1989, 28 (9): 985–96.

O'Dempsey TJD et al. Overlap in the clinical features of pneumonia and malaria in African children. *Transactions of the Royal Society of Tropical Medicine and Hygiene*, 1993, 87 (6): 662–665.

Ogden JA. Compliance versus adherence: just a matter of language? The politics and poetics of public health. In: Porter JDH, Grange JM, eds. *Tuberculosis: an interdisciplinary perspective.* London, Imperial College Press, 1999:213–233.

Ogden J, Porter J. The politics of partnership in tropical public health: researching tuberculosis control in India. *Social Policy and Administration*, 2000, 34 (4): 377–391.

Ogden J et al. Shifting the paradigm in TB control: illustrations from India. *International Journal of Tuberculosis and Lung Disease*, 1999, 3 (10): 855–861.

Ogden J et al. The politics of "branding" in policy transfer: the case of DOTS for tuberculosis control. *Social Science and Medicine*, 2003, 57 (1): 179–188.

Okeke IN et al. Socioeconomic and behavioral factors leading to acquired bacterial resistance to antibiotics in developing countries. *Emerging Infectious Diseases*, 1999, 5 (1): 18–27.

Okeke TA et al. Knowledge, attitude, practice, and prescribing pattern of oral rehydration therapy among private practitioners in Nigeria. *Journal of Diarrhoeal Diseases Research*, 1996, 14 (1): 33–36.

Okeke TA et al. Traditional healers in Nigeria: perception of cause, treatment and referral practices for severe malaria. *Journal of Biosocial Science*, 2005, 38 (4): 491–500.

Okumura J et al. Drug utilization and self-medication in rural communities in Vietnam. *Social Science and Medicine*, 2002, 54:1875–1886.

Olson KB. The household production of health and women's work: new directions in medical anthropology and households research. *Arizona Anthropologist*, 1994, 11:139–155.

Ong A. *Flexible citizenship: the cultural logics of transnationality*. Durham, NC, Duke University Press, 1999.

Ong A, Collier SJ, eds. *Global assemblages: technology, politics, and ethics as anthropological problems*. Malden, MA, Blackwell, 2005.

Ongore DL, Nyabola L. Role of shops and shopkeepers in malaria control. *East African Medical Journal*, 1996, 73:390–394.

Ongore D et al. A study of knowledge, attitudes and practices (KAP) of a rural community of malaria and the mosquito vector. *East African Medical Journal*, 1989, 66 (2): 79–89.

Opala J, Boillot F. Leprosy among the Limba: illness and healing in the context of world view. *Social Science and Medicine*, 1996, 42 (1): 3–19.

Orlandini B. Consuming "good governance" in Thailand. *European Journal of Development Research*, 2003, 15 (2): 16–43.

Orzech KC, Nichter M. From resilience to resistance: political ecological lessons from antibiotic and pesticide reliance. *Annual Review of Anthropology*, 2008. Forthcoming.

Paalman M et al. A critical review of priority setting in the health sector: the methodology of the 1993 World Development Report. *Health Policy and Planning*, 1998, 13 (1): 13–31.

Pablos-Mendez A, Shademani R. Knowledge translation in global health. *Journal of Continuing Education in the Health Professions*, 2006, 26 (1): 81–86.

Pablos-Mendez A et al. Knowledge translation in global health. *Bulletin of the World Health Organization*, 2005, 84:723.

Padmawati S, Nichter M. Community response to avian flu in central Java, Indonesia. *Anthropology and Medicine*, 2008. Forthcoming.

Padron M. Nongovernmental development organizations from development aid to development cooperation. *World Development*, 1997, 15 (suppl.): 67–77.

Paley J. *Marketing democracy: power and social movements in post-dictatorship Chile*. Berkeley, University of California Press, 2001.

Palis F et al. Our farmers at risk: behavior and belief system in pesticide safety. *Journal of Public Health*, 2006, 28 (1): 43–48.

Paluzzi JE, Farmer PE. The wrong question. *Development*, 2005, 48 (1): 12–18.

Pang T. Filling the gap between knowing and doing. *Nature*, 2003, 426:383.

Pang T et al. A 15th grand challenge for global public health. *Lancet*, 2006, 367:284–286.

Paral R. Health worker shortages and the potential of immigration policy. *Immigration Policy in Focus*, 2004, 3 (1): 1–13.

Parassitologia. The malaria challenge after one hundred years of malariology: papers from the Malariology Centennial Conference. *Parassitologia*, 1999, 41:1–528.

Parker M, Harper I. The anthropology of public health. *Journal of Biosocial Science*, 2005, 38:1–5.

Parker R. Sexuality, culture, and power in HIV/AIDS research. *Annual Review of Anthropology*, 2001, 30:163–179.

Parks W, Lloyd LS. *Planning social mobilization and communication for dengue fever prevention and control: a step-by-step guide*. WHO/CDS/WMC/2004.2. Geneva, World Health Organization, 2004.

Pathania V. Why the Indian TB control programme must stop ignoring private practitioners. *International Journal of Tuberculosis and Lung Disease*, 2001, 5 (2): 2013.

Patterson AE et al. Local terminology for medicines to treat fever in Bougouni District, Mali: implications for the introduction and evaluation of malaria treatment policies. *Tropical Medicine and International Health*, 2006, 11 (10): 1613–1624.

Paul BD, Demarest WJ. Citizen participation overplanned: the case of a health project in the Guatemalan community of San Pedro la Laguna. *Social Science and Medicine*, 1984, 19 (3): 185–192.

Pearce N. Traditional epidemiology, modern epidemiology and public health. *American Journal of Public Health*, 1996, 86 (5): 678–683.

Pearce N. The globalization of epidemiology: introductory remarks. *International Journal of Epidemiology*, 2004, 33:1127–1131.

Pearce N, Davey Smith G. Is social capital the key to inequalities in health? *American Journal of Public Health*, 2003, 93 (1): 122–129.

Pearl D, Stecklow S. Drug firms' incentive fuel abuse by pharmacists in India. *Wall Street Journal*, August 16, 2001:1.

Pellegrino ED. Is truth telling to the patient a cultural artifact? *Journal of the American Medical Association*, 1992, 268 (13): 1734–1735.

Percot M. From opportunity to life strategy: Indian nurses in the Gulf. In: Agarwal A, ed. *Exploring migrant women and work*. New Delhi, Sage Publications, 2006: 155–176.

Périn I, Attaran A. Trading ideology for dialogue: an opportunity to fix international aid for health? *Lancet*, 2003, 361:1216–1219.

Person B et al. Fear and stigma: the epidemic within the SARS outbreak. *Emerging Infectious Diseases*, 2004, 10 (2): 358–363.

Petchesky RP. Fetal images: the power of visual culture in the politics of reproduction. In: Lancaster RN, de Leonardo M, eds. *The gender/sexuality reader: culture, history, political economy*. New York, Routledge, 1997.

Peterson MA. The rhetoric of epidemic in India: news coverage of AIDS. *Alif: Journal of Comparative Poetics*, 1998, 18:237–268.

Petros G et al. HIV/AIDS and "othering" in South Africa: the blame goes on. *Culture, Health and Sexuality*, 2006, 8 (1): 67–77.

Petryna A. *Life exposed: biological citizens after Chernobyl*. Princeton, NJ, Princeton University Press, 2002.

Petryna A. Ethical variability: drug development and globalizing clinical trials. *American Ethnologist*, 2005, 32 (2): 183–197.

Petryna A et al., eds. *Global pharmaceuticals: ethics, markets, practices*. Durham, NC, Duke University Press, 2006.

Pfeiffer J. Cash income, intrahousehold cooperative conflict, and child health in central Mozambique. *Medical Anthropology*, 2003a, 22:87–130.

Pfeiffer J. International NGOs and primary health care in Mozambique: the need for a new model of collaboration. *Social Science and Medicine*, 2003b, 56:725–738.

Pfeiffer J. Civil society, NGOs, and the Holy Spirit in Mozambique. *Human Organization*, 2004, 63 (3): 359–372.

Philips J. The hookworm campaign in Ceylon. In: Teaf HM, Franck PG, eds. *Hands across frontiers: case studies in technical cooperation*. Ithaca, NY, Cornell University Press, 1955:265–305.

Phillips L. Women, development, and the state in rural Ecuador. In: Leon M, ed. *Rural women and state policy: feminist perspectives on Latin American agricultural development*. Boulder, CO, Westview Press, 1987:105–123.

Phillips L. Gender dynamics and rural household strategies. *Canadian Review of Sociology and Anthropology*, 1989, 26 (2): 294–310.

Pickles J, ed. *Ground truth: the social implications of geographic information systems*. New York, Guilford, 1995.

Pidgeon NF et al., eds. *The social amplification of risk*. Cambridge, Cambridge University Press, 2003.

Pigg SL. The social symbolism of healing in Nepal. *Ethnology*, 1995, 34:17–36.

Pigg SL. Expecting the epidemic: a social history of the representation of sexual risk in Nepal. *Feminist Media Studies*, 2002, 2 (1): 97–125.

Pigg SL, Adams V. Introduction: the moral object of sex. In: Adams V, Pigg SL, eds. *The moral object of sex: science, development and sexuality in global perspective*. Durham, NC, Duke University Press, 2005.

Pike I. The determinants of pregnancy outcome for nomadic Turkana women of Kenya [dissertation]. Binghamton, State University of New York, 1996.

Pike I. Age, reproductive history, seasonality, and maternal body composition during pregnancy for nomadic Turkana pastoralists of Kenya. *American Journal of Human Biology*, 1999, 11:658–672.

Pike, IL. The biosocial consequences of life on the run: a case study from Turkana District, Kenya. *Human Organization*, 2004, 63 (2): 221–235.

Pincock S. Poliovirus spreads beyond Nigeria after vaccine uptake drops. *British Medical Journal*, 2004, 328 (7435): 310.

Polanyi M. *The tacit dimension*. London, Routledge and Kegan Paul, 1967.

Porter JD. Epidemiologial reflections of the contribution of anthropology to public health policy and practice. *Journal of Biosocial Science*, 2005, 38:133–144.

Porter TM. Objectivity as standardization: the rhetoric of impersonality in measurement, statistics and cost-benefit analysis. *Annals of Scholarship*, 1992, 6:19–59.

Porter TM. *Trust in numbers: the pursuit of objectivity in science and public life*. Princeton, Princeton University Press, 1995.

Portes A. Social capital: its origins and applications in modern sociology. *Annual Review of Sociology*, 1998, 24 (1): 1–24.

Portes A, Landolt P. The downside of social capital. *American Prospect*, 1996, 26:18–21.

Poster M. *The second media age*. Oxford, UK, Blackwell, 1995.

Pottier J. Why aid agencies need better understanding of the communities they assist: the experience of food aid in Rwandan refugee camps. *Disasters*, 1996, 20 (4): 324–337.

Power M. *The audit society: rituals of verification*. New York, Oxford University Press, 1997.

Price J. Pharmaceuticals in popular medical culture: an exploration of unregulated circulation and consumption of biomedicines in a central African town [dissertation]. Cleveland, OH, Case Western Reserve University, 2002.

Price L. Ecuadorian illness stories. In: Holland D, Quinn N, eds. *Cultural models in language and thought*. Cambridge, Cambridge University Press, 1987:313–342.

Pronyk PM et al. Assessing health seeking behaviour among tuberculosis patients in rural South Africa. *International Journal of Tuberculosis and Lung Disease*, 2001, 5 (7): 619–627.

Putnam RD. *Making democracy work: civic traditions in modern Italy*. Princeton, Princeton University Press, 1993.

Putnam RD. Bowling alone: America's declining social capital. *Journal of Democracy*, 1995, 6:65–78.

Putnam RD. Health and happiness. In: Putnam RD. *Bowling alone: the collapse and revival of American community*. New York, Simon and Schuster, 2000:326–335.

Pylypa JJ. Healing herbs and dangerous doctors: local models and response to fevers in northeast Thailand [dissertation]. Tucson, University of Arizona, 2004.

Pylypa J. Healing herbs and dangerous doctors: "fruit fever" and community conflicts with biomedical care in northeast Thailand. *Medical Anthropology Quarterly*, 2007, 21 (4): 349–368.

Qingjun L et al. The effect of drug packaging on patients' compliance with treatment for plasmodium vivax malaria in China. *Bulletin of the World Health Organization*, 1998, 76 (suppl. 1): 21–27.

Quinlan MB. *From the bush: the front line of health care in a Caribbean village*. Belmont, CA, Wadsworth/Thomson, 2004.

Quinlan MB et al. Ethnophysiology and herbal treatments of intestinal worms in Dominica, West Indies. *Journal of Ethnopharmacology*, 2002, 80:75–83.

Rabinow P. *Making PCR: a story of biotechnology*. Chicago, University of Chicago Press, 1996.

Rabinow P, Rose N. Biopower today. *Biosocieties*, 2006, 1:195–217.

Radcliffe SA. Geography of development: development, civil society and inequality—social capital is (almost) dead? *Progress in Human Geography*, 2004, 28 (4): 517–527.

Radyowijali A, Haak H. Determinants of antimicrobial use in the developing world. *Child Health Research*, 2002, 4 (1): 1–36.

Rai S. Drug companies cut costs with foreign clinical trials. *New York Times*, February 24, 2005.

Ramaiah KD et al. Knowledge and beliefs about transmission, prevention and control of lymphatic filariasis in rural areas of South India. *Tropical Medicine and International Health*, 1996, 1:433–438.

Ramakrishna J et al. Treatment of malaria and febrile convulsions: an education diagnosis of Yoruba beliefs. *International Quarterly of Community Health Education*, 1989, 9:305–319.

Ramos-Jimenez P et al. *Immunization in the Philippines: the social and cultural dimension*. Netherlands, Het Spinhuis, 1999.

Rangan S, Uplekar MW. Socio-cultural dimensions in tuberculosis control. In Porter JDH, Grange JM, eds. *Tuberculosis: an interdisciplinary perspective*. London, Imperial College Press, 1999:265–281.

Rangan SG et al. Tuberculosis control in rural India: lessons from public-private collaboration. *International Journal of Tuberculosis and Lung Disease*, 2004, 8:552–559.

Rao P et al. North Carolina growers' and extension agents' perceptions of Latino farmworker pesticide exposure. *Human Organization*, 2004, 63 (2): 151–161.

Rathgeber EM, Vlassoff C. Gender and tropical diseases: a new research focus. *Social Science and Medicine*, 1993, 37 (4): 513–520.

Raufu A. Traditional rulers in northern Nigeria call for halt to polio vaccination. *British Medical Journal*, 2004a, 328 (7435): 306.

Raufu A. Nigeria postpones programme of polio immunization. *British Medical Journal*, 2004b, 328 (7451): 1278.

Rauyajin O et al. Socio-cultural and behavioural aspects of mosquito-borne lymphatic filariasis in Thailand: a qualitative analysis. *Social Science and Medicine*, 1995, 41 (12): 1705–1713.

Reddy KS. The burden of disease among the global poor. *Lancet*, 1999, 354:1477.

Reed H, Habicht JP. Sales of food aid as sign of distress, not excess. *Lancet*, 1998, 351:128–30.

Reeler AV. Anthropological perspectives on injections: a review. *Bulletin of the World Health Organization*, 2000, 78:135–143.

Reich M. Reshaping the state from above, from within, from below: implications for public health. *Social Science and Medicine*, 2002, 54 (11): 1669–1675.

Reidpath DD et al. Measuring health in a vacuum: examining the disability weight of the DALY. *Health Policy and Planning*, 2003, 18 (4): 351–356.

Reuben R. Women and malaria—special risks and appropriate control strategy. *Social Science and Medicine*, 1993, 34 (4): 473–480.

Rifkin SB. Lessons from community participation in health programmes. *Health Policy and Planning*, 1986, 1:240–249.

Rifkin SB. Primary health care, community participation and the urban poor: a review of the problems and solutions. *Asia-Pacific Journal of Public Health*, 1987, 1 (2): 57–63.

Rifkin SB, Walt G. Why health improves: defining the issues concerning "comprehensive primary health care" and "selective primary health care." *Social Science and Medicine*, 1986, 23 (6): 559–566.

Rifkin SB et al. Primary health care: on measuring participation. *Social Science and Medicine*, 1988, 26:931–940.

Rigau-Perez JG et al. Dengue and dengue haemorrhagic fever. *Lancet*, 1998, 352 (9132): 971–977.

Robins S. From "rights" to "ritual": AIDS activism in South Africa. *American Anthropologist*, 2006, 108 (2): 312–323.

Roe EM. Development narratives, or making the best of blueprint development. *World Development*, 1991, 19 (4): 287–300.

Roemer R et al. Origins of the WHO Framework Convention on Tobacco Control. *American Journal of Public Health*, 2005, 95 (6): 936–938.

Rohde JE, ed. *Learning to reach health for all: thirty years of instructive experience at BRAC*. Dhaka, Bangladesh, University Press, 2005.

Romney AK. Culture consensus as a statistical model. *Current Anthropology*, 1999, 40 (suppl.): S103–S115.

Rose G. Sick individuals and sick populations. *International Journal of Epidemiology*, 1985, 14:32–38.

Rose G. *The strategy of preventive medicine*. Oxford, Oxford University Press, 1992.

Rose N. *Powers of freedom: reframing political thought*. Cambridge, Cambridge University Press, 1999.

Rose N, Miller P. Political power beyond the state: problematics of government. *British Journal of Sociology*, 1992, 43 (2): 173–205.

Rose N, Novas C. Biological citizenship. In: Ong A, Collier S, eds. *Global assemblages: technology, politics and ethics as anthropological problems*. Malden, MA, Blackwell, 2005.

Rosenau J, Singh JP. *Information technologies and global politics*. New York, State University of New York Press, 2002.

Rosenberg CE. *Explaining epidemics and other studies in the history of medicine*. Cambridge, Cambridge University Press, 1992.

Roses AD. Pharmacogenetics and future drug development and delivery. *Lancet*, 2000, 355:1358–1361.

Ross SJ et al. Nursing shortages and international nurse migration. *International Nursing Review*, 2005, 52:253–262.

Rozemberg B. Representações sociais de eventos somáticos ligados à esquistossomose. *Cademos de Saúde Pública*, 1994, 10:30–46.

Rozemberg B, Manderson L. "Nerves" and tranquilizer use in rural Brazil. *International Journal of Health Services*, 1998, 28 (1): 165–181.

Ruebush TK II et al. Knowledge and beliefs about malaria on the Pacific coastal plain of Guatemala. *American Journal of Tropical Medicine and Hygiene*, 1992, 46 (4): 451–459.

Rueda-Baclig MJ, Florencio CA. Lay conception of hypertension and its significance to clients and professionals in nutrition and health. *Journal of Human Nutrition and Dietetics*, 2003, 16:457–466.

Rychetnik L et al. A glossary for evidence based public health. *Journal of Epidemiology and Public Health*, 2004, 58:538–545.

Sachs J. *Tropical underdevelopment*. Working Paper 8119. Cambridge, MA, National Bureau of Economic Research, 2001.

Sackett DL et al. Evidence based medicine: what it is and what it isn't. *British Medical Journal*, 1996, 312 (7023): 71–72.

Sackett DL et al. *Evidence-based medicine: how to practice and teach EBM*, 4th ed. Edinburgh, Churchill Livingstone, 2000.

Sadana R, Snow R. Balancing effectiveness, side-effects and work: women's perceptions and experiences with modern contraceptive technology in Cambodia. *Social Science and Medicine*, 1999, 49:343–358.

Sadana R et al. Importance of health research in South Asia. *British Medical Journal*, 2004, 328:826–830.

Said EW. *Orientalism*. New York, Pantheon Books, 1978.

Samuelsen H. Infusions of health: the popularity of vaccinations among Bissa in Burkina Faso. *Anthropology and Medicine*, 2001, 8 (2/3): 164–175.

Samuelsen H. Illness transmission and proximity: local theories of causation among the Bissa in Burkina Faso. *Medical Anthropology*, 2004, 23:89–112.

Sattenspiel L. Tropical environments, human activities, and the transmission of infectious diseases. *Yearbook of Physical Anthropology*, 2000, 43:3–31.

Sauerborn R et al. Low utilization of community health workers: results from a household survey in Burkina Faso. *Social Science and Medicine*, 1989, 29 (10): 1163–1174.

Sauerborn R et al. Age bias, but no gender bias, in the intra-household resource allocation for health care in rural Burkina Faso. *Health Transition Review*, 1996a, 6:131–145.

Sauerborn R et al. Seasonal variations of household costs of illness in Burkina Faso. *Social Science and Medicine*, 1996b, 43 (3): 281–290.

Scheper-Hughes N. Social indifference to child death. *Lancet*, 1991, 337:1144–1147.

Scheper-Hughes N. *Death without weeping: the violence of everyday life in Brazil.* Berkeley, University of California Press, 1992.

Scheper-Hughes N. The global traffic in human organs. *Current Anthropology*, 2000, 41 (2): 191–224.

Scheper-Hughes N. Rotten trade: millennial capitalism, human values and global justice in organs trafficking. *Journal of Human Rights*, 2003a, 2 (2): 197–226.

Scheper-Hughes N. Keeping an eye on the global traffic in human organs. *Lancet*, 2003b, 361 (9369): 1645–1648.

Scheper-Hughes N, Lock M. The message in the bottle: illness and the micropolitics of resistance. *Journal of Psychohistory*, 1991, 18 (4): 409–432.

Schoeph BG. International AIDS research in anthropology: taking a critical perspective on the crises. *Annual Review of Anthropology*, 2001, 30:335–361.

Schuler D, Day P. *Shaping the network society—the new role of civil society in cyberspace.* Cambridge, MA, MIT Press, 2004.

Schumann D, Mosley WH. The household production of health. *Social Science and Medicine*, 1994, 38 (2): 201–204.

Schwab M, Syme SL. On paradigms, community participation and the future of public health. *American Journal of Public Health*, 1997, 87:2049–2052.

Schwitzer G et al. What are the roles and responsibilities of the media in disseminating health information? *PLoS Medicine*, 2005, 2 (7): 576–582.

Scott J. *Seeing like a state: how certain schemes to improve the human condition have failed.* New Haven, CT, Yale University Press, 1998.

Scrimshaw NS, Gleason, GR, eds. *RAP: rapid assessment procedures.* Boston, International Nutrition Foundation for Developing Countries, 1992.

Scrimshaw SC, Hurtado E. Anthropological involvement in the Central American Diarrheal Disease Control Project. *Social Science and Medicine*, 1988, 27 (1): 97–105.

Sen A. Gender and cooperative conflicts. In: Tinker I, ed. *Persistent inequalities: women and world development.* New York, Oxford University Press, 1990: 123–149.

Sen A. The economics of life and death. *Scientific American*, 1993, 268 (5): 40–47.

Sen A. *Development as freedom.* New York, Alfred A. Knopf, 1999.

Sepúlveda J. Foreword. In: Jamison DT et al., eds. *Disease control priorities in developing countries*. Washington, DC, International Bank for Reconstruction and Development/ World Bank, 2006:xiii–xv.

Sepúlveda J et al. Improvement of child survival in Mexico: the diagonal approach. *Lancet*, 2006, 368:2017–2027.

Serquina-Ramiro L et al. Measles immunization acceptance in Southeast Asia: past patterns and future challenges. *Southeast Asian Journal of Tropical Medicine and Public Health*, 2001, 32 (4): 791–804.

Severe P et al. Antiretroviral therapy in a thousand patients with AIDS in Haiti. *New England Journal of Medicine*, 2005, 353 (22): 2325–2334.

Sewell WHJ. A theory of structure: duality, agency, and transformation. *American Journal of Sociology*, 1992, 98 (1): 1–29.

Sewell WHJ. *Logics of history: social theory and social transformation*. Chicago, University of Chicago Press, 2005.

Shah G. *Public health and urban development: the plague in Surat*. New Delhi, Sage Publications, 1997.

Shail A, Howie G, eds. *Menstruation: a cultural history*. Basingstoke, UK, Palgrave Macmillan, 2005.

Sharma R. India wakes up to threat of bioterrorism. *British Medical Journal*, 2001, 323:714.

Sharma R. The diagnostic rip-off. *Frontline*, 2002, 19 (23): 9–22.

Shields MD et al. Developing and dismantling social capital: gender and resource management in the Philippines. In: Rocheleau D, Thomas-Slayter B, eds. *Feminist political ecology: global issues and local experiences*. London, Routledge, 1996:155–179.

Shiva M. Malaria and tuberculosis: our concerns. *Health Millions*, 1997, 23:2–3.

Shore C, Wright S. Audit culture and anthropology: neo-liberalism in British higher education. *Journal of the Royal Anthropological Institute*, 1999, 5:557–577.

Simonsen L et al. Unsafe injections in the developing world and transmission of blood-borne pathogens. *Bulletin of the World Health Organization*, 1999, 77:789–800.

Singer M. The limitations of medical ecology: the concept of adaptation in the context of social stratification and social transformation. *Medical Anthropology*, 1989, 10:223–234.

Singer M. A dose of drugs, a touch of violence, a case of AIDS: conceptualizing the SAVA syndemic. *Free Inquiry*, 1996, 24 (2): 99–110.

Singer M, Clair S. Syndemics and public health: reconceptualizing disease in biosocial context. *Medical Anthropology Quarterly*, 2003, 17 (4): 423–441.

Singer M et al. Syndemics, sex and the city: understanding sexually transmitted diseases in social and cultural context. *Social Science and Medicine*, 2006, 63:2010–2021.

Singh J et al. Community studies on hepatitis B in Rajahmundry town of Andhra Pradesh, India, 1997–8: unnecessary therapeutic injections are a major risk factor. *Epidemiology and Infection*, 2000, 125:367–375.

Sirima SB et al. Early treatment of childhood fevers with pre-packaged antimalarial drugs in the home reduces severe malaria morbidity in Burkina Faso. *Tropical Medicine and International Health*, 2003, 8:133–139.

Sivin N. *Traditional medicine in contemporary China*. Ann Arbor, University of Michigan Press, 1987.

Slovic P (ed.). *The perception of risk*. London, Earthscan Publications, 2000.

Slovic P et al. The affect heuristic. In: Gilovich T et al., eds. *Heuristics and biases: the psychology of intuitive judgment*, vol. 2. New York, Cambridge University Press, 2002:397–420.

Smith BJ et al. WHO health promotion glossary: new terms. *Health Promotion International*, 2006, 21 (4): 340–345.

Smith GD et al. The cultural construction of childhood diarrhea in rural Nicaragua: relevance for epidemiology and health promotion. *Social Science and Medicine*, 1993, 36 (12): 1613–1624.

Smith R. Medical journals are an extension of the marketing arm of pharmaceutical companies. *PLoS Medicine*, 2005, 2 (5): 364–366.

Snyder RC. Social capital: the politics of race and gender. In: McLean SL et al., eds. *Social capital: critical perspectives on community and "bowling alone."* New York, New York University Press, 2002:167–182.

Sobel J. Can we trust social capital? *Journal of Economic Literature*, 2002, 40:139–154.

Sobo EJ. Bodies, kin, and flow: family planning in rural Jamaica. *Medical Anthropology Quarterly*, 1993a, 7 (1): 50–73.

Sobo EJ. *One blood: the Jamaican body*. Albany, State University of New York Press, 1993b.

Sobo EJ. *Choosing unsafe sex: AIDS-risk denial among disadvantaged women*. Philadelphia, University of Pennsylvania Press, 1995.

Sommerfeld J et al. Perceptions of risk, vulnerability, and disease prevention in rural Burkina Faso: implications for community-based health care and insurance. *Human Organization*, 2002, 61 (2): 139–146.

Spencer HC et al. Epidemiology of chloroquine-associated pruritis in Saradidi, Kenya. *Annals of Tropical Medicine and Parasitology*, 1987, 81 (suppl. 1): 124–127.

Sperber D. Anthropology and psychology: toward an epidemiology of representations. *Man*, 1985, 29 (1): 73–89.

Sperber D. The epidemiology of beliefs. In: Fraser C, Gaskell G, eds. *The social psychological study of widespread beliefs*. Oxford, UK, Clarendon Press, 1990.

Sperber D. *Explaining culture: a naturalistic approach*. Oxford, UK, Blackwell, 1996.

Spiegel J et al. Barriers and bridges to prevention and control of dengue: the need for a social-ecological approach. *EcoHealth*, 2005, 2:273–290.

Standing H, Bloom G. Beyond public and private? Unorganised markets in health care delivery. Presented at the "Making Services Work for Poor People" World Development Report (WDR) 2003/04 Workshop, Eynsham Hall, Oxford, 4–5 November 2002 (http://econ.worldbank.org/files/22482/_standingbloomWDR.pdf).

Staples J. Delineating disease: self-management of leprosy identities in South India. *Medical Anthropology*, 2004, 23:69–88.

Stein CE et al. Fetal growth and coronary heart disease in South India. *Lancet*, 1996, 348 (9037): 1269–1273.

Stepan NL. Race and gender: the role of analogy in science. In: Harding S, ed. *The "Racial" Economy of Science*. Bloomington, Indiana University Press, 1993:359–376.

Stepan NL. Tropical medicine and public health in Latin America. *Medical History*, 1998, 42:104–112.

Stepan NL. *Picturing tropical nature*. Ithaca, NY, Cornell University Press, 2001.

Stephens C et al. Knowledge of mosquitoes in relation to public and domestic control activities in the cities of Dar es Salaam and Tanga. *Bulletin of the World Health Organization*, 1995, 73:97–104.

Stewart MK et al. Acute respiratory infections (ARI) in rural Bangladesh: perceptions and practices. *Medical Anthropology*, 1994, 15 (4): 377–394.

Stock R. "Disease and development" or the "underdevelopment of health": a critical review of geographical perspectives on African health problems. *Social Science and Medicine*, 1986, 23 (7): 689–700.

Stone L. Cultural influences in community participation in health. *Social Science and Medicine*, 1992, 35 (4): 409–417.

Strahl H. Cultural interpretations of an emerging health problem: blood pressure in Dar es Salaam, Tanzania. *Anthropology and Medicine*, 2003, 10 (3): 309–324.

Strathern M. *The gender of the gift*. Berkeley, University of California Press, 1988.

Strathern M. From improvement to enhancement: an anthropological comment on the audit culture. *Cambridge Anthropologist*, 1996, 19:1–21.

Strathern M, ed. *Audit cultures: anthropological studies in accountability, ethics and the academy*. London, Routledge, 2000.

Streefland PH. Introduction of an HIV vaccine in developing countries: social and cultural dimensions. *Vaccine*, 2003, 21:1304–1309.

Streefland PH et al. Patterns of vaccination acceptance. *Social Science and Medicine*, 1999, 49:1705–1716.

Strong P. Epidemic psychology. *Sociology of Health and Illness*, 1989, 12 (3): 249–259.

Stryer D, Bero L. Characteristics of materials distributed by drug companies: an evaluation of appropriateness. *Journal of General Internal Medicine*, 1996, 11:575–583.

Sunyer J, Grimalt J. Global climate change, widening health inequalities and epidemiology. *International Journal of Epidemiology*, 2006, 35:213–216.

Surbone A. Truth telling to the patient. *Journal of the American Medical Association*, 1992, 268:1661–1662.

Suryakusuma JI. The state and sexuality in New Order Indonesia. In: LJ Sears, ed. *Fantasizing the feminine in Indonesia*. Durham, NC, Duke University Press, 1996:92–119.

Susser M. Does risk factor epidemiology put epidemiology at risk: peering into the future. *Journal of Epidemiology and Community Health*, 1998, 52:608–611.

Susser M, Susser E. Choosing a future for epidemiology: I. Eras and paradigms. *American Journal of Public Health*, 1996a, 86:668–673.

Susser M, Susser E. Choosing a future for epidemiology: II. From black box to Chinese boxes and eco-epidemiology. *American Journal of Public Health*, 1996b, 86:674–677.

Szreter S, Woolcock M. Health by association? Social capital, social theory and the political economy of public health. *International Journal of Epidemiology*, 2004, 33:650–657.

Tabor DC. Ripe and unripe: concepts of health and sickness in Ayurvedic medicine. *Social Science and Medicine*, 1981, 15B:439–455.

Talaat M et al. The social context of reproductive health in an Egyptian hamlet: a pilot study to identify female genital schistosomiasis. *Social Science and Medicine*, 2004, 58:515–524.

Tallo VL. Piang, panuhot or the moon: the folk etiology of cough among Boholano mothers. *Philippines Journal of Microbiological Infectious Diseases*, 1999, 28 (2): 59–67.

Tan ML. Traditional or transitional medical systems? Pharmacotherapy as a case for analysis. *Social Science and Medicine*, 1989, 29 (3): 301–307.

Tan ML. The meanings of medicines: examples from the Philippines. In: Etkin N, Tan M, eds. *Medicines: meanings and context*. Manila, Manila Press, 1994:69–81.

Tan ML. *Magaling na gamut*: pharmaceuticals and the construction of power and knowledge in the Philippines [dissertation]. University of Amsterdam, the Netherlands, 1996.

Tannen D, Wallat C. Interactive framer and knowledge schemas in interaction: examples from a medical examination. Interview in: Tannen D, ed. *Framing in discourse*. New York, Oxford University Press, 1993:57–76.

Tarimo DS et al. Mothers' perceptions and knowledge on childhood malaria in the holoendemic Kibaha District, Tanzania: implications for malaria control and the IMCI strategy. *Tropical Medicine and International Health*, 2000, 5:179–184.

Tarimo DS et al. Perception of chloroquine efficacy and alternative treatments for uncomplicated malaria in children in a holoendemic area of Tanzania: implications for the change of treatment policy. *Tropical Medicine and International Health*, 2001, 6 (12): 992–997.

Taylor AL. Global governance, international health law and WHO: looking towards the future. *Bulletin of the World Health Organization*, 2002, 80 (12): 975–980.

Taylor C. The concept of flow in Rwandan popular medicine. *Social Science and Medicine*, 1988, 27 (12): 1343–1348.

Taylor C, Jolly R. The straw men of primary health care. *Social Science and Medicine*, 1988, 26 (9): 971–977.

Tesler L. Now there is no treatment for anyone: health care seeking in neoliberal Nicaragua [dissertation]. Tucson, University of Arizona, 2005.

Thomas A et al. Predictors of relapse among tuberculosis patients treated in a DOTS programme in South India. *International Journal of Tuberculosis and Lung Disease*, 2005, 9:556–561.

Thomas P et al. Networks for research in primary health care. *British Medical Journal*, 2001, 322:588–590.

Thorson A et al. Health-seeking behaviour of individuals with a cough for more than 3 weeks. *Lancet*, 2000, 356:1823–1824.

Tripp K et al. Adherence to antenatal micronutrient supplementation: understanding community perspectives and attitudes. Dadaab Refugee Camps, Kenya, June–August 2001. Results of a qualitative field study. United Nations High Commissioner for Refugees, Centre for International Child Health, Institute of Child Health, 2001 (www.ich.ucl.ac.uk/ich/html/academicunits/cich/pdfs/MMNSupplementationDadaab2001.pdf).

Trostle JA. *Epidemiology and culture*. Cambridge, Cambridge University Press, 2005.

Tucker JB. Updating the International Health Regulations. *Biosecurity and Bioterrorism*, 2005, 3 (4): 338–347.

Tunstall HVZ et al. Places and health. *Journal of Epidemiology and Community Health*, 2004, 58:6–10.

Turshen M. The unnatural history of disease. In: Turshen M. *The political ecology of disease in Tanzania*. New Brunswick, NJ, Rutgers University Press, 1984:9–19.

United Nations Human Settlements Programme. *The challenge of slums global report on human settlements*. London, Earthscan Publications, 2003.

Uplekar M. Involving private health care providers in delivery of TB care: global strategy. *Tuberculosis*, 2003, 83 (3): 156–164.

Uplekar MW, Shepard DS. Treatment of tuberculosis by private general practitioners in India. *Tubercle*, 1991, 72 (4): 284–290.

Utarini A et al. Appraising studies in health using rapid assessment procedures (RAP): eleven critical criteria. *Human Organization*, 2001, 60 (4): 390–400.

Utarini A et al. Rapid assessment procedures of malaria in low endemic countries: community perceptions in Jepara district, Indonesia. *Social Science and Medicine*, 2003, 56:701–712.

Uvin P. *Human rights and development*. Bloomfield, CT, Kumarian Press, 2004.

Van Damme W, Van Lerberghe W. Epidemics and fear. *Tropical Medicine and International Health*, 2000, 5 (8): 511–514.

Van der Geest S. The illegal distribution of Western medicines in developing countries: pharmacists, drug peddlers, injection doctors and others. A bibliographic exploration. *Medical Anthropology*, 1982, 6 (4): 197–219.

Van der Geest S. "No strength": sex and old age in a rural town in Ghana. *Social Science and Medicine*, 2001, 53 (10): 1383–1396.

Van der Geest S, Whyte S, eds. *The context of medicines in developing countries*. Dordrecht, Kluwer, 1989.

Van der Geest S et al. The anthropology of pharmaceuticals: a biographical approach. *Annual Review of Anthropology*, 1996, 25:153–178.

Van der Veen KW. Private practitioners and the National Tuberculosis Programme in India. *Journal of Research and Education in Indian Medicine*, 1987, 6 (3–4): 59–66.

Van Hollen C. Invoking Vali: painful technologies of modern birth in South India. *Medical Anthropology Quarterly*, 2003, 17 (1): 49–77.

Van Sickle D. Silent treatment: what ails Cuban health care? *New Republic*, 1998, 218 (25): 14–15.

Van Sickle D. The rise of asthma and allergy in South India: how representations of illness influence medical practice and marketing of medicines [dissertation]. Tucson, University of Arizona, 2004.

Victora CG, Knauth DR. Images of the body and the reproductive system among men and women living in shantytowns in Porto Alegre, Brazil. *Reproductive Health Matters*, 2001, 9 (18): 22–33.

Vincent F. NGOs, social movements, external funding and dependency. *Development*, 2006, 49 (2): 22–28.

Vlassoff C, Manderson L. Evaluating agency initiatives: building social science capability in tropical disease research. *Acta Tropica*, 1994, 57: 103–122.

Vlassoff C, Moreno CG. Placing gender at the centre of health programming: challenges and limitations. *Social Science and Medicine*, 2002, 54:1713–1723.

Vuckovic N, Nichter M. Pharmaceutical practice in the US: research agenda for the next decade. *Social Science and Medicine*, 1997, 44 (9): 1285–1302.

Wacquant L. Comments (response to Farmer P, "An anthropology of structural violence"). *Current Anthropology*, 2004, 45 (3): 322.

Wadley S. Family composition strategies in rural North India. *Social Science and Medicine*, 1993, 37:1367–1376.

Wagner W et al. "I have some faith and at the same time I don't believe"—cognitive polyphasia and cultural change in India. *Journal of Community and Applied Social Psychology*, 2000, 10:301–314.

Wailoo K et al., eds. *A death retold: Jesica Santillan, the bungled transplant, and paradoxes of medical citizenship*. Chapel Hill, University of North Carolina Press, 2006.

Wakefield SEL, Poland B. Family, friend or foe? Critical reflections on the relevance and role of social capital in health promotion and community development. *Social Science and Medicine*, 2005, 60:2819–2832.

Waldby C. Stem cells, tissue cultures and the production of biovalue. *Health: An Interdisciplinary Journal for the Social Study of Health, Illness and Medicine*, 2002, 6 (3): 305–323.

Waldman A. Distrust reopens the door for polio in India. *New York Times*, January 19, 2003.

Waldram JB. The view from the hogan: cultural epidemiology and the return to ethnography. *Transcultural Psychiatry*, 2006, 43:72–85.

Wallace R. A synergism of plagues. *Environment Research*, 1988, 47:1–33.

Wallace R. Urban desertification, public health and public order: planned shrinkage, violent death, substance abuse and AIDS in the Bronx. *Social Science and Medicine*, 1990, 31:801–813.

Wallis P, Nerlich B. Disease metaphors in new epidemics: the UK media framing of the 2003 SARS epidemic. *Social Science and Medicine*, 2005, 60:2629–2693.

Walsh JA, Warren KS. Selective primary health care. *New England Journal of Medicine*, 1979, 301:967–74.

Walt G. Global cooperation in international public health. In: Merson MH et al., eds. *International public health*. Gaithersberg, MD, Aspen Institute, 2001a:667–700.

Walt G. Globalization and health. *Medicine, Conflict and Survival*, 2001b, 17 (1): 63–70.

Walt G, Buse K. Partnership and fragmentation in international health: threat or opportunity? *Tropical Medicine and International Health*, 2000, 5 (7): 467–471.

Walter FM, Emery J. "Coming down the line"—patients' understanding of their family history of common chronic diseases. *Annals of Family Medicine*, 2005, 3 (5): 405–413.

Walter FM, Emery J. Perceptions of family history across common diseases: a qualitative study in primary care. *Family Practice*, 2006, 23 (4): 472–480.

Walter FM et al. Lay understanding of familial risk of common chronic diseases: a systematic review and synthesis of qualitative research. *Annals of Family Medicine*, 2004, 2 (6): 583–594.

Wardlow H. Giving birth to *gonolia*: "culture" and sexually transmitted disease among the Huli of Papua New Guinea. *Medical Anthropology Quarterly*, 2002, 16 (2): 151–175.

Warren KS. The evolution of selective primary health care. *Social Science and Medicine*, 1988, 26 (9): 891–898.

Wayland C, Crowder J. Disparate views of community in primary health care: understanding how perceptions influence success. *Medical Anthropology Quarterly*, 2002, 16 (2): 230–247.

Weed DL. Epidemiology, the humanities, and public health. *American Journal of Public Health*, 1995, 85:914–918.

Weiner D, Harris TM. Community-integrated GIS for land reform in South Africa. *Urisa Journal*, 2003, 15 (2): 61–74.

Weiss B. Electric vampires: Haya rumours of the commodified body. In: Lambeck M, Strathern A, eds. *Bodies and person: comparative perspectives from Africa and Melanesia*. Cambridge, Cambridge University Press, 1998:172–194.

Weiss MG. The interrelationship of tropical disease and mental disorder: conceptual framework and literature review (part 1, malaria). *Culture, Medicine and Psychiatry*, 1985, 9:121–200.

Weiss MG. Cultural models of diarrheal illness: conceptual framework and review. *Social Science and Medicine*, 1988, 27 (1): 5–16.

Weiss M. Explanatory Model Interview Catalog (EMIC): framework for comparative study of illness. *Transcultural Psychiatry*, 1997, 34:235–263.

Weiss MG. Cultural epidemiology: an introduction and overview. *Anthropology and Medicine*, 2001, 8 (1): 5–29.

Weiss MG, Ramakrishna J. Stigma interventions and research for international health. *Lancet*, 2006, 367 (9509): 536–538.

Weiss MG et al. The Explanatory Model Interview Catalogue (EMIC): contributing to cross-cultural research methods from a study of leprosy and mental health. *British Journal of Psychiatry*, 1992, 160:819–830.

Weiss MG et al. Health-related stigma: rethinking concepts and interventions. *Psychology, Health and Medicine*, 2006, 11 (3): 277–287.

Weiss RA, McMichael AJ. Social and environmental risk factors in the emergence of infectious diseases. *Nature Medicine*, 2004, 10:S70–S76.

Weller SC. New data on intracultural variability: the hot/cold concept of medicine and illness. *Human Organization*, 1983, 42:249–257.

Weller SC. Consistency and consensus among informants: disease concepts in a rural Mexican town. *American Anthropologist*, 1984a, 86:966–975.

Weller SC. Cross-cultural concept of illness: variation and validation. *American Anthropologist*, 1984b, 86:341–351.

Weller SC et al. *Empacho* in four Latino groups: a study of intra- and intercultural variation in beliefs. *Medical Anthropology*, 1993, 15:109–136.

Wenger E. Communities of practice: the social fabric of a learning organization. *Healthcare Forum Journal*, 1996, 39 (4): 22–26.

Wenger E. *Communities of practice: learning, meaning, and identity*. Cambridge, Cambridge University Press, 1998.

Wenger E et al. *Cultivating communities of practice—a guide to managing knowledge*. Cambridge, MA, Harvard Business School Press, 2002.

Wessely S et al. Psychological implications of chemical and biological weapons. *British Medical Journal*, 2001, 323:878–879.

White C. Sociocultural considerations in the treatment of leprosy in Rio de Janeiro, Brazil. *Leprosy Review*, 2002, 73:356–365.

White L. *Speaking with vampires: rumour and history in colonial Africa*. Berkeley, University of California Press, 2000.

White SC. NGOs, civil society and the state in Bangladesh: the politics of representing the poor. *Development and Change*, 1999, 30:307–326.

Whiteford L. The ethnoecology of dengue fever. *Medical Anthropology Quarterly*, 1997, 11 (2): 202–223.

Whiteford LM, Manderson L. *Global health policy, local realities: the fallacy of the level playing field*. Boulder, CO, Lynne Rienner, 2000.

Whitehead M. The concepts and principles of equity and health. *Health Promotion International*, 1991, 6 (3): 217–228.

Whitman J. Political processes and infectious diseases. In: Whitman J, ed. *The politics of emerging and resurgent infectious diseases*. New York, St. Martin's, 2000:1–14.

Whittaker A. White blood and falling wombs: ethnogynaecology in Northeast Thailand. In: Rice PL, Manderson L, eds. *Maternity and reproductive health in Asian societies*. Amsterdam, Harwood Academic Publishers, 1996:207–225.

Whittaker M. Negotiating care: reproductive tract infections in Vietnam. *Women and Health*, 2002, 35 (4): 43–57.

WHO (World Health Organization). Declaration of Alma Ata, 1978 (www.euro.who.int/AboutWHO/Policy/20010827_1).

WHO (World Health Organization). Integrated management of the sick child. *Bulletin of the World Health Organization*, 1995, 73 (6): 735–740.

WHO (World Health Organization). *Framework Convention on Tobacco Control*. Geneva, World Health Organization, 2003.

WHO (World Health Organization). Safety of injections: global facts and figures. WHO/EHT/04/04. Geneva, 2004 (www.who.int/injection_safety/about/resources/en/FactAndFiguresInjectionSafety.pdf).

WHO (World Health Organization). *Revision of the International Health Regulations*. World Health Organization Document WHA58.3. Geneva, 2005.

WHO (World Health Organization). International migration of health personnel: a challenge for health systems in developing countries. Electronic document,2006a (http://cdrwww.who.int/gb/ebwha/pdf/files/SHA59/A59_18-3n.pdf).

WHO (World Health Organization). *Bridging the "know–do" gap: meeting on knowledge translation in global health*. WHO/EIP/KMS/2006.2. Geneva, World Health Organization, 2006b.

Whyte SR. *Questioning misfortune*. Cambridge, Cambridge University Press, 1997.

Whyte SR et al. *Social Lives of Medicines*. Cambridge, Cambridge University Press, 2002.

Wilcox BA, Gubler DJ. Disease ecology and the global emergence of zoonotic pathogens. *Environmental Health and Preventive Medicine*, 2005, 10:263–272.

Wilk RR, Netting R. Households: changing forms and functions. In: Netting R et al., eds. *Households: comparative and historical studies of the domestic group.* Berkeley, University of California Press, 1984:1–28.

Wilkes MS et al. Pharmaceutical advertisements in leading medical journals: experts' assessments. *Annals of Internal Medicine*, 1992, 116:912–919.

Wilkinson R. *Unhealthy societies: the afflictions of inequality.* New York, Routledge, 1996.

Williams HA, Jones COH. A critical review of behavioral issues related to malaria control in sub-Saharan Africa: what contributions have social scientists made? *Social Science and Medicine*, 2004, 59:501–523.

Williams HA et al. A community perspective on the efficacy of malaria treatment options for children in Lundazi District, Zambia. *Tropical Medicine and International Health*, 1999, 4:641–652.

Williams HA et al. The contribution of social science research to malaria prevention and control. *Bulletin of the World Health Organization*, 2002, 80 (3): 251–252.

Williams R. *Marxism and literature.* Oxford, Oxford University Press, 1977.

Williams SJ. Theorizing class, health and lifestyles: can Bourdieu help us? *Sociology of Health and Illness*, 1995, 17 (5): 577–604.

Winch P, Mehanna S. *Schistosomiasis in Egypt: an old disease and its new epidemiology.* Paper presented at the Annual Meeting of the American Anthropological Association. Washington, DC, November 20, 1995.

Winch P et al. Beliefs about the prevention of dengue and other febrile illnesses in Merida, Mexico. *Journal of Tropical Medicine and Hygiene*, 1991, 94:377–387.

Winch P et al. Vector control at the household level: an analysis of its impact on women. *Acta Tropica*, 1994, 56:327–339.

Winch P et al. A methodology for investigating local understanding of the seasonality of mosquito-borne diseases. Unpublished manuscript, 1995.

Winch PJ et al. Local terminology for febrile illnesses in Bagamoyo District, Tanzania, and its impact on the design of a community-based malaria control programme. *Social Science and Medicine*, 1996, 42:1057–1067.

Woelk GB. Cultural and structural influences in the creation of and participation in community health programmes. *Social Science and Medicine*, 1992, 35 (4): 419–424.

Wolf D. *Factory daughters: gender, household dynamics, and rural industrialization in Java.* Berkeley, University of California Press, 1992.

Wood K et al. Cleaning the womb: constructions of cervical screening and womb cancer among rural black women in South Africa. *Social Science and Medicine*, 1997, 45 (2): 283–294.

Woodward D et al. Globalization and health: a framework for analysis and action. *Bulletin of the World Health Organization*, 2001, 79 (9): 875–881.

Woolcock M. Social capital and economic development: towards a theoretical synthesis and policy framework. *Theory and Society*, 1998, 27:151–208.

Woolcock M. The place of social capital in understanding social and economic outcomes. *ISUMA Canadian Journal of Policy Research*, 2001, 2 (1): 11–17.

Woolcock M. Social capital in theory and practice: where do we stand? In: Isham J et al., eds. *Social capital and economic development: well-being in developing countries*. Cheltenham, UK, Edward Elgar, 2002.

Woolcock M, Narayan D. Social capital: implications for development theory, research, and policy. *World Bank Research Observer*, 2000, 15:225–249.

Woolhouse ME et al. Emerging pathogens: the epidemiology and evolution of species jumps. *Trends in Ecology and Evolution*, 2005, 20 (5): 238–244.

Worboys M. The emergence of tropical medicine: a study in the establishment of a scientific specialty. In: Lemaine G et al., eds. *Perspectives on the emergence of scientific disciplines*. Chicago, Aldine, 1976:75–98.

Worboys M. Tropical diseases. In: Bynum WF, Porter R, eds. *Companion encyclopaedia in the history of medicine*, vol. 1. London, Routledge, 1993:522.

Worboys M. Germs, malaria and the invention of Mansonian tropical medicine: from diseases in the tropics to tropical diseases. In: Arnold D, ed. *Warm climates and Western medicine: the emergence of tropical medicine, 1500–1900*. Amsterdam, Rodopi, 1996.

World Bank. *World Development Report 1993: Investing in Health*. Oxford, Oxford University Press, 1993.

World Bank. *Working with NGOs: a practical guide to operational collaboration between the World Bank and non-governmental organizations*. Washington, DC, World Bank, 1995.

World Bank. Social capital: the missing link? In: World Bank, *Expanding the measure of wealth: indicators of environmentally sustainable development*. Washington, DC, World Bank, 1997:77–93.

World Bank. *The World Bank–civil society relations: Fiscal 1999 progress report*. Washington, DC, World Bank, 2000.

Woronov T. *Consuming kids: Chinese children and/as commodity fetishes*. Unpublished manuscript, 2007.

Worrall E et al. Is malaria a disease of poverty? A review of the literature. *Tropical Medicine and International Health*, 2005, 10 (10): 1047–1059.

Worthman CM. Emotions: you can feel the difference. In: Hinton AL, ed. *Biocultural approaches to the emotions*. Cambridge, Cambridge University Press, 1999:41–74.

Worthman CM, Kohrt B. Receding horizons of health: biocultural approaches to public health paradoxes. *Social Science and Medicine*, 2005, 61:861–878.

Wright J et al. Direct observation of treatment for tuberculosis: a randomized controlled trial of community health workers versus family members. *Tropical Medicine and International Health*, 2004, 9 (5): 559–565.

Wu Z et al. Prevalence of HIV infection among former commercial plasma donors in rural eastern China. *Health Policy and Planning*, 2001, 16 (1): 41–46.

Wyatt HV. The popularity of injections in the Third World: origins and consequences for poliomyelitis. *Social Science and Medicine*, 1984, 19: 911–915.

Wyatt HV. Unnecessary injections and poliomyelitis in Pakistan. *Tropical Doctor*, 1996, 26:179–180.

Yach D. Globalization and health: exploring the opportunities and constraints for health arising from globalization. *Globalization and Health*, 2005, 1 (2), doi:10.1186/1744-8603-1-2.

Yach D, Bettcher D. The globalization of public health, I: threats and opportunities. *American Journal of Public Health*, 1998a, 88 (5): 735–738.

Yach D, Bettcher D. The globalization of public health, II: the convergence of self-interest and altruism. *American Journal of Public Health*, 1998b, 88 (5): 738–741.

Yach D et al. Epidemiologic and economic consequences of the global epidemics of obesity and diabetes. *Nature Medicine*, 2006, 12:62–66.

Yahya M. *Polio vaccines—difficult to swallow. The story of a controversy in northern Nigeria*. IDS Working Paper 261. Brighton, UK, Institute for Development Studies, 2005.

Yamasaki-Nakagawa M et al. Gender difference in delays to diagnosis and health care seeking behaviour in a rural area of Nepal. *International Journal of Tuberculosis and Lung Disease*, 2001, 5:24–31.

Yamey G. Malaria researchers say global fund is buying "useless drug." *British Medical Journal*, 2003, 327 (7425): 1188.

Yang N. Disease prevention, social mobilization and spatial politics: the anti-germ-warfare incident of 1952 and the "patriotic health campaign." *Chinese Historical Review*, 2004, 11 (2): 155–182.

Yeates N. Critical reflections and lines of enquiry. *International Feminist Journal of Politics*, 2004, 6 (3): 369–391.

Yeboah-Antwi K et al. Impact of prepackaging antimalarial drugs on cost to patients and compliance with treatment. *Bulletin of the World Health Organization*, 2001, 79:394–399.

Yen IH, Syme SL. The social environment and health: a discussion of the epidemiologic literature. *Annual Review of Public Health*, 1999, 20:287–308.

Yerly S et al. Nosocomial outbreak of multiple bloodborne viral infections. *Journal of Infectious Diseases*, 2001, 184 (3): 369–372.

Yoder PS. Examining ethnomedical diagnoses and treatment choice for diarrheal disorders in Lubumbashi Swahili. *Medical Anthropology*, 1995, 16:211–247.

Yoder S. Cultural conceptions of illness and the measurement of changes in morbidity. Annenberg School of Communications, University of Pennsylvania, 1989 (unpublished document no. 115).

Yoder S, Hornick R. Symptoms and perceived severity of illness as predictive of treatment for diarrhea in six Asian and African sites. *Social Science and Medicine*, 1996, 43 (4): 429–439.

Young A. Internalizing and externalizing medical belief systems: an Ethiopian example. *Social Science and Medicine*, 1976, 10:147–156.

Young A. The anthropologies of illness and sickness. *Annual Review of Anthropology*, 1982, 11:257–285.

Yumkella F. *Women, onchocerciasis and ivermectin in Sierra Leone*. Gender and Tropical Diseases Resource Paper No. 2, WHO/TDR/GTD/RP/96.2. World Health Organization, 1996, 2:1–16.

Zakus JD, Lysack CL. Revisiting community participation. *Health Policy and Planning*, 1998, 12 (1): 1–12.

INDEX

cholera, 47, 54, 66n44, 77, 120, 121, 180n40

climate, 20n44, 26, 27, 42, 51, 151, 153, 186n71

clinical trials, 3, 102n30; consent procedures and, 177n12, 181n46; in developing countries, 95, 102n28, 155, 183n61, 185n68

commodity chains, 173, 183n58

communicable diseases, 3, 46, 155, 163, 179n31, 186n71

communities of practice, 14n4, 106, 115, 130n21, 145n13, 164

Congo, 39n21, 47

contagion, 45, 46, 52–53, 55, 62n9, 63n15, 66n47

cotrimethoxazole, 97, 102n24

Cuba, 120, 128n3, 155, 183n61

data, 13n2; collection of, 7, 8–9, 167, 179n38; interpretation of, 9, 11, 23, 91, 167, 173, 179n35; representations and, 106n3, 109–14, 117n8

dengue, 2, 120, 128n2, 128n3, 153, 181n50; children and, 56, 82n9; as endemic disease, 27, 54; fevers and, 33, 77, 82n15; prevention of, 50, 124, 175n3; as vector-borne disease, 44, 48, 49, 63n21, 78, 108, 121, 122, 158

development, 118n18, 147n25; funding for, 105, 106n3, 106n4, 135, 138; global health and, 137, 151, 152n3, 154; government programs and, 99, 108, 138–39; health policy and, 99, 105–6, 117n8; metrics of, 111, 120; private sector and, 99; rhetoric of, 106, 109, 115n1, 116n2, 116n3, 133–34; social capital and, 135–36

diabetes, 47, 159, 177n17

diagnosis, 14n5, 58–59, 76; by treatment, 10, 21n46, 59, 64n26, 64n28, 71, 82n6

diarrhea: causality of, 35, 36, 42; children and, 26, 38n14, 43, 55, 75; as disease category, 2, 70–72; as symptom, 31, 58, 94; treating, 66n55, 71, 97, 103n33

diet, 11, 34–36, 37n5, 174, 178n25, 186n71; culture and, 6, 19n34, 25, 36; diarrhea and, 26, 35, 36; fever and, 27, 33, 39n18

directly observed therapy short-course (DOTS) programs: compliance in, 79, 98, 103n34, 122–23; education and, 46, 88; implementation of, 97, 116n4; restrictiveness of, 109, 116n7, 129n11, 129n12, 170

disability-adjusted life years (DALYs), 113–14, 163

disease, 14n5, 114, 120, 138; control programs, 30, 48, 49, 97, 115, 121; distribution of, 47, 152n3, 153–54, 157–58; reservoirs, 65n40, 68n64; transmission of, 63n23, 155, 160, 162–63, 165, 167, 173, 175n3

drug resistance, 64n26, 92–93, 101n21, 148n34; controlled use and, 33, 66n52, 102n25, 142; microbial disease and, 155, 162, 174

education, 47, 76, 117n15

Egypt, 36, 55

emergent diseases, 154, 171, 175n3, 175n5, 181n47

environment, 160, 176n11, 180n42; changes in, 11, 25, 51, 62n13, 164, 173; as risk factor, 54–55, 64n36, 123–24; vector-borne disease and, 48, 52

epidemic disease, 13, 47, 54, 63n17, 65n38, 120, 171, 181n51

epidemiology, 82n5, 83n18, 121, 155; conceptual frameworks for, 6, 8, 11, 17n20, 17n22, 117n8, 117n11, 117n14, 160–61, 177n16; ecosocial, 3, 9, 19n34, 19n36, 143n1, 160–61, 186n71; lay, 45–49, 62n12, 83n18, 92, 118n22; life-span, 160, 161–63, 174, 178n26; popular, 3, 8, 16n14, 83n18; research in, 5, 7, 17n25

Ethiopia, 27, 66n46

ethnicity, 9, 33, 63n17, 65n39, 76

ethnography, 1, 9, 13n2, 29n39

ethnophysiology, 2, 25–26, 37n1, 41, 51; children and, 26–27, 36; illness progression and, 31–33, 52; medication use and, 29–30, 32–34; women and, 28–31, 35–36; worms and, 27–28, 36

evidence-based medicine (EBM), 15n8, 95–96, 105, 106n3, 114, 117n8, 118n22

health care seeking, 130n16; clinics and, 34, 86, 88–89; culture and, 12, 20n44, 64n27, 74–75, 124; illness categorization and, 69, 71, 81n1, 100n1; medication and, 87, 90, 95, 103n36

health education, 77–79, 83n17, 93, 118n26, 129n13, 166; for health workers, 72, 99; malaria and, 48, 78, 79; negative focus of, 7, 11; risk and, 18n27, 123–24; TB and, 46, 47, 63n15, 79

health initiatives, 2, 5, 109, 114–15, 169

health social science, x n. 1, 3, 5, 69, 122, 138–39, 153, 163; applications of, 58, 63n24, 69, 92, 103n33, 147n28, 169, 179n34; development of, 154–55; epistemology of, 14n6, 21n47, 23, 79–81; predictive value of, 10–11, 164; syndemic approach to, 159–60, 165–67

"heating activities," 29, 34, 42, 51, 61

hepatitis, 60, 89

hereditary illness, 11, 46, 47, 51, 62n9, 63n18, 112

HIV/AIDS, 64n33, 67n59, 106n4, 141, 155, 169; as blood-borne disease, 68n62, 89, 100n12, 101n15, 177n16; as epidemic disease, 54, 65n42, 115, 128, 144n8; as sexually transmitted disease, 53, 66n53, 92, 100n12, 112, 158; stigma of, 46–47, 59–60, 65n39; treatment of, 102n24, 148n36

Honduras, 30, 49, 118n26

households, 122, 125–26, 129n13; economics of, 34, 96, 128, 179n32; health care seeking and, 32, 58, 63n25, 124–25, 129n13, 129n14; illness experience and, 14n5, 66n55, 71, 113, 163, 179n32; stability of, 123, 125

human rights discourse, 18n32, 137, 140–43, 147n25, 172–73, 174, 180n42, 182n53

humoral theory, 27, 38n10, 51, 87, 91, 93, 94

hunger, 42, 49, 51, 52

hygiene, 46, 63n16, 65n39, 66n44, 88–89, 124

illness, 14n5; as a biosocial experience, 12, 14n5, 18n25, 46, 61n1, 113, 178n24;

causes of, 2, 33, 35, 44–49, 52, 58, 61n1, 62n7, 62n11; chronic, 3, 19n36, 42, 47, 101n19, 102n24, 155, 162, 179n29, 179n32; cognitive schema for, 6, 8–9, 11–12, 25, 62n8, 70; exchange value of, 5, 10, 16n16, 81n2; labeling, 10, 20n46, 33–34, 76–78, 85; narratives of, 20n41, 42, 114, 141; predisposition to, 42, 51; prevention, 11, 61n1, 64n30; recurrence of, 75; severity of, 71, 73, 74, 85, 124, 130n15; taskonomy, 10, 20n45, 81n1; therapy management groups and, 10, 42, 125

India, 118n26, 155, 159, 174, 179n34; disease transmittal in, 46, 47, 48, 53, 65n37, 88, 89, 91; food and, 35, 36, 37n5, 39n22, 178n25; health care industry in, 99, 102n28, 103n39, 170, 183n61; humoral theory in, 27; illness and, 5, 31, 42, 45, 54, 55, 73, 77; medication in, 30, 33, 82n12, 86, 87–88, 92–93, 96, 97–98, 100n9, 101n20; politics in, 13n1, 53; tobacco use in, 159, 179n34; tuberculosis in, 46, 47, 55, 59, 60, 63n14, 97–98, 177n18; vaccination in, 38n14, 58, 68n63

indigenous medicine, 31, 33, 36, 73, 74, 78, 81n1

Indonesia: ethnophysiology in, 27, 30, 33; illness in, 58, 117n15, 181n50; politics in, 136, 171, 181n49, 181n52, 185n67; tobacco use in, 159, 179n34

infant formula, 170, 180n42, 180n45

infectious diseases, 171, 174, 179n29, 181n47; controlling, 115, 127; examples of, 114, 141; political factors in, 175n3, 175n4, 177n11

injections, 33–34, 76, 86, 100n10; safety of, 88–90, 100n12, 101n14

International Clinical Epidemiology Network (INCLEN), 15n8, 63n15, 105

international health, 89, 124–28, 154–55; focused funding and, 106n4, 121–22, 142; NGOs and, 137, 145n12, 145n13; social science and, 106, 141, 147n30; state governance and, 108, 120, 136

International Health Regulations (IHR), 168, 180n40, 180n41

ABOUT THE AUTHOR

Mark A. Nichter is Regents' Professor and professor of anthropology at the University of Arizona, with joint appointments in the Department of Family and Community Medicine and the Mel and Enid Zuckerman College of Public Health. Mark coordinates the medical anthropology graduate training program at the University of Arizona and has worked in the field of international/global health for thirty years. His research addresses health problems ranging from child survival to family planning, infectious to vector-borne diseases, pharmaceutical practice to tobacco control, and health-systems research to health policy and governance. He has served as a consultant to several international organizations; as visiting faculty to universities in India, Indonesia, the Philippines, Sri Lanka, and Thailand; and as health social science advisor to the International Network for Clinical Epidemiology for twenty years. He is former president of the Society for Medical Anthropology and is a recipient of the Outstanding Graduate Student Mentor Award, the Margaret Mead Award, and the Virchow Award from the American Anthropological Association. He is involved in ongoing research in South and Southeast Asia as well as the United States.